Beyond the Flow

Beyond the Flow: Scholarly Publications During and After the Digital

Niels-Oliver Walkowski

meson press

Bibliographical Information of the German National Library
The German National Library lists this publication in the Deutsche Nationalbibliografie (German National Bibliography); detailed bibliographic information is available online at http://dnb.d-nb.de.

Published in 2019 by meson press, Lüneburg
www.meson.press

Design concept: Torsten Köchlin, Silke Krieg
Cover image: Yuichiro Haga (www.flickr.com/photos/infinity-d/6781064978)
The print edition of this book is printed by Books on Demand, Norderstedt.

ISBN (Print): 978-3-95796-160-0
ISBN (PDF): 978-3-95796-161-7
ISBN (EPUB): 978-3-95796-162-4
DOI: 10.14619/1600

The digital editions of this publication can be downloaded freely at www.meson.press.

Contents

DIGITAL PUBLISHING

POST-DIGITALITY

MULTIMODAL ANALYSIS

MODELING

For the last twenty-five years, research on so-called digital publications was aimed at reconfiguring established modes of scholarly communication. Interest in the field is driven by the idea that the advent of digital technologies can solve a variety of past problems of scholarly publications, thereby constructing a conceptual space for negotiation of past and future. Issues at stake are epistemological commitments to strategies of production and representation of knowledge, as well as different understandings of the impacts of technology. The field thus shapes how we refer to scientific knowledge in the light of digital technologies. The present contribution examines how related research developed scenarios of the past and future of scholarly communications. Built on this enquiry, an alternative, more ecologically informed approach to understanding the changing landscape of scholarly publications is proposed. An attempt is thus made to put new light on a variety of conflicts that have dominated this research field throughout its existence.

Introduction

In the year 2006, Owen published *The Scientific Article in the Age of Digitization*. The goal of this work was to find answers to the question of "how the ongoing process of digitization has impacted on the substance of formal scientific communication as reflected in the scientific article" (15). There are several elements in this quote that are worth discussing. To begin with, it draws attention to the fact that an idea exists which presumes that the digital representation of the main method of communication in science — scholarly publications — could have a greater impact on such methods, beyond just representing them. While the term digitization suggests that articles are merely digitized, the whole of the sentence reveals a possibility for the representation to apply its own set of changes to the thing represented. The process of digitization is no longer a one-way relationship, and the digital form more than just a container. Another interesting aspect is the very relationship between the scientific article as an object and scientific communication as a practice. The quote calls to mind that the object happens to be not just an object within this practice, but that the shape of the article is an expression of the regularities of scholarly communication, in the same way as the qualities of articles facilitate and shape specific forms of scholarly communication. This relationship makes it possible to respond to the question of potential changes in scholarly communication, by having a look at what happened to the article form after articles were digitized. The final facet to be highlighted is an assumption that seems reasonable under the aforementioned circumstances: if digitization changed the substance of scientific communication, would such changes reflect a certain substance of the digital form?

In the above discussion of the dimensions of Owen's quote, the basic shape of a research field was outlined that formed nearly twenty-five years ago under the notion of *digital scholarly publishing* or *digital scholarly publications*. There is always a lot of contingency in the attempt to set a starting point for a slow transition. However, this stimulates the debate, and for the abovementioned context there are a bunch of reasons to define the year 1995 as a crucial year for something that could be called the transition from *Electronic Publications* to *Digital Publications*.

Electronic publishing was primarily about burning articles on CD-ROMs and putting print versions of articles online. The form of the article, its main features, had not been modified. Neither did those digital copies make use of more advanced possibilities of digital technologies, as comprehensively discussed by Hitchcock, Carr, and Hall (1996), Alsop, Tompsett, and Wisdom (1997), as well as Peek and Pomerantz (1998). In this sense, Hitchcock describes the time before 1995 as "the calm before the storm," with the term storm referring to more serious attempts of completely rethinking what a publication may be in the light of digital technology. Thus, the shift between Electronic Publishing and Digital Publishing was the shift from trying to represent something under new conditions to an attempt to let these new conditions change the thing itself. In other words, it refers precisely to the phenomenon Owen intended to evaluate years later.

Besides this line of arguments, there is also a quantitative measure supporting the claim of a shift in this period. A look at the *Google Ngram*[1] results for the use of the terms "electronic publishing" and "digital publishing," for instance, shows a decline for the first term after 1995, while the second term receives initial attention between 1994 and 1996.

Finally, there is an incident that well serves the purpose of having something like a symbolic event marking this shift. 1995 was the year in which Denning and Rous published their well-cited paper on "The ACM Electronic Publishing Plan." Besides its number of citations, this paper is significant because it calls for a radical rethinking of the extent up to which digital technologies should renew publications. It proclaims that "publishing has reached a historic divide" (69), demanding that publishers seriously consider these changes "if the system is to survive" (72).

Denning and Rous made some very precise suggestions how the structure and form of publications may change if digital scholarly publishing is understood as something more than moving historical publications into a new technological environment. One of the most concise statements, however, can be found in Nentwich's 2003 work *Cyberscience*, in which he argues that "hypertext and hypermedia will gradually become the standard ways of representing academic knowledge" (270). This general claim is a very good example for the issue Owen wanted to put to the test. It stresses key features of digital technologies, and assumes that these features will provide the new dominant structure for scholarly publications.

The idea that the main topic of academic publishing should be the modification of the publication format and structure, so that they are in line with the demands and opportunities of digital technologies, started a massive discourse on forthcoming revolutionary changes. In the introduction to his study, Owen (2006, 5–7) offers an impressive summary of nearly twenty statements from all over the field of scholarly publishing, proclaiming

1 The *Google Ngram Viewer* can be accessed at: books.google.com/ngrams.

"the electronic publishing revolution" (Hunter 2001), "a revolution in the communication of research" (Friend 1998, 163). Treloar (1999, 25) detected "revolutionized … attitudes towards communication as well as our ability to communicate ideas and research results."

Fourteen years have gone by since Owen's analysis of the discourse accompanying the "digitization" of publications. It does not come as a surprise that during that time a lot of new developments took place around the notion of digital scholarly publications. These developments have, nonetheless, not changed anything about the general impression in the field that the abovementioned revolutionary changes are yet to come. Remarks such as those gathered by Owen continue to frame research and developments until today. Accordingly, Shotton (2009) gives his account of the topic under the headline of a "Coming Revolution in Scientific Journal Publishing." Peroni (2014a, 7) continues to perceive in 2014 that "scholarly authoring and publishing are undergoing a revolution." Hall, Kuc, and Zylinska (2015, 3), in far more general terms, repeat the insight that the "digital revolution has facilitated the development of new modes of knowledge dissemination … as well as new forms of communication." Still, after decades of investment, research, and debate, Assante et al. (2015) feel that the "time for a Change in Scholarly Communication" has come, while Sofronijević (2012, 252) sees himself "on the verge of a revolution … in the area of communication." Bartling and Friesike (2014) aim "Towards Another Scientific Revolution," driven mostly by leaving behind the traditional publication model, and De Roure (2014b, 237) "calls for an overnight revolution" that should lead to "The Future of Scholarly Communications." The constellation of a coming revolution, the occurrence of which moves forward as new steps towards digital publications are taken, thus can be seen as a constant feature of the field.

In contrast to this situation, people such as Esposito (2013) state that the "The Digital Publishing Revolution Is Over." With the focus on a specific subtopic of digital scholarly publishing, Herb (2017) writes in "Open Access Between Revolution and Cash Cow" that in the year "2016 it must be noted that the hopes of open access advocates for a revolution will be disappointed." What seems to be a more recent critical reaction to the phenomenon described in the last paragraph is in fact a similar concomitant of the history of digital publishing. A study of the impressions and expectations of researchers about the impact of digital technologies on scholarly publications conducted by Eason et al. summarized in 1997 already:

> The growth in academic, refereed journals may well remain modest …. There also appears to be little reason to expect a growth in

> multi-media content. ... Hypertexts are the possible exception but there has been little enthusiasm so far for developing these .... (Eason et al. 1997, 81)

In 1998, Peek and Pomerantz (1998) published the results of a detailed analysis of changes scholarly journals had undergone in the previous decade. In quite a strong statement they conclude that "at a first glance, it may appear that the history of electronic scholarly publishing ... is littered with the corpses of failed efforts" (339). With respect to Owen's own overview of the revolutionary expectations in the field of digital publications, he remarks more generally at the end of his survey:

> The "revolution" in scientific communication that is supposed to be caused by information and communication technologies has often been compared to the so-called "Gutenberg revolution." But as we have seen, that revolution is more myth than reality as far as science and the media of scientific communication are concerned. (Owen 2006, 210)

Most recently Kaden and Kleineberg (2017, 1) summarized the results of a research project investigating *Future Publications in the Humanities* by remarking that "[es] lässt sich die grundsätzliche Erkenntnis festhalten, dass eine konsequente Digitalisierung des geisteswissenschaftlichen Publizierens bisher ausbleibt."[2]

To make a point, it could be emphasized that in the history of digital scholarly publishing, a narrative that always sees a revolution coming goes along with the proclamation of a failed revolution, or one that will never happen.

The last three quotes all came from evaluations of certain states of scholarly publications in the past. The authors were less involved in the design or the implementation of new publication forms than the "revolutionaries" were before. There are, however, plenty of statements in this research field resembling the observations of Peek and Pomerantz, Esposito or Herb in their own peculiar way. Throughout the whole history of digital scholarly publications, stakeholders, trying to introduce substantial changes to what scholarly publications look like, complain that despite all these attempts, no standards for new publication formats have emerged. This does not mean that they do not recognize their own contributions. These contributions, however, have produced a messy and

2 "the general fact could be recorded that a resolute digitization of publishing in the humanities fails to appear" (author's translation)

heterogeneous landscape instead of new reliable formations in scholarly publishing, and the ones that appear most frustrated about this fact are these specific stakeholders themselves. Castelli, Manghi, and Thanos (2013) remark that innovative approaches to scholarly publications are "poorly integrated" (155) because stakeholders do not want to focus on common solutions (167). It is not surprising that in 2003, Kennedy (2003) regrets that there is no standardized way to produce digital publications. The same regret, however, appears again and again, up to the present. Hence, Adriaansen and Hooft (2010) express their unhappiness with the fact that no supporting tools for digital publications exist — because there is no common procedure for their creation. This situation is considered a consequence of the fact that, more generally, there is no standard for digital publications in academia (8). In a similar fashion, Bardi and Manghi (2015a) lament the lack of any standardized framework for the installation of new publication forms in scholarly publishing. Bardi and Manghi (2014, 265) remark that digital publications are "a rich but foundationless realm" that finally needs "some kind of common understanding" (240). In fact, five years earlier, Sierman, Schmidt, and Ludwig (2009) already worked on such an understanding. They even called for the use of a specific standard which would support all aspects of this understanding. But as they announce this standard, they undermine it in an almost fatalistic remark, asking: "but who knows if this standard is the way of the future" (160). Candela et al. (2015, 1760) assert that "journal editors do not yet have a shared and consolidated strategy" regarding core elements of digital publications formats. "As a consequence of this state of affairs and the lack of standards in this area, there is great heterogeneity" (1752).

All the abovementioned authors, and others too, have tried to introduce or support the standardization process of digital publications that is supposedly the key factor in broader adoption. Each new attempt, nevertheless, refers to the general situation of digital publications. This pattern has been there for a considerable amount of time, suggesting that it is a constant of the history of digital publications so far.

As mentioned above, there is not just regret but also frustration. This frustration might not come as a surprise in a situation where revolutionary events are expected but do not seem to occur, at least not in the way they are expected. It is articulated in complaints about how much current scholarly publications available in digital environments are allegedly a copy of publications from the era of the printing press. In 1998, Singh et al. (1998, sec. Online Journals Today) write that "most of them [digital scholarly publications] are essentially a static visual form of their counterpart hard-copy journal" and publishing "has not kept pace with the changing research technology" (sec. The Need). Still, in 2014, De Roure (2014b, 233) asserts that no significant changes have been made to the format of the journal article since its introduction in 1665.[3] In 2009, Hogenaar (2009) launches a critique towards a new digital publication format, saying that "its end-product is still a publication rather than a communication object." Two years later, Bourne (2011) outlines the prospects of digital publications and contrasts them with the situation at that time. The bottom line of this comparison is summarized quite concisely by the title "Digital Research/Analog Publishing." Xu (2011, i) creates the same dichotomy. Consequently, "a highly semantic enriched publication always makes its information and data much easier to search, navigate, disseminate and reuse, whereas most online articles today are still electronic facsimiles of linear structured papers." Marcondes, Malheiros, and da Costa (2014) claim that "despite numerous advancements in information technology, electronic publishing is still based on the print text model." The announcement of a panel on publishing in 2017, organized by the *Institute of Network Cultures*[4] reads: although digital technologies promised a renaissance in the publishing industries, publishers still struggle with digital innovations and try to hold on to traditional workflows, production, form and business models" (Institute of Network Cultures 2017). Consequently, these complaints show that what was presented as the main distinction between electronic publications and digital publications never really developed.

The main object criticized is the *PDF* format, widely known inside and outside of academia as the most common format for the distribution of digital documents. Owen (2006, 146) had remarked already in 2006 that "perhaps the most conspicuous finding is the frequent use of pdf as a distribution format." According to his analysis, more than two-thirds of the investigated digital publications primarily used this format during that epoch. In 2018 Garcia et al. (2018, 2/26) state that "published papers are primarily available as HTML and PDF." Owen further finds this conspicuous, because the PDF, "in spite of its hypermedium and multimedia properties, is predominantly a print-document based format." For Owen, this conspicuousness mainly represents a good reason to reflect more broadly on certain elements in the discourse of the field of digital publications. For the field itself, observations such as those are a fundamental nuisance. In 2010, advocates for new publication formats thus began planning a conference with the title

3 De Roure refers to the *Philosophical Transactions of the Royal Society* launched that year by *The Royal Society of London.*

4 http://networkcultures.org/

"Beyond the PDF." A call for preparations, launched on the blogs section of the non-profit publisher *PLOS*, reads:

> PDF has become the standard way we consume scientific papers, but in fact is not a good format for this purpose at all. … *PDF is an insult to science.* (Fenner 2010)

In the same fashion, Lord, Cockell, and Stevens (2012, 1004) state that despite all the advantages for future publications that go along with digital technologies, digital scholarly publications today in fact "culminate in a lumpen PDF." Pettifer et al. (2011, 213) give an overview of some of the critiques in which PDFs are seen as "antithetical to the spirit of the web" and compared with the act of inventing a telephone and using it for morse code. And still, the authors assert that although much better choices are available, eighty percent of digital publications are published in PDF format. It stands to reason to assume that the PDF might also have been extended to make use of certain capabilities of digital technologies, and in fact such developments towards *interactive PDFs* and multimedia PDFs have taken place in the last years. These attempts to modernize the PDF, nonetheless, do not tone down the critique. Bourne (2010, 1) once commented with much polemic: "these pioneering publishers are now experimenting with interactive PDFs, 'articles of the future,' … but then what?"

It is indeed in the evaluation of the comportment of stakeholders involved in scholarly publishing where the frustration behind research on digital publication formats is most recognizable. Bourne, Buckingham Shum et al. remark:

> Producers and consumers remain wedded to formats developed in the era of print publication, and the reward systems for researchers remain tied to those delivery mechanisms. (Bourne, Buckingham Shum et al. 2012)

Oft mentioned reasons include that researchers behave selfishly (Markowetz 2015; Nüst et al. 2017), or think in terms of their self-interest (Cribb and Hartomo 2010), oriented towards the creation of competitive advantages (Borgman, Wallis, and Enyedy 2007). Publishers are distinguished by their occasional reluctance to even publish digital books (Humphreys et al. 2017) or think about making allegedly beneficial changes to what a publication is. From time to time, frustration also turns into open aggression, of which Neylon gives an illuminating example. He writes:

> Someone once said to me that the best way to get researchers to be serious about the issue of modernizing scholarly communications was

> to let the scholarly monograph business go to the wall as an object lesson to everyone else. After the last couple of weeks I'm beginning to think the same might be said of the UK Humanities and Social Sciences literature. … the problem is that people are focusing on the wrong problems and missing the significant opportunities to rejuvenate H&SS in the UK. (Neylon 2012)

If up to this point one thing is absolutely clear, then it is the fact that the topic of digital publications in academia is full of emotions. In it, the parallelity of fascination and resignation, between hope and frustration, form a weird but vibrant mixture. On the one hand, this mixture has been very productive insofar as a tremendous wealth of projects, initiatives, technologies, and models came to light. On the other hand, it has also shown itself to be extremely destructive, because resources and vigor often have been spent for nothing, while researchers, publishers, and other stakeholders are confronted with a growing amount of uncertainty about the publishing environment that should sustain their careers.

As Hall (2013, 497) puts it, today "all publishing is destined to become vanity publishing." The last paragraphs have shown that this might not only apply to concrete publications, but similarly to new forms or models of publications. Of the more than twenty publication concepts analyzed in the study at hand, many became relatively insignificant after funding had stopped. Others only survive in a small niche of experts and enthusiasts, of which many were directly involved in its development. While for Hall, vanity publishing constitutes the new, digital condition for publishing as such, it is not surprising that not everyone embraces this prospect as much as he does. The complaints about missing standardization and vast heterogeneity in the world of digital publications showed that there is much desire for more sustainable solutions, solutions that would be accepted by a broad academic audience and that could be sustained by bundling efforts and resources.

The insight that the imminent revolution and the revolution-postponed-until-further-notice are part of the same process and confront each other in a constant relationship within this process, puts a particularly interesting light on the question of what the reason behind all this might be. In brief, why does this relationship appear to be constant, and why have digital publication models not been more successful over the years? Missing standards and too many new publication formats seem to be more a symptom of a problem that is not immediately definable. The issue of heterogeneity, together with the nearly twenty-five years of developments, more than any other issue indicate that reasons exceed the scope of missing technological developments, or the need to just wait longer for stakeholders to finally adopt new publication formats. It would also be misleading to assume that broad funding would change this situation. In fact, substantial funding has taken place for more than ten years. In the European Union alone, it has brought to light multilateral research projects such as *DRIVER*, *workflow4ever*, and *OpenAIRE*, funded across several terms on a broad scale.

In the case of the UK, social sciences, and humanities, Neylon argued that people's way of reflecting on the topic of digital publications is inappropriate. As a strong advocate for innovative publications, he has a clear opinion of the actual problems and advantages of such publications. In the light of the current pattern, it seems, however, less obvious if certain problems are "wrong problems" and if opportunities are opportunities without restriction. Although time has passed, technological and conceptual implementations have taken place, and resources have been spent, advocates of digital publications nonetheless remain rather unhappy. It thus seems plausible to look for the underlying problem in a completely different place. This line of thought has become slightly old-fashioned these days, but maybe the problem is not some missing piece requiring a solution in order to turn digital scholarly publications into reality. Maybe the problem is in fact the awareness of the problem. Do stakeholders agree on the problem domain of digital publications? Do stakeholders evaluate problems in a similar way? Obviously, this is not the case. Does a way to look at things exist that could help balance the tension between certain expectations and the observations of researchers involved in the field? Is a way of engagement into scholarly publications and digital technologies conceivable that would make the distinction between revolutionaries and skepticists less paradigmatic?

Built on the abovementioned paradoxes, shaping the history of the research field of digital scholarly publications, it is indeed the hypothesis and the point of departure of the study at hand that the main obstacle for more sustainable publication formats is a problem of awareness about what is going on in the field, and what the relationships between digital technologies and publications encompass. The author is, moreover, convinced that conceptual work and the discussion of a problem can be as much a part of problem solving as implementation and modelling. It appears that this is not necessarily self-evident, especially in an environment in which "Building a Scholarly Digital Object" widely focuses on technological tasks (Meeks 2012). Owen (2006, 15) had already observed back in 2006 that related research has a “deficiency in terms of theoretical underpinning” and that this situation suggests “that the problem is more a lack of a coherent discursive formation.” Years later, Jankowski et al. (2012, 19) still note that the field is in “much need to extend theoretical understanding of the transformations that scholarly publication is undergoing.” This is not to say that theoretical research on digital scholarly publishing does not exist, but too often it exists only outside of and very much detached from projects, agents, and environments trying to build digital publication formats as well.

It sometimes feels as if there is an opposition between builders and theorizers, similar to the opposition between revolutionaries and skeptics. It would probably be more promising instead to have more builders with a healthy degree of skepticism and theorizers with a certain amount of capacity to build things. In the rare cases where theoretical discussions really become an integral part of the design process of new publication formats, it mostly happens as a means to an end. The by far most outstanding example for this is the “end of theory” debate, initiated by Anderson in 2008, and very much linked to the theme of the “fourth paradigm” (Hey, Tansley, and Tolle 2009). In both debates, it is argued that computers are not just new tools to carry out research. Instead, they could change the whole relationship between researchers and research objects. They basically allow to judge differently what counts as good research. It is then not surprising that particularly researchers, who want publications to better support computational analysis, intensively reference these debates. The real irony of this example, besides demonstrating the very pragmatic use of theory in digital publications environments, obviously is the performative contradiction it carries out. It makes a theoretical claim that undermines the feasibility of theoretical claims. Accordingly, the diagnoses made by Owen and Jankowski go well with observations about the role theory often plays in environments where future publication formats are defined.

If the claim that the conflict-loaded development of digital publishing stems from a lack of, or a paradoxical, conceptual framing is correct, the first task would be to identify explicit as well as hidden motifs driving this field of research. Having in mind the remarks of Owen and later Jankowski, it would not be enough to just analyze the written narrative in greater detail. This strategy would probably miss significant aspects of the whole development. Instead, it would be necessary to relate the narrative on digital publishing to something more concrete that can qualify and show its impact, as well as reveal aspects of the development that are not part of it.

A study of concrete formats and models for innovative, digital publications seems to offer exactly this type of access to the field of digital publishing. There is a tremendous amount of research literature evaluating the prospects of scholarly publishing in digital environments in general. In many cases, however, the authors are not part of developments in which the implementation of new types of objects happen, and which will have to carry and support the proposed ideas in real life. Research that is somehow tied to the task of implementing new scholarly objects, which in turn should serve the purpose of digital publications, reflects and reproduces the broader narrative. However, its analysis also facilitates the discovery and comparison of themes that are not openly discussed. It does so because the suggested and actual features of the newly designed publication formats allow revealing of such themes.

The strategy of reproducing the conceptual and mental environment around a topic out of an analysis of how the narrative, the relevant objects, artefacts, or installations are organized and structured, has a long tradition in humanities and social sciences research. Not least because of Michel Foucault's "Archaeology of Knowledge" (Foucault 1982), it has become a widely used methodology that did not remain without impact on the field of digital publishing. Owen (2006, 15) himself makes references to Foucault in order to put the background of his analysis into context. In more recent years, the French philosopher Bernard Stiegler (2012, 8) made use of Foucault's concept of the archive in order to outline some of the building blocks towards a new research field investigating "the emergence of digital technologies, of the internet and the web … as a new system of publication constituting a new public thing."

The inclusion of concrete publication formats into the analysis does not only add context to the analysis of the narrative, it also provides context in the form of the historical dimension in the development of digital publications. It allows to ask what the different turns in this history tell us about the issue of digital publications. Historical viewpoints, in fact, appear throughout the whole period defined above. In most cases, such viewpoints consist of comparing the situation of digital publications with the moment of the invention of the printing press or the formalization of the journal article (Dewar 2000; Kircz 1998; Buckingham Shum and Clark 2010; Willinsky, Garnett, and Pan Wong 2012; Bartling and Friesike 2014; De Roure 2014b). These comparisons, as helpful as they might be in some cases, are extremely ambiguous. It goes without saying that they may give orientation in a situation in which new conditions appear, with which there is trivially no long-term experience yet. It is this orientation, however, that might become a source of problems on its own, because, since experiences could not have been accumulated yet, it is uncertain which elements can legitimately be compared to each other. These comparisons pose a risk of withholding details that do not fit into them, resulting in biased interpretation. Owen (2006, 212) even goes so far as to speak of a "distorted view of history" which serves the purpose to suppose a direct and linear relationship between technological innovations and developing practices.

Fortunately, today it is actually no longer necessary to refer back to historical situations where publication formats were introduced that people are familiar with. More than twenty years of digital scholarly publishing constitutes its own historical horizon. This horizon is sufficiently broad to draw conclusions from it, supporting further engagement.

It will therefore be the task of the present study to analyze research on formats and models of so-called digital publications. The analysis will include both the models and formats themselves as well as the narrative, arguments, and leitmotifs surrounding them. It will attempt to map the conceptual and mental space in which digital publications emerged, in order to identify issues, inconsistencies, or tensions which might be able to explain the paradoxical situation summarized at the beginning. With reference to the abovementioned tradition of discourse analysis, it needs to be added that the parts belonging to such a strategy are not meant to be a goal in themselves. The goal is to use this approach as a means to find ways towards a less emotional discourse with less frustrated agents. Consequently, the present study will not stop at making a discursive formation explicit, but will intervene and try to reconfigure the discourse. The goal is to untie some of the elements in research on digital scholarly publications that appear to be indeed knots. For this to happen, parts of the analyzed discourse must be reconfigured.

For reasons of clarity, it makes sense to recall the specifications of digital publications that have been made so far, before beginning with the task described above. A digital scholarly publication is understood as a new type of publication. It might differ from historical publications in certain features, by including elements that have not appeared in historical publication, or by having a completely different "form and structure." A digital scholarly publication, furthermore, is a publication that is linked to certain understandings of digital technology. In other words, to count as a digital publication in the present analysis it has to follow that very idea that the possibilities of digital technologies define what it should look like. This conviction is a fundamental element of the field, which, as seen before, distinguishes digital publications from the notion of electronic publications or other types of variations of the form and structure of publications that might also exist. Digital publications are often described as "born digital," appreciated by "new digitally native researchers," as Goble, De Roure, and Bechhofer (2012, 7) put it. Where in this study the terms digital publication format, publication concept, or just publication are used without further specification, they refer to this specific notion of publications in academia.

The abovementioned specification defines conceptual boundaries around the research object of interest. There is, however, another challenge that needs attention before deeper analysis can begin. The cunning aspect of this specification is the fact that it defines the research field of digital publications in opposition to historical publications, but without providing any description of the concept of scholarly publications in general. This is intentional. It is the reaction to a constitutive problem of the topic. In the field of digital publications, the whole concept of publications is questioned, as will become clearer later on. Completely "new ways of publishing scholarship" (O'Hearn et al. 2017, 8) emerge, but these are very often "not recognized as a scholarly contribution" (Palmer et al. 2009, 33). This situation demands restraint from any normative definitions of scholarly publications at the very beginning. Instead, the present study will consider initiatives that place themselves in the context of scholarly publishing. Although it is not the primary goal of this study to define publications in times of digital technologies, the task of reconfiguring the conceptual space of digital publishing cannot be effective without a notion of publication up to a certain extent. Such notion will therefore gradually emerge out of the final part of this research. As far as the selection of research literature is concerned, literature will be included that affirms making a contribution to the topic of scholarly publications, agreeing on and supporting the prospects of digital publication as outlined before, and whose authors are in some way involved in concrete activities which define, model, or implement new publication formats.

The six chapters of this study can be split up into three different steps. The first step, as indicated already, consists of a historical analysis of the discourse and the design of digital publications. This analysis takes place in chapters one to four. Each chapter includes its own historical phase within this history. The organization of the history of digital publications into basically four phases is an outcome of this study and does not draw on other arrangements, of which there are hardly any. The first phase extends from the mid-nineties of the last millennium to the beginning of this millennium. It includes the first attempts and ideas completely revising the concept of scholarly publication, albeit within a technological environment that had just begun to appear on the horizon and which was rapidly changing. The second phase extended to approximately 2007. It saw a decrease of activities of the kind described above. Instead, there were a lot of changes in technological and organization infrastructure, from which the subsequent phase should benefit extremely. In the third phase, the most ideas revolving around digital publication formats appeared, and most activities and implementations took place. It is a direct consequence of the preceding phase which left the field with new possibilities to explore and test the scope of what it might mean to create a publication in academia. The final phase, which is still in an early stage, does not so much introduce new ideas as it tries to orient itself within the outcome of the vibrant period before. The beginning of this phase cannot be determined exactly, as it gradually emerges out of the deceleration of earlier activities. This takes place at different times, depending on the area in which specific activities took place. In most cases, this is between 2014 and 2016.

The last two chapters completely change the perspective on the topic. As mentioned before, the historical analysis brings to light central themes, key claims, and key arguments from the entire research field of digital scholarly publications. Ultimately, they are all facets of three fundamental questions: what are digital technologies, how does science work and what is the relationship between the two? The reference to the debate around "the end of theory" has already shown that Owen's original question, of how far the emergence of digital technologies has changed the scientific article, includes the question of how it has an impact on science and scientific methodology. It is then not unexpected that contributors to the field of digital publications frequently note that "researchers are envisaging a large variety of new research patterns that revolutionizing how science is being conducted" (Candela et al. 2015, 1747). Acknowledging the crucial impact of debates around these three questions on the developments of digital publications means that for the goal of reconfiguring the discourse of the field, it is indispensable to discuss them in greater detail.

Chapter five does exactly this. It starts with an evaluation of the concept of the digital and relates it to the notion of computation as the epitome of what is referred to as digital technology. Afterwards, the ways in which digital technologies can change the production and representation of knowledge are analyzed and compared with the arguments found in the history of digital publications. Both sections draw on the concept of the *post-digital* and the research field of *multimodal analysis*. This analysis reveals first insights into reasons for the paradoxical perception of digital publications, as well as for the frustration in the field. The final part of the chapter develops a hypothesis about how the emergence of digital technologies themselves might have contributed to the paradoxical debate. It uses the concepts of intermedial shifts and epistemic effects proposed by Sybille Krämer, and applies them to the appearance of digital technologies.

Chapter six, finally, lays the groundwork for a reconfiguration of the discourse on digital scholarly publications. It introduces some basic ideas in this respect, which continue to use concepts of multimodal analysis. At the beginning, a revision of publication formats with regard to the way these formats conceptualize their social dimension shows how much social aspects are simplified. This insight is presented as a result of the processes described in the chapter before. Afterwards, an empirical analysis of the social embeddedness of digital publication formats draws a more complex picture of this social dimension. It is then demonstrated how the issue of the social dimension of digital publication formats causes more tension, namely between the idea of communication and that of a publication. It turns out that in the research field of digital publications, both are hardly defined or distinguished. The chapter, and with it the current research, concludes with the application of three key concepts of multimodal analysis to the situation of digital publications. The application clarifies how the issues, conceived of as problems within the field, are not necessarily problems at all. It furthermore offers some conceptual orientation for future contributions, which draw on the viewpoint of this study.

[1]

Cyberpublishing

The ACM Publishing Plan

As has been argued in the introduction, the *ACM Electronic Publishing Plan* by Peter Denning and Bernard Rous, published in the year 1995, is one of the best and most often quoted references for a shift that took place in the way computers and network architectures are perceived from a publishing point of view. There are at least two interesting aspects about this manifest style paper. First, it already addresses many topics that were picked up, suggested, and partly developed later on and until today. Second, it states that digital publishing, without really giving it that name, was already taking place at the time of writing:

> These transformations have already begun. The clock cannot be turned back. ACM authors are already placing documents in databases on the "web" of information servers. (Denning and Rous 1995, 76)

This observation is significant because it highlights that the authors are one of the driving forces of digital publishing and that the *Association for Computing Machinery*[1] (also referred to as ACM) as a publisher needs to react to such developments. Hence, it is not the publishers who have the initiative.

The transformations Denning and Rous refer to are mainly social issues which themselves appear as a consequence of options presented by digital technologies. The authors (1995, 72–74) observe among other things that:

- scientists are not satisfied with the format of publications because it allegedly gathers too much information irrelevant to their interests;

1 http://www.acm.org/

- scientists are frustrated by the amount of time necessary for the traditional publishing workflow, especially in view of the scientific innovation cycle today;
- there is an information overload considered to be a consequence of the ever-growing amount of publications and research results;
- libraries are incapable of holding all publications that have been published;
- scientists therefore question the need for publishers as well as libraries;
- consequently, research output and publications are published more and more frequently on private servers and scientific work is perceived of as "living on the web";
- such content is therefore linked across documents, collaboratively created and continuously changing.

Based on such observations, Denning and Rous (1995, 75–77) outline a set of propositions that should be capable of dealing with the challenges posed by the aforementioned developments. In fact, these propositions are similar to themes which still shape a great deal of the research field of digital publication formats today. They can accordingly be called part of a collection of leitmotifs within the landscape of digital publishing. Such leitmotifs include:

- the need to increase the precision of information in publications;
- the need to accelerate the production chain of publications;
- the need to automate certain processes within the lifecycle of publications, in order to reduce publication time and to manage the information overload;
- the need to decentralize the organization of content of publications;
- the need to impose collaborative production workflows on publications;
- the need to conceive of publications as objects that are quickly obsolete and create a continuous demand for alteration.

Rous and Denning's work is also a good starting point for an inquiry into digital publications, because the authors make comprehensive suggestions as to how digital publications should be implemented in order to comply with the demands above. Accordingly:

- journals should become "streams" in which publishing takes place successively and without any interruptions imposed by concepts such as volume or edition;
- the "identity" of publications should be provided by means of "database categories";

- it should be possible to publish different states of a paper that can then be discussed online;
- technology should enable "repackaging" of the content of publications;
- the possibility to publish multiple resources as well as multi-media resources has to be offered;
- publishing has to include so-called "networked services";
- publications must be rendered in Standard Generalized Markup Language[2] (also referred to as SGML). They must provide explicit markup of images, graphs and other components.

It goes without saying that the authors understand these suggestions in a way that still is very much bound by the state of publishing at that time. Many of these ideas are radicalized in more recent projects. For instance, the database approach to articles just means the addition of meta-data to the articles. This should permit a grouping of articles different from the grouping in the journal volume in which these articles were published first. Despite such qualifications, Denning and Rous' work is one of the most comprehensive collection of ideas of its time and a pioneering contribution.

Additionally, it is important for present purposes to note that beyond the scale of innovative imagination Rous and Denning (1995, 82–83) also address a variety of social issues arising from technological changes in publishing. Challenges in this respect are: the system of copyright, the role of publishers and libraries, and the question of financial investment and responsibilities for long-term archiving of digital publications. As a publisher, albeit with limited economic interests, ACM needed to consider such issues by virtue of the very same reasons that were given in the quote at the beginning of this section. From their point of view their consideration was in fact a question of survival because "publishers that learn to provide well-structured knowledge through digital libraries and easy-to-use tools will be the main survivors and successful entrepreneurs in the new medium" (1995, 82).

The Roaring 90s

Few studies have tried to evaluate the state of digital publishing in the late 1990s. They show very well how innovative the scenario described in the ACM Publishing Plan must have looked. In 1997, Alsop et al. (1997) looked at three different digital journals examining their strategies in engaging

2 https://www.iso.org/standard/16387.html

with digital technologies. One of these journals added features to the publication which are not possible without these technologies. The pre-print database *Formations* implemented an open-review process by making use of a groupware software system in order to manage the publication process. The other two journals restrict themselves to putting published articles on web-pages or publish them separately on *CD-ROM*.

In 1998, Peek and Pomerantz (1998) conducted a survey which was much more comprehensive in terms of quantity and time frame of analyzed journals. They summarize the efforts of journals as activities that look to provide "alternative methods of access to scholarly" publications (1998, 331). Such access might be mediated by the *World Wide Web* or by CD-ROM. Common challenges and differences include the application and quality of *Optical Character Recognition*[3] (also referred to as OCR) for digitized articles or the inclusion of images and other resources in text exclusive archives.

These issues were not only evaluated in terms of technological challenges. Eason et al. (1997) studied different academic disciplines regarding their needs and preferences for linking between distinct information resources as well as for alternative access models. In the final analysis of their inquiry the authors observe that the role of online journals, as well as the need for capabilities like the ones above, varies significantly between disciplines. Consequently, three years after Denning and Rous, Peek and Pomerantz still stress that "the future of the electronic scholarly journal remains unclear" (1998, 344).

Other authors judged this situation quite differently. Singh et al. (1998, sec. Recommendations) are more convinced that the "time is right to revolutionize the 'Scientific Journal Publishing Technology'." They conclude that the reason why this revolution had not yet taken place at the time of their writing is primarily related to the "reluctance of the senior scientific community" (1998, sec. Acceptance) and only secondly to issues of infrastructure and financing. For further analysis, it is significant to highlight the different backgrounds of the authors which coincide with their distinct judgements. Accordingly, Singh et al. write from a computer science and engineering point of view while Eason et al. conducted their research in a "department of human sciences."

This distinction becomes even more significant when looking at some of the rare examples of more innovative journals tested at that time. In

3 Optical Character Recognition parses image files in order to computationally identify characters, letters and text which might be present on the image. Such segments are then turned into text representations in text files.

1998, Wheary et al. (1998) presented the Journal *Living Reviews* hosted at a *Max Planck Institute* and aimed at the field of gravitation physics. Burg et al. (2000) presented a bi-annual publication called *The IMEJ of Computer Enhanced Learning* (also referred to as IMEJ). IMEJ — sometimes also called IMMJ — is an abbreviation for *Interactive Multimedia Electronic Journals*. This term is one of the first propositions of a shared label for a bunch of more experimental digital journals.

These examples show that IMMJs are strongly linked to the field of computer science and the application of computation in day to day research work. The same link also applies to the assessment of the situation itself. Additionally, authors convinced of the benefits of digital publications are often the ones who also develop the underlying technologies. Some of the authors who designed new publication objects later on were first deeply involved in the fields of hypermedia research, like David De Roure (Carr et al. 1995; Carr et al. 1998), technological interoperability, like Jane Hunter (Lagoze, Hunter, and Brickley 2000; Hunter and Lagoze 2001), or information infrastructure projects, as in the case of Herbert van de Sompel (van de Sompel, Hochstenbach, and De Pessemier 1997).

The main concerns of IMMJs are already transparent in its name. On the one hand this includes a deeper integration of images and video into publications via embedding into html or referencing through links (Singh et al. 1998; Burg et al. 2000). On the other hand, there are attempts to evaluate the possibilities of interactivity enabled by computation. Such interactivity includes published simulations or interactive visualizations (Singh et al. 1998), but also for the first time software that would be re-runnable within a publication (Burg et al. 2000). Wheary et al. (1998) add the idea of evolving articles to these points. More precisely, authors are advised in the corresponding publication to continuously change their articles and to adapt them to the progressing state of research. The publication is thus not a stable entity any more. It constantly changes.

Another important if not immediately obvious type of innovation is offered by projects trying to explore how to represent books or documents in a digital way. Such projects did not design publication formats directly but generated ideas that have since been adopted by publishing projects. Outstanding in terms of public perception is the *Hypermedia Research Archive of the Complete Writings and Pictures of Dante Gabriel Rosetti* (McGann 1994). One goal of this project was "to use the Rossetti Archive as a model for exploring the theoretical structure of texts in general" (96). Likewise, efforts to represent ancient Japanese books in a "hypermedia model" can be named here, where books are perceived as a set of multiple compositions of networked nodes (Kitamura and Leggett 1996). Phelps and Wilensky (1996) went one step further by reflecting on the question, "What is a digital document?" In their view a digital document is just an abstract entity aggregating "complex content" from different physical sources. Such content can be presented in different ways, depending on the user's interaction.

Overall, it could be said that efforts on digital publications in the nineties took place under the impression of the hypertext or hypermedia theme. This theme is addressed most often as the idea of different resources that may be of different types and can be linked to each other in various ways. There are differences between the approach of questioning historical publication formats by way of application of this idea, and the approach of questioning this theme regarding its relevance for publishing formats. Another difference is the one between projects applying this idea to historical publication formats and those who use it to create publication formats. In the first case hypertext is used as a model for the representation of something that exists already. In the second case it is a paradigm for the design of something new. Later on, Nentwich (2003) will give this distinction a name by calling it the distinction between "weak" or "strong" hypertext structures.

As has been outlined before there were few innovations with a broader impact or ones that lasted longer. Most contributions to the issue of digital publications entered the scene on a more fundamental level, meaning by building general technological infrastructure, or as abstract reflections without any connections to particular publication formats (Kreitzberg 1989; Davenport and Cronin 1990; Brüggemann-Klein, Cyranek, and Endres 1995; Brüggemann-Klein 1995; Karisiddappa and Moorthy 1996; Thatcher 1996). In this context the ACM publishing plan is worth mentioning because it had a unique approach, not completely moving into one or the other of the aforementioned directions. It discussed changes on a meta level but also defined concrete technical and non-technical measures.

Publication formats implemented in the early stage of digital publications were affected significantly by technological problems stemming from general technological infrastructure that itself had just begun to develop. Singh et al. (1998, sec. Issues) mainly list infrastructural issues like bandwidth of internet connection, storage space for multi-media resources, secure connections, or even e-mail accounts for scientists. Further technical challenges concerned publication infrastructures and software itself, namely the support of digital publications through the development of tools to produce them. In the majority of cases the discussion of authoring tools referred to the conditions of word processors not well suited for the creation of more innovative publications formats like the IMMJ (Sørgaard and Sandahl 1997). Another problem implicit to the topic of authoring tools was the lack of formalized data and content models which technically model the publication. Denning and Rous as well as Wheary et al. (Wheary et al. 1998) propose the *LaTeX*[4] model while other journals and authors prefer SGML (Ishizuka 1997). This led to a clash of technological backgrounds. Furthermore, both options were also not well suited for the complex demands of IMMJs, which might be the reason why Singh et al. do not specifically mention any technological model. It will become clear later on that there is a greater challenge behind this issue.

Considering the state of the art of digital publishing as described by Eason et al. (above), it is of similar importance to emphasize that such discussions had limited influence on the broader landscape of scholarly publishing as such. In the final analysis both these problems — immature infrastructure and the lack of formats that match up with the abstract ideas — led to the fact that those digital publications trying to be innovative were only realized by applying highly context dependent solutions and making use of proprietary technology like *Java* applets. In consequence, corresponding publications only existed within concrete project environments and as objects in the browser.

The Modular Article

The concept of the *Modular Article* (hereafter referred to as MA), proposed by Frédérique Harmsze, Joost Kircz and Marteen van der Tol between 1998 and 2000 (Harmsze and Kircz 1998; Kircz 1998; Harmsze 2000; Kircz and Harmsze 2000), can be interpreted as a major milestone in the development of digital publication models. It was probably the first consistently designed and formally serialized digital publication model, developed on a large scale and tested for publications in different research fields. This might be why it is still used today as a point of reference for modelling digital publications (see Castelli, Manghi, and Thanos 2013; Bardi and Manghi 2014). It dramatically sharpened some aspects of the profile for digital publications that today have found publishing formats of their own, namely *Semantic Publications* (see chap. 3). Furthermore, it is one of the few

4 https://www.latex-project.org/

instances where a project modelling a publication format combines this with a broader theoretical context.

The Modularization of Content into Units of Information

One of the crucial achievements of the concept of MAs is the dissociation of certain concepts both from its terminological as well as its technological context within hypertext and hypermedia research (Harmsze, van der Tol, and Kircz 1999; Harmsze 2000). More precisely, MAs emphasizes the benefit of decomposing publications into smaller pieces which are then related to each other by links. This structure permits the independent dissemination and consumption or grouping of parts in different ways. In MAs such parts are called "modules."

The hypertext parallel is obvious but the concept of a module exceeds the nature of structural units in html documents or any technological distinction between media- or file-types. As a model existing independently from specific implementations, but also more technologically formalized than many ideas about publishing from the nineties, Modular Articles are aimed at an entity of particular importance for science. What in hypertext is a document and in hypermedia is a media-resource is called *information unit* in Modular Articles:

> A module is a uniquely characterized, self-contained representation of a conceptual information unit, which is aimed at communicating that information. (Harmsze 2000, 39)

Kircz (1998, sec. 2.3) argues that even the *URL*[5] is "an attempt to maintain to a certain level the tradition of a local archive," thus emphasizing the radicalism of his approach. The fact that by this definition a module is not framed in any technological or material way, as in the case of historical publications, turns decomposability into a general principle in the field of digital publishing (see also Bishop 1999). For Kircz this step is just a "natural consequence of the split between storage and presentation" (Kircz 1998, sec. 2.5). This split is allegedly suggested by the web architecture which delivers content from a server to any place within the web architecture. The rendering takes place in the *client* to which the content is delivered and can happen in many ways. Likewise, it should be mandatory to distinguish between *Form and Content in the Electronic Age* (Harmsze and Kircz 1998).

5 The *Uniform Resource Locator* is the technical term for links between resources like websites in the web.

As has been stated before, the novelty of the Modular Article approach is that it entangles theory and modelling. Accordingly, Kircz and Harmsze try to support their publication design by developing sophisticated claims. Such claims tackle the history as well as the goal of publications, and the nature of information. They configure the background for a clearly defined environment of digital publishing in which MAs are the key component.

The History of Publications Between Rigidity and Dissolution

In "Modularity: The Next Form of Scientific Information Presentation?" Kircz (1998) paraphrases the history of text as a monolithic linear object. He argues that the development of text into a publication in modern science is driven by the idea of persistence as a consequence of the persistence of its material carrier. With regard to McLuhan's *Gutenberg Galaxy* (McLuhan 2002) he describes that from oral culture to the medieval scriptorium up to the era of the printing press, text became increasingly structured and controlled, thereby facilitating a certain concept of scientific truth (Kircz 1998, sec. 2.1). The development of scientific journals with certain norms for the structure of its articles is presented as another step in this process. He attributes the general norm for this structure to Francis Bacon and his idea that knowledge is produced where the behavioral laws of the world match with the procedure and the strategy by which this world is described (Kircz 1998, sec. 2.2). In Kircz' overview both developments were only possible due to the facilities of the printing press.

From the end of the 18th century onwards the author identifies a destabilization of the scientific publishing system. This destabilization is presented as an overproduction of publications and thus an information overload. Curiously, for Kircz this process is socially and not technically motivated as was the case before. For instance, he identifies the entanglement between science on the one hand and economic as well as military competition on the other hand as a fundamental driver for this development (Kircz 1998, sec. 2.3).

Following the author, the presentation layer of publications is primarily the linearly structured narrative. The main problem of information overload is therefore the conflict between publications adhering to this linear and narrative structure while on the level of archiving[6] such structure allegedly does not exist anymore (sec. 2.4). Kircz repeats the argument about

6 When Kircz uses the term archive at this point he means publishing infrastructure which is delivered by digital technologies.

information overload as a driving force and a request to change the field of publishing already made by Denning. However, he substantiates this claim by adding a techno-historical argument.

Catching up on his evaluation of the role of the printing press for publishing, Harmsze and Kircz (1998, sec. 3) conclude that "we are now entering a new phase in which again a medium with superior capacities will change the form of the knowledge representations."

Once again, the quote distinguishes between form and content and constructs a notion of information and knowledge that can be clearly separated from the channel by which people become aware of it: "by a document we mean a symbolic representation of a quantity of information" (Harmsze 2000, 19). However, more important is the techno-historical necessity enforcing this distinction upon new publication formats.

The Hard Currency of Publications for the Communicative Endeavour of Science

If in the worldview of Modular Articles information exists independently of its narration, and presentation has no information value of its own, the question arises: "What is a scientific paper?" (Kircz 2001b, 266). In order to respond to this, Kircz refers to William Garvey's *Communication: The Essence of Science* (Garvey 1979). Accordingly, the key aspect in science is communication and the role of publications is that of being a "hard currency." In order to play this role Kircz states that publications have to be reliable and fulfill certain functions. More precisely, they have to guarantee registration, certification, awareness and archiving of information (Kircz 1998, sec 3.2). These properties therefore constitute something he calls the "trans-historical core" of publications. In contrast, the form of publications is only important up to the extent to which it seeks to achieve a design that best suits the needs of communication under the conditions of a peculiar historical period and the technology it delivers.

Harmsze (2000, 25) derives the needs of scientific communication from the general idea that such communication is primarily goal oriented. Defining the goals allows the definition of requirements which in turn lead to features for publications. Harmsze uses a sender-receiver model of communication in which goals are described both for readers and authors of publications. The evaluation takes place on the basis of an analysis of scientific communication in the field of experimental sciences. Within the frame of goal-oriented communication, the outcome of such analysis is that publications have to assure efficient communication. Communication is defined as efficient when it is clear, orderly, brief, and when it avoids ambiguity (Harmsze 2000, 22–24). While the trans-historical idea of publications is to communicate knowledge, the possibilities of realizing the specific type of scientific communication should shape their form at any given point of time. From an MA point of view modularity and explicitness in terms of formalization meet these requirements best.

The Biology of Information

At this point modularity is nonetheless still an abstract idea. It needs to become applicable to assure its potential for efficient scientific communication. The criterion for the implementation of modules is the identity of an *information unit*. An information unit is a piece of information or an aggregation of pieces of information focusing on a single concept (Harmsze 2000, 45). Furthermore, a module should be self-contained. This is the case when the meaning of a module makes sense without necessarily having to refer to other modules. An elementary module containing just one information is defined as the smallest piece of information that still holds the dependency of being self-contained.

The idea of concepts assures that it is possible to define modules as self-contained information units. They are strategical anchors from which it is possible to decide if an information should be part of an information unit or not. Without such an external viewpoint it would not be possible to define criteria to decide if a module is complete, is missing information, or includes unnecessary information. On the other hand, the problem would recur if the state of a concept was to be no different from the state of information. As has been noted, information as content detached from its presentation is an abstract entity according to Kircz and Harmsze. The difference is that for MAs, concepts are not abstract but embedded. The approach used by Harmsze refers to the work of Peter Gärdenfors (Gärdenfors 2000). Gärdenfors argues that three hierarchical levels of representation exist: a symbolical, a conceptual and a neurological level. Information is rendered on the symbolical level. In contrast, the neurological level does not really communicate. It is just a reflection of the world that is facilitated through our senses. The conceptual level in MAs should play the role of a mediator between the neurological and the symbolic layer.

The presented triptych allows judgements about the necessity, redundancy, or completeness of information and information units. It configures concepts in a way that makes them independent from the variation found in the application of the material in the symbolic layer. Indeed, common sense gives us the impression that it is possible to say the same thing in different ways. On the other hand, the idea that concepts are themselves anchored on a neurological level suggests that a conceptual level beyond symbolic heterogeneity must exist. By referring to the idea of concept classification of modules Harmsze (2000, 44) proposes that information is similar to atoms and molecules in the physical world.

To put it differently, the conceptual level is serialized by the idea of what Harmsze (2000, sec. 3.2) following Gärdenfors calls a "conceptual space." A conceptual space characterizes something in terms of its "quality dimensions." Harmsze offers the example of the concept "apple" which is characterized by color-, form- and taste- dimensions. It is possible to refer to the concept by making use of different quality dimensions. Each real-world object that is tackled by the concept instantiates a quality dimension differently (some apples are green, some red, some lighter and some darker). Nonetheless, the way in which the conceptual space takes this heterogeneity into account does not, in Harmsze's view, undermine but instead foster the idea of the existence of an underlying general concept. In turn, information units become definable and a modular approach to publications seems both appropriate and efficient.

Kircz describes very well what the goal of such efficiency is. Accordingly, the main idea behind modular articles is to prevent a problem which in the eyes of the author is the most significant problem of communication:

> … often information is repeated, whilst other information is missing. We try, in fact, to envision the information contained in the author's mind. (Kircz 1998, sec. 4)

Within the metaphor of hard currency, redundancy equates to inflation and missing information is deflation. What is important is that both aspects depreciate communication. Hence, the digressions about the conceptual level and the quality dimensions of information are not only an attempt to give evidence for the existence of information units, but also to offer approaches for better information retrieval. In order to really assure efficient communication, the conceptual level must be included in some way into the publication. Information overload demands not only a breakdown of publications into units which are easily consumable and correspond to its true nature. It also requires each module to be described by categories that make their true meaning processable. Modular Articles implement such categories as descriptive metadata attached to the modules. Harmsze (2000, 38–41) distinguishes between four types of categories to assure that the goal of efficient scientific communication is reached: categories referring to the conceptual function, categories addressing the type of scientific content, categories defining certain ranges like the temporal range, and finally bibliographic categories.

Semantic Links

A consequence of the theme of information efficiency on the one hand and modularity on the other hand is the design of *qualified links* between models. Harmsze (Harmsze 2000, 79–80) criticizes that in the web architecture of that time links only connect different resources but do not offer information on why the link exists. The goal of efficient communication however demands that a user has information about why the body and the target of a link — in the present case two modules — are connected to each other before she decides to follow the link.

That is why he proposes to add metadata not only to models abut also to links. Such metadata documents the creator, the time, and the type of relationship of the link. The type of relationship denotes the aspect by which two modules link to each other. Regarding scientific communication Harmsze (2000, 85) distinguishes between structural and discursive relationships. Structural relationships express which module contains what other modules, for instance in terms of the sequence of modules in a reading path, but also what concept a module represents, while discursive relationships document relationships in terms of logical reasoning.

Reflecting on Harmsze's work about MAs, Kircz (2002, 31) emphasizes that "relations which express themselves in hyperlinks become information objects in their own right." Thereby the modular article borrows heavily from the field of hypermedia research which had worked on this issue at the same time and before (De Roure and Hall 1997; Carr et al. 1998). It also anticipates the success of the *semantic web* (see chap. 3) introduced by Tim Berners-Lee in 2001 (Berners-Lee, Hendler, and Lassila 2001) and which influenced the course of digital publishing significantly. By doing so the Modular Article demonstrates its significance as a nexus between approaches in the nineties and developments that took place after the millennium. Furthermore, it illustrates how digital publishing at its very beginning is an effort that applies computer and information science concepts to the topic of publishing, in contrast to asking what possibilities for publishing exist by virtue of digital technologies.

Relevance and Limitations

Although at the verge of the next step of digital publications, MAs like IMMJs are still confronted with technology that is rapidly developing itself. Where no architecture for qualified links exists, there is also a lack of what today is called *web taxonomies* or *semantic vocabularies*, meaning formal vocabularies to consistently create classified links. Consequently, a lot of the work of Harmsze and Kircz consists of identifying appropriate viewpoints for classifications and defining terms. It is hence also not the goal of this present research to implement MAs and to further evaluate problems that become relevant after implementation. Nonetheless, those problems are listed and include issues of how to render and present them as well as how to author such complex objects. In association with the work of Harmsze, van der Tol (2001) develops an idea of how abstracts can be used to organize and comprehensively communicate MAs themselves. It could be said that such an idea partially opposes the whole point of the MAs insofar as it stresses that a type of composition is required for certain needs which is not dealt with by the concept of modules and links.

Another aspect is that MAs still focus on text modules. Kircz (2002, 29) is correct in mentioning that this is an unnecessary focus and also that non-textual resources can constitute modules. Nevertheless, there is no in-depth analysis of this viewpoint. The discussion of the question of how applicable the model of the MA is across disciplines is also problematic. The development of the model was bound to test cases from what Harmsze (2000, 97) calls "experimental sciences." Nonetheless, she claims that the model is generic and can be applied to publications from other domains (Harmsze 2000, 391–98), including the humanities. Significantly, she takes an example from the topic of "argumentation theory" to illustrate this. The field of application is thus a field that shares similar principles as those which lead to the definition of MAs.

Despite these remarks, MAs derive its major significance from the fact that it is the one publication format that most consistently represents the idea of decomposability of publications at that time.

Publication Formats Along the Path of Modular Articles

Although MAs develops the concept of modularity in its most radical form possible, by the turn of the millennium other projects existed which moved into a similar direction. Accordingly, McAdams and Berger (2001) present an alternative version of this topic. Traces of the discourse on modularity can be found up until 2008 (see de Waard and Kircz 2008). In 2007, Thomas (2007, 16) catches up on some propositions by McAdams and Berger in order to think about articles in terms of components. He presents his contribution to the *American Historical Review* in a "multisequential, multi-threaded, flexible, modular" way that "should break with the narrative structures." The unique contribution of this peculiar application of modularity is the fact that it was designed as an experiment in order to judge the actual usefulness of the approach. A long review process was associated with that aspect of the design of the article, leading to multiple revisions and a critical evaluation of modularity as such. Accordingly, Thomas asks to more clearly think on and define benefits and drawbacks of decomposing publications.

There are two more contributions which call their approaches "layered" publications. One has the form of a *layered article* (La Manna and Young 2002), the other of a *layered e-book* (Darnton 1999). The concept of a *Layered Publication* (hereafter referred to as LaP) is extremely similar to MAs. Again, it highlights the decomposition of publications into smaller pieces of information for the purpose of creating more efficient publications. It likewise defines efficiency in terms of the specific interests of goal-oriented readers and the possibilities of digital publications to comply with such goals. Finally, it also refers to publications mainly in the light of scholarly communication.

The difference between LaPs and MAs is the greater emphasis the first puts on precisely defined user roles. Accordingly, Darnton quotes the image of a pyramid in which the content is organized in different layers of complexity and information depths. Readers with different informational needs can approach the publication on different layers. Darnton's layered book is more traditional than MAs in the way that different information units are not really organized in separate forms. Instead the different layers are purposefully composed by the authors putting much more emphasis and effort on the authoring process. Nonetheless, the layered book needs to be stressed as one of few examples of digital publications that explicitly chooses the format of a book as a point of reference instead of articles.

Weiten, Wozny, and Goers (2002) made a contribution that focused much more on deeper technological issues than those discussed by Harmsze and Kircz. They rephrased the issue of efficient scholarly communication in terms of two problems: *interoperability*[7] and *information retrieval*[8]. By making use of the conceptual approach of MAs they emphasize the importance of technologies within the portfolio of the *Extensible Markup Language*[9] (also referred to as XML) in order to solve the first problem. Regarding the second problem, the authors highlight the need to define formal vocabularies, however this time in the form of sophisticated *ontologies* (see chap. 3). A more granular decomposition of publications than the one provided by MAs was offered by Caracciolo (2003). The author defines an approach in which a publication is reorganized around key concepts connected by relations comparable to those that can be found in thesauri.

7 Interoperability is a technical term in the field of computer science which tackles issues that assure that data can be processed consistently between different computers. A more technical definition of interoperability is given by the *interoperability-definition project (see http://interoperability-definition.info/en/).*

8 Information retrieval is a research field in computer and information science which develops means and strategies in order to provide the most relevant information in relation with a specific demand for such information. For further details see Jansen and Rieh (2010).

9 http://www.w3.org/TR/xml11

[2]

World Wide Publishing

Projects aiming at implementing concrete designs for digital publications declined in the first years of the new millenium. Instead, researchers like Leonardo Candela or Herbert Van de Sompel and others, who later engaged in the implementation of such designs, initiated projects that tried to create better conditions for the technological and social environment of digital publications. Such projects build on some of the key ideas of the discourse on digital publications, to be discussed more in depth later on. Some of these ideas were actually forged during this very period, such as the idea of open access and data science among others. This shift of attention from concrete publication projects to more global activities might in addition to other reasons also be caused by restrictions of technology and organization that have been pointed to more than once in the last chapter.

Position of Points in Infrastructure and Virtual Publishing Environments

Accordingly, Kennedy (2003) heavily highlights the meaning and potential of the *Open Archive Initiative*[1] (also referred to as OAI, see below) for the progress of the digital publishing ecosystem. He additionally argues with great passion that the project of the semantic web that had just been proclaimed by Berners-Lee, Hendler, and Lassila (2001) would be crucial for new digital publications. Furthermore, Hammond, Hannay, and Lund (2004)

1 https://www.openarchives.org/

explore how the *Really Simple Syndication*[2] (also referred to as RSS) model, another recent initiative at that time, could be used for in a digital publication context.

While MAs and similar activities explored how publications could be decomposed, another line of research started to prepare the design of completely new types of publications. These initiatives evaluated and defined models for the design of *aggregations* (Van de Sompel et al. 2010) of distributed resources and any media-types which would become *compound information objects* (Lagoze and Van de Sompel 2007, see chap. 3.2). The main shift behind such initiatives was the intent to not only structure and render a publication in a different way but to really set a new starting point for thinking about publications.

> This established system generally fails to deal with other types of research results in the sciences and humanities, including datasets, simulations, software, dynamic knowledge representations, annotations, and aggregates thereof, all of which should be considered units of scholarly communication. (Van de Sompel and Lagoze 2007, par. 2)

These resources may come from any point within the sphere of research. They do not depend on a final paper that synthesizes everything.

In 2003, Bekaert, Hochstenbach, and Van de Sompel (2003) already evaluated the potential of the *MPEG-21 Digital Item Declaration Language*[3] (also referred to as DIDL) format in order to model such compound information objects. A similar activity led to the definition of the *Document Model for Digital Library* (Candela et al. 2005, also referred to as DoMDL), meant to build the core schema of the *OpenDLib Digital Library System* (Castelli and Pagano 2002). This model would facilitate the organization of *Heterogeneous Information Spaces to Virtual Documents* (Candela et al. 2005). Lourdi, Papatheodorou, and Nikolaidou (2007) present a hierarchical model to aggregate resources of folklore collections which are part of one theme but represented in different media formats.

However, these and similar attempts had limitations. Some focus on the scope of a concrete repository, often for certain types of resources, and the use of XML as the foundation for the model. The limits of XML as a hierarchical data model for the representation of aggregations that should hold different types of resources from different repositories are

2 http://www.rssboard.org/rss-specification

3 https://mpeg.chiariglione.org/standards/mpeg-21/mpeg-21.htm

summarized by Brooking et al. (2009). Consequently, in 2006 the *Mellon Foundation* offered a two-year grant for the development of a new data model for compound information objects. This model was developed under the name of *Object Reuse and Exchange*[4] (also referred to as ORE) model. It was presented in 2007 (Lagoze and Van de Sompel 2007; Van de Sompel and Lagoze 2007) and was intended to realize the creation of scholarly digital publications as aggregations from the very beginning, even if its application nowadays exceeds such purpose. All these activities can be understood as infrastructure and technology developments. The reason for this is that they not only try to enable digital publications in the aforementioned manner but also that they constitute a significant extension to the web architecture in ways hypermedia research has worked on for a long time (Ossenbruggen, Hardman, and Rutledge 2006).

A different angle on infrastructure is introduced by Kennedy (2003). The author regrets that "until now, there has been no standardized framework from which organizations can freely explore and develop this option [electronic publishing]" (2003, sec. abstract). In this respect he describes and implements a service-oriented software that should manage the whole workflow of the production of digital publications. A comparable effort is presented by Sanchez, Morales, and Flores (2004). The service described aims at so-called *Digital Publishing Organizations* (also referred to as DPO). It tries to support the coordination process of agents involved in the creation of digital publications. The approaches that tried to act on a global scale were complemented by initiatives such as that presented in (Ghani, Suparjoh, and Hamid 2008), which did the same on an institutional level. All of them have in common that they focus on infrastructure in order to support interactions and workflows between stakeholders and agents in the chain of production of digital publications, while the former activities are aimed at facilitating the creation of publication data models as well as necessary computational interactions between them. In the same fashion Liew and Foo (1999; 2001) stress that the main innovation in digital publishing is not the publication, but an increasing level of possible interactions, especially for readers. Accordingly, they suggest investing more energy into the design of computational environments offering easy integration and usability of new publications.

4 https://www.openarchives.org/ore/

Programmatic Framing and Organizational Self-Awareness

The shift of interest regarding digital publications also led to a broader analysis of digital publications within a certain historical and social context. In the *Delphi Survey*, for instance, agents from the publishing, library, and research domain tried to evaluate the future of digital publishing in terms of design, financing, usage, and archiving, as well as the effects for the stakeholders (Keller 2001). In all these discussions the problem of the *serial crisis* — an alternative way of referring to the information overload — was a major topic guiding these reflections. Correspondingly, agents from the area of research libraries as well as researchers themselves argued that the development of digital publications in electronic journals may solve this serial crisis (Agosti et al. 2013). The development of such publications would help research libraries to gain autonomy from private publishers by providing cost efficient ways to produce, manage, and disseminate publications (Kennedy 2003). Thus, the development of computational services for the creation and curation of electronic publications can also be seen in a political light.

This political agenda behind the promotion of digital publications began to take shape in the formation of the *Scholarly Publishing and Academic Resources Coalition*[5] (also referred to as SPARC) around the turn of the millennium. One of the main goals of SPARC was to increase the possibilities of research libraries to strengthen their position in relation to publishers (Johnson 2001). In this respect they actively promoted an unrestricted access model for publications called *open access* from its very beginning with the *Budapest Open Access Initiative*[6] in 2001.

In contrast, publishers began to imagine new business models based on digital publications. Such activities built on the premise that publishers will transform from product centered to service-oriented businesses (Owen 2002). Hammond's evaluation of RSS mentioned above is one example of an early attempt to realize this claim. Following this premise, the implementation of digital publications should not so much alter the publication as it should connect publications with alerts about related activities, job notifications and other things. In this model the publication is deemed to be an interface that should facilitate the creation of profiles in order to deliver potentially interesting things for readers.

5 https://sparcopen.org/

6 http://www.budapestopenaccessinitiative.org/

The same period saw another theme come to light that will later on intervene with open access activities. Up to this point the re-design of digital publications was not closely linked to considerations about how science itself changes due to computational technologies. In contrast, Borgman, Wallis, and Enyedy (2007, 27) emphasize the emergence of "a new way of 'doing science'." In this new research model computation is the essential element. According to them research needs data as publications. The essential question is however what makes this type of data different from images, videos, text, and other media mentioned before. While a more comprehensive discussion of this question has to be postponed, a short response is that the argument is not so much about what the data is but how the interaction between researchers and data is conceived of. Such interaction privileges specific aspects of data presentation over others.

The idea of how research should or will take place then began to shape the design of publications. Borgman et al. continued to argue in favor of data libraries holding published data in a certain "reusable" way. This proposal is supported by a survey of Anderson, Tarczy-Hornoch, and Bumgarner (2006) who determined that at that time at least one fifth of the linked data from online publications was not available anymore. From a broader perspective on digital publications the issue of data publication equates to the emergence of publications that openly argued for building digital publications around its key component, that being data.

All of the topics outlined in the last paragraphs will reappear in the next chapter. The period of digital publications subsequent to the one in this chapter discusses and develops them in much greater detail. Nonetheless, the frame for much that is argued later on was set at the beginning of the millennium.

Early Theoretical Evaluations of Digital Publications

It is significant that in this period early attempts were made to comprehensively evaluate the state of the art of already implemented digital scholarly publications. In a highly theoretical perspective Nentwich (2003, chaps. 6.3–6.4) identifies a set of five different concepts of digital publication which consist of:

- Layered Article
- Modular Article
- Hyperdiscussion

- Hyperbook
- Knowledge Base

Some approaches already mentioned, such as IMMJs, are not completely covered by these categories. In contrast, concepts such as Hyperdiscussions and Knowledge Bases are not immediately understandable as publications in the first place. A Hyperdiscussion is an online discussion that is curated from time to time to be re-usable as a shared resource under academic terms. It is regarded as a publication because the online space is conceived of as a public space and because purposeful curation exists. A Knowledge Base is a resource which tries to comprehensively represent the state of the art of a defined field of inquiry. It is updated and modified consecutively to keep up with this goal. However, the content of a Knowledge Base does not necessarily focus on articles. A Hyperbook is something in between these two approaches and can be compared with the contribution of Wheary et al. (1998) discussed above. In the long run the distinctions were chosen by Nentwich to communicate two ideas about the prospect of digital publications at that time: modularization and liquefaction. Liquefaction is a term which in the study at hand will be used to refer to approaches that seek to undermine the different types of closures of a publication. In Nentwich's terms this means: (a) that the publication refrains from subtracting itself from the communicative flow (Hyperdiscussion), that it records it from the flow of communication with minor modifications; and (b) an ongoing update process (Knowledge Base).

Not long after the work of Nentwich was published Owen (2006) developed another attempt to classify digital publications. The temporal scope of his inquiry goes from 1987 to 2004. The typology of digital publications carried out by Owen does not classify new publications into any type of meta concepts as Nentwich does. Instead, the author defines a set of features which may apply to specific publications in different ways. Thus, electronic publications in comparison to historical articles may:

- include different multimedia resources;
- allow network access;
- be connected to other resources;
- grant the original author more control over the publication after submission has taken place;
- have dynamic content;
- may be adaptable to the context of use; and
- may therefore expose "quasi-intelligent behavior" (Owen 2006, 130),
- grant more control to the reader and her reading needs;
- appear in more flexible formats.

Owen's approach to evaluating digital publications reflects his primary research goal, which differs from Nentwich's. His main question is how much of an impact digital technologies really had on publications and not what general new publication formats exist. The results from his survey led him to the final remark that "the experiment, in so far as it really was aimed at transforming the scientific article, has failed" (Owen 2006, 223), mainly because very few of the electronic publications incorporated the features which he describes. He explains this by claiming that many of these features are incompatible with the abstract goal of publications to implement norms for the manifestation of the scientific idea of objectivity, a criterion he derives from his theoretical thoughts at the beginning of his book.

Meadows (2006) takes a more critical stand as well. He highlights the need to look from above at how digital publications are actually used by scholars and thereby extends Owen's argument. He argues that for the state of digital publications at that time there have been too few analyses of reader practices. His research shows that the type of interaction of scholars with digital publications differs significantly depending on different informational needs in different disciplines. Therefore, digital publishing would probably remain a field of experimentation for a period of time yet.

The appearance of highly theoretical surveys that evaluate digital publications after an initial period of five to ten years really demonstrates that the phase from the beginning up to the middle of the first decade of the new millennium is a phase of transition and consolidation. On the one hand research had led to a sufficient amount of digital publication concepts calling for further analysis; on the other hand, a variety of shortcomings became obvious, leading to activities such as those described in this chapter. Having said all this, it might seem likely that the critical remarks on the success and impact of digital publications might also have been a consequence of such shortcomings. It will have to be the task during the analysis of the following periods to determine how far digital publications from such periods have reflected the points that were raised.

[3]

Publishing 3.0

If the beginning of the millennium can be understood as an episode in which most relevant developments for digital publishing formats took place in fields such as infrastructure development or community building, and if the evaluation of such formats often happened rather critically, then the years 2007 and 2008 clearly mark the shift to a new phase for digital publications. From that time on, the field is again dominated by new experiments and new implementations of publication formats. The following years brought such concepts to light as:

- Scientific Publication Packages
- Open Laboratory Books
- Research Objects
- Scientific Compound Objects
- Liquid Publications
- Enhanced Publications
- Semantic Publications
- Nano Publications
- Transmedia Publications
- Rich Internet Publications
- Liquid Publications
- Unbound Books
- Living Books
- Hybrid Publications
- Self-Contained Publications
- Single-Resource Publications

This list is not complete, but it suffices to show that the years between 2008 and 2013 were probably the most vibrant ones in the history of digital publishing.

As if it was meant to be a starting signal, the commercial publisher *Elsevier*[1] initiated the *Article 2.0* contest by asking: "What if you were the publisher?" (Elsevier 2008). Later on, Elsevier announced a second contest in which they looked for the *Article of the Future* (Elsevier 2011). Both times the goal was to imagine and prototype innovations for scientific articles. Researchers and research projects were at the center of innovation in digital publishing once again. It can be seen throughout this chapter that this is much more than a shining marketing message. However, additional interdependencies emerge as well. In both calls, Elsevier emphasized publication issues, pertaining to articles instead of approaches completely refraining from the concept of articles and text publications. This of course highlights Elsevier's corporate interest of maintaining their market position and identifying new revenue options. Both interests are reflected in the approaches which won the prizes. These approaches focused on the enrichment of articles that however remain the constitutive unit in publishing (Elsevier 2011). Additionally, they demonstrate implementations of services that make use of such enhancement. Such an approach has been rolled out by Hammond before and is also reiterated by more recent contributions from this environment (Aalbersberg et al. 2014).

The Open Laboratory Book

The scope of the Elsevier contest directly addressing researchers goes together well with the so-called *Open Laboratory Book* approach (Clinio and Albagli 2017; Carter-Thomas and Rowley-Jolivet 2017). Open Laboratory Books (hereafter referred to as OLB), sometimes also called *Open Notebooks*, are an initiative by researchers from the domain of chemistry and biology with a strong involvement in experimentation. The concept alludes to the laboratory notebook, in which scientists of certain fields take notes during experimentation. The main question behind OLBs is what such laboratory books would look like if they were to be imagined in digital form from the beginning.

The Transformation of the Laboratory Notebook

Two major aspects of the laboratory notebook are highlighted in the discussion of this concept (Neylon 2009). One is the fact that a laboratory notebook is a tool used *in* the research process. It is not written at the end in a reporting fashion but for documentation purposes, to document

1 https://www.elsevier.de/

the research process itself. The second aspect focuses on the fact that due to this, a laboratory notebook holds records of each step and each experiment, even of failures. Both of these aspects contrast with historical publications which narratively re-organize research processes and refer to experiments in a summarizing manner, only cherry-picking "'typical' results" (Bradley et al. 2010, 260) fitting into the narrative. In contrast, the weakness of the laboratory book lies in the fact that it does not fulfill publication needs and cannot really stage the experiment. Bradley (2007) argues that this is not necessary in times of the web and in an environment of computer aided research. The author advocates the use of online-blogs and -wikis to write notebooks publicly, as a replacement for conventional publications. Additionally, he argues that the increasing digital nature of experiments and the data they produce facilitates their inclusion into channels like those mentioned above. The OLB is still considered to be a publication insofar, as it is explicitly designed against historical publications. Accordingly, Neylon (2009) seeks to make historical publications obsolete and to substitute them with an ongoing publishing activity forming an interface to the live stream of research.

As previously mentioned, the issue of authoring created certain challenges for the success of digital publications in earlier approaches. The creation of digital publications was time consuming and demanded a mastery of technical skills. By recommending blogs and wikis, OLBs explicitly responds to this general problem. The basic approach is the idea of starting within the environment immediately accessible to researchers instead of waiting for tools and services to be implemented. Accordingly, supporters of the OLB concept criticize the development of such tools by arguing that they are inefficient and not generic in terms of functionality (Neylon 2009, 5). The meaning of generic — presented as a criterion of quality — is important in this context. Within the critique of existing tools in the field of OLBs, it means building tools that focus on one specific task instead of creating a software environment combining functionalities in order to tackle multiple parts at once. In this respect it is in line with famous software development principles asking to "make each program do one thing well" (McIlroy, Pinson, and Tague 1978, 1902).

Furthermore, Neylon criticizes tools as too complicated to use which had been developed in the closely related field of the Semantic Web. In correspondence with the approach of blogs and wikis, OLBs therefore recommends the use of third-party tools like *Google Spreadsheets*[2] or *Google*

2 https://docs.google.com/spreadsheets

Charts[3]. Although there were supporters strongly advocating the use of technical standards and standardized vocabularies in a way comparable to the one that was indicated in the last chapter, OLBs delegated such issues to other stakeholders and to higher-level services (Bradley et al. 2010). Those services took over the necessary tasks of identifying data resources in the web, converting them into standardized formats, and neutralizing other drawbacks caused by using proprietary tools. Later, Bourne (2010, 2) more clearly addressed the problem of responsibility. He insisted that "I want the publisher of the future, or the publisher in collaboration with a third party, to be the guardian of these workflows." The drawback of such approaches is emphasized by Poole (2015) in more recent time. Accordingly, he diagnoses that the OLBs field "remain inchoate" (106). The following sections show that the question of how tasks and efforts should be distributed across stakeholders causes ongoing debate.

Regardless of who carries responsibility for these embedding processes, they are the key aspect through which OLBs really become publications beyond just online documentation. In order to facilitate them, Neylon (2009) suggests the use of the RSS facilities of blogs, providing a computationally accessible wrapper around the text and data posts of the OLB. This is reminiscent of Hammond's et al. consideration of RSS for the field of publishing. However, in OLBs it is not the publication providing an interface to related research delivered by RSS. The RSS feed is actually the publication itself, insofar as it provides a public interface to the research process. Therefore, two core components of this type of publication are its ongoing and potentially infinite extensions on the one hand, and the availability of an online reference to ongoing research published in real-time on the other. Supposedly, every resource used during the research process is published. Any step is an event which alerts the consumer of the feed; the narrative of the research process is the narrative of the publication.

Neylon emphasizes that especially the last point is a remarkable advantage over historical publications. Open Laboratory Books attribute the summarization aspect of historical publications to the needs of the publication format, as has been mentioned before. By referring to the often-quoted *knowledge pyramid* (Ackoff 1989), Neylon (2009) argues that a historical publication represents knowledge as systematized data, while OLBs expresses data itself. In his point of view this significantly limits the risk of interpretative fuzziness, manipulation, and other problems. He assesses the

3 https://developers.google.com/chart/

open-ended character of OLBs in the same way, corresponding to the fact that research never really has an ending.

Instigating Open Science with Open Laboratory Notebooks

The design of OLBs is part of a broader movement towards a way of doing science in an unrestricted, public, and collaborative way. This movement started as an initiative driven by researchers and is strongly linked with the open access initiative previously mentioned. According to Suber (2004), one of the most prominent advocates of open access, the goal of open access is to make research literature "digital, online, free of charge, and free of most copyright and licensing restrictions." Such principles can be easily extended to cover more than just research literature or other research results, as highlighted by Nüst et al.:

> Open access is not only a form of publishing such that research papers become available to the large public free of charge, it also refers to a trend in science that the act of doing research becomes more open and transparent. (Nüst et al. 2016, par. 2)

One of the first drivers of this movement was the *Science Commons*[4] initiative of the non-profit organization *Creative Commons*[5]. In order to extend the scope of open access, Creative Commons (2005) focused on the following three aspects:

1. The evaluation of licensing models which guarantee accessibility for everyone
2. Formal description models for the licensing of research results
3. Technological strategies to overcome heterogeneity in the ways research results are stored and which prevent from reusing them

As has been highlighted above, the understanding of research results comprises not only text publications, but more importantly research data and other supplementary resources. The case of research data provoked a debate over the question of whether licenses provided for the creative industries by Creative Commons are suited for licensing research data. Scientific Commons was driven by initiatives stemming from experimental sciences, claiming that experimental results are facts and accordingly not products of creative work. Thus, it should not be possible to legally treat them as such either. In consequence, new activities developing within the framework of *open data* tried to evaluate the legal state of data

4 http://sciencecommons.org
5 https://creativecommons.org/

in the broader frame of open science. One of such activities led to the release of the *Panton Principles for Open Data*[6] in 2009. These principles give four practical and legal recommendations for the "open" publication of research data. The process was supported by the *Open Knowledge Foundation*[7], whose definition of openness (Open Knowledge Foundation 2015) is explicitly mentioned in the principles. Correspondingly, content is open when it "can be freely used, modified, and shared by anyone for any purpose" (par. 3).

Cameron Neylon, an author who appeared as one of the leading figures behind OLBs in the last section, was a member of the core team that developed these principles. Similarly, members of the team behind the Panton Principles participated in the open science working group of the Open Knowledge Foundation. That is why Open Laboratory Books do not only borrow terminology from the open science movement, they are in fact a driving fraction of the movement itself. Accordingly, Lyon (2009, 39), in her study about open science refers to OLBs as a radical open science approach. In a similar way Whyte and Pryor (2011) call OLBs an exceptional example for "Open Science in Practice."

It has however been indicated that open science is not just a legal extension to open access for data resources. In a summary of definitions of open science terminology Frank Gibson (2007) indicates that above all open science is a combination of other open practices, such as open access publishing, open source programming and open data. Other authors highlight certain additional aspects. David, den Besten, and Schroeder (2008, 2), for instance mention the need for a more developed digital infrastructure and a stronger adoption of digital principles into science. Scientific Commons noted at the beginning that technological heterogeneity in publishing prevents openness from being realized even where it is legally possible. Likewise, Hunter (2006, sec. 7) stresses that digital infrastructure at the time of 2006 "is inadequate for the task" of open science. Thus, open science calls for the implementation of this infrastructure, for doing science in a consistently digital environment (Creative Commons 2008; David, den Besten, and Schroeder 2008), and for a radical commitment to open standards where ever research data is produced (Gibson 2007).

Beyond changes in infrastructure and standards, advocators of open science stresses the value of collaboration in science (David, den Besten, and Schroeder 2008, 299–302; Lyon 2009, 12; De Roure et al. 2009, 3).

6 http://pantonprinciples.org/
7 https://okfn.org/

Openness is conceived as a social commodity that creates value whenever researchers interact with each other as much as possible. Accordingly, Lyon (2009, 8) coins the term "team research." Bradley and Owens (2008) take an even more radical stand. They argue that the idea of collaboration in the context of open science blurs the boundaries between scientific and non-scientific domains, seeking to put open research in the context of crowdsourcing[8].

The legal, technological, and social changes necessary in order to realize open science are significant. It is therefore not surprising that the benefits are heavily promoted. Whyte and Pryor (2011, 4) try to group those benefits proclaimed by advocates of open science into five categories:

- Speed and efficiency of the research cycle
- Capabilities to identify new research questions
- Research effectiveness and quality
- Innovation, knowledge exchange, and impact
- Research group and career development

It stands out that all these benefits have a tendency to focus on notions of efficiency and productivity. Such an impression is substantiated by the following list of benefits extracted from Lyon (2009, 16). It renders the abstract values above in a more concrete form, often alluding to aspects of economy. In order to illustrate the use of language, the whole list is quoted below (emphasis in original) despite its verbosity. It consists of:

> *Increased return on investment of public funds* allocated to science and research, by making data outputs openly available for re-use.
>
> *Faster dissemination of research outputs* including methodologies, data, models, and scientific outcomes.
>
> *Greater academic rigor*, robustness, and scholarly integrity from transparent data practices.
>
> *Higher potential for new discoveries* and new knowledge arising from data re-use contributing to growth in UK economic and intellectual wealth.

8 Crowdsourcing which is an artificial term constructed by using the words crowd and outsourcing refers to a strategy to use the internet to the end of acquiring information and contributions from the public within a project context (see also Estellés-Arolas and González-Ladrón-de-Guevara 2012).

> *Accelerated ability to predict scientific outcomes* and behaviors based on large-scale open data analysis, shared complex models, and simulations.
>
> *Efficiency gains* from open research practice leading to reduced unnecessary repetition of research activity and associated wasteful funding allocations.
>
> *Enhanced opportunities for student learning* from open sharing of experimental methods and results data.
>
> *Increased human capacity and capability* from professionals, amateurs, volunteers, and citizens to assist in collecting, curating, and preserving the growing scientific record.
>
> *Enhanced public engagement and understanding of science* principles and practice through raised awareness, pro-active participation, and direct contribution to research.
>
> *Significant wider societal gains* through more inclusive and participatory approaches which facilitate public empowerment and ownership of global challenges. (Lyon 2009, 16)

Both surveys are part of more general research on open science. Lyon's work relates to the viewpoint of policy makers and funders. Different agent groups thus emphasize different possible advantages. Similarly, it is worth mentioning that the notion of open science circulates among different social contexts. One result of this is a process translating academic arguments into a highly mercantile terminology, as can be observed from Lyon's list. The observation of different interests conflating in the topic of openness coincides with the fact that later on, governments of countries such as England and the United States caught up on some of the arguments of the openness movement by promoting their own open data programs. Correspondingly, *data.gov*[9], an initiative for open governmental data in the United States, was launched in 2009. One year later England followed suit by opening up *data.gov.uk*[10]. The release of the portal in the US was part of a broader *Open Government Initiative* (The White House 2013) launched by the Obama administration. These initiatives went along with the big data initiative, also by Obama in 2012 (Weiss and Zgorski 2012), and the massive support of big data by the research councils in the UK (Research Councils UK 2015).

9 https://www.data.gov/
10 https://data.gov.uk/

Beyond economy, politics implements ethics. This is no different in the case of open science. At the beginning of this section a certain ethos of doing science was mentioned. Ethical aspects of open science in a political sense already appear in the last bullet point of Lyon's list of benefits. In fact, they were a crucial part of open science from the very beginning. The discourse on ethics is not separable from the pragmatic and scientific goals of open science. The homepage of the Scientific Commons initiative shows a quote by Alan Dove, in which he denounces patenting of pharmaceutical discoveries by private companies. Hence, the message of the arrangement is that the ideas of open science reduce social injustice. Cribb and Hartomo argue more committedly in their comprehensive and programmatic work on open science:

> The need to share human knowledge has never been more urgent. As the world grapples with the acute challenges of resource scarcity, climate change, poverty, illhealth, pollution, rapid urbanization and food insecurity, it has never needed its science and technology more. However, if anything is to secure the future of civilization and human wellbeing, it will not be science alone, but the knowledge it yields being shared and employed both widely and wisely. For science and technology to deliver full value to society, they must be accessible to as many people as possible and their messages must be easily understood. (Cribb and Hartomo 2010, 1)

The message is clear: only science that follows open science principles is capable of maintaining a world and a human race existing at the edge of possible catastrophes. Consequently, Goble, De Roure, and Bechhofer (2012, sec. 4) frame the issue of open science in a remarkably decisive way when saying that it represents the decision between "the common good vs. self-interest."

Related Activities

Despite the fact that OLBs are deeply embedded into experimental sciences Shaw, Buckland, and Golden (2013) tried to transfer some of the ideas behind OLBs into a project they call *Open Notebook Humanities*. Instead of emphasizing data publication activities the Open Notebook Humanities stressed the role of notes as a primary research object in humanities disciplines. Notes are considered pieces of thought that go along with research in humanities, and which are therefore never complete or finished. Shaw asserts that the exposure of such notes in an open environment and in a structured form accessible for computation can support a humanities research process, as can the publication of any kind of experimental data in scientific disciplines.

Until now the area of blogging has not been discussed in greater detail in the context of publishing. It is significant that Bradley (2007) has put the OLB in the context of blogs. In fact, they share so many features that it is possible to argue that OLBs try to generalize the blogs in the context of scholarly publishing, open-science, and data-driven science. Thus, the topic of blogs and blogging will not be discussed further within this inquiry. An insightful analysis of blogs as an approach between formal and informal scholarly publishing is presented by Puschmann and Mahrt (2013) and Puschmann and Bastos (2015).

Aggregations

More or less at the same time as the development of OLBs, the notion of publications as aggregations, sometimes also referred to as *Scientific Compound Object Publishing* (Hunter et al. 2008) or *Compound Information Objects* (Lagoze and Van de Sompel 2007) started to become prominent. A crucial backdrop for such publication concepts is some of the infrastructure developments indicated at the end of the last chapter, described in greater detail below. Although such developments took place earlier, it is between 2008 and 2010 that they led to the creation of real publications.

Aggregations interpret the decomposition of publications in a slightly different way than MAs or OLBs. Also, the design logic of aggregations starts from the opposite direction. The question is not how to decompose pre-existing publications into smaller units but to stress quite literally that the idea of an aggregation in science is enough by itself in order to speak about a scholarly publication. A favorable reason for this emphasis is the fact that aggregations are developed by agents involved in activities different from those of OLBs and MAs. Publications like those discussed in this section are associated with computer and information-scientists, mostly involved in the field of digital infrastructure development.

The main theme behind such publications is best described by citing the title of Van de Sompel et al. (2010): “From Artefacts to Aggregations.” In order to entirely distinguish this phrase from ideas like modularization or the inclusion of additional resources such as data or visualizations into blogs, it is important to stress that aggregations completely abstract from any idea of qualitative connectivity. In technical terms, that means connectivity going beyond linking between two resources or defining what can be linked. While MAs decompose articles into smaller units, they still very much refer to the article as a conceptual framework and to a positive description of information. Open Laboratory Books include resources which could not be integrated in paper notebooks, but this notebook is much more than an aggregation. Resources are packaged within a software environment, that being the blog, and thereby connected within a narrative, by time, and by layout through the design of the publication environment. Open Laboratory Books are defined from a perspective that comes out of the research process, because it is mostly developed by researchers.

In contrast, aggregations represent a curator's point of view, who is less invested in the value of specific resources and the way such resources affect each other, than with the fact that in any case she needs to take care of a certain set of resources that are in some way entangled with each other. Lagoze et al. (2012, 15) make this shift in perspective very clear when they provide the example of a webpage from the *JSTOR*[11] archive that they decompose into a model of resources and links, as well as another example from astronomy, in order to showcase the possibility of building a publication from resources of any digital type that could be connected in any definable way. Assuming this point of view, the image of the aggregation tackles both the decomposition of resources perceived as artifacts into aggregations, and the accumulation of artifacts into bigger aggregations.

The key component for publications as aggregations is the OAI-ORE data model, developed to gain more interoperability in certain contexts of the web (Van de Sompel and Lagoze 2007; Lagoze and Van de Sompel 2007). The capacity to generally aggregate digital resources requires both a consistent way of referring to resources, and of describing the resulting aggregation. Flaws in existing approaches with comparable purpose were the reasons leading to the implementation of OAI-ORE (Van de Sompel et al. 2010, 3). The most important design decision behind OAI-ORE is based on the claim that the goals of such a model could be best accomplished by sticking to the mechanisms of the web itself (Lagoze et al. 2012). One of the main mechanisms of the web is the URI (see sec. on Linked Open Data). In OAI-ORE such URIs are not just used as addresses of websites, but to identify anything, even abstract concepts. In the context of aggregations, URI identify: (a) the complete description of aggregations in a metadata-like web document, (b) the terms that are used to describe the relationships between resources and (c), the resources that are linked together

11 https://www.jstor.org/

themselves. This approach has two consequences. First, anything that has a URI is a resource itself, which may serve as a resource in other resources that define aggregations. Second, in consequence to the web approach an aggregation does not exist in any other way than as a metadata description called resource map. The resources remain somewhere in the web and are only referenced in the same way as websites. Thus, aggregations form publications, the parts of which are distributed all over the web.

Collections

The epitome of a scholarly aggregation, especially in the case of the humanities, can be seen in collections. The gathering of material for a collection and the selection of items in the context of a specific research topic is an important curatorial process supposed to contain a lot of intellectual work already (Palmer et al. 2009, 11–13). Additionally, collections of a certain type have always been presented, for instance in libraries or archives. Thus, it does not surprise that creating collections as a form of academic publishing became increasingly attractive at the same time as OAI-ORE created better conditions to do so. Abargues, Granell, and Huerta (2010, 1) accordingly put the publication of collections into the context of a new paradigm of publishing.

Publications as aggregations are collections if there are no further specifications describing the type of relationship of the aggregated resources. In other words, the dominant aspect linking the resources in a collection is the theme of the collection itself.

A very early approach tightly connected to the development of OAI-ORE itself is *oreChem* (Lagoze 2009). oreChem publishes collections of resources from molecular chemistry. The resources are hosted in different repositories. Abargues, Granell, and Huerta (2010) presented the same approach, but for geo-referenced places instead of molecules. Another approach from the humanities, especially scholars from the literature domain, is presented by Hunter and Gerber (Gerber and Hunter 2008; Hunter and Gerber 2009; Gerber and Hunter 2010; Hunter and Gerber 2011). The *Literature Object Reuse and Exchange* (also referred to as LORE) project enables the formation and publication of collections on top of Australian repository infrastructures hosting resources critical for philology and literature studies. LORE provides a sophisticated authoring component implemented as a browser plugin, an idea which resembles that of distributed resources and networked research.

The main reason for the publication of collections shared by all authors in the aforementioned example is the reduction of technological and semantic heterogeneity between published resources within in a certain domain. The motivation behind reducing heterogeneity is the creation of better conditions for information retrieval. The example of oreChem and *chemSpider*[12] makes this very clear, as it was also initiated as a complement to approaches such as OLBs (Clark, Williams, and Ekins 2015), which have excluded these problems in order to be able to create publications to their liking (Bradley and Owens 2008).

Workflow Publications

Scientific Publication Packages

As mentioned above, collections gather resources pertaining to a certain topic. The way in which these resources link to each other is not necessarily a crucial issue. This distinguishes them from other approaches which decisively try to answer the question how resources are linked within the scholarly domain in general. In an attempt to define the appropriate point of orientation for the modelling of collections in science, a new type of publications emerged. This publication concept makes use of the OAI-ORE

facilities and an online data-publication approach called *linked open data* (see next section), but adds organizing principles to the way resources are gathered within the OAI-ORE aggregation.

The key idea of corresponding formats like *Scientific Publication Packages* (hereafter referred to as SPP) or *Research Objects* (hereafter referred to as RO) is the claim that the most significant theme for the design of publications in science should be a so-called workflow. The concept of workflow is derived from the claim that science is organized in lifecycles (Van de Sompel et al. 2010). In more concrete terms, advocates of corresponding publications argue that science and its dynamic of innovation is organized into three phases: (a) the production of knowledge that is the research process itself, (b) the creation of publications, i.e. the communication of knowledge, and (c) the use of the represented knowledge by researchers who therefore need to interact with publications. This setup is conceived of as "remarkably stable" (Van de Sompel et al. 2010, 567) despite historical changes of the scientific field.

12 http://www.chemspider.com/

The way this lifecycle is described presents publications primarily as a necessary mediator between the first and the third phase. Following this description, it is possible to argue that a good mediator brings the two ends of the mediation process together as closely as possible. With this argument in mind, workflow-oriented publications argue that the whole research process needs to be published instead of just a summary. Within the research process, knowledge is produced and thus only the research process can give testimony about the adequacy of scientific knowledge. Workflows are introduced as a formal model for the representation of research processes, which make it possible to turn research processes into objects. They describe a "series of structured activities and computations that arise in scientific problem-solving" (Bechhofer et al. 2012, sec. 1), which in turn "support reproducibility and reuse in sciences" (De Roure et al. 2012). Thus, workflow publications try to let readers be observers of the research process itself.

A workflow publication may embed all resources of a particular research process, like primary data, processed resources, software, text, and media among other things. However, collecting such resources is not enough to really gain reproducibility (Yuan et al. 2018). Workflow publications, thus, attach descriptive metadata to each resource, representing their temporal position and role within the research process, itself defined as a goal oriented consecutive process (Hunter 2006, sec. 1; Hunter 2008, 36).

Scientific Publication Packages were the first example of workflow publications. They were first presented as *Scientific Model Packages* by Hunter (2006) in 2006. The term *model* explicitly emphasizes the paramount theme of the scientific workflow. The work was part of the *FUSION*[13] project at the *University of Queensland* which evaluated the impact of grid technologies[14] in computer-driven research in the fields of bioengineering and nanotechnology. The Scientific Publication Packages two years later (Hunter 2008) were a slightly modified version. The approach makes use of a comparable attempt by Coleman (2002), albeit benefiting from the aforementioned technological environments and the context of infrastructure development.

It is obvious that SPPs and OLBs share the same focus on the research process in terms of its processuality. However, even with that common

13 http://www.itee.uq.edu.au/eresearch/projects/fusion

14 In computation, a grid is a network of linked computers that could be used together in order to carry out one specific task. It enables to use resources from all the computers in the grid which facilitates computations that very expensive (see also Magoules et al. 2009).

ground, SPP make a very different choice regarding the consequences of this priority. Most notably, SPPs confirm the closed nature of research processes, whereby OLBs emphasize that those endings are artificially set up and that research never really comes to an end. Scientific Publication Packages are in consequence authored all at once, while OLBs emerge in a dynamic and fluent way. The idea of defined research processes that have a starting point and an end point demands more decisions explicitly in the design process of the publication format as such. In the case of SPPs, this leads to a much higher degree of formality in the SPP model compared to OLBs. For instance, SPPs use the so-called *ABC* (Lagoze and Hunter 2006) model in order to define formal terms and entities that build the workflow description (Hunter 2008, 38). Having said this, SPPs are more concerned with the notion of publications as objects while OLBs are intent on publishing as an activity.

The aforementioned difference underlying the two formats is discussed explicitly in the context of SPPs. From a methodological point of view, Hunter highlights the distinction between *workflow* and *lineage* (Hunter 2006, sec. 3.1). The workflow describes steps to be carried out in order to reach a goal, before such steps are actually taken. A workflow is like a work schedule. Lineage describes what really happened after the workflow has been applied. To this end, lineage makes use of information gathered within the process, especially in computer-driven science where it is literally recorded and called provenance. However, Hunter also emphasizes that data conversion, acquisition, and inference need to be applied in order to get an informative picture of lineage. It is then possible to also categorically distinguish between provenance and lineage. From the viewpoint of this discussion, OLBs favor the provenance perspective. Provenance in OLBs is nonetheless mostly told rather than recorded.

Scientific Publication Packages were developed mainly by computer scientists and infrastructure projects, as noted above. This situation offered more possibilities for a more sophisticated publication format, but more importantly it included the development of software facilitating the creation of and interaction with such publications. An example of this is the *SCOPE virtual research environment*[15] (Hunter et al. 2008). In SCOPE, scientists have the ability to investigate and visualize workflows, to automatically infer new workflows from existing workflows, and to link web resources

15 A virtual research environment is a design concept for the creation of software that seeks to support research in specific domains across different steps in the research process and in completing different tasks within one consistent product (see also JISC 2013; Candela, Castelli, and Pagano 2013).

with the workflow. For the purpose of publishing, it offers the possibility to attach licenses in a machine-readable way and to define rules that restrict access.

Research Objects

The concept of ROs is a derivate of the project *myExperiment*[16] (De Roure et al. 2009; De Roure, Bechhofer, and Goble 2011). The goal of this project was to create an infrastructure around the idea of sharing workflows as a primary research output comparable to SPPs. The myExperiment project created a web-portal around the notion of ROs in which scientists are able to retrieve, review, repeat, reuse, and re-purpose previously published workflows. This portal provided data for the analysis of user behavior (De Roure et al. 2009, sec. 3; Bechhofer, De Roure, et al. 2010, sec. 4), where one of the outcomes was the insight that workflows alone are not considered sufficient by scientists who want to use other researchers' workflows (De Roure 2014b).

MyExperiment developed the possibility of creating a *pack* in which test data, presentations, articles, and other "supplemental" material were put together with the workflow into a downloadable zip (see below) file (De Roure, Bechhofer, and Goble 2011). Research Objects are more elaborate versions of packs which refer to open technologies (see below) and standards. They make use of the OAI-ORE data model and of a set of related best practices known as linked open data. However, they also address situations where such best practices do not suffice (Bechhofer, Ainsworth, et al. 2010; Bechhofer, De Roure, et al. 2010).

For the purpose of advancing ROs as a publication concept, an international infrastructure project with several partners, funded by the European Union, was launched in 2010. The project, which lasted until 2013, was called *workflow4ever* (Gómez-Pérez 2013). At the end of the project, related activities moved into a *W3C*[17] community group (W3C Research Object for Scholarly Communication Community Group 2013) as well as into a loosely organized consortium (Goble 2015). Among other things, such initiatives provided a set of formal semantics for the description of ROs (Bechhofer et al. 2014) as well as low-level tools for their creation and management (De Roure et al. 2012). The social dimensions of ROs as a publication format were evaluated further. This led to a schematic illustration of the lifecycle

16 https://www.myexperiment.org/home

17 W3C is the acronym of the *World Wide Web Consortium* which organizes the standardization of technologies related to the world wide web (see https://www.w3.org/

of published workflows (Bechhofer et al. 2012) and to a way of automatically modelling access rights as well as personal relevance of ROs (Gamble and Goble 2010).

Research Objects are mainly used in the domains of biology and chemistry (De Roure, Belhajjame, et al. 2011, 3). However, there are some examples from the fields of musicology, (De Roure, Page, et al. 2011; De Roure 2011; De Roure 2014a; McGarry et al. 2017), facilities science (Matthews et al. 2013), and computer science (Crick et al. 2014) as well.

The overview of ROs above shows clearly that more effort was put into them by more partners over a longer time period. Clearly, ROs could be described as a more elaborate and explicitly designed version of SPPs. In his short comparison with SPPs, Bechhofer et al. (2014, 5) break down the conceptual difference between SPPs and ROs into two points: (a) links between the resources of the workflow exists as a resource on its own and independently from any final format such as the zip file in myExperiment; (b) emphasizes the use of open standards, assuring the highest degree of interoperability for the description of the logical structure of RO. Both points directly refer to the LOD approach without mentioning this explicitly as the point of comparison.

The Impact of Linked Open Data

The term "linked open data" was first used by Berners-Lee (2009). It does not so much introduce a new piece of technology, it is rather a request to make use of existing technologies in order to build a web of machine-readable data side by side to the web of HTML[18] documents which primarily suits the needs of humans. Thus, it is a paradigm for the publication of data (Heath and Bizer 2011, sec. Abstract) in a form that corresponds with web principles (Bizer, Cyganiak, and Heath 2007). The mechanisms that are used are the same as those used to link websites. A data source A, for instance, asserts that a symphony is written by Shostakovich. However, Shostakovich is not just written down in plain text but represented by an URI[19] which

18 HTML is an acronym for Hypertext Markup Language which is a set of formal semantics used to structure the content of websites.

19 An URI is a more general form of an URL which is used to define links between websites. Not only entities are expressed as links but also the links themselves. Modular Articles introduced the notion of meaningful links as links that specify in which way the two resources that are linked together relate to each other. In the sentence "Shostakovich composed the Leningrad Symphony" the predicate "composed" links together the subject and the object. It is a term which in the LOD world is part of a formal vocabulary, interpretable by computers. It is represented

links directly to a data source B that contains biographical data about Dimitri Shostakovich. This data may have the form of values such as dates and strings, but may also consist of an URI pointing to other data sources. Another assertion about a recording of this symphony, for example, can directly link to a data source C.

In a workflow, a piece of software has a link to a data resource on which it is applied. Once again, it is not just a link but a link with meaning. In the case of workflow publications, this meaning could say dataset X was generated by software Y. The predicate *wasGeneratedBy* is part of the *W3C-PROV*[20] ontology, referenced by the fact that the term is represented by a URI. The fact that the link between the piece of software and the data source is modelled as a link itself, pointing to the ontology, assures that the formal meaning of this term can be evaluated by humans or computers within the same technological framework in which the workflow is modelled.

It is not the case that SPPs do not provide proper standardized semantics. They use and extend the ABC model in order to model workflows. The main difference is the way these semantics are serialized under the same conditions as the data by following LOD guidelines. This is what Bechhofer et al. meant with the second distinction between SPPs and ROs.

Research Objects were introduced slightly later than SPPs. The time span is significant, however, because in the interim the web of data had grown 1700 percent (Cyganiak 2015). Research Objects were therefore capable of making full use of LOD. The extent to which this aspect is crucial for the success of aggregations in general and ROs in particular can only be fully appreciated when taking into account the extent to which LOD and OAI-ORE implement theoretical ideas that had been around in digital publishing for some time in a very pragmatical way.

While the techniques behind LOD enable online data publishing, LOD being just a term to refer to the world-wide data-web, OAI-ORE provides the mechanisms to formally refer to a subset of these resources in order to create aggregations such as workflow publications (Bechhofer, Ainsworth, et al. 2010). It enables descriptions of aggregations of LOD resources. Accordingly, it sets boundaries for a group of resources that

as a URI which itself links to the vocabulary that it is part of. Thus, there is a link between Shostakovich and the Leningrader which is realized by the meaningful link that is the predicate of the sentence, but in the same structure three more links refer to other data sources which hold data about Shostakovich, the symphony and the act of composing.

20 https://www.w3.org/TR/prov-overview/

belong together in the context of an aggregation. Consequently, De Roure, Bechhofer, and Goble (2011, 4), Bechhofer, Ainsworth, et al. (2010, 13), and Bechhofer, Ainsworth, et al. (2010, 1322) call ROs "boundary objects." The only thing which make resources a part of an aggregation is a link, and the very same resource can be part of many other aggregations. Such links can be gathered in a web document or stored in a database which is accessible on the web. The important aspect is the fact that the aggregation is no more than a formal description of (data) resources on the web. It is now clear why the LOD movement and the OAI-ORE model fundamentally belong together in the context of aggregations, and why ROs became a more successful version of workflow publications than SPPs.

From Workflows to Packs to Research Objects

As has been previously mentioned, the design of ROs was a process starting with the development of an infrastructure in order to share workflows. Similarly, to Hunter, Bechhofer et al. (2012, sec. 3) distinguish between three workflow layers: the first describes the abstract idea of what a workflow is, the second defines templates for workflows before they are applied, the third layer contains the data that is recorded in order to document the applied workflow. The main concern at the beginning of myExperiment was the second layer as well as the creation of a social space around workflows (De Roure, Bechhofer, and Goble 2011, sec. III). This space follows the idea that by sharing one's workflows others could reuse them or put together parts of different workflows into new ones. In the best case such workflows can be executed automatically and thereby enable scientists to easily test workflows and "accelerate discovery" (Goble, De Roure, and Bechhofer 2012, sec 2.2).

De Roure, Bechhofer, and Goble (2011, 3) mention how the possibility to reuse other people's workflows created a demand to have access to resources that are associated with the workflow in a broader perspective. This does not only mean data. It includes articles, presentations, and other supplemental resources bundled into a so-called pack. At its core a pack is a list of links to these resources and the workflow data, which itself remains the key component (De Roure et al. 2013, 304). Sometimes, a pack is packaged with its supplemental resources into a *ZIP*[21] file (Roos et al. 2010,

21 ZIP is a file and container format which enables to bundle multiple files into one file. Since ZIP uses a compression algorithm the resulting file is most often smaller in size than the original files altogether.

14). In this scenario it obviously relinquishes the conceptual and theoretical approach of LOD and aggregations.

Bechhofer, De Roure, et al. (2010, sec. 4) distinguish between seven different types of packs. Packs for the purpose of publishing are only one possible scenario. Thus, ROs are a concept building on basic packs, for the specific tasks of publishing. The relation between packs and ROs is described in a concise form by De Roure, mentioning that packs are "prototypical examples of Research Objects" De Roure (2010, 3).

Bechhofer, De Roure, et al. (2010, 4) highlight several tasks crucial for the conversion of packs to ROs. The most important issue is the definition of a consistent way to add metadata. Four kinds of metadata are mentioned in this respect: (a) metadata regarding the lifecycle of ROs, version information about ROs, ownerships and access rights metadata, and finally metadata about the relationship between ROs as a whole and it parts. Bechhofer et al. (2014) outline the semantics which were defined in the workflow4ever project mentioned at the beginning of section on ROs.[22] A repository with the name of *ROHub* has been set up providing basic access to ROs meant for publication. In order to support the publication process, a small piece of software, usable from within a terminal[23], was programmed.

The path from myExperiment to Research Objects is a path in which certain objects (workflows) in a well-defined environment are developed further to become publications. In a similar way it gives testimony about the impact of LOD and OAI-ORE on the discourse about digital publications.

The E-Science Narrative

A curious characteristic of ROs is the emphasis they put on experimentation and research cultures, including experimentation, as a crucial aspect. Experiments are not only the name of the original project of RO, they are also very close to the concept of workflows. In principle, a workflow follows the same pattern as experiments do. An experiment has to be set up, it follows a linear temporal logic when it "runs," and the incidents that happen during runtime are documented together with the results for further interpretation. The similarities between the experimental model of doing science and the theme of workflows is the reason why workflows

22 Machine-readable versions of these semantics can be found at Goble (2015 sec. Specs and Tooling)

23 A terminal is an interface for the control of computers which has no graphical components like windows or buttons. It works by writing commands which are consecutively evaluated.

are the core model behind ROs. In the case of computational workflows, research processes are described in three steps: (a) data and algorithm are selected, (b) the algorithms are applied to the data, and (c) the result is viewed, interpreted, and published (2011, sec. 3). The steps of an experiment and a computational workflow are identical. Even more important than the steps themselves is the fact that workflow and experiment share the same temporal-linear logic in which each step has its time. The striking detail about the description of the three steps of computational workflows is that it was derived from an article about research in musicology, or more precisely "computational musicology." Hence, it describes a research process in the context of a field which historically has few connections with experimenting sciences. Thus, ROs try to bring the notion of experiments far beyond experimenting sciences:

> ... we should say "research" rather than science, because the Web is agnostic about research discipline: it is as much a home for digital arts and digital humanities as digital science and engineering. (De Roure 2010, 90)

Such a generalization refers to a much broader discourse on the state of research. Research Objects were not just developed by computer scientists, but by computer scientists who belonged to a peculiar field of activity called *e-Science*. De Roure defines e-Science as:

> ... characterized by global reuse of tools, data and methods across any discipline .... Research is significantly data driven and we see increasing automation and decision-support for the researcher as the environment. (De Roure 2011, 10)

The generalization from one specific practice doing research to a global model for research as such is framed by a political and epistemological discourse, the key features of which will be outlined in the following paragraphs. The section about OLBs has already introduced a peculiar discourse frame called open science. Indeed, open science and e-Science are strongly linked to each other. On the one hand, ROs would not work well without an open web environment of accessible resources from which they arise. On the other hand, open science advocates agree that the most scientific benefit of open science will arise from computational processing. The open science discourse is more politically and ethically loaded than e-Science, which is more concerned with methodology. Due to this, both complement each other. Thus, for De Roure (2011, 8) open science is just the final step in the realization of e-Science.

The terminology of "a final step" and its "realization" implies a historical argument about the development of science, society and technology. E-Science not only makes references to such a socio-historical frame, it decisively perceives itself as the main driver for a peculiar vision of socio-historical progress. Correspondingly, two viewpoints emerge when analyzing the e-Science discourse. One characterizes its key features, the other analyses the past and the future it describes.

The omnipresence of arguments of progress in research literature about ROs and e-Science in general is striking. In "The Future of Scholarly Communication" De Roure (2014b) writes about a thought experiment that looks back on publishing today and describes why it has to disappear in its current form. The main argument is presented in terms of a linear vector within a diagram that illustrates how society and science become continuously more collaborative and automated. In between, the "digital research ecosystem" will develop in "three generations" which De Roure outlines like this:

> ... the early adopters of new tools, followed by a phase of embedding and re-use and then, building upon this new sociotechnical platform, a world of open science and radical sharing. (De Roure 2011, 1)

The fact that he refers to the article as an obsolete heritage of the historical publishing system (De Roure 2011, 12), as well as the claim that disciplines are at different stages of their "computational turn" (De Roure 2011, 12), clearly show that e-Science is not meant to be one field of research among others. Instead, it is just a separate concept for as long as there is a need to mark the avant-garde, which in time will become normality. Similarly, this viewpoint is not only presented in the sciences, there are also the e-Humanities as well.

Before it is possible to go into the details of the historical process as illustrated by the e-Science agenda, certain characteristics of this agenda need explanation. Obviously, the center of e-Science is its focus on computation as the dominant mode of scholarly engagement. In this sense the rise of e-Science corresponds with the term "computational turn" used by De Roure before. The question what computation means can be answered by referring to the self-descriptions of e-Science. De Roure states that:

> This can be characterized as the "Big Science" view of e-Science: scientists working with heroic computational power and volumes of data, targeting breakthroughs in the modelling of everything from

> storms and earthquakes to fly brains and nanoscale transistors. (De Roure 2010, 1)

This quote implicitly contains many of the important qualities of e-Science, but in a form that communicates well the mission it represents. Key issues are addressed by power, volume, data, modelling, and the plural form of the word scientist. This plural refers to collaboration as a key element of e-Science. De Roure presents another description of e-Science in "Machines, Methods and Music" (De Roure 2011, 12). This description remains a bit fuzzy as well. It can be reduced to the following six terms, terms that will be used in the present study to characterize the e-Science approach. Beside collaboration, e-Science builds on the themes of automation, data, acceleration, connectivity, and preservation.

The goal of automation is linked to a topic which has been denoted as a serial crisis or information overload in the previous sections. In e-Science this issue turns into a situation in which advocates proclaim that the "volumes of data" cannot be processed by human minds. This situation demands automation in order to prevent the *data deluge*:

> The data deluge is caused by, and needs to be handled by, innovation in automation and by the new scale of participation of scientists in the digital world." (De Roure 2011, 1)

However, in e-Science automation does not stop at automating tasks within research processes, which could hardly be handled otherwise. Automation becomes an ethos, and as an ethos e-Science tries to significantly extent the scope where automation is applied. Automation in e-Science aims at automation of research itself. Correspondingly, Neylon (2009, sec. Introduction) uses the term "automated experimentation."

Research Objects are publications designed to facilitate this very goal and not just for reasons of transparency and openness. The idea of workflows itself links closely to the ethos of automation, for it provides a viewpoint on research that is formalizable. The redesign of publications in this field is strongly motivated by the goal of preparing publications for the sake of automation (De Roure 2010, 92–93) and to facilitate automated processing of its contents (Shotton 2009). It implies that automation is always useful, wherever it is possible. The data deluge is one of the key arguments behind this claim.

The next step to automated science after automated experimentation is automated knowledge discovery (Pan 2010). In automated knowledge discovery, tasks such as data selection, aggregation, and method selection among others are automated within a self-learning computation seeking to adequately solve defined problems. In another step, scientific robots or "bots" (Kuhn 2015) operate self-responsibly (Sofronijević 2012), thereby becoming agents of their own. These "social machines" (De Roure 2014a, 237) are the final stage on the way towards fully automated science.

Once again thoughts of the future of publishing are tightly coupled with a discourse that uses the argument of scarce resources in order to make a certain vision more convincing: "we can anticipate an increasingly automated future — we will run out of humans and yet the technology axis goes on" (De Roure 2014b, 234).

The topics of automation and data deluge also lead to another issue: acceleration. Bradley and Owens (2008, 2), like most authors in this research field, emphasize that the of goal automation is the acceleration of the scientific progress. Names of related software such as *ChemSpeed Technologies AG, Accelerator SLT100 Synthesizer* (Bradley and Owens 2008, 4) give ample evidence of this ideal.

There are few examples in which the ideal of acceleration is discussed explicitly. Cribb expressed one of the reasons implicitly in the phrase quoted in the section on open science and the open laboratory book. The number of urgent problems in the world forces science to find quicker ways of dealing with the problems outlined by the author. In e-Science, acceleration is understood as a reduction of the "time-to-discovery" (De Roure 2013, 1) in "scientist's knowledge turns" (Goble, De Roure, and Bechhofer 2012). A knowledge-turn is conceived as the time needed for results of one research process to be processed into the new results of subsequent research processes. Marcondes (2005, 119) calls this shift the embodiment of research results within the scientific knowledge base.

Another point of reference in e-Science regards the conditions necessary for e-Science to become the main mode of doing research. In other words, everything that is of value within an e-Science research process has to be available in digital form, or at least to be easily digitizable. A computational workflow is not capable of taking things into account that have no digital representation. There is no methodological concept for how to deal with non-digital things within e-Research and its publications. Digital representation is conceived as the most outstanding as well as dominant mode of representation. Thus, already in 2010 Bourne (2010, 1) stresses that "computation has impacted science to the point where every aspect of it is touched by computation."

A further restriction regarding representation is the fact that in most cases digital representation refers to an abstract notion of data. *Executable Music Documents* (De Roure 2014a) are thus not publications meant to be listened to. They contain music data in a form that suits the algorithms with which this data is packaged. The concentration on data as a form of appearance and not just as a means of representation led to e-Science often being called *data-driven science* (Hey, Tansley, and Tolle 2009; De Roure 2014b, 234).

Complementary to the discourse in open science and its ethos of collaboration, e-Science, and here especially the research field of ROs, develops the notion of "social infrastructure" (De Roure et al. 2009, 3). Driven by the claim that "the majority of scientific advances in the public domain result from collective efforts" (Goble, De Roure, and Bechhofer 2012, 21) this infrastructure is a primary concern in corresponding discussions. De Roure, Bechhofer, and Goble (2011, 1) clearly references this when he uses the term "Science 2.0." As the development of the web 2.0 caused a new type of engagement of web users in the web, the implementation of social infrastructure will engender a new type of science.

The concept of ROs building on the model of distributed web resources, reproducibility, and reuse depends on another given: the availability of these resources. Such availability has been partially addressed by the ethos of openness and digitization. However, openness and digitization do not assure that resources are here to stay. Consequently, another ethos builds upon the topic of preservation.

Major players in the field of e-Science advocate a radical form of archiving that tries to preserve as much as possible from what is produced digitally. The argument behind this approach is the claim that the future value of resources cannot be anticipated (Bourne 2010) at the time where archiving decisions are made. Accordingly, ubiquitous preservation is demanded. This demand is well addressed by remarks that without radical archiving, a "digital dark age" (Choudhury et al. 2008, 20) will arise in which "knowledge burying" (De Roure et al. 2009, 10) is an omnipresent problem.

Now that the characteristics of the e-Science agenda are clearer, it is easier to follow the arguments of history and progress in which e-Science posits itself. The avant-garde status, which e-Science claims for itself, is only convincing when there is a past that directly leads to the e-Science mode of research and a future to which this particular avant-garde leads in the most direct way. In both viewpoints e-Science has strong opinions. The state of affairs which presents e-Science as a necessary step, and which is the result of a history that focus on the history of technological innovation, has already been discussed on several occasions. At its end there is the data deluge. Data deluge was introduced as an updated version of information overload and the serial crisis. While information overload is indifferent to the form of the information, data deluge is more precise. It completely adheres to the mode in which e-Science is trying to do science, a mode which focuses on data and computation. A more concrete definition of the data deluge specifies it in terms of the so-called "three Vs" (Hendler 2013). Accordingly, the *velocity* with which information is produced, as well as its *volume* and *variety* dominate science in such a way that only e-Science is capable of dealing with it. This issue is likewise not presented as *an* issue in science but as *the* issue of science today. From the viewpoint of e-Science, this challenge is primarily a failure of the historical publishing system (Neylon 2009, 2), where modes of production do not match modes of consumption any longer. Insofar as e-Science appears to be the way out of this crisis ROs have to become the new publication format.

According to Borgman, Wallis, and Enyedy (2007, 7), the topic of the data deluge is one of the main drivers behind funding investments into e-Science. At the other end of the discussion are advocates like David De Roure, affirming that "this new sociotechnical situation means we are better equipped to cope with the data deluge that predicated the e-Science program" (2011, sec. 4). Research Objects and other workflow-oriented publications are the means which "deliver systematic pipelines to deal with the data deluge" (Bechhofer, De Roure, et al. 2010, 91).

The discourse about the future is dominated by arguments about the epistemological environment this future will bring. One part of these arguments was provided by the anthology on *The Fourth Paradigm* published by Microsoft Research (Hey, Tansley, and Tolle 2009). The other point of reference is the article "The End of Theory: The Data Deluge Makes the Scientific Method Obsolete" published 2008 in *The Wire* (Anderson 2008).

In the letter publication Chris Anderson argues that the amount of data produced does not just bring a quantitative but also a qualitative change to science. He asserts that the amount of data already available at the beginning of research does not allow the derivation of a hypothesis from it before any statistical exploration has taken place. On the other hand, the results of data driven research processes make it difficult to derive any model that is more expressive than its description. In consequence, he concludes that hypothesis driven research and theories as models for world explanation do not lead to promising research anymore.

Contributions in the former publication also include more balanced views which, however, have a similar direction. The main claim behind the proclamation of a fourth paradigm is the claim that computation will eliminate the epistemological difference between empirically and theoretically driven research, making each of these approaches available within the same research process.

These discussions are not really taking place within the e-Science field but are cited here in order to describe the relevance and future success of its research program. It partially resembles the discourse about the essence of information discussed in the section about MAs. However, where MAs try to connect the issue of meaning with neuroscience in order to empirically anchor information, ROs harness epistemology in order to give primacy to the unit of the (computational) experiment as a way of organizing the research process. The consequence of this way of thinking is also well expressed when remarks are made about the role of texts within the new methodological setup. In this context, text is a social asset that provides no unique truth value on its own (2011, 3). The workflow is in fact meant to be a replacement for articles that only remain due to historical reasons. In contrast, workflows will be the primary object by which scientists get credit (Bourne 2010, 2).

The e-Science program that maintains a strong relationship with the project of open science was presented in connection with ROs, because ROs are the most prominent publication format inheriting e-Science principles in an extremely unfiltered way. Nevertheless, around three quarters of the publishing concepts that are presented in this research openly posit themselves within the same ideological frame or share key aspects, that being more of a justification for the extended space given to the topic here.

Semantic Publications

The next approach to digital publishing to be discussed here are *Semantic Publications* (hereafter referred to as SPs). SPs are not completely new. As will be shown later on, they share many ideas with Modular Articles. Harmsze, for instance, is sometimes referenced as a pioneering figure in this respect (Giunchiglia, Xu, et al. 2010, sec. 1). The decrease of research activity regarding digital publications and the different key interests in the remaining activities, however, led to the development from MAs to SPs being not without interruption. After 2009, SPs became one of the most active research areas on digital publications as well as a concept with a significant degree of implementation. Additionally, it could be argued that in fact the concept of MAs entails both the idea of aggregations and of SPs.

The key difference leading to this opposition between aggregations and SPs has to do with the understanding of the concept of a module. Aggregations, and RO in particular, radicalized the main idea introduced with the metaphor of modularity. They conceive of modules in a way that resembles physical separation, and in fact the distributed nature of aggregations includes servers that are physically quite separated. The path that leads from MAs to SPs, however, leaves the unit of the object, first known as the physical object of an article, intact. While the second perspective focuses on the modular structure within things conceived as given objects, the first focuses on how such objects are always part of a modular structure that precedes them.

Modularity in SPs is achieved by markup. Markup is a way to explicitly identify and denote fragments in text objects by placing it inside the text. As such, it does the same as was done by OAI-ORE in the JSTOR article example. However, the identification and description in the OAI-ORE example exists independently from the article, as has been made clear. It stands out from the object and is therefore also called standoff markup while markup in SPs is put into the object and addressed as embedded markup. Although both create information units on their own, which in the language of the turn of the millennium could be called modules, they take different steps in realizing modularization. Consequently, Bechhofer, Ainsworth, et al. (2010, 2) put a lot of emphasis on the distinction between ROs and SPs.

From Modular Articles to Semantic Publications

In the transition process from MAs to SPs, the three contributions by Marcondes (2005), Mons (2005), and Seringhaus and Gerstein (2007) stand out. Building on the same arguments summarized in the last sections, Marcondes highlights that scientific communication is slow and difficult to verify via text publications. In order to accelerate science, he proposes to model the "deep structure" (Marcondes 2005, 119) of articles. Similar to Harmsze, deep structure means the formalization of structure and topics in articles. These aspects should be made explicit by using XML markup and standardized formal terms. In this respect Marcondes proposes the

Scholarly Ontology Project[24] (also referred to as ScholOnto), which offers formal terms in order to reproduce the rhetorical structure of an article.

The issue of standardized semantics, contrasted with the contingent forms of natural language, is the main concern of Seringhaus and Gerstein (2007). Only if the semantics used are shared by all stakeholders, the formalization of deep structures in articles can really help to integrate "the ever-growing body of information" (1). Accordingly, Seringhaus highlights standardization as one of the most important goals to ensure progress in digital publishing.

Besides standardization of semantics for purposes of formalizing the structure and discourse of articles, Mons (2005) stresses that the same need exists for the things (entities) articles are about. He argues that "text is a nightmare for computers" because there are always many ways to refer to the same topic or thing. Hence, Mons asks the rhetorical question: "Which Gene Did You Mean?" (title). In his example, markup is used in order to link a text passage that refers in a narrative way to a codified standardized representation of this entity.

The term Semantic Publications was first used in the article "Adventures in Semantic Publishing" (Shotton et al. 2009). In this work the author offers an illustrative definition of the term, as well as a sophisticated example of a Semantic Publication. Following Shotton's own words:

> We define the term semantic publication to include anything that enhances the meaning of a published journal article, facilitates its automated discovery, enables its linking to semantically related articles, provides access to data within the article in actionable form, or facilitates integration of data between articles. (Shotton et al. 2009, 1)

This definition also takes features beyond those already discussed into account. However, the important thing is that all these features are achieved by revealing the possibilities of formally codified markup, which is attached to the original article in the example. The features implicitly addressed in the definition show up in the example in terms of:

- actionable data, meaning data sources that are de-referenceable and which possess a persistent link that can be processed while the publication is read;
- data fusions, meaning automatized merging of data sources within the publication with data sources outside of the publication, but which are about the same things;

24 http://projects.kmi.open.ac.uk/scholonto/

- highlighting of terms representing important concepts, persons, and other entities during the reading process for faster reading;
- authored or inferred links to external information sources;
- supporting claims tooltips on the basis of a functional analysis of citations;
- automatically created machine-readable summary of the article;
- tag clouds and a tag tree representing the topic of the article. The tag tree is created on the basis of formal taxonomies representing the knowledge domain of the article;
- interactive elements like changing data views, visualizations and re-orderable reference lists;
- citation-networks for the article and the authors cited in the article;
- deep structured markup of the article which express its composition.

All these features are enabled by explicitly adding markup to the article, facilitating computational processing of the content. Nonetheless, these computations still have to be implemented on their own and by the institutions which present the publication.

The Primacy of Formality and Standardization

The last paragraphs demonstrated how ideas from MAs continued even after their development had stopped. The use of markup for making aspects of articles explicit, the formal representation of logical and rhetorical structure as well as of meaning are fundamental pillars for MAs. Shotton's contribution gave an idea of possible benefits of this approach that has not been described with such level of detail before. The ability to achieve this derives from the developments of the so-called *Semantic Web* (hereafter referred to as SW), discussed on several occasions above. In short, the Semantic Web provides the technological means for making data interchangeable over the world wide web. It is the technological foundation for previously discussed initiatives, like the linked open data and OAI-ORE, but also for developments responsible for SPs. The Semantic Web also provides the means of embedding markup into web documents by virtue of a very sophisticated version of embedded markup, which in turn is completely compliant with SW principles. This approach is called *RDFa*[25]. It enables linking from within HTML elements of webpages to SW data and concepts outside of the document. RDFa was approved as a standard by the W3C at the same time OAI-ORE was finalized, and is heavily used in SPs.

25 https://www.w3.org/TR/rdfa-primer/

However, in correspondence with the two ways of interpreting modularity, Hunter et al. (2008, 15) classify OAI-ORE and RDFa into two profoundly distinct approaches for digital publications.

Another aspect of the Semantic Web needing further specification in the context of the present study is the use of the adjective *semantic*. In the current context, this term, which has appeared several times already in the preceding sections, has a meaning very specific to the field of information science. Evidently, text as such has meaning and uses semantics in order to create meaning. However, in the context of the Semantic Web and Semantic Publications, this adjective denotes the use of formally standardized knowledge representations, for instance taxonomies, thesauri, or ontologies. Accordingly, a publication becomes semantic the moment it adds a layer of formalized and standardized terms.

The name of SPs is a direct reference to the Semantic Web. They are the application to the field of publishing of ideals of formalization and standardization in the Semantic Web. Buckingham Shum and Clark (2010, 2) state that SPs are a response to the question: "what does the scientific article look like on the Semantic Web."

However, in view of the two notions of modularity, the quote of Buckingham, Shum, and Clark needs qualification: Semantic Publications are only one of two possible answers to the question of what articles look like on the Semantic Web. Semantic Publications, in contrast to aggregations, stick to the form of the article. This is why they use embedded markup instead of isolated metadata descriptions, as in the case of aggregations. The background for this decision is given by Shotton et al. (2009, 2). He argues that articles and databases represent two very different goals in research. An article is defined as a rhetoric object representing a certain state within research, from which the underlying hypothesis should be argued convincingly. A database in contrast would contain up-to-date information and is analytical in nature. Consequently, Shotton asserts that it is not desirable to replace one with the other. He adds social value to the two possibilities to achieve modularity in different ways.

Nevertheless, he also very much argues in favor of "frictionless interoperability" (Shotton et al. 2009, 2) between the two. This frictionless interoperability is achieved by including the aforementioned semantic layer on top of articles, putting the data view on the rhetoric object. In a certain way SPs thereby make databases out of articles. The difference highlighted by Shotton is thus not as big as it seems. It is a difference of deciding how to socially embed the database paradigm into publishing, but not a difference of objects. As has been noted by the example of the JSON article, a database-oriented first approach can likewise produce objects that are used as a rhetoric object.

The key effect of the Semantic Web for publications can therefore be summarized as the implementation of a dataset-oriented view on resources, and the attempt to treat digital scholarly objects as databases. The Semantic Web could achieve this, because in contrast to the situation MAs experienced it provided better means for formalization and standardization. The metaphor of a database as a model for the re-design of publications is openly proposed by Bourne (2005) when he asks: "Will a Biological Database Be Different from a Biological Journal?" (title), and has been used all over since. Within the developments instigated by the Semantic Web, the research field of SPs is the one that focuses on the development and propagation of formally standardized semantics in the context of scholarly publishing (Peroni 2014b, 121). It does so because it leaves the form of the article intact. While in MAs and aggregations the issue of semantics follows the issue of decomposition, provoking a deeper debate on formats, it is the primary concern of SPs. The current study therefore includes among the publication formats the concept of SPs, which do not use Semantic Web technologies, but do share the concern for formal and standardized semantics for the purpose of isolating aspects of scholarly text publications.

Models and Ontologies. The Many Forms of Semantic Publications

In most cases formal semantics are represented in ontologies. Ontologies are specific forms of multi-dimensional knowledge representations, which use a Semantic Web-compliant format such as the *Resource Description Format Scheme*[26] (also referred to as RDFS) or the *Web Ontology Language*[27] (also referred to as OWL). Apart from offering the possibility of defining terms, which give shared names to certain phenomena, ontologies permit the definition of how these phenomena relate to each other. This aspect facilitates automated inference on logical relationships between the phenomena. Early models of those outlined below are not always implemented with this technology. However, newer ones sometimes also use different implementation technologies, because they explicitly aim at different technological environments. Decisions against the use

26 https://www.w3.org/TR/rdf-schema/

27 https://www.w3.org/TR/2012/REC-owl2-primer-20121211/

of Semantic Web technologies therefore are not just bound to historical circumstances. Still, Semantic Web compliant ontologies are at the heart of SPs.

One of the first semantic models consistently implemented in the context of digital publications, albeit before the definition of RDFS or OWL, was again provided by Harmsze. Her struggle to identify core information units resulted in a scheme of splitting articles into modules called meta-information, positioning, methods, results, interpretation, and outcome. Each of these defines the boundary of a self-contained model. Even if an article is not completely split up into pieces, these concepts provide the means to markup parts of articles and thereby express their goal.

A little bit later than Harmsze's model, *ScholOnto* was developed as an attempt to represent the discursive structure of research articles (Li et al. 2002). In ScholOnto, the term discourse has a very open and flexible meaning. It provides three different types of semantics. The first distinguishes important from interpretative from epistemologically oriented parts in the text. The second defines links between parts, which correspond in terms of rhetoric structure, logic structure, similarity, or problematization. Finally, there is a mechanism to weight links in order to express how strong the relationship is. Thereby, ScholOnto also tries to formalize some qualitative aspects.

When it comes to the use of standardized terms in order to annotate topics and entities, it was Harmsze once again who argued in favor. Examples of early projects following this approach in a more systematic way are provided by the *Concept Wiki* of the *Concept Web Alliance*[28] (also referred to as CWA) and the *Unified Medical Language System*[29] (also referred to as UMLS). While the concept wiki was mostly used in biosciences, UMLS, as the name suggests, includes terms from the field of medicine. The problems addressed by these and similar subsequent projects are similar to the one Mons tried to highlight in the question about the correct gene cited before, to provide uniform names for things that are supposed to be the same thing.

Although UMLS started with the definition of terms for entities and topics, it was later extended by another vocabulary called *Semantic Network* (also referred to as UMLS-SN), which defines 54 terms for the representation of discourse around these entities (Marcondes, Malheiros, and da Costa

28 https://conceptweblog.wordpress.com/
29 https://semanticnetwork.nlm.nih.gov/

2014). The reason behind a unique definition of discourse representation in UMLS was the perceived peculiarity of discourse in medicine. Another example from the domain of medicine is the *Semantic Web Applications in Neuromedicine* ontology[30] (Gao et al. 2006; also referred to as SWAN). Originally rooted in research on Alzheimer, SWAN is used to model scientific discourse in articles on life science and neuromedicine (Ciccarese, Ocana, and Clark 2012). SWAN is comprised of several modules which, adhering to Semantic Web principles, import other ontologies for the description of bibliography and citations. The unique parts of SWAN provide topic-related terms for discourse elements, research statements, research questions, as well as so-called structured comments. Additionally, they define canonical entities from the life sciences as well as mechanisms for representing the lifecycle of articles and the agents involved.

The Text Encoding Initiative (also referred to as TEI) is a model not specifically defined to semantically enrich research publications, but to model aspects of digital editions in the context of scholarly editing. It still plays an important role for digital publishing in the humanities in general. Examples of journals that use TEI are the *Zeitschrift für Digitale Geisteswissenschaften*[31], the *Review Journal for Digital Editions*[32] and of course the *TEI Journal*[33].

Another important model that seeks to markup rhetorical blocks in articles is informed by the so-called *IMRaD* style. The IMRaD style is the name of a prominent concept for the structure of research articles in the second half of the 20th century, and again originates in the fields of medicine and biology (Sollaci and Pereira 2004). The acronym refers to the sections of a specific type of a research article: introduction, methods, results, and discussion. The ABCDE model was built on the IMRaD approach. Here the acronym resolves to annotation, background, contribution, discussion, and entities. de Waard and Tel (2006) try to adapt IMRaD to the needs of semantical annotation of research articles in digital form as such.

The *Semantically Annotated LaTeX* model (also referred to as SALT) stands out because it specifically aims at the LaTeX community. LaTeX is a text processing software suite which processes elements in texts, similar to markup, in order to create well layouted documents. It is used in research domains such as computer science, but is not compatible with

30 https://www.w3.org/TR/hcls-swan/
31 http://www.zfdg.de/
32 http://ride.i-d-e.de/
33 https://journal.tei-c.org

web technologies. The goal of SALT is to bring SP ideas into publication workflows with LaTeX. It provides three ontologies addressing document components, rhetorical structures, and document metadata.

The *Scientific Knowledge Object Pattern* (also referred to as SKO) is another attempt to represent the logical structure of articles. Giunchiglia, Xu, et al. (2010) offer further insights on the use of articles thus annotated. They demonstrate how this model is used to outline and automatically process inductive, deductive, and abductive argumentation patterns.

Buckingham Shum and Clark (2010) made an attempt to classify all models seeking to represent discourse, a goal that most of the models presented in the last paragraphs also try to do. They distinguish between rhetorical and argumentative or logical discourse. Rhetorical discourse is concerned with narrative strategy and strategies regarding the presentation of research.

Finally, Peroni (2014b) describe the *Semantic Publishing and Referencing Ontologies* (also referred to as SPRO), the most diverse set of ontologies in this list. It describes very different aspects of articles. Each ontology can be used on its own or together with others. Some of these ontologies, such as the *Citation Typing Ontology* (Shotton and Peroni 2012; also referred to as CiTO), were created by David Shotton himself. However, many other SP initiatives, like for instance the SWAN ontology, are involved in SPRO, too. Further ontologies in SPRO include:

- DoCo to markup document components of articles (Shotton et al. 2015);
- FaBio and FRBR to highlight bibliographic information (Shotton and Peroni 2012);
- BiRO to markup bibliographic reference lists;
- C4O to model the context and number of citations in an article;
- PRO to attach information about roles of agents involved in the publishing process of an article (Shotton, Peroni, and Vitali 2012);
- PSO to communicate the publishing status of an article that is semantically enriched;
- PWO, a workflow ontology for publishing workflows (Shotton, Peroni, and Vitali 2012).

The list of models presented in this section was extensive. The purpose behind such level of detail was the substantiation of a recent observation by Ruiz-Iñiesta and Corcho (2014). The authors noticed (1) that the concepts of SPs caused a significant increase in models seeking to describe structures and aspects of publications. Several other surveys try to give an overview of the landscape of these publication ontologies that were not even mentioned before (Buckingham Shum and Clark 2010; Ruiz-Iñiesta and Corcho 2014; Xu et al. 2014). Peroni (2014a) counts seven of those ontologies in the domain of law alone, and 12 that focus on bibliographic information.

The examples of SP ontologies offered so far can be systematized into at least six groups. These groups include ontologies concerning:

- administrative aspects
- discourse aspects
- structural aspects
- biographical aspects
- citation purposes
- topics and entities

This variety of aspects also offers some explanation for the quantity of existing models. The quest to describe the deep structure of articles leads to very different prioritizations and interpretations. Following Ruiz-Iñesta's observation, an ironical aspect of SPs is the fact that their focus on standardization and interoperability has the opposite effect in some areas. In the majority of cases, multiple ontologies exist for the same category, due to specific domain needs, different requirements for information precision, different technology backgrounds, and historical reasons. All of these have in common that they respond to social demands and backgrounds. The meaning of this phenomenon will be analyzed in the second part of this work.

The Burden of (Digital) Extra Work and its Distribution Across Human and Non-Human Agents

Obviously, the effort it takes to manually markup every research article within the plurality of viewpoints listed above, and with such a high level of detail, poses a problem for the whole approach of SPs. This challenge is a crucial point of discussion within the field of SPs from the beginning until today. Shotton (2009) determines in his introductory piece of work that a "cost-effective" implementation of SPs requires significant automation in the creation of markup. In the same way, Giunchiglia, Xu, et al. (2010 sec 2.7) highlight the huge effort in metadata generation and maintenance necessary to deduce and attach a formal representation of the line of argument to a research article.

Although Mons (2005) is one of the earliest agents who advocates SPs, he emphasizes another aspect behind this issue. Besides the fact that human markup creation on the scale required by SPs does not seem feasible for the author, he also stresses that it is not desirable. The normative and static encoding schemes would lead to a kind of writing and restriction of the "creative" minds of authors that would significantly reduce the quality of articles.

There are several responses to this challenge. One already mentioned is the attempt to let computers do the work of creating the markup. Other answers just stress that the resulting benefits are worth the effort, or that these efforts are inevitable and can therefore not be discussed because they are part of social changes in the publishing sector that are without alternative.

It is worth mentioning that in SPs there is in general more reflection on issues of stakeholder groups and the publishing system to which they belong than in many other projects. Most often the role of publishers is briefly criticized but rarely evaluated in greater depth. In contrast, both Shotton (2009) and the "FORCE 11 Manifesto" (Bourne, Buckingham Shum, et al. 2012), sustained by the protagonists of SPs, provide extensive discussions on new roles for different stakeholders within a digital publishing system shaped by the SP approach.

Regarding the distribution of necessary efforts for the creation of markup in articles, Shotton (2009, 91–92) refers to three agent groups: publishers, editors, and authors. The publisher should organize a machine-readable version of the bibliography, as well as a structured version of article components such as sections. The editors with their domain knowledge should assume the task of researching and markup entities, context, and logical meaning. Finally, the authors should provide functional classification of their citations, that is highlight formally why they cited a particular source, by using semantics like the ones provided by CiTO.

A complementary strategy to the distribution of effort is to gradually scale the effort. This approach is suggested by Lord, Cockell, and Stevens (2012). The authors call it a "measured and evolutionary" (1013) semantic enrichment. Here, the extent up to which formal markup is applied by the authors depends on technical and non-technical aspects of the authoring process, and may vary from publication to publication. The goal is to define a strategy that can be easily included in existing research and publishing workflows of authors. Additionally, the effort demanded from the authors should reflect the extent up to which the benefits can actually be made transparent to the authors. The goal is to slowly move away from the "lumpen pdf" (see Introduction) to SPs, so that the effort becomes a natural part of the publishing process without dominating the discourse on digital publishing.

Regardless of strategies to minimize markup-efforts by sharing it between people or gradually postponing it, such effort remains a critical aspect of SPs. Abundant research on the automation of this task gives evidence of this. Very similar to the argument of De Roure, Shotton (2009) claims that techniques of automation will more and more solve problems that digital technologies have produced in the first place. The importance of the issue of effort, so the assertion goes, will therefore decline over time. Nonetheless there are still more examples for semi-automated enrichment of SPs (Pavlopoulos et al. 2009; Fink et al. 2010; Marcondes, Malheiros, and da Costa 2014) than of fully automated enrichment. Furthermore, the level of automation significantly depends on the aspects that should be recognized automatically. Automatically identifying document structures (Shotton et al. 2013) is more reliable than the discursive functions of citations (Ciancarini et al. 2013). The disambiguation of terms for instance requires the assistance of authors and their "tacit knowledge" (Shotton 2009, 7).

Revisiting Progress, Data Deluge and Information

As has been mentioned, another way to approach the obstacles of SPs is to show that there is no alternative to SPs in the near future. There is no better way to give evidence for this argument than to cite Penev et al. (2010, 2), who apply the "adapt or die" principle to the situation of publishers and SPs. Terminology that strongly commits to the theme of progress is used all over within the SPs community. Correspondingly, Shotton (2009) calls SPs "the coming revolution in scientific journal publishing," while Peroni (2014a) shortens this into just "The Digital Publishing Revolution." Moreover, innovation in publishing is reduced to the concept of SPs when he makes the equation: "today's publishing revolution, aka semantic publishing" (7). In contrast, Bourne (2011) complains about the growing "problems of outdated communication."

Shotton (2009, 93) observes "raw text decreasing in value," a phenomenon that makes relinquishing semantic markup in publications an act of digital censorship (94). Having said all this, SPs share the same certainty about the development of digital publications, albeit based on slightly different visions.

The similarity between key themes in the discourse on SPs and other publication formats include more than reflections on automation and progress. The belief that SPs are without any alternative corresponds with the emphasis that is again put on the often-cited theme of data deluge. Thus Shotton (2009) argues that data deluge does not permit researchers to really read all the articles that are published. Similarly, Renear and Palmer (2009) state that the overload of information requires a more strategic form of reading. They claim that digital technologies are exactly the kind of technologies that permit reading differently. Seringhaus and Gerstein (2007, 1) state that the amount of information already published, and continuing to grow, is the main challenge of publishing. The only solution he sees that can face this challenge is to "modernize academic publishing to exploit the power of the Internet."

Comparable with MAs, SPs make their arguments in a nexus between the social-historical issue of the quantity of information, a positive definition of information, and a publishing environment which has to integrate both. The peculiarity of SPs, compared to former applications of the same setup, is the extend up to which the last point in this setup is discussed. While the Modular Articles focus on the application of the information paradigm to the publication format, SPs extend its application into a vision for the whole publishing environment. This extension derives from the experience that libraries struggle to offer appropriate services for dealing adequately with the digital "chaos in the laboratory" (Bourne 2011, 120).

Accordingly, Sefton (2009) introduces his model of SPs as an element within the bigger picture of an "integrated content environment." Gradmann (2010) develops the idea of a vast "knowledge space of data," enabled by SPs and turning publications into heuristic objects for the creation of this space. Bourne, Shotton, et al. (2012) express the same idea in a very colorful way when they argue that:

> We see a future in which scientific information and scholarly communication more generally become part of a global, universal, and explicit network of knowledge; where every claim, hypothesis, argument — every significant element of the discourse — can be explicitly represented, along with supporting data, software, workflows, multimedia, external commentary, and information about provenance. (Bourne, Shotton, et al. 2012, 45)

Having said this, SPs are associated with attempts to create better conditions for information retrieval and for information infrastructure:

> The goal is to pave the way towards a Semantic Publishing Ecosystem that will alleviate, at least partly, the information overload problem. (Groza 2012, sec. Abstract)

The call for a more strategic reading as a consequence of the quantity of information extends the evaluations of the status of information given so far. Renear and Palmer (2009) add another formalization to this: one of the main points in their article claims that this type of reading is not only necessary, but that it is the epitome of reading in science. Consequently, they argue that scientists have always read strategically. In this light, SPs become the most natural way to design publications and the effort to markup information appears as a key scientific activity difficult to question. A minor survey with researchers in order to support this claim was carried out by de Ribaupierre and Falquet (2014). In summary, they stress that the act of looking out for a publication in science always corresponds with a search for specific information.

Additionally, this argument supports the positive definition of information as it was highlighted on several occasions above. The equation between the information-seeking purpose of readers and the application of standardized markup obscures the possibility of an agency of the reader in the creation of the information content. This line of thought goes beyond the unit of individual information in the field of SPs, and includes narrative aspects of publications. Accordingly, "such discourse structures are trapped within the content of the publications" (Groza 2012, sec. Abstract).

The positive notion towards a formal understanding of information in the context of SPs is less theoretical and more pragmatic than in the case of the MAs. Nevertheless, the outcome is the same. For Marcondes (2005), markup is the real information in text. Yet it is necessary to add this markup to text because the characteristics of narrative transform it into an "invisible knowledge unit" (Giunchiglia, Xu, et al. 2010, sec. 2.1). In this respect markup reconfigures the hierarchy between text and information in favor of information, like it adheres to the concept of SPs. Marcondes (2005) correspondingly continues to imagine a world of publishing in which publications are dissolved in communication, similar to the vision of Gradmann. This is possible because formal semantics, like ontologies, would dissolve the semantic heterogeneity inherent in text publications (Sierman, Schmidt, and Ludwig 2009, 63).

The Role of Domains and Stakeholder Groups

The previous paragraphs have given some indication of the close connection of SPs to activities in the field of library and information science. Many contributions in SPs are made within infrastructure projects, for instance in Digital Libraries. Prominent advocates of SPs, like Allen Renear and Stefan Gradmann, are information scientists themselves. In Germany, the working group on digital publishing that was founded by the *Association for Digital Humanities in German Speaking Countries*[34] (DHd) mostly equates SP principles — "the codified text" (Stäcker et al. 2016) — with digital publishing in general. This observation is important insofar as the initiator and convener of this working group is a librarian by profession.

As has been indicated in the introduction to this chapter, publishers are another stakeholder group closely linked to SPs. A superficial phenomenon demonstrating this entanglement further is the quantity of references to the Article of the Future contest made by authors in the field of SPs. Giunchiglia, Xu, et al. (2010) as well as Marcondes, Malheiros, and da Costa (2014) explicitly include these initiatives in the list of SP-like activities. Peroni (2014a, 8) and Shotton et al. (2009, 2) discuss Elsevier's *Grand Challenge* initiative as an active attempt by Elsevier to propagate SP ideas to a broader community, and to create better conditions for SP compliant versions of articles. On the other hand, Elsevier sponsored a prize for the best contributions at the *SePublica* conference, a sub-conference of the *European Semantic Web Conference*[35] that focuses on SPs. Elsevier also participated in the first FORCE11 workshop, which produced the aforementioned manifesto.

The example of Elsevier is given here because Elsevier is one of the biggest commercial publishers in science. Nonetheless, the connection between SPs and publishers include other publishers with other business models as well. Thus, Shotton (2012) mentions *Pensoft* as another publisher who intensively implements SP principles into its publications. Likewise, the pioneering showcase for SPs provided by Shotton (2012) was a cooperation with *PLOS*, an open access publisher most active in the fields of biology and medicine.

There are several explanations for this strong entanglement. The first is the strong emphasis SPs put on the unit of articles. In contrast to other approaches like ROs, the article remains the core unit. Some of

34 https://dig-hum.de/

35 https://eswc-conferences.org/

the reasons for this preference were mentioned at the beginning of this section. Without doubt, this makes it easier for publishers to associate with innovations in digital publishing, because they do not require substantial modification to the main element of their business plans. Instead, SPs are "semantic overlays" (Clark 2014) on top of well-established objects of revenue. Consequently Pellegrini (2017, 9) asserts that "semantic metadata" such as produced in SPs begin to show up as the "core of their [the publishing companies] innovation strategy having a profound impact on existing business practices and new strategies of value creation."

Furthermore, SPs offer exceptional possibilities of implementing the way publishers will develop business models on the basis of services rather than content. Since markup significantly facilitates processing of articles, it eases the implementation of these services significantly. With the ongoing success of open access, publishers are meant to be forced to develop this option and explicitly advertise SPs in this respect (Shotton 2009, 86; Bourne, Shotton, et al. 2012, 49; Peroni 2014a, 8–9).

Essentially, new business models may arise from the need to create, derive, and disseminate "semantic assertions" from SPs (Peroni 2014a, 8–9). In the FORCE11 initiative such prospects are transformed into more substantial product descriptions. Accordingly, tools are needed to produce semantic publications and enhanced products may be offered to researchers. The information provided by markup can also be used for advanced "reputation management" services, which should be of interest to institutions and funding bodies (Bourne, Shotton, et al. 2012, 54–56). Another good example of features that enhanced products can provide is the list of views and inferred information which Shotton presents in his initial paper.

The above section on SPs demonstrated that the integration of digital technologies into publishing in general, and of Semantic Web technologies in particular, does not require substantially invalidating publishing concepts. In comparison with ROs, SPs do not question either the form or the content of publications. While ROs position publications on top of a networked, multi-media, and multi-resource environment, in the vision of SPs this environment is derived from publications in a subsequent step. It can be achieved by information infrastructures, like in the examples of library and information science projects, or through services provided by publishers. Regardless of the specific variant, in the field of SPs the article comes first. Semantic markup, in the form of embedded markup, provides the gateway to what lies beyond.

Liquid Publications

Liquid Publications (hereafter referred to as LP) are a publication format that appeared more or less at the same time as SPPs, slightly earlier than ROs and SPs. Liquid Publications are the outcome of the Liquid Publishing project that was funded within the 7th Framework Program for research funding in the European Union.

The basic idea of LPs is the claim that the current mode of publishing has deficits, causing major problems for any agent group related to publishing, most notably for researchers, who are the creators and the consumers of publications. Casati, Giunchiglia, and Marchese (2007) highlight the problem that researchers take more time to write publications than to do research because reputation is based on publications. They describe situations in which issues are created only for the purpose of writing a publication that solves the problem, a practice the authors call "sudoku research" (Casati, Giunchiglia, and Marchese 2007, 8). Furthermore, they stress that the current publication model does not support reuse of publications or publications really representing the continuous evolvement of knowledge. Instead for every new finding a new publication is created. Additionally, the historical mode of publishing would delay the dissemination of new findings and is insufficient in giving granular credit to specific types of contributions in publications with multiple authors.

Beyond the aforementioned issues LPs are very much concerned with the topic of peer review. Casati, Giunchiglia, and Marchese (2007) harshly criticize the model of closed, expert-based peer review for quality control. They state that it "kills good papers and is inherently flawed" (7). The viewpoint is presented on a personal basis and not supported by actual research. Yet arguments are given which include: (a) that the results of reviews are contingent and do not always match the quality of the paper, (b) that reviewers are biased and that there are groups of reviewers who are generally more positive or negative.

The critique of the historical mode of publishing is presented together with a judgment about researchers' motivation when publishing. These motivations are: (a) the wish to communicate research to the public, (b) the wish to get symbolic capital back, and in the case of conference papers to establish and maintain relevant research contacts. In this context the authors assert that digital technologies have created completely new ways of knowledge production and, in correspondence with the judgments in the last sections, invalidate historical modes of publishing (7). They particularly highlight the meaning of network technologies and storage. Only these two resources create ways of making research output available and of interact with without limits. The authors express irritation about the fact that insufficient and outdated present modes of publishing remain conceptually and often also physically paper based, thus "lagging behind." In this light Casati, Giunchiglia, and Marchese (2007, 8) introduce LPs as a publishing model designed as if "academic research was born after the Web."

Architecture: Analogies of Hard- and Software

The key topic guiding the design of LPs is a presupposed analogy between software and knowledge. Casati, Giunchiglia, and Marchese (2007) stress that both the creation of software and of knowledge is an effort by many people and an endeavor that will never be finished. Publications should accordingly enable collaborative work and permit permanent modification. This analogy is also provided for the purpose of showing that in software engineering, mechanisms are already in use that resemble both ideas. It is extended to the changing relationship between what is conceived as hardware resp. software. Like the logical structure of software becoming increasingly independent from the underlying hardware, publication will see a decoupling between the structure of a publication (software) and the former hardware (the paper). The most successful strategy in order to achieve digital publications is to transfer these software development mechanisms to the world of publishing. Concrete references are made to the principles of *agile project management*[36] and *open source software development* (Casati, Giunchiglia, and Marchese 2007, 3). Liquid Publication research literature consequently applies a bunch of further concepts in computer science in order to design the shape of digital publications. Publications become *data warehouses* and the publishing process is defined and rendered in correspondence with *pushing*, *pulling*, and *branching* processes as they appear in the context of *version control systems*[37].

36 Agile project management or software development is a dynamic and highly flexible strategy for project management that tries to reduce bureaucratic overhead as much as possible in order to be able to quickly adapt to unforeseen issues during the realization phase of a project (see also Larman 2004).

37 Version Control Systems (also referred to as VCS) are specialized are a specialized software that is able to track changes in files — mostly textbased files like programing code —, to recover the state of these files for a certain point of time and to organize contributions (commits) from multiple contributors working with different copies of the repository containing the files (see also Hinsen, Läufer, and Thiruvathukal 2009).

Entities: Persons, Processes and Objects

Another significant aspect of the background of LPs is its partial critique of alleged viewpoints in the open access movement. Although principles of open access are welcomed and acknowledged as a fundamental dependency for the realization of LPs, Casati, Giunchiglia, and Marchese (2007, 22) claim that these principles focus too much on the accessibility and the usability of knowledge, but do not reflect the dynamic and multi-faceted ways in which publications float between different stakeholders. LPs in contrast address this issue systematically. Publishing is accordingly defined as a nexus of three entities: *agents*, *processes*, and *knowledge objects*. A specific constellation between these three elements forms a Liquid Publication. Three different examples for LPs are given in the project: Liquid Books (Casati et al. 2011), Liquid Journals (Baez et al. 2009; Baez and Casati 2010), and Liquid Conferences (Xu 2011). The three versions of LPs will be described in greater detail below.

In order to be able to implement and describe LPs as the product of collaborative work, it is necessary to index all the different roles in which agents can contribute to a publication. Casati, Giunchiglia, and Marchese (2007, 13) note that in times of digital technologies agents appear in changing roles more frequently and that many contributions are subtle, like for instance aggregation, classification, or blogging, among others. In contrast to earlier formats, LPs sustain a certain notion of a monolithic object at the center of publications, which they call *Scientific Knowledge Object* (hereafter referred to as SKO). Scientific Knowledge Objects are also referred to as "the IT aspect of the knowledge creation and dissemination problem" Casati, Giunchiglia, and Marchese (2007, 13). Scientific Knowledge Objects are the way by which the complexity demanded by the features summarized above and the complexity of processes and actors indicated in the last paragraph should become manageable. On a very basic level SKOs are defined as *repositories*[38] which — beyond content of any typ — contain a description of the social network of agents and processes involved in their creation and modification. The concept of a repository is again derived from software development. Here it is technological infrastructure that is able to store software and organize the interactions of multiple developers within the development process.

38 A repository is a software infrastructure that facilitates the storage and management of digital resources.

Functional Requirements

Looking at the research literature, it is hard to grasp what LPs are precisely. In varying levels of abstraction Casati, Giunchiglia, and Marchese (2007) refer to them as papers, publications, or just organized scientific knowledge. Likewise, no clear distinction exists between the term Liquid Publication and the term Scientific Knowledge Object. In correspondence with the last paragraph, however, the interaction patterns as well as the functional requirements enabling these patterns will be discussed in greater detail. Four functional requirements guided the design process of SKOs are listed. First, SKOs need to permit non-restricted modification of any aspect for the time people in a collaborative setting are willing to contribute. This includes the possibility of several versions of an SKO representing different states of research and work. The notion of snapshots is used for this purpose (Baez et al. 2009, sec. 3). Secondly, SKOs must permit the organization and reflection of different types of work between different contributors to an SKO. This means that different contributors might have different control over elements in the SKO and that their contributions are individually tracked and categorized. Third, every contributor should be able to maintain and work on her own version of an SKO. This option is compared with the concept of branches[39] in decentralized version control systems like Git[40]. Finally, SKOs should not just resemble the principles of software repositories, but indeed be technically implemented as software repositories for the creation of publications from the start. Thus, they are also called "content repositories," or, for the example of Liquid Books, "LiquidBook Repositories" (Giunchiglia, Chenu, et al. 2010, 49).

Stack: Layers of Liquid Publications

The possibility to have different people administering different content in different versions is called a low-level capacity of software repositories. It offers basic technical and semantic means of referring to elements in SKOs, their creation history and their contributors. Advocates of SKOs are

39 Branches in software repositories permit to develop certain features independently from each other and from the main state of development. It enables changes to software that only exist for the people working on a specific branch. When the developments in a branch have reached maturity the whole set of changes of the branch can be merged back into the main development line. Branches are used in software repositories where many people work on many different things at the same time. Due to branches the integrity of the core of the software is not jeopardized but still offers the highest degree of flexibility for software developers.

40 https://git-scm.com/

aware that publications have more specific interaction models. Scientific Knowledge Objects address this issue by defining more granular categories in order to describe the elements of SKOs and their relationship. Furthermore, these categories should make it possible to represent types of interactions between contributors and the publication. This is an important aspect for SKOs because the goal of improving the review process is partially built around the idea that different contributions to publications should be identifiable on their own.

Formally, four different semantic levels are defined, this is an important aspect, each generating specific types of metadata (Giunchiglia, Chenu, et al. 2010, 10–13). These levels are:

1. The file level
2. The semantic level
3. The serialization level
4. The presentation level

The elements described within these levels are called nodes. The file level holds the content itself. The content in turn is represented in terms of URLs. These URLs can link between nodes, fragments of nodes, or groups of nodes.[41] As mentioned above, the file node may contain content of any file type. The semantic layer holds any type of metadata which describes what a node represents scientifically as well as in which context it was included into the LP.

The serialization level is meant to arrange the content or filter file nodes and semantic nodes to create specific LPs versions. It has been noted before that a SKO may lead to different publications, for instance a blog post or a poster. The blog post has a linear structure while the poster might arrange content in columns or as a graph. Likewise, the poster probably uses less of the text content of the SKO. The serialization level describes this ordering. The presentation layer finalizes the implementation of specific LPs out of SKOs. In general, it applies styles to publications. This refers to things like the font used for text or the size of a video. Additionally, it defines the output file format.

The four levels do not only introduce certain distinctions between aspects of publications, they also reproduce the software engineering view on publications. The relationship between these layers is hierarchical. There are

41 Considering the definition of URLs that has been given before it is important to repeat that the content of LPs, different from ROs, is not distributed on the web, but stored in a repository. Here, the URL only defines a certain mechanism of making digital resources technically identifiable.

aspects which are considered crucial and aspects that are made contingent. Accordingly, Giunchiglia, Xu, et al. (2010, 10) call the addition of serialization metadata to LPs an "execution" of a SKO and the presentation of metadata the "rendering" of the content. The terminology resembles the distinction between programming and running software as well as programming and compiling. Furthermore, it updates the distinction between form and content that was made in other publication concepts. In any case, LPs suggest a specific way of judging essential and contingent aspects of publications.

State: Versions and Continuous Modification

Giunchiglia, Chenu, et al. (2010, 19–21) try to advance the concept of liquidity. First, the basic idea of continuously evolving publications is separated into three different types of dynamics. By referring to physical states, such types are called the gaseous, the liquid, and the solid state. These states are analyzed in terms of properties and technical requirements. Properties mainly address the modification rate and the level of maturity that can be expected from a publication in each of these states. In contrast, requirements define different levels of effort applicable to the task of assuring the persistence of SKOs. LPs thus call for the definition of different levels of sustainability, an approach which is reminiscent of Hunter's decay factor.

In the long run the three states of liquidity in LPs equate to traditional notions of a work being a work in progress (gaseous state), a draft (liquid state), or the final version (solid state). However, the main point of the whole argument about liquidity is that publications are already publishable in all states. The liquid state is also considered to be the crucial state of future publishing. Accordingly, publishing ceases to refer to a certain state in knowledge production. Giunchiglia, Chenu, et al. (2010, 22–23) outline the type of practices that a publication in the liquid state attracts. Most of these practices concern collaboration, feedback, and review. The fact that a publication can be reviewed in its liquid state already, together with the elementary structure of nodes, is perceived as a major contribution to a more open and more specific review process.

Model

It is significant that the LP project actually fails to elaborate specifications for the different metadata levels of LPs described above. The final project report does not comprehensively define more fine-grained elements than those that have been discussed already. The vocabulary referring to the file-layer, for instance, proposes only a *file_node* element that may have an attribute containing the URL. There are few things in the formal SKO model that substantiate the perspectives described in prose above, meaning: (a) the fact that there are four semantic levels, (b) that within these levels a publication is a group of elements (nodes) that (c) refer to each other in a certain ways (relations).

No definitions of concrete relationships defining specific structures are made, like in the case of workflows in ROs. The same holds true for elements in the serialization and presentation level. What is offered is a random integration of some vocabularies already mentioned in the SPs section, more precisely the ABCD and the SALT vocabularies (Giunchiglia, Chenu, et al. 2010, 56). Additionally, an unsystematic selection of style features like *font* and *paragraph_style* is mentioned. However, these features hardly serve any other purpose than to illustrate the mechanism.

Indeed, the more concrete research on LPs gets, the more the approach turns away from its original complexity and radicalness and thus from the need to define usable vocabularies. The last step in the aforementioned report is again an illustration of a set of three *SKO patterns*. Patterns are common implementation structures of the SKO model. The three patterns presented are: inductively, deductively, and abductively organized journal articles. In these examples, as can be expected, the serialization of the content is sequential, and the semantic level includes logical relationships.

Later work by Xu (2011) confirms the tendency of LP research to give preference to the journal article form in order to discuss issues of publishing and LPs. While this fact is especially prominent for LPs, due to the tension between the level of critique and the LP showcases, this observation can be made for many contributions to the field of digital publication formats. Accordingly, Xu (2011, 67–70) continues to investigate the three SKO patterns that were mentioned above and transposes the rather technical concepts in the LP project to concepts that are more familiar to the publishing domain. Lifecycle, for instance, is a far more restricted variation of the theme of general "liquidity" structured by snapshots within a repository (Xu 2010, 425–27). Correspondingly, the rich and open space of options for the design of publications that was chased by Candela, Casati, and others at the beginning is reduced to a set of commons features later on. What were once the levels of serialization, semantics, and presentation as well as the feature of liquidity turns into basic structures of text documents, rhetorical relationships, and subsequent annotations (Xu 2010, 428).

Reference Implementations

Further examples try to deepen the analysis of dependencies between agents, practices, and SKOs. The three showcases are Liquid Books (Casati et al. 2011), Liquid Journals (Baez et al. 2009; Baez and Casati 2010) and Liquid Conferences (Xu 2011, chap. 6). The goal of these examples is to investigate how the concept of liquidity might change historical publishing setups understood as a conflation of aforementioned entities. Although these examples offer more concrete insights into LPs, these insights substantiate the notion of liquidity, not the model of the LP format.

For instance, Liquid Journals are defined as thematic streams which continuously include and exclude links to scientific contributions. The important aspect of these journals is no longer providing final versions of research papers, but offering an interface to currently relevant research at every state of maturity. Liquid Publications in the gaseous state could be linked in the same way as solid ones. Likewise, links could be included and excluded at any time. Issues of journals are transformed to journal snapshots that represent "collections of links" (Baez and Casati 2010, sec. 4.2). This proposition also makes clear that holding content is no longer the primary function of journals.

The re-specification of historical formats keeps the historical agents associated with a specific concept intact. However, it asks for the types of activity such agents might engage in within a continuum of different levels of "liquidity." For example, there are still editors in Liquid Journals, but they now curate the list of links in Liquid Journals instead of accepting and editing content.

Liquid Publications are in many aspects in between MAs, SPs, and ROs, enriched with the unique idea of liquidity. From MAs they inherit the strong emphasis on fragmentation and modularization. The use of URIs in order to technically represent elements and entities in a publication as well as the intent to formally classify each of its entities comes close to SPs. However, it is worth mentioning that despite comparable technological approaches and goals there is rarely any reference to SPs. The management of LPs in repositories, finally, resembles some of the characteristics of the early ROs in the myExperiment environment.

The term liquidity is a metaphor. By putting together all aspects apparent in its presence it is possible to say that most often it defines a higher rate of interaction between agents and publications. Interactions that are outlined for the liquid state include giving feedback, reviewing, and modification. The modification of content as an instant reaction to the feedback resembles the idea of direct communication. Accordingly, the Liquid Journal was characterized as a channel that no longer holds content but controls the flow of information. The focus shifts from the object to the phenomena the object is supposed to mediate. Such communicative turn is also supported by the aforementioned analogy between the history of publishing and the decoupling of software from hardware. One could therefore claim that LPs aim at the highest degree at which publishing can be grasped as communication.

Enhanced Publications

Next in line is the concept of *Enhanced Publications* (hereafter referred to as EPs). The term Enhanced Publication is used in two different ways. On the one hand it represents an effort to define an integrative concept to digital publications. Sierman, Schmidt, and Ludwig (2009), Castelli, Manghi, and Thanos (2013), Bardi and Manghi (2014), and Simukovic (2012) even use it as an umbrella term for digital publications as such. On the other hand, it is used by projects or journals trying to advertise innovative components of their digital publications. The term integrative concept highlights that some of the related work consists in comparing and systematizing different approaches, identifying common problems, and in undertaking the first attempt to define a technical and formal model that includes all the others. This is a significant difference to former evaluations by Nentwich and Owen. Furthermore, EPs seek to create better conditions for infrastructure that supports their creation.

The reason for this significant difference is the professional background of the concept's main contributors. Enhanced Publications arose out of the digital library and digital research repository domain, and first appeared in the *DRIVER*[42] project (Digital Repository Infrastructure Vision for European Research). They were used in a variety of reports which were combined in a publication funded by the Dutch *SURF*[43] Foundation (Sierman, Schmidt, and Ludwig 2009). The definition of this term as well as the content of the reports built upon earlier work on research repositories which also

42 https://web.archive.org/web/20120113023439/http://www.driver-repository.eu/
43 https://www.surf.nl

took place in the Netherlands. Correspondingly, Peters and Lossau (2009, 250–51) highlight the impact of the *DARE* (Digital Academic Repository, see Koninklijke Bibliotheek 2006) for the realization of the DRIVER project as well as for the *COAR*[44] (Confederation of Open Access Repositories). Hogenaar (2009, 2–3) likewise relates the activities to the Dutch project *ESCAPE*[45] (Enhanced Scientific Communication by Aggregated Publication Environments). Most of the authors of DRIVER's reports had worked in one of these projects before.

The peculiar viewpoint of these domains not only shaped the specification of EPs, it also led to activities of a type that were new in the context of digital publications. Despite these peculiarities EPs are obviously part of the same discourse on digital publications as the concepts discussed earlier in this work. They repeat large parts of the major themes that have been outlined already, among them the information overload (Woutersen-Windhouwer and Brandsma 2009), the acceleration of science (Verhaar 2009, 38), and open access (Peters and Lossau 2009). Nonetheless, research on EPs focuses more than others on the evaluation and discussion of environmental and infrastructural problems of digital publications. This aspect is very well documented by Woutersen-Windhouwer's and Brandsma's (2009, 81) intent "to help to structure the environment of scholarly publishing."

The alternative usage of the term Enhanced Publications builds on the attempt of the DRIVER project to establish a generic perspective. Accordingly, people and projects use it to give a name to the innovative potential of publications as such, regardless of their type. Some of these projects were intentionally initiated by the same SURF foundation that was involved in the DRIVER project (Jankowski et al. 2012, 2). Other initiatives like the *Information Bulletin for Variable Stars* appropriated the term independently (Holl 2012).

The *W3C Incubator Group on Library Linked Data* (W3C Library Linked Data Incubator Group 2011) provides a random list of EP projects relating to the engagement of SURF mentioned above. It also describes their entanglement within the strategic frame of infrastructure development in the Netherlands.

44 https://www.coar-repositories.org/

45 https://escapesurf.wordpress.com/

Specifications and Features

As mentioned above, any description of EPs is pragmatically motivated. The primary goal of such descriptions is finding a starting point from which to answer the question of whether research repositories need to invest in further development of their technologies or not (Woutersen-Windhouwer and Brandsma 2009). Hogenaar and Hoogerwerf (2009) state that the examples of what they consider to be an EP are so new that they lack an overarching model in order to refer to them. In fact, the most important aspect of this argument is the underlying claim that different approaches to new publication objects do belong to a unifiable idea.

Judging by the quantity of publication concepts available at that time, the number of concepts considered in the evaluations is relatively low. Basically, two concepts are repeatedly mentioned and discussed in greater detail. These are the Modular Article and Scientific Publication Packages (Hogenaar and Hoogerwerf 2009; Woutersen-Windhouwer and Brandsma 2009; Hogenaar 2009). Woutersen-Windhouwer and Brandsma (2009) also discuss Marcondes "web published scientific articles" while Verhaar (2009) posits Seringhaus as a reference point for EPs. Both contributions were discussed as early examples of SPs in the present study. In fact, Woutersen-Windhouwer and Brandsma (2009) use the section title "Semantic Publishing" in their presentation of Marcondes but then include SPPs under the same title. In contrast, they differentiate between MAs and SPs even though both can be described as referring to similar key concepts.

The reason for this fuzziness depends on which aspects are given priority in the analysis. The key point behind the results of each of these analyses is the claim that publications need to be conceived of as aggregations of components, similar to approaches in the section on aggregations. This also prepares the field for another claim, that of saying that the main innovation of digital publication concepts is the inclusion of components that have not or could not have been included before. Hogenaar writes:

> … the information object will play a central role. It may be any kind of object: a traditional publication, a comment on that publication; a dataset; an image; an audio fragment, and so on. (Hogenaar 2009, 1)

Accordingly, Verhaar (2009) argues that EPs appeared in consequence to the incapacity of historical publications to include supplementary research materials. The function of these newly included materials in different publication concepts as well as the evaluation of concrete information units and resources is of secondary importance. Van der Poel (2007) and Woutersen-Windhouwer and Brandsma (2009) distinguish between components of three different "information types": data as evidence, extra materials as illustration, and post publication data. The level of abstraction behind this classification is one of the reasons why Hogenaar and Hoogerwerf (2009) conclude that SPPs and MAs are basically the same approach, despite the differences described in the current study. In an even more concise definition, the authors (136) write that EPs have an "object-based structure with explicit links between objects."

A significant substantiation of the types of information objects that became a constitutive component of EPs is given in Verhaar summarization:

> In conclusion, Enhanced Publications can be defined as compound digital objects, which combine ePrints with one or more metadata records, one or more data resources, or any combination of these. (Verhaar 2009, 101)

The Question of Text

In comparison with the earlier specifications, the above quote highlights the centrality of text, referring to it as ePrints. Indeed, later specifications of EPs promote this idea more often. Hogenaar and Hoogerwerf (2009, 136) accordingly state: "we assume Enhanced Publications have at least one textual resource." This is significant because both authors add that publications are conceivable in which there is no central textual resource (Hogenaar and Hoogerwerf 2009, 154), an idea for which examples have been described in the current study already. They argue that this scenario is out of the scope of EPs. This argument is striking insofar as the concept of SPPs, which does not make text mandatory, is one of the more prominent objects of study in EP research. In the light of this point the EP approach therefore cannot fulfill its ambition to be generic.

Despite Hogenaar's and Hoogerwerf's pragmatic decision, the role of text remains an issue. Within the article that introduced the concept of information objects and which was published in the same year, Hogenaar (2009) does explicitly not distinguish between articles and other information objects. Jankowski et al. (2012) tone down the definition given by Hogenaar and Hoogerwerf by saying that an EP consists of a central publication which only most often is a textual resource. Diender (2010) instead not only states that EPs are primarily textual resources to which other resources are added, but that text is also its primary interface.

Despite this inconsistency the question of the role of text is addressed more often than in other publication designs. Semantic Publications are an exception. However, SPs are able to make a decision about the role of text by virtue of a very specific approach to digital publications. Enhanced Publications are not able to do the same, because their concept is grounded in an evaluation of the state of the art. In the light of the issue of text, this state of the art therefore appears to be less consistent than EPs assume.

The Question of Methodological Differences and the Humanities

Enhanced Publications also offer minor attempts to evaluate dependencies between specific needs of disciplines, especially the humanities and EPs. In fact, the cluster of EP projects created more example publications in the domain of the humanities than in other projects not originating in the humanities. Around 2011 several projects were funded with the goal to evaluate the potential of EPs for publishing in the humanities. Among them are the *Veteran Tapes* project, which publishes research on the second world war (van den Heuvel et al. 2010), and the *Enhancing Scholarly Publishing in the Humanities and Social Sciences* project (Jankowski et al. 2012).

In the latter project, several books from media and cultural sciences that were already published in paper form were transformed into EPs. Jankowski et al. (2012) propose that the selection of added features in the project should resemble the particular needs of the humanities. However, no deeper analysis of these methodological needs and the way in which they relate to these features is provided. The paper focuses on descriptive and technical aspects of EPs and on the implementation process of the use-cases. However, it documents some of the experiences the designers made together with the humanities researchers within the implementation process.

In contrast to the original goal of these projects, the Veterans Tapes project also lacks a substantial evaluation of the experiences of humanities researchers involved in this type of project. It was instead meant to function as a lighthouse project, to attract a broader humanities audience. More precisely van den Heuvel et al. (2010, 2688) state: "We consider this project as exemplary for the paradigm shift that is taking place in the field of humanities." The paradigm shift itself, however, is only proclaimed.

Hogenaar and Hoogerwerf (2009, 137–39) discuss concerns about the fact that the DRIVER project chose to only implement one EP "demonstrator" that should represent all scientific domains. Once again, the discussion indicates the possibility of different needs between different disciplines when it comes to the design of new publication formats. The authors respond negatively to this question in two ways. First, they relativize these needs by arguing that methodological differences between disciplines will become increasingly unimportant due to the growing phenomenon of interdisciplinary research. Thus, like in other publication concepts, the design process is led by certain claims about how technological innovation will change scientific practice. Second, they reduce the question of methodological differences an observe that only different resources are important in different disciplines. More precisely, they link different disciplines to different resource types such as text corpora for the humanities and measured data to science. Due to this simplification, the authors can argue that EPs are able to handle any resource type and are therefore capable of representing research in any discipline.

Another contribution in which Jankowski and Jones (2013) is involved does indeed approach the topic of methodological differences and EPs more seriously. The authors present the research of Meyer et al. (2011). This study tried to investigate different uptakes of digital tools, especially so-called web 2.0 tools, by disciplines in the humanities and the sciences. Jankowski et al. deduces from that work that the Humanities tend to work less collaboratively and use "computationally less complex" tools than the Sciences do. Although Jankowski et al. highlight the importance of this and comparable studies for EPs, they intentionally leave the interpretation to the readers: again, this topic is introduced but left behind without further clarification.

Functional Requirements

Enhanced Publications are not only defined by extracting features from existing digital publication formats. Further strategies to gain insights into requirements for a sustainable meta model of EPs are considered as well. Woutersen-Windhouwer and Brandsma (2009) substantiate specification of EPs by putting the abstract idea of EPs in the context of research literature on publishing as such from the repositories domain. They follow Van de Sompel and Lagoze (2007), mentioned already, by claiming that scholarly communication consists of the areas of registration, certification, awareness, archiving, and rewarding. These areas are translated into technical specifications[46], calls made to stakeholders in the publishing

46 An example of such a specification is the use of so-called persistent identifiers (PIDs). Persistent identifiers are URIs that are not supposed to change in the future. While

field[47], but also recommendations for changing related practices, such as the review process and the measurement of the impact of publications.

Hogenaar (2009) defines six further requirements for EPs based on a questionnaire of "users" which address different facets of publishing. Following the questionnaire, an EP must (a) be citable, (b) have metadata for itself and its components, (c) must contain explicit relations between components, (d) be capable of being stored in a network environment, I able to be versioned and continuously modified, (f) be machine-readable, and finally, (g) be stored in an environment that provides an *Application Programming Interface*[48] (also referred to as API). These properties are strongly reminiscent of the discussion on aggregations, and indeed several references to this community have already been highlighted. However, the list of requirements provokes the question which user base was selected in the questionnaire. Unfortunately, no further information is given.

In "Identifying Properties for Enhanced Publications" Gielkens and Hulman (2011) also build their research on the basis of an evaluation of users. However, the area of interest in which these properties are defined is significantly different from the studies described above. Gielkens and Hulman analyze readers' comments about a contribution to Elsevier's Article of the Future contest. In these comments, readers judge the different properties of the article and thereby offer an opportunity to draw inferences and to guide further research. Consequently, the authors derive properties for the areas of usability, layout, content quality, and readability. The selection of properties shows that here, EPs are defined from the angle of their presentation. The key claim behind any further specification is that EPs turn into interactive websites and are published as HTML, a development that takes place after the main phase of the DRIVER project.

Adriaansen and Hooft (2010) take a similar approach to Gielkens and Hulman. They select five different journal websites and call them EPs without further explanation of the relationship between former definitions (see above), the meta-model (see below), and the application of

domain URIs might change due to a variety of reasons, a PID should always link to the same place and remain "stable".

47 The DRIVER project calls for the creation of so called "trustworthy repositories", meaning repositories which for various reasons are sustainable, respected, and integrated into the publishing landscape.

48 An API is a technical mechanism by which software can be accessed from other software. In this context it means that software and software services can obtain metadata and content out of repositories hosting EPs.

this concept in their study. Recommended features of EPs in this study are interactive navigation or the option to have downloadable PDF versions.

It was mentioned in the introduction to EPs that the term EPs is sometimes also used by certain journals trying to express that they form part of a development towards new publication types. In this context the specific set of features these journals provide is of minor importance: the term is appropriated as a political concept. Holl (2012) is a good example for this type of usage. He presents the astronomy journal *Information Bulletin of Variable Stars* and calls it an EP. He tries to backup this classification by just summarizing features of the journal website in a non-systematic manner. These include links to databases and data sources, interactive visualizations, and a search facility on specific entities using normalizing name resolution.

Model

One of the most important contributions to EPs is the attempt to provide a high-level formal model for digital publications. Corresponding to the original intention to establish EPs as an umbrella concept, this model intends to represent the minimal intersection of all digital publication concepts investigated by the DRIVER project. As such, this model is meant to be a reference model that should facilitate the implementation of EPs and of supporting repository infrastructures.

Hogenaar and Hoogerwerf (2009) define what a publication model is in the context of the DRIVER project. A publication model defines the components of a publication and the way they are arranged in it. More technically, it describes relevant entities and their relationships. Consequently, Verhaar (2009) transforms the approach into a so-called *entity-relationship model* (see figure 3.1), a common modelling approach in computer science, especially in the context of databases. In this model Verhaar defines five entities: e-prints, data objects, metadata, compound datasets, and EPs themselves. The difference between data objects and compound datasets is mainly technical. It addresses the possibility that resources belonging together on the level of meaning might be split into different physical resources. It is also worth mentioning that EPs may contain other EPs.

It is also significant that the model for EPs does not provide any other relationship between components than *consistsOf*. Likewise, there are no further semantics included in the further discussion of this model. Evaluations of relationship types exist outside of the high-level publication model (Verhaar 2009, sec. 10.6; Woutersen-Windhouwer and Brandsma 2009, sec. 5). Nevertheless, these evaluations are hardly systematized and serve the purpose of merely illustrating the usage. The aforementioned demonstrator introduced by Hogenaar and Hoogerwerf (2009, 154) also only mentions the need to model sequential relationships, they do not implement this information in the core description of the demonstrator itself. The implementation of the demonstrator is built upon the OAI-ORE standard. In fact, the last paragraph showed that the semantics of the EP model and those in OAI-ORE are nearly identical, a fact that is confirmed by Verhaar (2009) as well.

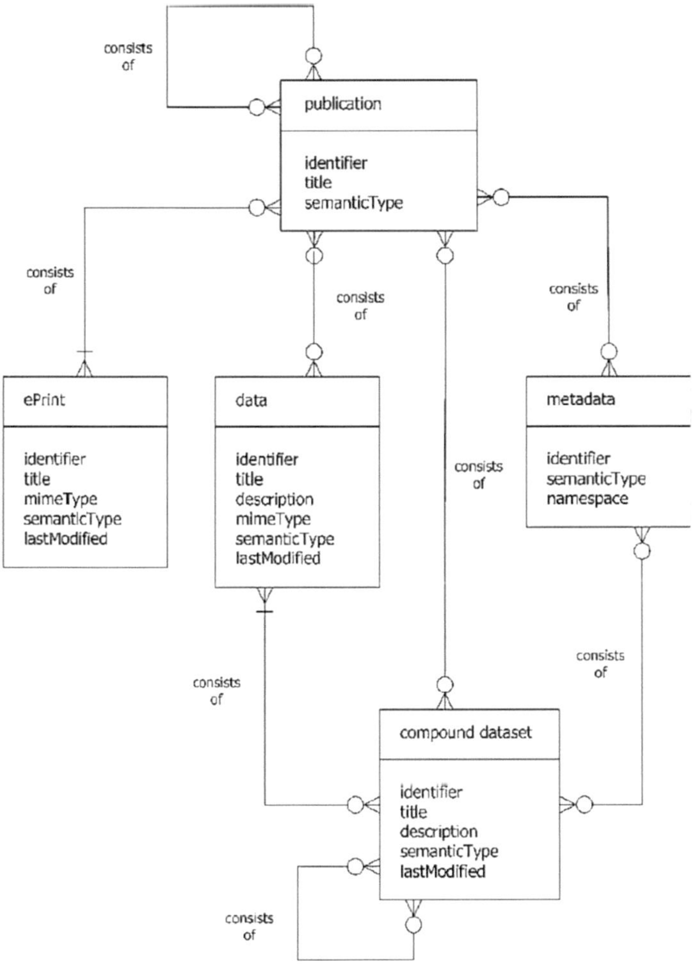

[Figure 3.1] Basic entity-relationship diagram of EPs taken from Verhaar (2009)

It was mentioned before that the concept of EPs was defined among other things in order to be able to evaluate the digital repository landscape at that time. This task is carried out by Woutersen-Windhouwer and Brandsma (2009). In the evaluation the authors (79) make an interesting observation: "The main conclusion is that publishers and repositories have the building blocks and the tools, but in general do not use them to create an Enhanced Publication."

From Enhanced Publications to Rich-Internet-Publications

It has been indicated that the definition of EPs changed over time. This change is more than an addition of features within another perspective. It is a modification of the conceptual core of EPs. In the DRIVER project, the core of EPs was constituted by technical requirements of EPs modelled within a compound object meta-model. In later contributions, the core is an interactive website, while technical aspects become secondary. Some of these examples have already been mentioned. For instance, the EP of the astronomy journal is created by a script (a small computer program) only. There is no independently modelled version apart from the HTML page that could be archived in a repository. Interactive visualizations, moreover, are created on the fly by means of another script that is not even part of the website.

The shift that takes place creates a new term within the research field of EPs. Consequently, some authors begin to use the term *Rich Internet Publications* (Voutsinos 2010; Breure, Voorbij, and Hoogerwerf 2011; Breure 2014, hereafter referred to as RIPs). The term was initially introduced by Breure, Voorbij, and Hoogerwerf (2011). Although some of the authors formed part of research groups that developed the EPs model, and although they emphasize the strong connection to EPs, they argue that there is a qualitative change in the development of EPs. More precisely, they state that little research has been carried out on the presentation layer of EPs. They claim that there are few connections between research about the structural layer of EPs and its presentation layer. At the same time the browser is implicitly defined as the place where EPs are presented.

In a survey, Breure et al. look at different websites of publications and publication-like research output. They categorize them into three different types. The first are EPs, type two and three are RIPs. The two main criteria which enforce these distinctions are the level of interactivity with which a user can navigate and manipulate the content of the website, as well as the capability to render components of a publication in a multi-media like style. They argue that there are more investigations of the integration of components in the manner mentioned above, and that therefore a new term should highlight this shift. In continuation, RIPs refer to phenomena such as interactive multi-media presentations created with technologies like Flash[49] or Java. The distinction between EPs and RIPs is also expressed as the low-end and the high-end point of view on digital publications.

Another use of the term RIP highlights alleged benefits of visual forms of communication in publications, in comparison to textual forms. By using the phrase "Show What You Tell" Breure, Voorbij, and Hoogerwerf (2011) introduce a hierarchy of digital publications, ordered according to the extent to which they use visual elements in favor of textual elements. Thus, RIPs also engage again and in a new manner with the debate about the role of text in digital publishing.

Other contributions such as those by Voutsinos (2010) and Jankowski and Jones (2013) put RIPs in the context of the *Web 2.0* debate. The Web 2.0 debate focuses on the capability of web technologies to blur differences between producers and consumers of web content. In the Web 2.0, a website is an interface of mutual communication and editing by both the provider of a website and its visitors. In this spirit, Voutsinos (2010) defines a "reference design pattern" for RIPs which contains communication features only. It includes the ability to comment, to annotate, or share content of RIPs with other web environments. This approach to RIPs is less substantial than the definition by Breure et al. because it focuses on aspects that were already part of the original EPs model under the name of post-publication data (Woutersen-Windhouwer and Brandsma 2009).

Although Jankowski and Jones (2013) share the same fascination for Web 2.0 features, they refrain from making a clear distinction between EPs and RIPs. Consequently, EPs are "an initiative to incorporate web functionalities into scholarly publishing" (349), while RIPs are an alternative term "for basically the same development" (355).

The characterization of RIPs as "interactive web-site like environments" (Diender 2010, 1) leads to research on ways of incorporating such interactivity. For instance, de Boer and Verkoolj (2011) evaluate visualization software like Google Charts or *Microsoft Pivotviewer*[50] in order to see if they can be used for RIPs. Breure, Hoogerwerf, and van Horik (2014) and Breure (2014) introduce a Flash based application in order to author and render

49 https://get.adobe.com/de/flashplayer/

50 https://www.microsoft.com/silverlight/pivotviewer/

RIPs with a high level of interactivity. More standardized technologies, like HTML with CSS for the design, and JavaScript for interactivity are addressed but do not seem to be implemented in software. Many of the showcases of the project website need Flash to be presentable. Therefore, an interesting aspect of the shift from EPs to RIPs is the fact that it is also a shift, from trying to elaborate a generic approach that uses standardized vocabularies and technologies, to an engagement into real-world discussions and established technologies at that time.

Reality Check

Beyond the basic evaluation of the role of text and disciplines for EPs, another very important difference from other concepts needs to be mentioned. Research on EPs also includes accompanying research on the development of EPs. Thus, studies exist which try to investigate aspects like feasibility, problems, and acceptance of EPs.

The first critical evaluations are already provided by the DRIVER reports themselves. After the implementation of the demonstrator, Hogenaar and Hoogerwerf (2009) conclude that the concept of EPs has a conflicting aspect. More precisely, there is the approach of potentially including everything that is available in the web into EPs, which endangers the EPs due to technical and social issues. These issues include the lack of necessary metadata for components, its potential anonymity on the web, different access rights, the changing state of resources — for instance a database that is being updated — and finally the phenomenon of dead links. All of these problems address the lack of control over publications which built in a network environment like the web. They jeopardize the stability, integrity, and last but not least the quality of an EP.

In a slightly later article, Hoogerwerf (2009) repeats these problems and adds another three: first he admits that EPs are hardly creatable and maintainable in an efficient way, second, he states that the EP model is underspecified both in terms of semantics for relations between components and of obligatory fields and finally, he remarks that researchers are not really aware of EPs.

The issues of sustainability, authoring, and of the attitude of researchers as key stakeholders are the main issues which recurrently mentioned and further studied. Diender (2010) carries out a survey on usability and asks researchers: are "Enhanced Publications an Enhanced Experience?" Jankowski et al. (2012) set up working groups with author collectives from three print publications to explore and test their transformation into EPs. Farace et al. (2012) also provide a survey, but on the willingness of researchers to actually enhance their publications with extra material.

The results of all these studies are challenging. According to them half of the interviewees are willing to provide research materials, half are not. A little more than a half question if these materials are of use for other researchers. Although beneficial elements were discovered within the transformation of books to EPs, the original authors also put in question the benefit of such EPs on a broader perspective. Additionally, they stressed the lack of time to curate such publications. There is no clear picture for the issue of usability. Although interviewees gave an overall positive feedback, many details were criticized. Farace et al. (2012) interpret this contradiction by highlighting that people considered the potential in what they had evaluated more than their concrete experience. All authors agreed on the fact that more research needs to be done in these directions in order to help spreading EPs.

The issue of authoring is further investigated by Adriaansen and Hooft (2010), Breure, Voorbij, and Hoogerwerf (2011), as well as Breure (2014). Breure, Voorbij, and Hoogerwerf (2011) remark that sophisticated RIPs cannot be created without programming capabilities. This assertion only substantiates the concern that the tools to create EPs by many authors are missing. In order to evaluate these problems in greater detail, Breure (2014) describes the demands of an entire authoring process. In the end he concludes that in comparison to the benefits, the effort it takes to create EPs questions the concept as such. Adriaansen and Hooft (2010) evaluate the landscape of available authoring tools for EPs. They find that none of these tools actually support work on all of the crucial aspects of EPs and that their usage is often very complicated.

Doorenbosch and Sierman (2011) report on the results of a comprehensive study on the feasibility of long-term-preservation of EPs. Hogenaar and Hoogerwerf (2009) and others have argued that the complexity and quantity of resources in EPs needs re-distribution of archiving responsibility. In contrast, EPs and also many concepts emphasized the fundamental network nature of publications as living in the web beyond institutional nodes. In this context Doorenbosch and Sierman find out that a distribution level exceeding two repositories in a network jeopardizes EPs, due to related problems also mentioned. Furthermore, they distinguish between technological and organizational reasons, most of which belong to the organizational area. Despite these pessimistic results and the strong emphasis EPs and other concepts put on the network as a fundamental organizing principle of digital publication, the authors are positive that these issues will be resolved.

With the concept of EPs, an attempt was made for the first time to define a systematic and overarching framework and technical model for the description of digital publications. The attempt was driven by a community which was only indirectly engaged with most publication formats discussed before: the repository domain. In consequence, some of the issues of digital publications which had not raised much attention before have been highlighted more explicitly. Such issues notably include the role of text in digital publications and possible dependencies between research disciplines and certain features of digital publications. Similarly, the attempt to establish an overarching concept for different approaches to digital publishing raised more awareness about social complexities, namely a different evaluation of the feasibility of long-term preservation, of the costs-benefits relationship, and the integration of associated research to the development of more abstract and technical concepts.

The impact of these reflections are unfortunately limited, for a variety of reasons. Regarding the role of the text a further evaluation of the meaning of this issue is blocked by a pragmatic decision to comply with the centrality of the text at project time. The question about differences between scientific disciplines is rejected immediately after it was raised, without giving further arguments than the confirmation that it is the attempt of EPs to carry out a generic approach. Issues of feasibility are mentioned but have no effect on the generic model or on the perception of digital publications.

The shift to RIPs furthermore makes this tension worse for some of these issues, especially for long-term preservation. Although no technical generic model for digital publications as such existed before, the usability of the EP data model can be challenged. As mentioned before, it is built on a comparison between publication concepts that ignores important differences and neglects other publication concepts that were available already. In addition to other reasons this might also have contributed to the fact that the generic EP data model does not differ substantially from the logics of the OAI-ORE model. Perhaps it is the consequence of missing perspectives deriving from the EPs data model that leads to the shift towards RIPs. Since RIPs have a strong focus on aspects of the user interface, and since they deal with very concrete, partially proprietary technologies they are, however, not capable of enriching the EPs data model. If the term

EP refers to the higher level of digital publications and the term RIPs to the lower, in other words to the viewpoints of a generic model and the presentation layer, then the research domain of EPs shows well how often both angles lack conceptual integrity in digital publishing.

Nano-Publications

The next publication concept to be introduced differs substantially from those of the last sections. This concept is that of *Nano-Publications* (hereafter referred to as NPs). It is also built on top of the Semantic Web infrastructure and the linked open data principles, but it interprets their consequences for a model of digital publications quite differently. This difference can best be described by again referring back to Bourne's metaphor of a database. In many approaches discussed so far, the database referred to the publication itself. More precisely, the publication should be usable as a database. Nano-Publications are pushing this metaphor one step further. Kuhn and Krauthammer offer a first starting point for understanding this shift when they claim that:

> Small RDF-based data snippets — i.e. nanopublications — rather than classical narrative articles should be at the center of general scholarly communication. (Kuhn and Krauthammer 2012)

The technical term "RDF-snippet" basically means one specific scientific assertion. To put it differently, NPs consist of one claim (Kuhn et al. 2013, 1) or fact (Mons and Velterop 2009) and one only. This claim should be representable in one sentence. Such a sentence is normally expressed as an RDF triple. RDF triples are at the heart of the Semantic Web approach. They are called triples because they consist of three entities which together build a subject, predicate and object structure. Hence, a triple represents the smallest form of a statement about something and it is such a statement that constitutes the (Nano-)publication. Statements may take the form of observations, hypotheses, or claims (Mons and Velterop 2009). The granularity of the publication is its key characteristic and thus stands behind the term "Nano."

Similarly, to Kircz and Harmsze, the scope of such an assertion is defined as the smallest, unambiguous unit of thought (Groth, Gibson, and Velterop 2010, sec. 2). The difference however is the exclusion of anything else in the publication that goes beyond one instantiation of such a unit. Former approaches with similar goals tried to formally identify and leverage many of these units within a much bigger publication. In Nano-Publications there is essentially nothing else than this piece of information. While other approaches group or semantically relate such pieces of information together, NPs do not have this intention.

Going back to the metaphor of the database, it is not the publication anymore that creates a database with information but the (Semantic) Web itself becomes a huge database in which each publication is one piece of data. Correspondingly, the point is not extracting the pieces of information in a publication anymore, but to treat one piece of information as a publication itself, which in conjunction with others builds a global "knowledge network" (Schmidt 2014). Even the MA did not equate the boundaries of information units with the syntactical unit of a formalized minimal sentence. Instead, NPs break down the scope of publications to the simplest formal form that an expression may have in communication as such.

The strong link between the Semantic Web and NPs has been repeatedly indicated already. In fact, NPs, like many other approaches which try to exploit the potentials of formalized semantics in computation, are not imaginable without the technology provided by the Semantic Web. The extent of this in the case of NPs is the identity between the core unit of the Semantic Web (RDF triple) and the scope of the main part of the publication (statement). The specific application of these technologies in the case of NPs results from issues that influenced the creation of OLBs and SPs as well.

The concept of NPs in particular was developed out of the Concept Web Alliance. This initiative attempts to normalize and standardize relevant concepts from the field of the life sciences and biosciences. For each concept a Semantic Web compliant URI is offered, consistently and persistently linked to it. By doing so, CWA wants to create better conditions for the discovery and alignment of related research.

This goal follows the line of arguments of Mons who was already introduced in the section on SPs. It was also Mons and Velterop (2009) who published the first set of key ideas of NPs in 2009. These were followed by technological specifications written by Groth, Gibson, and Velterop (2010). Possibly due to its simplicity, the concept of NPs was quickly adopted by some services in the life sciences that used SW technologies before. Among them are the *Open Pharmaceutical Triple Store*[51] (Open PHACTS), the *Leiden Open Access Variation Database*[52], *Prizmas Database*, and the *COEUS Semantic*

51 https://www.openphacts.org/
52 http://www.lovd.nl/3.0/home

Web Application Framework (Lopes, Sernadela, and Oliveira 2013; Sernadela, Lopes, and Oliveira 2013; Sernadela et al. 2014). The latter also tries to offer tools for the creation of NPs. The Open PHACTS project was responsible for the publication of the first NP guidelines as well, which received the status of a W3C Community Draft (Open Phacts 2012). Later on, the curation of the guidelines moved to the Concept Web Alliance itself (Concept Web Alliance 2015).

Redundancy, a Non-Technical Interpretation of the Data Deluge

As outlined in the section on SPs, huge effort is put into the standardization of semantics in the Semantic Web domain. Nano Publications push this approach even further. A first hint of this radicalization could be observed by reconsidering the data deluge theme in the form that is presented by NPs. In a first reference Mons and Velterop (2009, 1) comply with the prevailing interpretation that the data deluge is a "chasm between data production and data handling." However, Nano-Publications do not stop here. They build on the claim that beyond pure quantity the data deluge multiplies the production of redundant research and research results. Thus, the issue is not only to make the amount of research results manageable and processable, but to merge allegedly identical research output together. Consequently, and above all, Chichester et al. (2015) states that Semantic Web technologies are data integration technologies in the first place.

In none of the research papers used for the current research any evidence or quantitative analysis of the phenomenon of redundancy itself was given. However, the issue is illustrated by assumptions and fictional show cases. Accordingly, Velterop (2010) claims that the simplification of eight million PubMed articles to core statements would reduce redundancy by a factor of a thousand. Kuhn et al. (2013) tell the touching fictional story about two authors researching a similar topic but not finding each other before similar research is carried out twice.

The transformation of an approach where existing articles are "semantically enriched" to find further integration, to an approach where these articles are substituted with one formal assertion is the effect of this specific interpretation of the publishing situation today. However, the whole concept of NPs is not wholly described by just addressing the substitution of a publication with an assertion. There is another important level of integration. The assertions of NPs are not published on their own but in combination with data that supports the claim expressed in the assertion. Finally, NPs build a collection of data sets by means of linking to them in the context of the assertion.

The final integration step is the main point behind the whole concept and justifies the semantic web compliant formalization in which the assertion has to be expressed. Advocates of NPs hope that when research results are published this way, a complete knowledge base of relevant claims in a scientific domain will automatically show up. There may be many NPs with the same claim and each may reference different data sets. By virtue of the standardized form of expressing the claim in the web a search for that claim with semantic web technologies will instantly bring them up together. A reference implementation of such a *Nano Browser* is implemented by Kuhn (2013) and described by Kuhn et al. (2013).

This radicalization of the application of Semantic Web technologies and their standardization efforts in the context of publications is in fact also meant as a critique of the application of SW technologies in other publishing approaches. For instance, Kuhn et al. (2015) ironically refer to ROs as "megapublications" which are not necessary in order to gain similar benefits. Additionally, they criticize *SPARQL*[53], a widely used search mechanism for the Semantic Web as poorly performant. Thompson and Schultes (2012) criticize SPs by arguing that they underestimated the effort needed to formally annotate articles. Finally, Kuhn et al. argue that:

> Basically, nanopublications could become the basis for the entire Semantic Web. Whatever information one wants to share, it could be published in the form of one or more nanopublications. (Kuhn et al. 2013, sec. 3.1)

Consequently, Velterop (2010) asks the question if NPs might be the true realization the SW idea.

The Issue of Text Revisited

Nano-Publications are as resolute in eliminating text and narrative elements form publications as ROs were. While the latter concept expunges text due to its interpretation of the role of computation for future science, NPs do it in consequence of arguments comparable with those behind MAs. They just radicalize this approach by putting the assertion in the place of

53 The *SPARQL Protocol and RDF Query Language* (also referred to as SPARQL) is, as the name suggests, a query language in the context of the Semantic Web. A query language is comparable with a programming language, limited and specialized for the purpose of querying a database like environment.

the module. On the other hand, authors in the field of NPs do not completely reject all importance of text-based publications in science. At first the goal is just to clearly separate both types. Along the way this strict separation is put into question. This process is an illustrative example for the challenges of approaches situating the realm of meaning within a purely information- or data-oriented context.

The idea of such separation in the area of NPs was first presented by Mons and Velterop (2009) and Mons et al. (2011), at the beginning of the NP initiative. In concrete terms, the authors assert that the historical article and its textual profile are not well suited for the honest presentation of research results. The authors describe text as being redundant, filled up with context dependent terminology which they classify as "jargon," and ambiguous in terms of meaning. Its nature is rhetorical and thus aims at "readers and writers" needs in contrast to the precise representation of facts and claims that is the ideal of science.

On the other hand, such qualities would turn text into an exceptional tool for things like project reports, because reports are primarily meant to be read. Mons and Velterop accordingly call textual publications "minutes of science." They propose to use them for reports to funders or in order to make a plea for something. The separation between NPs and text is therefore extended in terms of specific functions that each of the two is able to fulfill. Consequently, Mons et al. (2011) depict text as a way to give provenance information for research results which themselves are better published by NPs.

The extent to which textuality and its narrative structure are separated from the presentation of research results is also observable where NPs address the SWAN ontology, introduced in the section on SPs. It is an ontology for the purpose of modelling research discourse based on research articles. SWAN, although originally defined earlier than NPs, is also capable of modelling assertions like those addressed by NPs. However, Kuhn et al. emphasize that in contrast to SWAN:

> None of these persons "owns" the sentence [the assertion which creates the core of a NP], but the sentence has an existence on its own and just happens to be mentioned (i.e. claimed, challenged, refuted, related, etc.) by people from time to time. (Kuhn et al. 2013, 4)

Thus, for NPs the assertions are not facts that are isolated and extracted from discourse, they ontologically precede discourse.

After the NP model was introduced, several suggestions tried to extend it. The extensions put an interesting perspective on the ontological status of formal assertions proclaimed at the beginning. Gibson et al. (2012) for instance propose to implement so-called cardinal NPs. Cardinal NPs respond to the issue of quality and trust. More precisely, normal NPs offer a way of discovering how much evidence exists for an assertion, but do not include any information about the reliability and quality of this evidence. Cardinal NPs are the result of a "harvesting" process which is supposed to automatically gather relevant information about quality and reliability and which transforms this information into a quality assertion that is itself a NP. If a NP is understood as a sentence, then the network of NPs now creates meaningful, multi-sentence units.

Kuhn and Krauthammer (2012) also propose extending NPs in such a way that it is possible to publish informal statements as a NP as well. Informal statements would be statements that are not representable as an RDF triple and by using Semantic Web vocabularies. The list of reasons the authors present is quite comprehensive. It reaches from the fact that there are entities where no formal vocabulary exists to the observation that especially innovative and new claims are often difficult to represent formally.

Kuhn et al. (2013) develop this approach further by presenting the *AIDA* model as a way to describe the key concepts of NPs in a non-technical manner. The acknowledgment that not everything can be represented in an SW-oriented approach to NPs goes hand in hand with the shift from a primarily technological description of NPs to a prosaic one. Correspondingly, assertions in NPs are not always RDF triples, but expressions which are atomic, independent, declarative, and absolute. This definition allows publishing a "continuum between formal and non-formal claims" with NPs (Kuhn et al. 2013, 4). Nonetheless, the formal version remains the primary goal, which is why Kuhn et al. (2015) propose to work on best practices for the use of vocabularies in NPs.

Additionally, Kuhn et al. (2013) seek to comprehensively "broaden the scope of Nano-Publications." The scope referred to here is the notion of a scientific assertion. The authors suggest using NPs also for assessing, interlinking, or correcting other NPs, representing output from mining algorithms and to represent insights derived from existing NPs created by curators or "bots."

Finally, some contributions to the field of NPs remark that NPs should be possible that do not comply with the AIDA rules. Golden and Shaw (2015,

4–5) stress that many assertions in the humanities are not even falsifiable because they describe purely discursive objects. Thus, the scope of a NP should follow whatever the need of the researcher is.

At this point the clear distinction between the realm of discourse and the realm of facts and statements that gave birth to the concept of NPs turns upside down. When taken seriously, the outcome of this approach with all its modifications and additions would create a huge "knowledge network" (Schmidt 2014, sec 5) of interconnected NPs. These connections, however, resemble logical but more importantly also qualitative functions of language. Thus, instead of building a reliable space of the presupposed positive essence of scientific communication clearly separated from the realm of discourse, in text publications the advancement of the current approach heads towards a space where colloquial discursive form is reconstructed with NPs.

Another consequence worth mentioning is the fact that all these different NP-flavors require reconsideration of the founding theme of NPs, and with minor modification and additions also of MAs, SPs and others: redundancy. Assertions will probably appear that are represented in these flavors but that would represent the same statement within the original understanding of meaning and language. Since these contextualized and faceted statements are the outcome of NPs themselves, they really challenge the overarching theme of redundancy in the field of NPs and beyond.

From Ecology to Infrastructure

In the introduction to this section the database metaphor was used to highlight the dimension of the shift introduced by NPs. Nano Publications were contrasted with SPs where the article is treated like a database. Instead, they are pieces of data in a data space, or something which could be called a scholarly publication web.

If NPs try to turn the web into a publication space in the same way as SPs tried to turn articles into databases, it does not surprise that much effort in NP-research is spent on technologically promoting this turn. A model for NPs is one thing, but a technological environment in which these objects behave like publications is another. In this very sense Kuhn et al. (2015) propose the idea of "Publishing Without Publishers" which follows "a decentralized approach to dissemination, retrieval, and archiving of data." Consequently, the term decentralized concerns the web architecture.

To achieve the aforementioned goal, NP-advocates stress the need to first define the requirements for the web as a scholarly publication space. The research literature suggests three different properties: trust, reliability, and quality. Kuhn and Dumontier (2014) define trust as the possibility of assuring that a link to a NP will always and in any situation give back the same NP. According to Kuhn et al. (2015), reliability is achieved by guaranteeing permanent and performant access to NPs. The aspect of quality is addressed by Chichester et al. (2015). They define it as a mechanism to assure that NPs comply with a certain quality standard.

There are services and environments which have taken these issues up in the context of NPs as well. The *neXtProt*[54] portal, for instance, offers hosting capabilities for NPs which facilitate the fulfillment of the first two requirements. However, the creation of services offered by particular agents is not the kind of solution addressed by the quote before. Kuhn et al. (2015) consequently criticize initiatives like *Figshare*[55] for building centralized services to find solutions to the aforementioned publishing requirements. They argue that such services depend on the survival of their owners and their servers do not guarantee one hundred percent reachability.

In contrast, Kuhn and Dumontier (2014) propose to solve the issue of trust in a technical fashion by creating URIs which contain a so-called hash[56] string generated from the NP itself. When the content of the NP changes or if it is delivered incompletely, the hash changes automatically and thus would not match the URI any longer. A similar approach is taken by Chichester et al. (2015) for guaranteeing quality. The authors propose to partly derive quality from the provenance information of NPs (author, date, and source) and to define a scheme for links which encode the result of this automatic assessment.

Another example for "decentralizing" publishing infrastructure is given by Kuhn et al. (2015). In the same way as quality control is distributed and semi-automated, hosting and curation should dissociate from specific agents such as publishers. The authors explicitly criticize agent-focused hosting strategies for digital resources. Instead they propose a grid-like

54 https://www.nextprot.org/

55 https://figshare.com/

56 Hashing is a method that allows to turn a huge set of input information into a unique and short set of output information, normally a sequence of characters. The same quantity of input information always leads to the same output hash. In doing so, a hash is well suited for checking on the integrity of data in a compact way.

publication infrastructure. Comparable to *peer-to-peer*[57] filesharing services, NPs should always be available from several publication servers. The aspect of curation should take place on specific servers which focus on hosting NPs of only one topic compared to servers which mirror NPs regardless of the subject matter. The consistency regarding subject matter is achieved by also encoding the subject into the URI of NPs, like it was done in the case of NP hashes. Hence, topic related grouping is not the product of a curator or editor any longer, it happens automatically when the URI of NPs are parsed within the server network.

All these efforts have in common that they try to delegate publishing tasks from stakeholder roles and individual manual work to apparently self-regulating elements in the web architecture. Indeed, the confidence in this strategy is big enough that Sofronijević and Pavlović (2013) claim that due to its technologically mediated bottom-up approach and resource management, NPs will significantly push forward open access publishing in developing countries.

Publication Formats in the Spirit of Nano-Publications

Referring to the informational content scope of NPs an initiative by the *GitHub*[58] service called *Gist* (GitHub 2018) should be mentioned. GitHub is a provider for hosting version-controlled software repositories. They also cooperate with the *Mozilla Science Lab* and the aforementioned Figshare service. Gists are complete version-controlled repositories, which basically consist of one text file. This text file can provide text, code, or data. In conjunction with the initiative by Mozilla these Gists can become mini-publications comparable in scope to NPs but more flexible.

In fact, Gists are already used for the publication of specific resources. The article of Pfaff et al. (2015) published at Wiley is a good example, where a significant part of the publication is hosted as a Gist. Becker et al. (2017) describe an approach where something that resembles the idea of a resource map in OAI-ORE is published as a Gist in order to create better conditions for reproducible publications in data-driven-science.

It has been argued that under the perspective of reducing the scope of the information unit, NPs introduced the most radical concept possible.

57 The peer-to-peer principle is a horizontal organizational principle in which computers in a network have equal right to offer and make use of services within a computer network. Thus, no computer owns a specific service or is restricted by any type of role management.

58 https://github.com/

Likewise, it was demonstrated that this approach led to an enhancement of the web architecture in order to create a scholarly publication web. This web is more than just a web of data, because it implements regulatory and classificatory mechanisms which in historical publishing setups are carried out manually by stakeholders, or which are part of the argument of historical publication itself. As Kuhn has indicated, trust and quality were the outcome of curation and editing by related stakeholders as, of course, is assured by specific sections, writing style, and other aspects of text publications themselves.

It is significant that after NPs were introduced a new publication concept appeared, positioned in between approaches like NPs and historical text publications. This concept is called Micro Publications (hereafter referred to as MPs). The name clearly alludes to the wording of the concept of NPs and is once again announced as the "Next Generation Scientific Publishing" (Clark 2014) approach.[59]

Micro Publications were introduced in 2014 by Clark and Ciccarese (2013) and Clark, Ciccarese, and Goble (2014). There are some significant differences of this concept compared to approaches like NPs or SPs. First, the authors observe that previous approaches to formalize and normalize publications in the sense of the Semantic Web have not succeeded enough, or may have even failed, as in the case of semantic abstracts[60]. In contrast, MPs try to define an approach which mediates between former models and which permits the formalization and normalization of articles step by step and up to the extent necessary in a given situation.

This demonstrates that for MPs it is not the intent to remove the narrative form found in historical publications. Clark, Ciccarese, and Goble (2014, 1) state: "The linear document publication format, dating from 1665, has survived transition to the web." Corresponding with this nuanced evaluation, MPs envision digital publishing as a nexus that makes use both of the "Web of Documents" and the "Web of Data" (Clark 2014).

An incremental or scaled approach to the formalization and normalization of articles was also already proposed in the SP field itself. The difference is that SPs leave open what ontologies are used, and which entities are formalized in such a process. Micro Publications define very clearly how

59 A less technologically focused version of the MP approach is proposed by Poo and Wu (2017).

60 Semantic abstracts were discussed by Harmsze and Shotton as a starting point for the use of semantic technologies for publications because it requires less effort than creating a whole Semantic Publication.

this space between articles and pure data should look like by building upon "defeasible reasoning" and argumentation theory, as well as selected models in artificial intelligence (Clark, Ciccarese, and Goble 2014, 5). Thus, while the level of formalization is a compromise, the decision as to the type of important semantics is not.

In many situations, MPs are also defined as arguments to support claims (Clark, Ciccarese, and Goble 2014, 5). In this respect they seem to comply with the original NP approach. However, they criticize NPs and similar models as a "statement" focused approach and as not being sufficient for scholarly communication.

This argument is raised in two ways. First, they respect the use of natural language in research communication, especially for innovative research which needs qualification. Second, they state that a claim with unqualified evidence is not enough to prevent the misuse of this claim. Studies on MPs assert that in scientific publishing the level of misuse of citations and evidence is tremendous (Clark 2014; Clark, Ciccarese, and Goble 2014). In fact, the appropriate use of citations is presented as the driving force behind MPs. This goal is also ethically framed in a use case for MPs concerning the *Drug Interaction Knowledge Base*[61] (Schneider, Collins, et al. 2014; Schneider, Ciccarese, et al. 2014). Here, bad citation and integration of evidence would lead to "preventable medication errors." Micro Publications approach this problem by assuring the right use of evidence and citations in publications, by enforcing more subtle citation semantics.

The last paragraphs showed that MPs are bound to discourse-oriented approaches in publishing. However, as an approach seeking to provoke the use of formal semantics in an incremental fashion, they permit the creation of on-statement publications in the same way as the creation of an entire "knowledge base with extensive evidence graphs" (Clark, Ciccarese, and Goble 2014, 5). Curiously, the seamless integration between formalized and unformalized perspectives in MPs also seems to create its own set of difficulties. Schneider, Ciccarese, et al. (2014) summarize that in the aforementioned use case challenges arise from the fact that the database requires both a natural language and a formal language representation for an assertion.

61 https://dikb.org/

Automated Publications

The following publication concept does not really look like a new and genuine concept in the first place, at least not when looking at the final product, which is a research paper. On the other hand, it does appear audacious if one considers the way this paper is produced within this concept. *Automated Publications* (hereafter referred to as APs) are publications which a computer algorithm creates with only partial or even no involvement of humans. The term Automated Publications is not part of the discourse on these publications. It is introduced at this point in order to gather different loosely connected activities which (semi-)automate the production chain of scientific publications regardless of their relationship to any other publication concept.

The topic of APs is more widely known in the area of news media and journalism, where it is discussed under the "Robot Journalism" (Latar 2015, title) or "algorithmic journalism" (Dörr 2016). In robot journalism, news agencies algorithmically produce stories on topics which provide rich statistical material such as sports or finance news (van Dalen 2012), but also short breaking news, as in the case of an earthquake on the west coast of the U.S. (Lobe 2015).

In academia the strategy of automatically producing research papers is broadly discussed in the context of so-called "fake papers" or "nonsense papers" (van Noorden 2014). These types of papers are produced by algorithms such as the well-known *SCIGen* (Stribling, Krohn, and Aguayo 2005) which resembles a certain type of jargon by contingently combining scientific phrases. Fake papers became famous because there is a long story of them being accepted in which culminated in the removal of more than 120 papers from publications by Springer and IEEE (van Noorden 2014).

Whereas the scandal behind fake papers is the fact that their content makes no sense when they are read and the intention behind them is fraud, APs take this approach seriously. Until now the issue of automation in publications was generally considered in two ways: the modelling of publications towards automatized research processes (Research Objects, Scientific Publication Packages), and the automated extraction of content from publications by mining algorithms (Semantic Publications). Under the first point of view the research paper was abolished. Automated Publications share the binarity between factual content and text often met in the latter approach. However, they turn the workflow upside down. The point is not to derive factual content from written papers but to derive written papers from factual content.

Accordingly, authoring tools about datasets exist, for papers which require that the author enters information and gives reference to data in order for those tools to automatically create text articles (Candela et al. 2015, 1755). Robertson et al. (2014) present such a tool in greater detail, called *GBIF Integrated Publishing Toolkit* (see also chap. 4.3.1). Resulting papers are published in journals like the *Biodiversity Data Journal*[62] or *Zookeys*[63].

Although APs turn the procedural relationship between factual and written content around, they comply with the assumption that no genuine level of meaning belongs to the written form of articles. This is the very reason why writing is considered automatable. In "Publishing Against the Machine" by Sofronijević (2012), this fact is quite obviously presented in an analogy between writing and clothes. As clothes are put around a body text coats the facts. Sofronijevic illustrates the idea of future science in which human and computational agents build hybrid research clusters, due to exponentially growing capacities of computers. This vision resembles ideas that have been summarized in the section on e-Science already.

The argument is supported by the presentation of research in computational linguistics: rules were found for language phenomena which had been considered too complex for the identification of rules before. At the same time, Sofronijevic equates rule-based work with routine work and argues that scientists should focus on the creative work. These arguments demonstrate that APs are inspired by a much broader theme on the relationship between computers and humans. In this line of thought APs are only one element in fully automated scientific processes. These processes are carried out by "Science Bots" (Kuhn 2015) or "Laboratory Bots," that (King et al. 2009) also publish the results on their own, as their human counterparts do.

Sofronijevic makes it clear that at the moment APs are publications with very structured text, or where the text is produced on the basis of comprehensive data. However, the way he historically frames APs as well as his assumptions about the future make it clear that this is just a current state and that this concept is supposed to be extended.

62 https://bdj.pensoft.net/

63 https://zookeys.pensoft.net/

Unbound Books

As for now, all publication concepts presented root in disciplines like information science, computer science, or in the hard sciences, in particular life science, bio-science, or physics. Although implementations from the humanities exist for most of these concepts, humanities disciplines did not shape these concepts. In some cases, the concept was slightly modified or re-interpreted to build a bridge for the needs of specific implementation contexts. Accordingly, the TEI Journal and DHd Journal use other semantics than those ontologies most common to SPs. They refer to the TEI schema because it is the most popular model for the markup of text in the humanities. Furthermore, NPs have also been discussed in fields like archaeology, but without sharing the same rigorous understanding of the status of claims enrolled by the original proposal.

The following publication design is different in this respect. It is not only widespread in the humanities but also theoretically grounded in a cultural scientific perspective. The term which is most often used to name it is *Unbound Book* (hereafter referred to as UBs). As the term suggests UBs perceive publications as objects that are always updated and modified, without the development towards a final version.

This theme is not new and has been included in other designs too. The term "Liquid" in the LPs project addresses comparable ideas. Wheary even uses the same metaphor in his *Living Reviews* journal back in 1998. However, the Living Reviews journal remained an isolated example in a specific context, which was not extended or generalized beyond this context. Likewise, LPs are distinct from UBs both in terms of the object which is "put to life" as well as of the implementation of this idea.

Grounded in the humanities, the idea of UBs is in fact very much concerned with books as historic-cultural entities. Thus, they add a native perspective inherent to the humanities to the discourse about digital publications.

The Genealogy of Liquidity

Unbound Books, among which the present study also counts the concepts of Liquid Books[64] or Living Books, go back in large parts to research

64 The concept of Liquid Books in this context is not to be confused with the concept of Liquid Books that has been developed in the Liquid Publications project. In order to minimize the potential for confusion the term Unbound Book used less often but being more open conceptually was chosen as an umbrella term for publications in this section.

activities carried out by Hall and Birchall (2009) and Birchall and Hall (2006) in the middle of the first decade of the new millennium[65]. Both researchers work in the field of cultural sciences and media theory. In their work they try to reshape cultural studies in a way that makes use of a concept they call "liquid theory." Both authors are also editors of *Culture Machine*[66], an online journal which is published by *Open Humanities Press*[67]. In 2008 they used the journal to apply certain aspects of their theory to their publishing activities. They did so by launching the so-called *Culture Machine Liquid Books* series[68]. The first book published in this series was *The Liquid Theory Reader* (Hall and Birchall 2009).

The concept of UBs was further developed and discussed in the outstanding *The Unbound Book Conference* (Institute of Network Cultures 2011), which took place in 2011 in Amsterdam and The Hague. Although the program shows a significantly broader scope, the UB concept was a crucial part of it (Hall and Amerika 2011). At the same time Hall and Joanna Zylinska released a derivate of the Liquid Books approach called *Living Books about Life* (Hall, Zylinska, and Birchall 2011), also published by Open Humanities Press and funded by the British *Joint Information Systems Committee*[69]. The *Living Books about History*[70] series emerged in 2016, published by the *CLIO*[71] network in Switzerland. Finally, there is a strong entanglement with the "remixthebook" project (Amerika 2011a) by Mark Amerika. In this project which goes in parallel with the publication of a book (Amerika 2011b), Amerika theorizes the strategy of remixing for writing texts.

Later, the concept was adopted by another participant of the editorial board of Open Humanities Press, the sociologist Bruno Latour. Latour used the UB concept for his project *An Inquiry into Modes of Existence*[72] (also referred to as AiME), which engendered fairly huge attention for this type of publication after results went public in 2013.

65 The term "Unbound Book" was chosen in study to avoid confusion with LPs project. There are now connections between these two efforts.
66 https://www.culturemachine.net
67 http://www.openhumanitiespress.org/
68 http://liquidbooks.pbworks.com/
69 https://www.jisc.ac.uk/
70 https://www.livingbooksabouthistory.ch/de/
71 https://www.infoclio.ch/
72 http://modesofexistence.org/

A Culture of Liquidity and the Living Against Binding and Scientism

As noted earlier, UBs grew out of the humanities and are consequently concerned with the book and not with articles. However, UBs are not only embedded in the humanities as a field, they also form part of certain critical narratives. More precisely, supporters of UBs see the design of these publications as a part of an analysis of the book as a cultural object that imposes certain boundaries and organizational mechanisms on the production of knowledge.

In "The Unbound Book" Hall, for instance, introduces a significant difference between book and text. Following this distinction, text has precedence over the book in the sense that what an author writes is text in the first place. The book binds text together after it is written, in order to serve a specific purpose, address an identifiable audience, or to assure delivery into defined places. Hence, the book adds a layer of politics to the text. Adema (2015) is significantly clearer on this. She evaluates the cultural concept of the book as a nexus between commercial interest of publishers, issues of power in academia, and questions of epistemological authority. Thus, while the interests of authors are to produce text, the book represents interests, which alienates the author from her text.

The moral weight of this description is intended and further radicalized when Hall quotes Jacques Derrida:

> What then do we have the right to call a "book" and in what way is the question of right, far from being preliminary or accessory, here lodged at the very heart of the question of the book? This question is governed by the question of right, not only in its particular juridical form, but also in its semantic, political, social, and economic for — in short, in its total form. (Hall 2013, 496)

Consequently, for Hall a book is a result of "the force of binding" (Hall and Amerika 2011) and the UB is, using the terminology of postmodern philosophy which is addressed in this quote, an attempt to *deconstruct* the concept of the book. It intends to implement a possible answer to the rephrased version of the aforementioned question: "What do we have the right *not* to call a 'book'" (Hall 2013, 496).

Obviously, these answers come from an evaluation of the qualities of text. Text unbound from its book form is presented as an ever-changing decomposed and recomposed thing. Hall describes current scholarly writing practices like pre- and post-print publishing, blogging, and tweeting among others in order to demonstrate these qualities. In these activities, text pieces are cut out of longer pieces to put them into transitory communication channels. Different blog posts are put together for the publication of articles and post-publication publications correct and adapt the text in reaction to classical publication. After the illustration of text as something that cannot and should not be "fixed," Hall shows that the same can be said about historical texts like the Codex Sinaiticus. According to Hall it is the oldest preserved bible which collect texts that existed independently before, but also contain texts which are not part of modern bibles. It is thus a shining example of the text-book relationship.

Adema (2015, 70–75) extends Hall's critique by re-connecting text and book, but now in a different hierarchical relationship than the one that forced Hall to approach text and books as an opposition. More precisely, Adema criticizes a certain notion towards books by applying the aforementioned features of the text back to books. The opinion she criticizes conceives books as representation of stability and integrity. It is built on the idea that in scholarly communication the book assures quality, trustworthiness, authority and responsibility. Corresponding with Hall's line of argument Adema stresses that these opinions are fictions and that the book as a cultural object has always changed. Thus, these opinions are a projection from the present into the past. In her opinion to fall victim to this idea of the book would mean to make a conservative and boring entity out of it. Unanimously, Hall summarizes that:

> We could therefore say that books have always been liquid and living to some extent; digital technology and the internet has simply helped to make us more aware of the fact. (Hall 2013, 501)

For Bruno Latour the concept of the UB is a crucial aspect for the realization of an academic goal. In his book *We have Never Been Modern* (Latour 1993) argues that modernity instigated scientistic ideas of progress and emancipation which obscured other cultural and geographical configurations to the benefit to cultivate an occidental fiction of socio-cultural history. It does so because these configurations express themselves by virtue of more strategies than just scientific truth. However, these strategies are not recognized within the theoretical and historical theme of modernity. In the occident where this line of thought appeared the emphasis on scientific reasoning furthermore concealed the multiplicity of factors which actually shaped the development of modern science beyond rationality.

Correspondingly, Latour tries to identify these factors and their influences as well as to look out for other cultural configurations. These configurations which he calls "modes of existence" can only be discovered appropriately when the theme of the modernity is abolished. For Latour this means to also abolish the established mode of knowledge production. In his counter approach the presupposed occidental notion of scientific truth is one object of study but only one among others. Additionally, it is never the author or scientist alone who produces scientific results but a cluster of people and other entities (human and non-human agents) which interact in the field of scientific process. Latour calls this interaction negotiation by which science becomes a "diplomatic enterprise" (Leclercq 2011). Putting emphasis on this structure means to democratize science for the purposes that have been described before.

In the UB[73] *An Inquiry into Modes of Existence* Latour (2014) tries to implement an online book which supports the idea of science as a diplomatic endeavor. He created this book to facilitate the identification and description of other modes of existence in the way described above. By making use of a book form which roots in Latour's theoretical reflections about the nature of the problem of modernity the goal to reveal hidden modes of existence should become more successful. Additionally, the project provides a step-stone for his broader project to establish a philosophy which is built around the idea of diplomacy instead of representation (Latour 2014).

The detailed description research background of the creators of UBs should clarify the tight connection between both angles. This connection goes far beyond the attempt to test possible conveniences digital technologies might bring to scholarly publishing. Nonetheless, it is also important to have a look at how this background is actually implemented formally and technologically. Without having it said explicitly, the last paragraphs have already indicated that UBs are created in order to support three core ideas:

1. the first idea defines that UBs need to support ongoing modification of its contents,
2. the second idea defines that UBs need to enable and stimulate the engagement of multiple authors and contributors which are not selected or defined in advance,
3. additionally, UBs encourage to re-use existing content.

Accordingly, Hall (2015) defines the term "liquid" or "living" in the two series he edits and curates as being "open to ongoing collaborative process of writing, editing, updating, remixing and commenting by readers."

73 Latour calls this project an augmented book. However, as it becomes obvious later on it belongs to the same conceptual framework as the Living or Liquid Books.

While the Culture Machine Liquid Books series has a stronger focus on the first two principles the Living Books About Life series is very much concerned with the third one. A Living Book starts with the compilation of at least ten existing articles from both the sciences and the humanities about a specific topic (Hall, Zylinska, and Birchall 2011). Afterwards, they can be modified, extended or content can be erased again.

Technology Beyond Its Cultural Critique

Since re-use of other people's materials commonly requires legal permission, the implementation of this facet of UBs is social and not technical. Thus, the field of UBs is also a profound supporter of the OA principle (Hall 2008).

Most advocates of UBs come from the fields of Media Theory and Cultural Sciences. Developments show that they do not pay as much attention to the technical context of their concepts as they do to their evaluation. Hence, they do not discuss critical aspects of specific key technologies and the influence that decisions on that level might have on the operational phase of UBs. It goes without saying that in contrast to most of the publication concepts that have been discussed so far, conceptualization and implementation are strictly separated, meaning that in some cases the technological implementation is carried out by contractors. In other cases, contributors to this concept looked for existing pieces of technology which they feel can represent the features of the UB concept well.

One type of software considered to meet these requirements are *wikis*. A feature of wikis is the possibility to let content be updated by users, who are provided with the necessary tools to do so. At the same time wikis document the modification process and are very accessible for non-technical users. Another reason might also have contributed to the prominent choice for wiki software: despite its appreciation of any kind of media for the sake of publishing — even exotic ones like augmented reality and interactive visualizations are considered (Hall and Amerika 2011) — UBs remain text focused publications. Apart from text, UBs sometimes include *YouTube*[74] videos or images. The wiki approach on the other hand, despite all its flexibilities, still adheres to the format of documents and texts. The key component of a wiki is an article or a post. This situation, and the fact that certain technological issues of this choice only appear when more complex

74 https://www.youtube.com/

digital media objects are in use, or interactions other than reading are added, might also have influenced the decision.

In the case of the Culture Machine Liquid Books and the Living Books About Life series the backend is provided by the proprietary wiki software *PBWiki* by the *PBWorks*[75] company. The AiME project has developed its own software[76], which resembles wiki functionality but extends the idea of documents. In the AiME software there are four different types of content. The main content, glossary content for the explanation of terms, and apparatus content with meta-information and commentary.

All three projects combine their UBs with so-called "frozen" versions (Hall 2015). These take the form of PDFs or printed books. In the case of Liquid and Living Books, frozen versions are edited and published by Open Humanities Press. Frozen versions contain the content of a UB at a given point in time, without the content that is not supported by the PDF format or by printed books. It is important to stress that in both cases this does not include the hierarchical categorization of publishing concepts. Latour and Davis (2014) call the AiME software a software for publishing, while Hall associates frozen versions with the need to monitor and control the modification process of UBs.

The decision to choose wikis was partially explained by the lack of interest in technological challenges and the dependence on other stakeholders due to the lack of necessary know-how. However, this explanation only addresses one side of the relationship of UBs and technology. Evidently, UBs put emphasis on very different issues when it comes to the definition of aspects in science and scholarly publication that deserve to be changed. In Adema's and Hall's description of the book, the material or technological aspects of the book are only sufficiently understood when they are put into their corresponding social and cultural context. Likewise, digital publishing can also only be developed successfully if new publication formats consider first the affordances, expectations, and conditions of the social environment in which they are implemented. The publication concept thereby materializes itself while in use, and not before. This approach is in contrast with the decision to solve technological issues first made by other publication concepts. Adema (2015) consequently titled her work "Performing the Scholarly Monograph in Contemporary Digital Culture." Additionally, Zylinska (2011) remarks that Living Books About Life should not only allow collaborative curation of content, but also enable new methods for

75 http://www.pbworks.com/
76 https://github.com/medialab/aime-core

teaching, thus connecting different stakeholders like publishers, scientists, or students in new ways with each other in order to stimulate new forms of using existing content.

The lack of any formal or technical model for UBs is compensated by the great emphasis put on the role of curation and moderation, at least within the AiME project. The missing publication model is substituted here by a sophisticated lifecycle model that mediates contributions and modifications in the UB. In order to stimulate contributions, workshops were frequently carried out. These are organized by a team of eight people who were specially assigned and prepared for this task. Individual contributions made on the AiME platform must be forwarded to a moderation team, who can send it back with demand for corrections. In the next step the contribution is handed over to an expert assigned by the moderation team for final review. At a certain point of time, contributors whose submissions were accepted to extend the UB were invited to a conference in order to discuss the new state of the book and its contents. Thus, the design process which took place for this UB more than anything else concerned itself with processes and interactions instead of format.

Despite the fact that the emphasis put on the complexities of social and cultural aspects of publishing identified a blind spot in many digital publication formats, it caused other issues as well. More precisely, the focus shift causes technical issues which demonstrate a certain potential to undermine the UB concept. For instance, the whole online issue of "Force of Binding" by Hall and Amerika (2011) was not accessible from time to time, due to Flash related issues. In contrast to the emphasis put on open access, the Living Books About Life and Cultural Machine Liquid Books series use proprietary wiki software and third-party services. The negative effects such approaches have on the ability to reuse and remix UBs is barely considered anywhere.

Furthermore, media resources are often not identifiable in a persistent way, or separable from the surrounding wiki environment when uploaded into the wiki. When content comes from third party services like YouTube, as is often the case, the video files are just embedded by mechanisms provided by YouTube. Both strategies endanger the integrity and stability of UBs. In contrast to the goals of UBs it also reduces options of reuse dramatically.

Finally, it is also important to mention that despite the intent in most cases no print-on-demand option for frozen versions is provided. It is very likely that this fact relates, at least in parts, to the technological issues as well. Due to the wiki approach, frozen PDF versions of Living Books About Life are badly layouted and hard to read. The possibility to enable quality print publications on the ground of digitally curated content does often not go well with so-called *WYSIWIG*[77] environments. The prioritization of accessibility and inclusion suggests that important technical issues were underestimated.

Single-Resource Publications

Many of the concepts described above stress the possibility of using any kind of media resource in digital publications. There are however differences regarding the exact use of media resources other than text. Particularly the early publication concepts, but SPs as well, refer to these resources only vaguely and in a general way: the use of the prefix "multi" in multi-media, and the umbrella term "supplementary" in supplementary material demonstrate this very well. The latter term also adds the notion of a hierarchy between different media types, a hierarchy which appeared in concepts such as ROs. With this in mind, there are few important aspects of particular resources or media types that should be discussed.

A common and broad way of referring to the benefits of publishing different media resources is to highlight how they present evidence in research. Often, this approach does however not add more specification, which becomes obvious in the case of ROs. In ROs the differences between media resources conflate, since for ROs these resources are important only as data. Semiotic or perceptual differences between different media-types are not even considered. This is because ROs are just about computation, and computation treats all resources as data. The evidential value of image data within a workflow is derived as the result of a computation, not by an evaluation of how an image represents a situation differently than other media types.

Finally, many publishing concepts calling for the inclusion of different media resources do not always take care of questions such as how these resources might form publications of their own right. For instance, OLBs

77 WYSIWIG is the acronym for "what you see is what you get". It is an approach for the authoring of content in which the user interface makes it possible to curate content in the way it should appear. In contrast the "what you see is what you mean" (also referred to as WYSIWYM) approach only permits to curate functional aspects of the content. Its appearance is addressed in another step. In the WYSIWIG approach, for instance, a header is defined by visual properties while the WYSIWYM would use certain syntactic elements in order to annotate a passage as having the function of a header.

advocate the publication of data and visualizations by any means possible. The publication concept, however, remains the concept of OLBs. This is different when Long and Mobley (2015) discuss the new form of *Single Figure Publications*. Some authors have equated publishing to the act of uploading resources to the web. This might be a blog environment, or a Google service, or anything else. This way any resource which could be found on the web would constitute a publication, because the web as such is considered a public sphere.

By not accepting this simple definition, a variety of projects evaluate what it might mean to publish different media resources as individual publications. "Individual" means that presented models do not describe publications as consisting of several and different media resources. The scope of publishing that is addressed refers to resources of one specific media type and one type only.[78]

With some limitations the UB series Living Books About Life could also have been mentioned in this section. Despite the fact that this series forms part of a broader concept, it also builds on the idea that videos should be treated like written articles. By leaving aside the scope of an anthology or the edition of a journal, the article is a publication of its own right and Living Books About Life advocate considering video files in this very self-sufficient light.

A similar case is provided by the *Journal of Digital Humanities*[79] (also referred to as JDH). One of the key ideas of this journal is to look out for resources of different media types that are already accessible online somewhere else. Again, a YouTube video is considered such, but the JDH more frequently addresses blog posts from private research blogs, conference posters, or tweet sets on *Twitter*[80]. In this context the term media is used to denote a specific communication channel. The element these resources have in common is the fact that the environment in which this content appears is more volatile than one would expect when applying common publication principles. Within this changeable situation the Journal of Digital Humanities looks for resources and content considered to be high quality. If such content is identified, it initiates a review and editing process and

78 The author is aware of the fact that the term media is hard to define and often used in a very fuzzy and problematic way. The second part of the study at hand provides more information on the present understanding. Up to this point the use of the term just reflects its use in the discussion itself. This normally means that text, images, audio, and video files are treated as media of their own right.

79 http://journalofdigitalhumanities.org/

80 https://twitter.com/

finally publishes the content in one of its issues, thereby pulling it out of the ongoing stream of communication.

In the examples above the publication of different media resources was tested as a substitute for research articles in the historical frame of a journal or anthology. The informal *bl.ocks.org*[81] platform sets up a whole website for the publication of one specific type of resource only, that being software code. Driven by the opinion that online software repositories alone do not suffice for publishing, bl.ocks.org defines a set of components which need to be attached to the code so that it meets the expectations people have of a publication. The contents added to the code are automatically parsed by the software in order to create a publication as a website. Effectively, the platform became a platform for the reproducible publication of data visualizations.

The bl.ocks.org project is a private initiative and focuses on the identification of metadata components and mechanisms for the publication of software code. Due to its informality, it has the status of a reference project and does not integrate with services other than GitHub. Beyond this, it deals with no other publishing issues, such as for instance long-term-preservation. Accordingly, bl.ocks.org presents and promotes software as a resource worthy of being considered an academic publication, but it does not create sustainable publications out of it. This, however, is the very goal of the *Code as Research Objects* initiative initiated by *Mozilla Labs* (Mozilla Science Lab 2013a; Mozilla Science Lab 2013b).

This initiative brings together GitHub, Figshare, and Mozilla in order to provide an easy workflow for the creation of sustainable publications out of software. In this context, sustainable means that the software becomes citable and is stored in an environment that claims sustainability. One of the outcomes is a bookmarklet[82] and a website which automatically creates a *DOI*[83] for the underlying software repository in GitHub and for the duplication of the contents in Figshare.

Figshare is a freemium service maintained by the *Macmillan Publishing Group*[84]. Its goal is to create a trustworthy and sustainable environment

81 https://bl.ocks.org/

82 A bookmarklet is a small piece of code that can be added to browsers as a bookmark. Instead of opening a specific webpage the bookmarklet runs its code when the user clicks on it.

83 A DOI is a provider of persistent identifiers, supported by a consortium and implementing a standardized scheme for the creation of DOI URLs.

84 http://macmillan.com/

for the publication of non-textual research output. It is therefore also the attempt of a commercial publisher to get involved into the publication of digital resources. Figshare does not focus on particular resource types, as the name might suggest. It nevertheless implicitly introduces a minimal standard of requirements necessary in order to level up such resources to the status of publications. In this point of view, it is of particular importance that the company behind Figshare is a publisher, since the credibility the company possesses as a publisher was a great influence on the perception of non-textual research output as resources worthy of publishing.

The key components of the aforementioned standard are: (a) descriptive metadata, (b) a persistent identifier, (c) and a long-term archiving environment that feels trustworthy for many researchers. The last criterion raises the question of whether a private company in a competitive environment with its own interests is really able to provide such a trustworthy environment. As mentioned above this capacity is challenged in particular by NPs. Chapter 4 will provide an example of a comparable project, but one which is funded by the European Union as part of a broader initiative towards OA publishing in Europe.

The final example for single-resource publications is a particularly interesting one because it invalidates certain distinctions that are common in the field of digital publications. Distinctions between data and representation, form and content, research object and research results are harder to make for this example and so is its assignment to the current or the following section. It takes the form of the so-called *video-essay*.

A video-essay is a short video produced by film-critiques, film-scholars or film-passionates. The exact properties of video-essays as scholarly publications are still a matter of debate (Bernstein 2016). McWhirter (2015, 396) argues that a video-essay "is essentially a short analytical film about films or film culture." As such it reuses footage from existing films and rearranges it in order to make a point. Visosevica and Myersb (2017) even go so far to assert that it is "thesis-driven" and is produced within an "analytical framework." There are, however, also viewpoints which emphasize the artistic and poetic dimension of the audio-visual form: "while one [video-essay] has an overt lesson with evidence and research and bullet points, the other simply has a series of images and leaves it up to the viewer to take from it what they will" (Renee in Bernstein 2016).

In any case authors tend to highlight the hybrid nature of video-essays. They are supposed to bring together the allegedly conflicting sides of language and discourse and visual aesthetics, of film and essay and thereby of a historically collaborative endeavor and the explorative work of an individual (Bresland 2010) who is enabled by digital technologies.

Although the origins of the video-essay are tracked down to the nineteen-forties and the similarly underspecified genre of the film-essay (McWhirter 2015, 371) and although examples of video-essays are given that come from the nineteen-eighties (Bresland 2010) nearly all advocates agree that digital technologies play the most significant role in its development. The reasons include the decrease of costs of production, the advanced technological control of aspects of film making by individuals with possibly minor technological know-how, the potentials of remixing offered by the digital representation film material and, of cause, the internet as an accessible dissemination and publication space. Consequently, McWhirter (2015, 377) notes that "the video essay is clearly one element of the digital revolution that genuinely offers the possibility of a transformative change to film criticism and film scholarship."

This being said, the video-essay is on its way to become a significant element of film and media studies scholarship. Accordingly, in 2012, the *Society for Cinema and Media Studies*[85] conference offered a workshop on video-essays as "film scholarship's emergent form" and the University of St. Andrews asked whether video-essays represent the "film and moving image studies re-born digital" (quoted in McWhirter 2015, 375). Film studies journals such as the *Frames Cinema Journal*[86] or the *European Journal of Media Studies*[87] include video-essays into their issues while the journal *[in]transition*[88], a cooperation between the *media-commons* network[89] and the Society of Cinema and Media Studies offers the first video-essay-only peer-reviewed journal.

Video-essays adhere to the principles of single-resource publications insofar they are one-file digital resources, relatively small in scope (up to fifteen minutes) and, most importantly, insofar they try to give the status of scholarly publications to objects that were not considered as such before. There are, nonetheless, some differences compared to the abovementioned approaches. Although video-essays become part of common film studies research culture they often continue to live in technologically questionable environments. Even when published in journals like the ones mentioned above, they are most often hosted on

85 http://www.cmstudies.org/
86 http://framescinemajournal.com/
87 https://necsus-ejms.org/
88 mediacommons.org/intransition/
89 mediacommons.org/

proprietary platforms such as *Vimeo*[90] and only embedded into the journal. This and other reasons lead to the fact that technical requirements proofed to be necessary or, at least, beneficial for publications to fulfill certain functions (see above) are hardly met. Services such as the *AV-Portal* of *German National Library of Science and Technology*, therefor, try to offer more sophisticated services for the publication of audio-visual resources (regardless of the research field) in a more trustful environment (Drees, Kraft, and Koprucki 2018).

Transmedia Publications

The last section addressed the issue of specific media resources which, by virtue of digital technologies, should become publications in their own right. It has been argued before that terms media and multi-media often refer to unspecified inclusions of non-textual resources to publications. This section presents a publication concept that in contrast to the aforementioned observation builds upon a very precise idea of the entanglement between different media types. A term which seems appropriate for including all publications in this section is the term Transmedia Publications (hereafter referred to as TPs).

The term Transmedia Publications is derived from one of its early projects, more specifically from *The Institute for the Future of the Book* (Meade 2013), one of whose major protagonists used the term "transmedia writing" in order to describe the type of work the institute wanted to support. It is introduced as an umbrella term in the study at hand for a variety of projects sharing a common view of the specific use of media for publishing, which could be well described by the term transmedia meaning across media.

In some contexts, the term "multimodal" is also used instead of transmedia in order to refer to the same aspects (McPherson 2008; Svensson 2010). Nonetheless, transmedia seems preferable at this point, because the word multimodal will be used in the second part of this work in order to describe properties of digital publications that are broader in scope. Another term that sometimes appears in related discussions is "webtexts" (Ball and Eyman 2015). The disadvantage compared to the term Transmedia Publications in this particular case lies in the fact that webtexts address a particular technological environment for TPs. However, this environment is not a necessity for the main elements of this concept.

90 https://vimeo.com

It is now clear why video-essays are in fact an edge case. Obviously, they also combine different modalities in order to carry out a multimodal discourse. Video-essays are not only one medium because its technological representation packages it into one file associated technologically with a so-called *media type*[91]. In the context of the analysis of digital publication formats the media type aspect, however, is not without value. Publication formats are a conflation between conceptual and technological definitions. The present study, accordingly, refers to Transmedia Publications as publications combining both different media in the sense of presenting a multimodal discourse as well as of different technological media types.

The Story of Transmedia Publications

The beginning of the TP concept could be set around 2005 with the release of *Vectors*, a *Journal of Culture and Technology in a Dynamic Vernacular*[92] as well as *Sophie*, an authoring tool for the creation of "networked multimedia" publications[93]. In their brief overview on TPs Ball and Eyman (2015) pinpoint the beginning of TPs much earlier, starting from 1996 with the release of the *kairos*[94] journal of which the authors are the editors. Nevertheless, they admit that at that time these publications were not fully transmedia but html documents on the web.

The Institute for the Future of the Book, which was behind the development of Sophie, was a project of the University of South Carolina with different partners around the world. Its goal was the exploration of the "book's reinvention in a networked environment" (Institute for the Future of the Book 2008). For this purpose, several tools were developed. Similarly, the Vectors journal became not just a journal but a project which led to institutional cooperation and the creation of social infrastructure, as will be described in greater detail in the next section.

In 2014 the international *Anthropocene Project* at the *Haus der Kulturen der Welt* in Berlin[95] tried to imagine new ways of doing and representing science, intended to match up with the scale of problems today (Welt 2015). It awarded three examples of so-called "Future Storytelling" which

91 https://www.iana.org/assignments/media-types/media-types.xhtml
92 http://vectors.usc.edu
93 http://web.archive.org/web/20150206051256/http://www.sophieproject.org/ (archived version from the Internet Archive)
94 http://kairos.technorhetoric.net/
95 http://hkw.de/en/programm/projekte/2014/anthropozaen/anthropozaen_2013_2014.php

were supposed to best represent this attempt. These publications were all designed as TPs. More recent examples of TPs comprise the journal *Thresholds*[96] and the project *Vega-Pub*[97] (Ball 2017). Vega-Pub tries to develop an editorial management software for the publishing workflow of TPs.

Due to the theoretical background of TPs explained in the next paragraphs, TPs are mostly created in the humanities. Nonetheless, examples like the *Rich Interactive Narratives* authoring tool developed by *Microsoft Research* (Takeda et al. 2013) or e-book-oriented approaches from the field of medicine (Stirling and Birt 2014) provide examples from other domains as well.

Transmediality, the Outcome of a Another Perspective on Digital Technology

When defining transmedia in TPs, it is helpful to review the ways in which the inclusion of different media has been discussed until now. In many cases, the issue of multiple media resources was addressed by the phrase of "supplementary material." This points to a certain hierarchy between media. At the top of that hierarchy there might be text, or in the case of digital publications, data. As has been argued before, other resources are delegated the function to support what is written or computed. The latter case is more complicated insofar as data may represent any type of modality such as sound or images. However, if ROs or SPPs speak of supplementary material instead of data they are referring more to the type of engagement with this material. Thus, while audio files as data in the workflow are computed, audio files as supplementary material are most likely meant to be listened to.

In TPs the use of different media serves a completely different purpose, which precisely emphasizes the different ways in which media resources are produced and perceived. They do so because they follow the idea that the unique features of different media offer unique ways to represent and communicate knowledge. Compared to the concept of supplementary material, there is no conceptual hierarchy between media resources as such. Each media may contribute its own truth values to the scientific discourse in a publication. The relationships between these ways of representation are multiple and no use of one media can be fully substituted by the use of another one. Accordingly, it does not make sense to maintain any hierarchical relationship between media as it is problematic

96 http://openthresholds.org
97 https://vegapublish.com/

to view different media only from the viewpoint of a specific media type. The Vectors journal stresses that "we publish only works that need, for whatever reason, to exist in multimedia" ("Vectors Journal" 2013).

Nevertheless, the term multimedia remains ambiguous, since it is also used in earlier and different applications of multiple media resources. It does not make any strategy behind these usages clear, at least none that goes beyond aggregation. This is the reason why the term transmedia suits better. It emphasizes:

> ... a fusion of old and new media in order to foster ways of knowing and seeing that expand the rigid text-based paradigms of traditional scholarship. ("Vectors Journal" 2013)

Transmedia publications seek to represent a form of knowledge which does not reside within the media resources but "in the spaces between" (McDonald and Trettien 2016).

README

Preamble

Each act of digital production is an opportunity to shrug off the burden of opaque software and to focus instead on the medium of the production itself. Each act is therefore an invitation to embrace writing as digital expression's central activity: Not gestures, not menus. Not visual interfaces or resource-intensive all-in-one software packages, which embed production knowledge so deeply and invisibly that it can no longer be acted upon or understood.

In digital form, writing is nothing but strings of characters, endlessly and potentially losslessly manipulable under conditions that menu-driven graphical software short-circuits in the name of intuition and user-friendliness. More than any other mode of expression, writing demands revision. There is no hope of getting it right the first time. Or the second.

When writers write and revise by hand to make digital things, they introduce a missing human element and human timescale into the process and the production. The tenuous distinction between natural and computer languages dissolves, revealing itself as a construct that thrives on and maintains fear and ignorance of many core affordances and constraints of the digital medium.

[Figure 3.2] The "Lo.-Fi. Manifesto" published in the Kairos Journal. The picture was modified for print. In order to get the authentic color impression refer to http://kairos.technorhetoric.net/20.2/inventio/stolley/.

In his "Lo-Fi Manifesto 2.0," Stolley (2016) gives a good example of how simple transmediality is used by publications in the Kairos journal (see figure 3.2). The Manifesto is a plea for the use of simple technologies, mostly in the spirit of the KISS[98] principle that was coined in the *UNIX* world back in the 80s. Stolley wants to challenge the development of complex pieces of digital technology and software in current time.

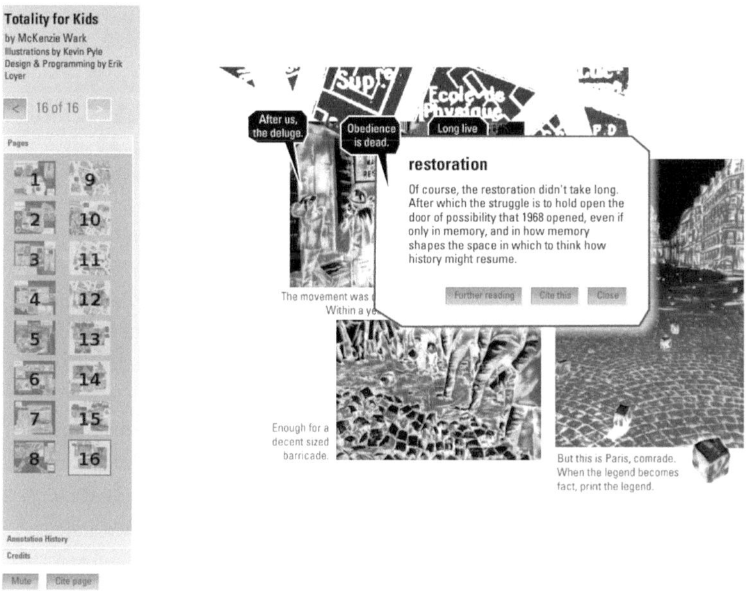

[Figure 3.3] "Totality for Kids," a Transmedia Publication from the Vectors Journal. The picture was modified for print. In order to get the authentic color impression refer to http://vectors.usc.edu/issues/7/totality/ .

However, this challenge is not only presented by arguments. The article is written in a monospaced font and uses colors from the solarized color palette. It refrains from using any images or media other than text. In fact, there are iconographic elements such as the header, but the author uses characters in order to draw the image. Both font and color scheme allude to terminal environments and to minimalistic editors like vim[99] which are operational before any graphical desktop environment has been loaded. By doing so, color and font link to a certain discourse and environment which matches the main argument of the text. In this respect, the absence of

98 KISS is an acronym for *Keep It Simple and Stupid* which describes a common ethos for the design of software.

99 http://www.vim.org/

other media is an explicit transmedial design decision. There is not just no media but by not using it, multi-media is addressed explicitly.

McKenzie Wark's "Totality for Kids" (2013) chooses a completely different approach (see figure 3.3). Stolley's transmedia strategy can be described as a repetition throughout one non-textual media strategy. The visuals of the article reaffirm the statement of the written text. Nonetheless, the strategy does more than just illustrate the argument. In fact, it could be said that this constitutes more a contradiction to Stolley's intent, insofar as it makes the whole resource technically more complicated than it needs to be. In contrast to Stolley, Wark designs a dense entanglement between text, sound, drawing, time, and interactivity, in which the line of argument truly grows out of all these components combined.

The publication investigates the story of the *situationist international* in Paris, between the early fifties and the seventies. It does so by embedding snippets from the line of arguments in situationist theory into historical events that are presented as a graphic novel. Thereby the visuals speak of history while the text develops a theoretical discourse. Another peculiarity is that there is the notion of pages. However, the shift between pages is automatic and is always scheduled in such a way that the reader cannot get everything that is on the screen. This decision creates the effect of transitoriness, which does not only emphasize the historicity of the whole discourse, but also produces the feeling that something is lost or situational. This feeling coincides with the end, in which the objective of the movement itself is lost, an objective that consisted of changing the socio-cultural reality of capitalism.

It is also possible to interrupt the automatically scheduled flow of pages by mouse clicks, enabling the reader to get further text explanations, passages from theoretical texts, and other material. More than just giving context information, this feature enables a shift between a theoretical and a historical perspective on the very same content, by means of designing time and interactivity as medium to create discourse.

Another strategy to relate different media together to create an argument is presented by *Scalar*[100]. Scalar offers the possibility of rendering the publication or parts of it in different views. Views vary in terms of text-focused or visually focused presentation of content. For instance, the path view enables to see how different components in a publication might relate with

100 https://scalar.usc.edu/scalar/

each other in other ways than the intended reading path. Other views may provide statistical information or visual access to the content.

Sayers and Dietrich (2013, 11) call this strategy a design of multiple "modes of attention," in which the narrative strategy behind those views is the construction of specific types of perception of components in a publication. The underlying claim is that there is no argument or information which is independent of the environment in which it is created, and which has to be experienced (Svensson 2010, para. 150). In fact, this claim turns the whole approach of radically isolating content from form experienced in other digital publication formats upside down. Accordingly, digital technologies allow a clearer view of the fact that form is always content, and permit making use of this aspect for more powerful publications.

The ability of the user to actively change between views, or to decide when she wants to interrupt the automatic flow of the default line of arguments introduces interactivity as its own "medium" for strategic narrative purposes. The design decisions concerning interactivity not only shape how much freedom a reader has but also in which aspects within the line of arguments interactivity takes place and in which not. Thereby, interactivity does not necessarily undermine the authored line of argument. It can also make it more convincing. For instance, certain points may seem more authentic when they are experienced by the reader "on her own."

These examples for the term transmedia substantiate an understanding of digital media which is fundamentally different from those found in other concepts. The approach to technology, in this case digital technology, informed by common arguments from cultural theory and the humanities, is very different as well.

Correspondingly, McPherson, in a lecture at the *Rewiring the Future of Publishing* conference (summarized by Adema 2014), criticizes the so-called stack model of computer architecture. In this model, computer architecture is represented in a hierarchy which from the bottom up consist of: platform, code, function, interface, and reception. It has been shown that in approaches to publishing that are informed by computer science, this hierarchy equates to an epistemological hierarchy. Form can be subtracted from content because levels below the interface level do not interfere with the reception level.

McPherson argues that this model is inconsistent in two ways. First, it neglects that the fabrication of the platform is the result of a cultural decision-making process and thereby equally as contingent as the interface. Second, the different levels might be useful for understanding digital technology, but only if their relationship is considered non-hierarchical and reciprocally influential in continuously changing ways. Thus, it could be argued that the proliferation of different digital devices and platforms is provoked by the reception level which, far from being passive, strongly influences the refurbishing of platforms.

> Ultimately, no one view is a direct representation of data. Rather, each shapes audience perception and constructs both a subject and an argument (which are steeped in disciplinary histories of interpretation). (Sayers and Dietrich 2013, 10)

Views and their entanglement with different media address different ways of perceiving the world, but also different ways of engaging with it. The array view of an image as a numerical three-dimensional array[101] is meant for a computational context, while the "image" view suggests "experience." Yet the effect of one type of consideration can change the activities of the other and vice versa.

The framing of technological concepts as socio-cultural angles which interact with other socio-cultural concepts on an equal level is pushed further by McPherson (2010). In this paper she criticizes computational approaches to digital publishing, as well as certain types of disapproval of digital publications from humanities scholars. The author remarks that both discourses deal with narrative organization of arguments, linear structure, and interpretative methodology as properties that belong to the text and print world, while digital technologies have a need of different methodological and organizational principles (network structures and quantitative methodology).

McPherson argues that this assumption is wrong, since a text does also provide non-linear relationships, and digital technologies enable authoring of much more than what is done in e-Science. She states that this mismatch is caused by two binaries: the binary of databases and monographs on the one hand and of interpretation and quantification on the other. While both binaries are two different things — artifacts and methodology — they are treated as one and the same thing in the discourse about digital publishing, just as it is suggested by a purely technical interpretation of the stack model above.

101 The openCV python client for the implementation of software projects in computer vision does represent images in a three-dimensional numpy-array where each dimension encodes information about one color channel in the Red, Green, Blue spectrum.

The concept of TPs is therefore part of a broader scientific endeavor in the humanities, that of challenging the usage of certain binaries that are often driven by common viewpoints of digital technologies:

> Thus, it [Scalar] mediates a whole set of binaries: between close and distant reading, user and author, interface and backend, micro and macro, theory and practice, archive and interpretation, text and image, database and narrative, and human and machine. (McPherson 2014, 185)

Transmedia Publications as Humanist Forms of Experimentation

It would fall short to only present the theoretical background of TPs in contrast to other viewpoints. Transmedia Publications are also part of a research program in the humanities which sets and promotes its own goals. It could even be said that up to a certain extent TPs are not just a new type of presenting research results, but the primary goal of a certain research line itself.

Accordingly, Svensson (2010), in his pioneering overview "The Landscape of Digital Humanities," calls the Vectors journal the epitome of a certain type of humanities. Alluding to McPherson, he calls this research field "Multimodal Humanities." He describes it as driven by the attempt to challenge common ideas of form and content, leading to a notion of research as artistic practice and science as an area of activism and intervention. The last point is based on the argument that scientists never just represent the world, but by representing it automatically shape it to the liking of the representation.

In this respect TPs investigate "what might count as scholarly argument" (McPherson 2010, 2). It was indicated that even outside of a political notion of science this research question does by no means constitute a goal in itself. Accordingly, the Future Storytelling contest was set up around the argument that the problems of our time can only be adequately represented in a transmedia fashion. There has been a strong base for such thinking in humanities research for a long time. In 1991, Flusser (1994, 40) already wrote that "es ist offensichtlich geworden, dass die Probleme, die sich vor uns auftun, es erforderlich machen, sie durch sehr viel raffiniertere, exaktere und reichere Codes und Gesten als die des Alphabets zu denken."[102]

102 "... it has become evident that the problems we experience today require thinking in terms of codes and gestures that are much more sophisticated, exact, and richer than those of the alphabet." (author's translation)

The plurality of representation strategies, however, does not mean that TPs are all about the creation of new publications. They sometimes make explicit references to a historical publication format that is closely related to the humanities and that is considered to be in danger today: the monograph. Consequently, McPherson asserts that:

> ... new forms of experimentation and bookishness are necessary if we are to advance (and perhaps save) scholarly publishing in the humanities. (McPherson 2010, 2)

Corresponding with the cultural critique of a techno-deterministic angle on publications and with the field's interpretation of research as an act of social engagement, the preservation of the humanities monograph cannot be carried out in a normative top-down manner. Instead it needs to be laid out as a social process in which new forms of publishing should be the result of a hopefully democratic process of negotiation:

> ... the book should be seen as a process of mutual becoming: a form of intra-action between different agents and constituencies (human and non-human). (Adema 2015, viii)

This is also the reason why McPherson talks about new forms of bookishness in terms of experimentation and why she encourages experimentation. Accordingly, a broad range of approaches will provide more input for the future of the monograph and assure the democratic character of the process. In this respect McPherson remarks that "Vectors is part and parcel of this broader culture of experimentation and change" (McPherson 2010, 5).

This ethos of experimentation is very much celebrated across all TP projects. Thus, the *if:book* initiative, which forms part of the project behind Sophie, defines its primary goal in "exploring digital possibilities for literature and the future of the book" (Meade 2013). The Future Storytelling contest is set up on the question: "What kinds of crossmedial stories can be told about the Anthropocene" (Welt 2015) and TP journals choose names like the *Journal of Visual Experiments, and Audiovisual Thinking*.

Two Types of Consequences of a Different Notion of Technology

It has been pointed out several times that all the significant differences between TPs root in a different evaluation of technology in general, and of digital technology in particular, for the prospect of scholarly publications. Svensson (2010 par. 31) explains this difference by stressing that the research field in which TPs are created is concerned with digital technologies as a cultural phenomenon and a research object instead of technology as an "instrumental tool." The last paragraphs explained why this is so and what the consequences of this fact for the many goals of TPs are. The consequences for the technological implementation for TPs and their environment, however, still need to be discussed.

A crucial issue also stressed by other projects already concerns the support of the authoring process of digital publications. For obvious reasons, the creation of TPs is an extremely demanding process, varying according to the transmedial complexity of the particular case. Maybe it was the fact that this challenge is so evident that made the field of TPs, in contrast to other approaches, respond to it from the very beginning and why they have created a set of sophisticated authoring tools. Besides, it can also be seen easily, from what has been described so far, that this is also the result of efforts to enable researchers in the humanities to engage in digital technologies.

Among these tools are Sophie, the *Rich Interactive Narrative Framework*[103], Scalar or the *Dynamic Backend Generator* (Vectors Journal 2008) some of which were even awarded in general purpose computer magazines (Fenton 2013). The main purpose of these tools is to make different digital resources manageable for the construction of multimedia narratives and to make the result exportable. The tools intentionally try to abstract from a view which reflects technological needs and perform the task of transforming the conceptually defined publication into a technological implementation.

Although these tools exist, they are often not used. The cases where a TP is designed by a team consisting of humanist researchers and computer scientists are not so rare instead. This situation might also reflect the fact that the perspectives of transmediality create needs which can never be fully supported by standardized tools, because the areas where standardization takes place in other contexts have to be available to the individual purposes of researchers simply by concept design. This aspect also indicates how resource intensive the creation of TPs can be.

So far, the discussion of the theoretical background of TPs has mostly highlighted issues that benefit from a transmedia approach, while the last paragraph indicated that there are also issues which become more problematic and which have not been wholly sorted out. At least one of these issues is tightly bound to the theme of the critiques of binaries, given by McPherson,

103 https://www.microsoft.com/en-us/research/project/rich-interactive-narratives/

especially the goal of "melding form and content to enact a second-order examination of the mediation" ("Vectors Journal" 2013).

Although serious arguments for this critique exist on the theoretical level, all of which are discussed above, the binary of content and form does also reflect some very pragmatic needs. For instance, it enables a distinction between core and contingent properties of an object of interest. Theoretically and politically such a prioritization might appear problematic, but when it comes to the question of maintaining and sustaining multimedia narratives as publications, prioritization of additional criteria is valid. When related stakeholders are able to develop a profile for certain publication types, it means that they are able to support, maintain, and build an environment around it. This is one of the reasons e-Science-oriented publication concepts so eagerly and radically separate the two. Striving for a complete conflation between form and content jeopardizes the sustainability of publications as socio-cultural objects, as will be shown in the following paragraphs. Thus, the issue is not that a line between form and content exists as such, but that imposing and implementing such a line is a conceptual tool to make digital publications manageable. Consequently, Ball (2016, 52) admits that "webtexts [TPs] can be difficult to stabilize due to their technological and media innovations."

Ball and Eyman (2015) give a very good example for the aforementioned consequences. In 2015 already, the authors stated that no editorial workflow exists for TPs. In their study they list a variety of reasons, all related to the individual complexity of TPs and the topic of the conflation of form and content. They illustrate how these issues create complicated conditions for requirements such as the review, citation, dissemination, or archiving of TPs.

The problem of archiving can be demonstrated well using the Scalar project. Compared to other projects Scalar does in fact provide a sophisticated model for the export of TPs. For the publication of TPs, Scalar provides a web platform which organizes some of the aforementioned tasks. Nonetheless, the export model (in 2016) only describes parts of a TP. More precisely, it only considers the resources included in a TP as well as the links (paths) between them. The Scalar views which, as has been said, form a crucial aspect of the Scalar logics are not part of the export model. Additionally, some design elements that are provided by the authoring software and the Scalar platform are not represented either. In consequence, the data model re-introduces a separation between core elements of a publication and its representation, a separation that was substantially challenged by the project before. Only the platform assures the status of TPs as transmedial. The export into the aforementioned data model only turns them into an aggregation such as those described in section 3.2.1 without the possibility of reproducing them as TPs somewhere else.

Scalar is still a positive exception. It exports publications as RDF, thereby complying with certain technical standards. Other TPs are even more dependent on their environment and often do not provide a machine-readable or software-independent version.

Issues regarding archiving, long-term-preservation, and integrity belong to the most substantial challenges caused by the peculiar relationship of TPs to technology. Svensson (2010, para. 149) even goes a step further and remarks that "the technology itself does not seem to be a primary focus."

Although this assertion is quite harsh, many observations support it. Many TPs, for instance, are implemented in Flash. Flash is an old proprietary technology which, for example, is not supported anymore by browsers in mobile devices and which poses much more challenges to the issues of the type discussed concerning archiving before.

Vector publications like the "Roaring Twentieth" (Thompson 2013) do not provide either a linted[104] nor persistent citation URL. In a modern browser environment[105] audio streams sometimes work and sometimes do not work. This is a substantial issue in a publication which is primarily concerned with sound.

Many Vectors publications let the browser get stuck in the tab of the publication so that the browser had to be restarted in order to be able to change tabs again. The *Photomediations* (Zylinska et al. 2015) publication by Joanna Zylinska creates a second scroll bar on the website for design purposes. However, in certain situations this seems to conflict with the browser scrollbar and scrolling is not possible at all anymore. Some links from the index page do not open the corresponding page after a certain sequence of previous steps.

104 In the present context linting means to use an understandable, clean, and standardized structural scheme to define links that subtracts from the technological environment in which the link is defined.

105 The publication was rendered in a Firefox browser version 46.

Summary

All things considered, TPs introduce a substantially new approach to the design of digital publications. This approach is so radically different from those that were outlined already that TPs seem to represent an opposing point of view. The difference is based on a very specific evaluation of the role of digital technologies for publishing. More precisely, TPs address technology as a catalyst for new forms of meaning and communication, and not as a mechanism to make scholarly communication more efficient, implying an understanding of the term shaped by information and computer science. This is based on the fact that for TPs digital technologies are themselves expressions of cultural constructs and thus can also be appropriated in different ways. They are thereby not able to impose a certain type of logic.

Transmedia Publications resemble a line of argument which common in the humanities. Without doubt these arguments are a blind spot in the conceptual space of other publication concepts. On the other hand, it has been demonstrated that more complex reflections on technology in digital publications instigate more complex challenges for the socio-technological environment of corresponding publications. Hence, the question of efficiency remains, albeit in a different guise. Beyond sustainability, it calls for additional viewpoints such as the readability of TPs. While other concepts were focused on the readability of publications for machines, TPs need to consider the readability for humans and for the sake of scholarly communication as well. Unfortunately, the discourse on TPs rarely approaches this question.

The benefit of existing TPs can furthermore be challenged, if it is compared with the field's goal to create new types of meaning and more powerful modes of representation. Many media properties of TPs concentrate on atmospheric aspects or on mirroring the main points of the text. While supporters of the concept would probably argue that the term atmospheric already introduces a problematic distinction between necessary and unnecessary features, the application of multimedia is without question far removed from the "more exact and richer codes" that sometimes frame the discourse.

[4] Publishing-Com Bubble

The period between 2007 and 2013 was indeed highly dynamic and shaped by an impressive number of individual projects and initiatives. Despite their fundamental differences, all these activities, from ROs to TPs, had one aspect in common. They all emphasize the "revolutionary force" of digital technologies in one way or another. The way in which this force is interpreted varies.

The success of these activities, in contrast, remains limited, especially if evaluated by their key agents. Consequently, De Roure (2014b, 233), a key figure behind ROs, remarks in 2014 that "scientific publication still looks remarkably as it did in years past." A group of prominent contributors to SPs and NPs similarly state that:

> ... two decades of emergent and increasingly pervasive information technology have demonstrated the potential for far more effective scholarly communication. But the use of this technology remains limited. (Bourne, Shotton, et al. 2012, 41)

In a more emotional manner, Bardi (2014), involved in LPs, asks the rhetorical question: "Scholarly Communication: What's Wrong with It?" At the same time these judgements were made, the funding for many of the project environments maintaining these activities ended.

Another possible observation is the emergence of a greater number of publication concepts stemming from the humanities at the end of this period. As has been emphasized, these concepts introduce new ideas about digital publication or re-interpret existing ideas. There is one aspect among these differences that stands out regarding its meaning for future developments, especially visible in the AiME project. This project put an amount of effort into the organization of reliable social structures around its UB publication that is unequalled by other publication concepts up to that time. It is true that the scope of funding behind this project facilitated this. However, it also represents a higher appreciation of social aspects influencing the success of digital publications.

The next phase in research on digital publications distinguishes itself by the way it takes into account the social context of scholarly publications. There are differences between different publications concepts when it comes to the exact way by which this context is acknowledged. Nonetheless, its being considered in the first place marks a sea-change for all of them.

Hybrid Publications

One of the publication concepts belonging to those mentioned above is that of Hybrid Publications (hereafter referred to as HPs). It makes sense to start with HPs insofar, as they are a development that involved people who also contributed to the last publication concept of the chapter above (TPs). HPs are a concept representing substantial ideas that have not been discussed yet in this form.

The first time that the term Hybrid Publishing was used in conjunction with a clearly marked research agenda was probably by McPherson (2010) in her already cited article "Scaling Vectors." In the second part of the article, the author describes insights from experiences gained during the years of the Vectors Journal. Additionally, she introduces the formation of the *Alliance for Networking Visual Culture* (also referred to as ANVC), an organization of researchers, libraries, archives, and university presses, as a means of solving issues that had been identified during the publishing of the Vectors Journal.

One of the key insights from the Vectors project reflects on the status of TPs as experimental spaces. McPherson states that this approach has certain limitations and concludes that:

> ... we need to evolve more "standardized" structures and interfaces that will allow us to delineate more stable genres and to scale multi-modal scholarship. (McPherson 2010, 6)

This standardization should enable the creation of technological and social infrastructure, as well as minimize the effort for scholars when producing TPs. On the other hand, the quote shows that TPs are not considered capable of allowing such developments. The Scalar publication platform mentioned above is one of the outcomes of this process and the alliance. The relationship between the two names "Vectors" and "Scalar" highlights very well how the alliance and the Scalar platform are shaping the issue of digital publications. The goal is to find scalars on the vectors of digital publishing.

The section on NPs contained a dense description of strategies by which those publications try to transfer certain requirements of publications from social agents to technological platforms. This transfer should make it possible to remove stakeholders, namely publishers and editors, from the ecology of publishing. The HPs' approach and its underlying convictions are the opposite of NPs in this. Both the evaluation of stakeholders and their relationships, as well as the social function of reference implementations are based on different points of interest.

The difference starts with the type of discussion that takes place around the issue of standardized structures. In the spirit in which they are addressed by the NPs example, standards are often conceptually taken for granted. They follow a strategy where certain standards are advocated against existing social structures, which need to adapt. Accordingly, Cameron Neylon discusses in his blog:

> ... that the best way to get researchers to be serious about the issue of modernizing scholarly communications was to let the scholarly monograph business go to the wall as an object lesson to everyone else (Neylon 2012, para. 1)

In the HPs approach, many of the issues that in the eyes of people like Cameron Neylon are already sorted out actually are not. The identification of standardized structures — social and technological ones — depends on greater insights into questions like: "how will editorial functions and their temporalities shift ...?," "who will be responsible for updating and sustaining digital publications?," "what relationships might evolve between presses, libraries, and archives?" or "how best to organize the digital archive to facilitate scholarly analysis?" (McPherson 2010, 10–12), questions that have not been answered comprehensively enough.

It is true that HPs ask these questions mainly for publications following the TPs and related concepts. Nevertheless, the attitude is very different, and the Scalar portal is a means, not of establishing a point of reference, but of creating an "experimental space for publishing focused on understanding the entanglement between publishing technology and culture" (Adema 2015, 38). Furthermore, this new type of experiment is a joint venture of all stakeholders in the publishing sector, as the alliance consists of representatives of all of them.

An Integrative Perspective on Digital Publications

The difference with this fresh attempt to digital publications is visible in a variety of discussions and activities that take place in the context of HPs.

The best example are the topics of open access and open science. It is transparent throughout this work that strong ethical arguments are made about open access publishing. However, of similar importance is the aspect that the success of many of the publication concepts depends significantly on the availability of open access resources. The discussions of these publication designs and open access mutually support each other.

As Hall, Kuc, and Zylinska (2015) point out in their "Guide to Open and Hybrid Publishing," this is not significantly different for HPs. Hybrid Publications do not reject open access. The title of the guide mentioned above even extends the name of HPs with the term "open." The Vectors journal, furthermore, was an open access publication from the very beginning. However, advocates of HPs also stress the difficulties of open access.

More precisely, they argue that there are lots of unanswered questions barring open access from becoming a socially and economically sustainable endeavor, especially, but not limited to, the case of new digital publication formats (McPherson 2010, 11). As it will become clear later on, HPs do not reject historical publication formats. In the humanities, this format is typically the monograph that people like Neylon want to see going to the wall.

Burkhardt (2015) from the Hybrid Publishing Lab, as well as Eve and Edwards (2015), clearly state that common open access business models do not work out for monographs.[1] Reasons relate to the format itself and to different social conditions such as funding schemes in the humanities.[2] However, instead of giving up on these formats, initiatives of HPs try to form alliances with open-minded presses like those involved in the ANVC, in order to develop special open access models that might work within

1 In the common open access publishing business model it is the author who has to pay a fee that covers the publication and dissemination costs. Arguments for why this is problematic in the case of the monograph are given by Herb and Schöpfel (2018).

2 For further details on this matter see also Collins, Milloy, and Stone (2015), Milloy and Collins (2016), Ferwerda, Pinter, and Stern (2017).

particular environments. To this end, the Hybrid Publishing Lab formed the OA publisher *Meson Press* and also contacted *De Gruyter*, an important publisher in the humanities but not particularly known for pushing open access forward. Vectors became part of the Open Humanities Press, an open access publisher for the humanities, when this initiative was launched in 2009 (Open Humanities Press 2015). Finally, Scalar cooperates with more than one press.

Another integrative approach to open access, regarding the issue of revenue and financial sustainability, is proposed by Hall, Kuc, and Zylinska (2015) in their "Guide to Open and Hybrid Publishing." The authors define a strategy called "subsequent monetization." Subsequent monetization does not undermine the core of open access in HPs, but proposes derivatives and reformatted versions of the original content. They summarize that:

> Open and Hybrid Publishing learns from open access, it sometimes borrows from OA; it may incorporate OA strategies, but it can also go beyond them. (Hall, Kuc, and Zylinska 2015, 4)

The discussion of open access is probably the one topic in which peculiarities of an integrative approach to digital publications can be illustrated best. Significant differences can nevertheless be observed in other areas, too. Scalar, for instance, follows best practices of the *Critical Commons* initiative (Critical Commons 2016). As the name suggests, Critical Comments refers to the Creative Commons initiative. However, instead of just focusing on licensing issues, Critical Commons evaluates best practices of fair use and reuse of media. The ethical issues of open access are thereby crucially extended. Additionally, the approach emphasizes that positive effects on the field of publishing do not just derive naturally from the introduction of certain licensing models.

It is also significant that Scalar publications — which are also aggregated publications — use semantic web technologies for the integration of resources but do not limit the issue of interoperability to this one solution. Scalar makes contracts with partner archives such as the *Internet Archive*[3]or the *Visual History Archive*[4] of the *Shoah Foundation*[5]. These contracts assure that criteria of fair use in the sense of Critical Commons are kept beyond issues of licensing, and that interoperability is maintained beyond the technological protocol. From the study of (Doorenbosch and Sierman 2011),

3 https://archive.org/
4 http://vhaonline.usc.edu
5 https://sfi.usc.edu/

outlined in the EPs section, it became obvious that such an approach is critical when dealing with distributed media resources.

This type of interoperability, which could be called social interoperability, extends the perspectives of technological, structural and semantic interoperability of computer science addressed in previous publication designs. In the ten recommendations to creating HPs by Hall, Kuc, and Zylinska (2015), none actually tackle issues of technological interoperability. Furthermore, the transformation of one publication version into another — for instance, a website which is turned into a print book — is described as a process based on human intervention. The authors do not just ignore aspects of interoperability, but follow the implicit critique in HPs that technological and formal perspectives on interoperability are not always the most effective ones and have limited impact on the social world on a general level.

Defining Hybrid Publications

A clear definition for HPs, albeit addressed as a specific publication type, does not exist. It is true that the concept of HPs emerged partially out of TPs. Hall, Kuc, and Zylinska (2015) furthermore reference UBs as one of its predecessors. Nonetheless, its key aspect is an argument by which it opposes the attitude of many other publication formats. Accordingly, HPs argue that it is not possible anymore to focus on one specific publication format as the new model for publications. Instead, a plurality of formats is the way to go, including non-digital formats.

McPherson (2010) first used the term Hybrid Publication in order to summarize that digital publishing is successful — as early as 2010 — wherever it does not try to substitute print or text publications. As Liu et al. (2016, 31) put it in the context of their hybrid book approach: "previous research suggests that, while digital content has its advantages, printed content still offers benefits that cannot be matched by digital media." McPherson, furthermore, draws upon experiences in the Vectors Journal, revealing that Vectors articles were often re-edited and re-published in print or in a blog publication. In the opposite direction, existing publications were sometimes re-edited in order to become articles in Vectors. She outlines that the background of such strategies is the need to address different audiences and different media needs, making it impossible to address all of them in just one format.

Hall, Kuc, and Zylinska (2015) similarly call HPs collections of resources, remixed and reformatted in order to satisfy the need of different devices, economical needs, and social channels, and which only completely exist when all are considered together.

More clearly, the authors state that HPs are the one principle which undermines the top-down, one-to-many, and "one size fits it all" approach of other publication concepts. In the author's view the one player who controlled publishing in a top-down fashion was the publisher, whose mechanism of control was the print publication. In contrast, HPs advocate publications in multiple formats using different resources by potentially different agents, where the network of related publications forms the abstract notion of a HP.

Having said all this, the task of HPs is not to define a publication but to catalogue and support different publication formats as well as the conversions between them. The first effort was started by Worthington and Furter (2014). Even if incomplete, of low quality, and not a taxonomy in a strict sense, their *publication taxonomy* was still the most comprehensive attempt to list publication designs up to that point in time.

Examples of Hybrid Publication Bundles

The *Photomediations* project is an outstanding example for a Hybrid Publication. Photomediations started in March 2013 with *Photomediations Machine* (Zylinska 2015). Ever since then, it has been a journal-like online publication, associated with the Culture Machine journal previously mentioned. It publishes reviewed and curated text as well as visual content around the topic of photography.

In the year 2015, Joanna Zylinska, the main editor of Photomediations Machine, published *Photomediations: An Open Book* (Zylinska et al. 2015). This online book is comprised of eight chapters differing both in content and form. The first chapter is a comprehensive introduction into photomediation as a specific theory on photography. The next four chapters include over two hundred images grouped and described in terms of light, motion, hybridity, and relationship. The photos were not originally created for the book, they are reused versions of mostly open-licensed photos gathered from Photomediations Machine, *Europeana*[6], *Flickr Commons*[7], or *Wikimedia*[8], following the spirit of remixing.

Whereas the beginning chapters are meant to be in a finished state, chapters six to eight are open for ongoing updates and extensions. Chapter six is an open compilation of general essays about photography, while chapter seven consist of a *Tumblr*[9] blog, conceived as a "social space" for discussion on the topic of the book. The last chapter reorganizes selected contents of the book into an "exhibition" designed in conjunction with *Europeana Space*. Last but not least, Open Humanities Press published a print publication of the sixth chapter of the open book in 2016 (Kuc and Zylinska 2016).

Hall, Kuc, and Zylinska (2015, 6) call the whole Photomediations Hybrid Publication "an experiment in open and hybrid publishin — as well as a celebration of the book as a living object." It is an outstanding example of this publication concept because it showcases excellently how the concept of hybridity in HPs responds to the so-called binaries introduced by McPherson (see 3.11.2): it contains multimedia content, it is a cluster of work in progress and finished parts, it remixes existing content and creates new contents, there are digital and non-digital versions, and finally it includes other publication concepts. This list also provides a better understanding of the difference between TPs and HPs, even if there is a deep entanglement between the two.

Further examples of HPs focusing on particular issues of the research field are provided by the Hybrid Publishing Lab (Worthington 2015), for instance the *Hybrid Lecture Player* developed here. The Player is more like a web environment for publishing recordings from academic lectures in combination with images, other additional materials, and transcriptions. The idea is again to republish material already published somewhere else, but in a new format that creates its own additional value.

In the *Merve Remix* use-case, the Hybrid Publishing Lab digitized existing print monographs published by the publisher Merve and turned them into web-publications (Worthington 2016, 4–7). The goal was to get certain insights about the reformatting processes. The use-case is also well suited for highlighting again that HPs are not necessarily "digital-first" publications. A publication becomes part of HPs the moment different

6 https://www.europeana.eu/portal/de
7 https://www.flickr.com/
8 https://commons.wikimedia.org
9 https://www.tumblr.com/

publication formats — digital and non-digital — exist. The *Debates in the Digital Humanities* series (Gold 2012; Gold 2016a) presents a HP approach in which the printed books are published in parallel to a web version, providing sophisticated tools for annotation-based discussions and computational analysis of reading behavior (Gold 2016b).

Tensions

In contrast to the obsolescence of the "one size fits it all" principle declared by Hall, and as the main point of the last paragraph, the understanding of the multi-format aspect in HPs remains contradictory. Accordingly, Burkhardt (2015, 4) also calls multi-format publishing "single-source publishing" (see also Rasch 2017). However, they are not the same. The concept of hybridity as it is used in Photomediations, Scalar, or Merve Remix is intentionally not set up around the principle of one source from which all other formats emerge. The abovementioned principle and the concept of social interoperability are in fact precisely arguing against it. Nevertheless, the Hybrid Publishing Lab has designed a software called *A-Machine* which seeks to provide a tool for single-source publishing as part of HPs (Hybrid Publishing Consortium 2015).

Hall called Photomediations an "experiment" (above). McPherson (2010, 6) similarly depicts Scalar as a space for "experimental work." On the other hand, it was said at the beginning of this chapter that HPs somehow overcome the phase of experimentation inherent to TPs and e-Science approaches. The difference is a different type of experimenting that is going on even if the term is still used.

While in the field of e-Science, experiments or so-called reference implementations are made to push forward the idea of a future considered to be clear, HPs, if experimental, are such in order to evaluate possible futures. While in the spirit of e-Science reference implementations serve to make clear how agent groups should adapt, in HPs they serve to find out what the reconfiguration of the publishing roles might look like.

This significant difference is well expressed in the self-description of the Hybrid Publishing Lab. It says that "Unser Ziel ist das Produzieren von Wissen durch den Prozess des Machens"[10] (Burkhardt 2015, 4). Thus, experimental implementations are necessary in HPs because publishing is in a phase of radical change where many things become uncertain (McPherson 2010, 1) and not because they can be considered certain but not realized yet.

10 "Our goal is to create knowledge using the process of doing" (author's translation).

Resume

The HP concept further develops the unique attitude chosen by some concepts of the humanities, in order to deal with the challenges in digital publishing. It has been shown on multiple occasions that this unique attitude consists of a cultural perspective on digital technologies and a more open understanding of digital publishing.

Hybrid Publications nevertheless do not leave certain tensions — already experienced with TPs — completely behind: those between a theoretical evaluation of digital publications and the application of technology. The issue of multi-format versus single-source publishing is part of this tension. Single-source publishing exactly represents the stack model in computer science, criticized by McPherson and Adema. Likewise, there is a great tension between the attempt to foster the publishing ecology and that of creating better conditions for sustainable publications, outlined by McPherson and the set of HPs best practices listed by Hall. These practices include recommendations to use services like WordPress, Flickr, Google, or GoDaddy, which create serious issues for publishing on a technical, legal, and ecological level. These issues are not evaluated in a serious manner, instead the ease of use is emphasized.

These tensions also continue to frame the theoretical discourse in HPs. The publication taxonomy, for instance, introduces a simple binary between new and old publication formats. It thereby reproduces an essentialist way of thinking, criticized above, and contradicting the base line of arguments in HPs. Correspondingly, Burkhardt (2015) reproduces the motif in the e-Science discourse on digital publications, stating that the sciences are far ahead of the humanities in this topic. Contrastingly, the original attempt of HPs was to escape this very logic.

Scaling Digital Publication Concepts

The Hybrid Publishing approach might have been the first publication concept to take up a different approach to the social aspects of technology in publishing. It did, however, not remain the only initiative to choose this direction. In the previous chapter, the concept of Liquid Publications was introduced. It was argued that a dominant aspect of LPs is the idea of applying principles from computer science to publications. The LPs literature is full of concrete suggestions and metaphorical terminology in this respect. In the end, a publication is compared to a software repository.

Many authors like Manghi and Castelli, who participated in the LPs project, re-engaged with the topic by taking part in the *OpenAIRE*[11] project. This project took up many of the activities carried out by the DRIVER project, namely a database of open access publications in the European Union and the concept of EPs. Apart from maintaining the work of projects that had ended, OpenAIRE was launched to "supporting the diffusion and adoption of the European Commission Open Access mandate" (Manghi et al. 2010, 31). Additionally, the project was to make it possible to evaluate the impact of this mandate.

The first OpenAIRE project started in 2009 and ended in 2012. OpenAIRE plus, which extended the activities of OpenAIRE, went on between 2011 and today. While OpenAIRE focused on the inclusion of EU-funded open access article publications and the provision of core services, the OpenAIRE plus project extended the scope to all article publications in the EU region and to data publications. The service portfolio was extended, and a conceptual framework introduced to update the concept of EPs later on and under the new funding scheme of *Horizon 2020*[12].

Manghi, Bolikowski, et al. (2012, 3) list four different goals for both OpenAIRE and OpenAIRE plus. According to this, the projects are aimed at "building support structures for researchers in depositing FP7 research publications," the "establishment and operation of OpenAIRE e-Infrastructure for peer-reviewed articles and other forms of scientific results," the "exploration of and experimentation with scientific data management services," and the "sustainability of the OpenAIRE e-Infrastructure."

It is worth mentioning that compared to the language used in the LPs project, these goals are expressed far more moderately and open. This is significant in so far as the progress could also have in time permitted the expectation of more defined and ambitious goals. In fact, the step back from the highly innovative but also very specific ideas offered by projects like LPs is the major one in the OpenAIRE projects. This will become more transparent when the problems behind digital publications as presented by OpenAIRE are described below. It will become obvious that the OpenAIRE approach is motivated by comparable reflections on the situation of digital publications, such as have been presented by Tara McPherson. However, the reaction to these issues is still fundamentally different and emphasizes a different way of thinking.

11 https://www.openaire.eu/

12 Horizon 2020 is the programmatic framework for research funding in the European Union between 2014 and 2020.

A New Problem Awareness

Like McPherson, Bardi and Manghi (2014) now acknowledge the richness and variety of existing digital publication formats. The authors similarly began to realize that this situation is the result of broad experimentation on possible scenarios, with the aim of integrating scholarly publications and digital technologies. In correspondence with the experiences of the Vectors Journal, they also stress that this notion of experimentation is a significant reason for the lack of broader success of newly defined digital publication objects in real life. Moreover, and now in contrast to HPs, they regret that a conceptual common ground for these publication objects is missing.

The OpenAIRE project is the first environment discussed in this work in which people from the area of information and computer science acknowledge that conceptual heterogeneity is the major characteristic of digital publications and also its major challenge. It is true that the topic of heterogeneity is crucial to all of the approaches connected to these domains. In all of these cases, the discussion, however, focused on heterogeneity in terms of formal semantics and technological implementation, not on the heterogeneity of approaches to digital publications as such. Even the DRIVER project evaluated different approaches as part of the same development.

Another new and significant aspect is the fact that the problematization of heterogeneity is now also applied to protocols used for data exposure. Castelli, Manghi, and Thanos (2013) specifically mention OAI-PMH, OAI-ORE, and the LOD, among others. Curiously enough, these protocols were originally introduced to reduce heterogeneity. By stating that just these three protocols already create significant confusion around the implementation of digital publication services, the authors implicitly admit that the goals of these protocols could not be reached. Indeed, in the current study approaches were described which use "pure" LOD strategies (NPs), or which adopted OAI-ORE (ROs) by claiming that "Linked Data is not enough for scientists" (De Roure et al. 2013).

According to OpenAIRE, all the abovementioned problems cause another type of problem: stakeholders hesitate to invest into digital publication infrastructures due to uncertainty about the direction into which digital publications will develop (Castelli, Manghi, and Thanos 2013). In contrast, digital publication producers hesitate to make use of existing services or are unable to find service providers that meet the requirements of a certain type of digital publication. Consequently, these environments are most often set up from scratch, use standards and technologies from the environment in which they were built, and are therefore considered non-reusable by OpenAIRE (Bardi and Manghi 2015a).

Although the notion of standardization as the only valid solution remains in the background of this evaluation, it is the wording that marks a contrast with former evaluations of the same type. This difference is the fact that the situation of stakeholders within the changing landscape of digital publishing is addressed in a more understanding way. Agents not only refuse to use standards and technologies, they are themselves faced with a complicated situation. Accordingly, Castelli, Manghi, and Thanos stress that:

> The problem is mainly cultural, since shifting behavioral norms is a slow process and requires all stakeholders, from librarians and repository managers to data managers, to understand and disseminate the benefits of data citation for researchers. (Castelli, Manghi, and Thanos 2013, sec. 4.1)

In the quote, data citation is meant to be the crucial condition for EPs. Thus, while the authors share the old claim that the main problem for digital publications is the mental state of stakeholders, they differentiate this by acknowledging that changes need to be introduced in a subtle process. Another quote by Manghi et al. (2010), presenting the goals of the OpenAIRE project, shows the consequences of this apparently tiny distinction:

> Experiences ... show that acceptance and broad take-up by the scientific community critically depends on accompanying support mechanisms, ... (Manghi et al. 2010, 33)

Hence, implementers of digital publications started to shift from just demanding standardization to evaluating how to achieve standardization. A major goal of OpenAIRE is to define and develop the aforementioned support mechanisms. Likewise, support mechanisms are a much broader concept than tools for the creation of digital publication concepts. The first quote, furthermore, gives testimony of the fact that OpenAIRE attempts to address specific stakeholders in a specific way.

Castelli, Manghi, and Thanos (2013) look at the situation of data centers and research libraries. In the eyes of the authors, these are the most important stakeholders for the development of digital publications. Besides the uncertainty about future directions mentioned above, they argue that there is another uncertainty about the service profile both institution types would have to provide in the future. Digital publications, so it is argued, require the implementation of completely new services. Castelli, Manghi, and Thanos (2013) stress that it is not clear which stakeholder should include which service, i.e. how specific tasks are distributed within the network of existing stakeholders. In consequence, different stakeholders respond differently, and the already existing heterogeneity in digital publications increases further, resulting in more expensive infrastructure development.

Assante et al. (2015) similarly investigate the role of different types of digital research infrastructures for digital publications. They argue that infrastructures following different purposes are not sufficiently integrated with each other to leverage the real value of the publications that they provide.

The examples clearly demonstrate that OpenAIRE does not seek to promote digital publications by creating new demonstrators or formal models again. This also distinguishes OpenAIRE from its predecessor DRIVER. Instead, it highlights problems that suggest engaging with stakeholders and reconsidering their relationships. Accordingly, Castelli, Manghi, and Thanos (2013, 167) argue that digital publication initiatives need to integrate into larger "eco-systems."

Scaling the Network

Different measures were taken in order to provide orientation and support for stakeholders following the definition of the problem above. Manghi, Bolikowski, et al. (2012) summarize some of these efforts. Accordingly, OpenAIRE tries to "efficiently disseminate best practices, guidelines, initiatives, and events" (sec. 1) and seeks to engage with existing projects such as *DataCite*,[13] *Mendeley*[14], *ORCID*[15], *EUDAT*[16], *REIsearch*[17].

In order to sufficiently achieve this agenda, OpenAIRE establishes a "European helpdesk system" (Rettberg and Schmidt 2012; Manghi et al. 2010; Koukounidou 2017). This helpdesk is a centrally coordinated network of national agents from the research repository domain. According to Manghi et al. (2010), it is used for several purposes. First, being a network, it should facilitate the aforementioned dissemination process; secondly, it should provide help for issues regarding the management of open access repositories and for facilitating the publication of research results in it; finally, the helpdesk should foster relationships with external stakeholders

13 https://www.datacite.org/
14 https://www.mendeley.com/
15 https://orcid.org/
16 https://eudat.eu/
17 http://reisearch.eu/

in order to extend the network of open access publishing stakeholders. The helpdesk explicitly addresses multiple stakeholders and not just repository managers. Among them are also individual researchers as well as research institutions.

The same applies to the *OpenAIRE Guidelines* (OpenAIRE plus 2013; Príncipe et al. 2014). These guidelines consist of three different sections targeting data archives, document repositories and *Current Research Information Systems* (also referred to as CRIS) services[18]. It mainly describes how metadata should be presented by repositories and what metadata formats should be used in order to describe resources in repositories in a machine-readable way. The guidelines aim in two different directions.

One goal is to enable easy harvesting of information by OpenAIRE for the creation of the OpenAIRE platform (see below). Another goal is the definition of a minimal set of best practices and standards which are communicated from above by using the "hierarchical organization" (Manghi, Bolikowski, et al. 2012, sec. 1) of OpenAIRE. By doing so, OpenAIRE addresses the stakeholder's lack of orientation described above. Consequently, Príncipe et al. (2014) note that these guidelines will facilitate the creation of EPs and promise that OpenAIRE will do so on top of collected information.

Scaling Engagement

Guidance and leadership are one way to harmonize the landscape of digital publications. The other one is direct intervention. The last paragraph indicated that OpenAIRE collects digital publication metadata from all over Europe. The platform is supposed to provide an overview of open access publications and European research funding, in line with the general goals of the project described at the beginning of this section.

As a result of this, OpenAIRE is confronted with the same heterogeneity as data centers and repository managers. In this respect, Castelli, Manghi, and Thanos (2013) regret the lack of best practices in data publications. The authors stress that the format of metadata, its granularity and quality vary significantly. Manghi, Bolikowski, et al. (2012) diagnose that the integration of digital resources in a publishing environment struggles with missing information and redundancy. Thus, the orientation returns to a narrative familiar from former publication concepts.

18 CRIS services present information about research activities in Europe. It will be discussed below in further detail.

Kobos et al. (2014) offer detailed insights into the efforts OpenAIRE carried out to process data from repositories. Metadata was not only harmonized and corrected, it was also created by virtue of content mining techniques, applied to resources where such metadata did not exist. The outcome of this curation process is not only the creation of the OpenAIRE platform but an improvement and enhancement of the situation of available publication metadata as such. Since truly digital publications in the eyes of many authors related to OpenAIRE are metadata descriptions of linked published resources, the machine-readable exposure of this metadata automatically impacts the conditions of creating these publications.

Scaling Technology

The harmonization and exposure of information on research publications in Europe is not the only objective of the OpenAIRE platform. As a service on its own, it represents a specific approach to solving the technological issues of digital publications. This approach is generalized and presented by Castelli, Manghi, and Thanos (2013) under the name of *Scholarly Communication Infrastructures* (SCIs). Scholarly Communication Infrastructures is a reaction to the need for extended service requirements in order to create and use digital publications (above).

The main point behind SCIs is a specific response to this problem, because it is claimed that neither data centers nor research repositories should extend their service profile. They should focus on the work they have done before. Instead, a new type of service should be implemented, a service which integrates existing but isolated services. Scholarly Communication Infrastructures is the initiative to organize and harmonize fragmentation of digital publications on a higher level and by infrastructural means.

Castelli, Manghi, and Thanos (2013) present the main ideas of SCIs in a diagram which shows four layers of abstraction and which is presented in a simplified version in figure 4.1. The lowest layer, which could be called the *source layer*, consists of existing stakeholders such as research libraries, data centers, and similar, common workflows as well as digital resources. Each of these provide different content and services, thereby reflecting the current heterogeneous situation. The second and third layer form the SCI approach. First, the *mediation layer* connects the different interfaces by which content and functionality of the first layer are exposed. This allows access to different environments within a new environment. Secondly, in the SCIs' *application layer*, there are three types of services in these layers:

- organization of a consistent access to all the underlying environments,
- harmonization and linking of all of the content metadata from the underlying environments,
- abstraction and exposure of functionality from the underlying services.

The fourth layer consists of scientific stakeholders, already involved in the first layer, but not interacting directly with this layer. Instead, they interact with it by means of the services provided by SCIs.

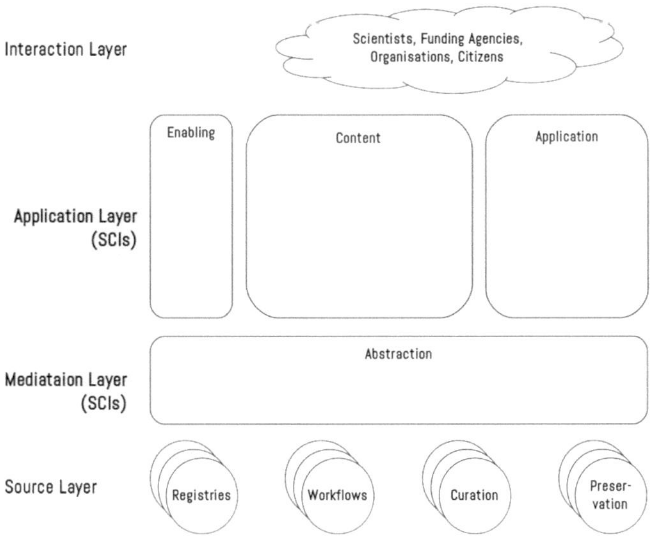

[Figure 4.1] Simplified and slightly modified version of the concept of SCIs as defined in Castelli, Manghi, and Thanos (2013)

A Fallback Solution

While the OpenAIRE portal tries to harmonize and bundle existing environments, the *Zenodo*[19] research repository addresses another problem. In the description of its goals at the beginning of this section, OpenAIRE notably seemed to emphasize article publications. Indeed, the publication of other resource types was considered mainly in the second project phase.

Corresponding literature now also chooses to put a stronger focus on conceptual components of publications, as can be seen in Assante et al.

19 https://zenodo.org/

(2015), or Bardi and Manghi (2015a). This seems reasonable if the project's underlying analysis revealed that the efforts existing at that time had not brought to light the conditions necessary to realize truly digital publications. The fact that most of these issues were social or cultural does not mean that technical and infrastructural issues did not also remain.

Zenodo is a direct intervention in this situation. It is a research repository for the deposition of so-called "orphan" resources (Manghi, Bolikowski, et al. 2012). The term "orphan" denotes resources which have no other place to be stored. The lack of access to appropriate repositories by researchers is one reason for this situation, as highlighted at the beginning of the section. However, the term is not misused when applied to situations in which no repository exists for a specific resource type. Consequently, Zenodo notes on its website that it accepts "all research outputs" and "any file format."

Zenodo contributes to this situation in multiple ways. First, it implements a research repository following the guidelines OpenAIRE seeks to establish. Secondly, it establishes an operational infrastructure for a service that is rare within the scope of its goal. Third, it thereby provides better conditions for the future creation of digital publications, which can make use of its services, its content, and its assured sustainability in a consistent way. Fourth, it extends the OpenAIRE platform by integrating Zenodo in the spirit of SCIs. Finally, it substantiates and materializes a certain notion of digital scholarly publishing which remained silent in earlier activities, but start to be heavily promoted in this situation.

Accordingly, Assante et al. (2015) introduce "modern scientific communication workflows" which are defined by two main criteria. One is to publish "during" the research activities as opposed to "on date" (sec. 4). The other was already addressed in the last paragraphs and states that any type of resource — technical as well as conceptual — should be published. Thus, in the eyes of the authors, modern scientific communication workflows are increasingly "blurring the distinction between research life-cycle and research publishing" (sec. 1).

This model needs the support of a special type of repository yet to be created. The authors call such repositories *science 2.0 repositories*. These repositories are closely integrated with Virtual Research Environments as "the place where research is conducted" (sec. 1). The strong references to themes discussed under the term of e-Science above are obvious. Zenodo is a service which implements a small selection of the ideas of science 2.0 repositories.

Scaling Standardization

Despite these similarities with many digital publication concepts, there is a significant difference. This difference becomes obvious when OpenAIRE changes the focus from infrastructure and ecology of publications back to the structure of publications themselves. The main point of similarity between the publishing process described above and e-Science publication concepts is the notion of a publication that integrates most of the output of an entire research process.

The model of science 2.0 repositories, completely in line with its general approach to resolve obstacles in the creation of digital publications incrementally, provides a pragmatic model for the design process of such publications. For instance, it simplifies the act of single-resource publication, because curating an entire digital publication is more expensive than publishing a single resource. It detaches the description of relationships between resources from publishing these resources in the first place. The full benefit science 2.0 repositories intent to provide will nevertheless be experienceable only if published resources are semantically put together by forming a digital publication as a compound object.

In fact, OpenAIRE creates EPs on its own. More precisely, the project creates and uses specific metadata on publications, collected from research repositories, in order to make connections between single resources. The semantics used by the project are described in the "Data Model of the OpenAIRE Scientific Communication e-Infrastructure" (Manghi, Houssos, et al. 2012). This model is primarily a re-use of existing semantics, namely from DataCite and CRIS (see above). While DataCite focuses on the appropriate citation of digital resources, CRIS provides classes and terms that really connect resources.

As the name suggests, CRIS defines entities and terms that should make it possible to formally describe research activities, their output, and their context. It particularly offers possibilities of expressing which institutions were involved in a research process, the project context, the relevant line of funding, and comparable mostly administrative information. By doing so, EPs in the OpenAIRE portal form broad agent-networks in which research output is the result of socio-economically meaningful actions.

The EPs model of OpenAIRE is consistent with the approach expressed in science 2.0 repositories in two ways. First, it supports the publication of individual research output, independent from publications as compound objects and simultaneous to research itself. Secondly, the semantics that connect resources prefer social relationships in research in favor of any epistemological or methodological relationship found in concepts like ROs. This means that the level of semantic integration of research output scales up with the possibilities and the need of doing so.

It could be argued, however, that this approach just resembles the fact that the projects follow a clear political agenda (above). The semantics of the OpenAIRE model allow monitoring of the impact and success of this agenda. Grassano et al. (2016) evaluate the OpenAIRE infrastructure in just such a way.

Following the same logic, OpenAIRE also made attempts to contribute to the model of digital publications at the end of the second project phase, and after other goals had been pushed forward. In 2014, Bardi and Manghi (2014) presented a significant evaluation of digital publication concepts dating back to the nineties and to MAs. Although it tries to be comprehensive, the presentation still ignores some concepts, mainly those belonging to the humanities. Compared to the same attempt in the DRIVER project, it is nevertheless more consistent and systematic. It does not only pick out some aspects of selected approaches to assert a homologous development, it is precise enough to grasp significant differences. Accordingly, the study aims at "introducing common terminology and classification schemes in order to shed some light and put some order in such a rich but foundationless realm" (265).

The authors try to introduce this terminology without making too many implications. For instance, they try to give orientation to existing approaches by grouping them according to "scientific motivation." These motivations are: "packaging with supplementary material, improving readability and understanding, interlinking with research data, and enabling repetition of experiments" (253).

Despite this attempt, the evaluation clearly reveals its foundation in e-Science and computer science. This becomes even more obvious when not only motivations of publication objects but also components are evaluated. The authors follow the categorical distinction between text and data as description and evidence (241), which appeared in e-Science approaches and which was cemented by the EP model in the preceding DRIVER model. Like DRIVER, it refers to EPs as an overarching concept for digital publications, although its basic elements already exclude some of the concepts presented in this study.

The entanglement between certain practices in research and specific resource types can be found in most of the motivations and components presented by the article. The implicit decisions about which practice corresponds with which resource type also clearly follows the e-Science agenda. Accordingly, the attempt to re-approach EPs differently, lying at the center of many related activities in OpenAIRE, fails when it comes to a conceptualization of EPs themselves.

This conceptualization, nevertheless, is not an end to itself but a means to realize *Enhanced Publication Management Systems* (Bardi and Manghi 2015b; Bardi and Manghi 2015a). The term alludes to *Database Management Systems*, a software environment built around a database in order to organize user and software interactions on data and data models in a database. In the same way, Enhanced Publication Management Systems (also referred to as EPMS) should support and facilitate the creation of EP models and EPs.

The strategy of EPMS is comparable to the one behind SCIs. One the one hand, it accepts that context specific heterogeneity exists, on the other hand it tries to standardize EP under OpenAIRE's specific notion of generic features of digital publications. In the context of EPMS, it led to the proposal of an *Enhanced Publication Data Model Definition Language* (Bardi and Manghi 2015a, sec. 2). They intended to create a consistent starting point for the development of new digital publications and publication environments. This is the point where a self-declared ecological approach to digital publications finally goes back to the more common top-down approach of former concepts.

At the beginning of this section, OpenAIRE was introduced as a project forming part of a general tendency to address social issues of digital publishing over the last years. Indeed, OpenAIRE reflected on the situation of some stakeholders, tried hard to offer multifaceted explanations of obstacles, and tried to work with the situation as it is instead of as it should be from the project's point of view. In this respect, it differs from many former approaches. The value of recognizing and engaging with this situation and its stakeholders, however, remained a means to an end. In other words, OpenAIRE's strategic orientation in this respect is based on the acknowledgment that the creation of models and reference implementations is insufficient for the broader uptake of digital publication objects. In contrast, the main ideas about these objects, their features, and the focus on specific conditions that need to be satisfied for digital publication objects to succeed remain the same as in former approaches from the last phase. These aspects became more and more dominant in the work on SCIs and EPMS.

This is significantly different from the direction taken in HPs. Partnership organizations like the Alliance for Networking Visual Culture were formed because people were convinced that sustainable solutions will arise only in such an inclusive environment, solutions that are not yet known. In HPs, the evaluation of means and end are thus part of the same process. Correspondingly, OpenAIRE falls back on the creation of infrastructure, whereas HPs maintain their emphasis on social organization. Infrastructure creates the boundaries for thematically related future activities. This holds true especially where its creation is so closely connected to research-policy making, and where its funding is set on a continental level. In this respect, the infrastructural approach is an efficient way to steer social processes into a certain direction. For OpenAIRE, this direction and the way to get there is concisely summarized by Castelli, Manghi, and Thanos:

> The idea of enabling a "global scientific communication infrastructure," unifying and giving access in a systematic, discipline-specific, authorized, and reusable way to the whole outcome of world's research, must rely on common practices and standard ways .... (Castelli, Manghi, and Thanos 2013, 167)

Thus, the OpenAIRE approach is indeed a top-down, globally oriented approach, driven by certain ideas about the shape of future scientific communication that are supposedly generic. Moreover, the totality of scholarly communication is conceived of as a derivative of a consistent technological environment.

Data Papers

Compared to OpenAIRE, the concept of *Data Papers* (hereafter referred to as DPs) concentrates on a certain type of publication only. The key aspects highlighted in DPs, however, vary significantly from those promoted in other publication concepts. Obviously, DPs are about the publication of digital data, even if the term "paper" seems strange in this respect. In order to clarify this apparent contradiction, it helps to refer to the working paper of Rees (2010) which was an important stepping stone in the broader adoption of the data paper approach. Rees (2001, 1) states: "A data paper is a publication whose primary purpose is to expose and describe data, as opposed to analyze and draw conclusions from it." This description normally includes a de-referenceable reference to the described dataset in the form of a URI. However, this description still does not reveal why data papers are different in a way that would suffice to include it as a concept of its own. The main argument is the fact that the publication of data itself is only a superficial reason. Common declarations on the value of data sharing are not lacking. Chavan and Penev (2011, 2) highlight the problem of "dark data" (unpublished data), and Robertson et al. (2014, 1) stress the need for massive "data mobilization." Similarly, strategies for the publication of data as a resource existed before, as has become clear throughout the last sections. Accordingly, DPs are perceived in the research community as one specific strategy to publish data in addition to others (Reilly et al. 2011; Garcia-Garcia, Lopez-Borrull, and Peset 2015). Following Pampel and Dallmeier-Tiessen (2014) and Garcia-Garcia, Lopez-Borrull, and Peset (2015), and in line with the present analysis, other strategies publish data as a resource of its own (single-resource) or as an isolated component of a broader publication (ROs, EPs).

Compared with these two approaches, DPs were the latest to appear in the field. Their development was driven significantly by the observation that the situation of data publication is precarious, even though the aforementioned strategies existed already. Thus, Rees (2010, 1) declares that a "data re-use failure" exists. Additionally, Chavan and Penev (2011, 4) quote earlier research in which results show that at the time of writing, only three percent of published research data could actually be located. Consequently, the authors summarize: "However, these efforts are yet to yield any significant results because existing data remain unpublished, undiscovered and thus underused" (Chavan and Penev 2011, 4).

There are several weaknesses in data publication, addressed in greater detail by the concept of DPs, which will receive more attention below. The key aspect of DPs is the fact that most advocates do not consider specific issues to be the main reasons for the aforementioned evaluation. Instead, they argue that the problem resides in a different way of dealing with all these issues. Rees argues:

> We encourage everyone involved in data sharing and reuse to take a holistic view of the data reuse problem. The attention that the various pieces of the problem are receiving is welcome, but it's not just about review, or publication, or deposit guidelines, or archiving. All parts of the system must work together if we are to create the incentives needed for adequate publication .... (Rees 2010, 3)

Thus, the initial statement that DPs stand out in the area of digital publication concepts was made because of this shift of perspective.

Rees' paper is a working paper, published in 2010. The context was his engagement with the Creative Commons initiative mentioned above. This working paper was the first attempt to promote the concept of DPs on a broader scale. There were two articles the year before, presenting comparable initiatives (Callaghan et al. 2009; Newman and Corke 2009). These initiatives, however, focused on specific environments, i.e. meteorology and robotics. These efforts were furthermore linked to a concrete project and an existing journal. A significant step towards the later success of the DP concept was the cooperation between the publisher *Pensoft*[20] and the *Global Biodiversity Information Facility*[21], presented by Chavan and Penev (2011). This initiative produced one of the most successful data paper projects as yet. It is thus reasonable to argue that 2010 marks the beginning of the DPs approach.

Garcia-Garcia, Lopez-Borrull, and Peset (2015), Candela et al. (2015) and Chen (2017) made the first attempts to summarize the recent history of DPs.[22] While the first survey presents examples and compares submission guidelines, the second and third extracts key features in a more systematic form. In contrast to the last paragraphs, Garcia-Garcia, Lopez-Borrull, and Peset (2015) set the starting point of DPs in the year 1956. More precisely, the authors include six journals founded between 1956 and 2002 in the concept of DPs. The reason for this deviation is the fact that the authors do not focus on any technological linkage between a dataset and a paper but instead on the main purpose of describing a data set.

The accentuation of different facets of the DP approach across projects is a general phenomenon in this research field (Candela et al. 2015). It does not reflect inconsistency, but is an immediate consequence of its general approach. In total, Candela et al. (2015) count 116 *data journals* already in 2015 that permit the submission of DPs or exclusively publish DPs. The subject matters range from health sciences, life sciences, physical sciences, social sciences, and humanities to multidisciplinary journals. Additionally, stakeholders like *Thompson Reuter* begin to show interest in the DP format (Force et al. 2016).

20 https://pensoft.net/

21 https://www.gbif.org/

22 A list of data journals, i.e. journals which focus on publishing DPs was temporally curated by Akers (2014).

A Family Resemblance Between Different Key Functions

The next paragraphs will summarize how different functions of DPs are accentuated in different environments. This will help to elaborate a more substantial idea of DPs. It will also clarify the small distinctions which led to different evaluations of the temporal frame of DPs.

Rees' quote from the beginning of this section indicated that the concept of DPs is often described in a very minimalistic way. Rees highlights exactly one function of DPs, the need to contextualize data sets that are available on the web. Newman and Corke are even more minimalistic by stressing that:

> A data paper should provide a crisp statement of how the data was collected and a summary of its salient properties and intended audience. (Newman and Corke 2009, 1)

In this respect DPs have the purpose of bridging an information gap between articles that present research results on top of a dataset and metadata about this dataset, which in turn might be available in the corresponding data repository. The main argument behind this function is the claim that neither resource provides the type of information necessary to reuse the dataset efficiently. Filling this gap with information is the content function of DPs.

Newman and Corke further writes that beyond the necessary properties to fulfill this function:

> ... data papers will be treated in the same fashion as regular papers, undergoing the standard peer-review process and appearing in print in regular journal issues, and authors should expect their data papers to be cited just as regular papers are. (Newman and Corke 2009, 1)

Chavan and Penev (2011, 3) similarly state that the creation of DPs should require as few technological skills and resources as possible. Furthermore, the creation and publishing workflow of DPs should be closely connected to existing stakeholders and publishing processes. By doing so, advocates of the DP approach hope to develop data publication practices more efficiently than has been the case for more ambitious attempts before. This function of DPs could also be called the embedding function of DPs.

Embedding for now takes the form of conceptual congruence with historical article publications. However, the main point addressed here is not the form of the article but the already organized social environment existing around this form. This fact becomes more evident by analyzing more ambitious DP projects, such as the *Biodiversity Data Journal*. In the context of this journal, the publisher Pensoft developed a sophisticated authoring tool called the *Pensoft Writing Tool* (Smith et al. 2013).

One of the major benefits of this tool is the ability to distribute different tasks in the context of technologically very ambitious data publications across different stakeholders, and within existing stakeholder roles. The development of the tool is contrasted with data publication strategies that requires stakeholders to be technologically specialized themselves (Chavan and Penev 2011, 2), or sophisticated infrastructure such as in OpenAIRE (Robertson et al. 2014, 2). A "data paper enables a division of labor" (Chavan and Penev 2011, 9).

Accordingly, the embedding function does not mean that only a few things should be changed. Actually, the Pensoft Writing Tool provides a lot of automated processes for including features of SPs and HPs. Embedding means that the design of DPs is intended to activate stakeholders and resources where they currently are, in order to advance data publication and digital publishing. Hence, the creation of authoring tools like the Pensoft Writing Tool or the *GBIF Integrated Publishing Toolkit* (Robertson et al. 2014) are not only ways to make the creation of a new type of publication easier. They are active interventions into a publishing ecology, for the sake of better connecting its pieces. Compared to OpenAIRE, this intervention is neither top-down nor motivated by policy (Smith et al. 2013).

Another closely connected function is the scaling function of DPs, comparable to the OpenAIRE approach. By starting with the simplest idea, consisting of only changing the topic and content of articles, the level of innovation introduced for specific DPs can be defined in a flexible way. DPs exist on a scale of innovation that adapts to the conditions found in a specific context. Depending on the capabilities of a publisher, for instance, the size of the data and authors' access to it is sometimes embedded in the paper, stored in a repository owned by the publisher, or in an official data archive (Garcia-Garcia, Lopez-Borrull, and Peset 2015).

Data Papers are sometimes also published as printed articles (Newman and Corke 2009), as websites[23], as a parsable "metadata documents" (Chavan and Penev 2011), and sometimes all options exist together as in HPs. An overview of similar variations of DPs is offered by Candela et al. (2015). Together with the goal of embedding the concept of DPs into social reality, the idea of scaling enables to "downstream" (Robertson et al. 2014, 5)

23 http://dhcommons.org/journal/

technological sophistication without preventing it. With downstreaming, the authors refer to a stepwise enrichment of DPs with features commonly discussed in the field of digital publishing, a process which takes place while DPs move from the author across other stakeholders in the publishing process to specific environments with specific needs.

Another feature of DPs, of particular interest for some authors, is the fact that DPs create a layer of abstraction among datasets. Therefore, these authors also sometimes call DPs *Overlay Papers* (Moyle and Polydoratou 2007; Callaghan et al. 2009).[24] This function does not introduce something completely different compared to the aforementioned functions. However, it is a generalization of an aspect implicit to the other functions.

By highlighting this function, the possible scope for the application of DPs can also be extended. More precisely, authors like Callaghan et al. (2009) or Whyte et al. (2013) propose that this type of article can also be used to create articles about software and models, among others. In fact, many online journals appearing in the last years had this very purpose. Especially in the humanities, publication series like DH Commons Journal, or RIDE (see also Steinkrüger 2016) give evidence of the success of this approach.

Callaghan et al. define the function of their overlay journal as followed:

> The overlay journal database itself consists of a number of overlay documents, which are structure documents created to annotate another resource with information on the quality of the resource. (Callaghan et al. 2009, sec. Overlay Journals)

Apart from illustrating the overlay function of DPs, the quote also addresses another set of arguments for why this abstraction is necessary. It has been mentioned before that the discourse on DPs also concerns specific data publication problems, despite changing the whole perspective on data publication issues itself. Here, one of the concrete problems is the lack of assessment of the data meant to be published.

Callaghan et al. (2009) make no exception here. There is no article about DPs that does not stress that DPs are a means of offering necessary review and quality control for resources other than text publications. From Callaghan et al. (2009) and Rees (2010), to Chavan and Penev (2011), to the DH Commons Journal and RIDE, each initiative would confirm that these

24 An overview of different terms used to denominate the concept of DPs is presented by Candela et al. (2015, 1752-1753)

publications “bridge the ‘evaluation gap’” (Jackson 2014, 544) between making something accessible and considering it a fully published resource.

Similar to the issue of quality is that of credit. In most contributions about DPs “the lack of professional reward structures of incentives” (Chavan and Penev 2011, 4) is addressed as a, if not the major obstacle for the implementation of successful data publication practices. Accordingly, Callaghan et al. (2009) present results from a survey in which sixty-seven percent of researchers said that they would publish data if reliable reward mechanisms existed.

Such a credit system requires that the creation and curation of data can be rewarded independently from the presentation of research results in a common article, and also from the act of deriving research results from a dataset. Thus, data publication requires a more specific attribution system, sometimes called “micro-attribution” (Candela et al. 2015, 1754) in its extreme form. Data Papers try to support this development by exposing a publication which permits rewarding the creation and curation of a dataset independently from other scientific achievements.

Both quality-control and rewarding address publications as important means to arrange the research as a socially organized space. Data Papers stand out compared to many of the concepts that have been discussed in the last chapter, by putting related issues first, and by the strategy they choose in order to achieve this arrangement.

While the ethics of “radical sharing” in approaches close to e-Science discourage any attempt to decide whether publications are worth publishing, this decision constitutes a crucial condition for the success of data publishing in the viewpoint of DPs. Additionally, DPs complete this task strategically by review and selection, in contrast to approaches like NPs in which the social field of research is supposed to organize itself. Therefore, DPs tend to carry out a social management function. The underlying question is how much a process that considers itself innovative must abstract from the materiality of technology, the unit of information, the logic of sharing, and other aspects, so that digital publications might be better received.

In contrast, Candela et al. (2015) accentuate the linkage function. In their survey on DPs, cited here several times already, the authors complain that there is a “lack of standards in this area” (1752). Standardization of DPs is conceived as a necessary step to create better conditions for data publications. In order to achieve such standardization, they present an entity-relationship-model, as the DRIVER project has done for EPs. In this model the structure of DPs is related to the structure of traditional articles (see figure 4.2).

Consequently, the data paper is a subclass of the common journal article form. The one thing that distinguishes it from this form is its connectedness to a data resource, as shown in the figure. Framing DPs like this obviously implies more than making the link feature of DPs more understandable. It suggests a certain judgment which becomes transparent in the summary of the survey. In this summary, DPs are described as a concept that lags behind other concepts developed earlier (1761). The authors suggest that DPs should borrow ideas from EPs in future versions, to overcome the problems of "no, slow, incomplete, inaccurate, or unmodifiable communication" (1760).

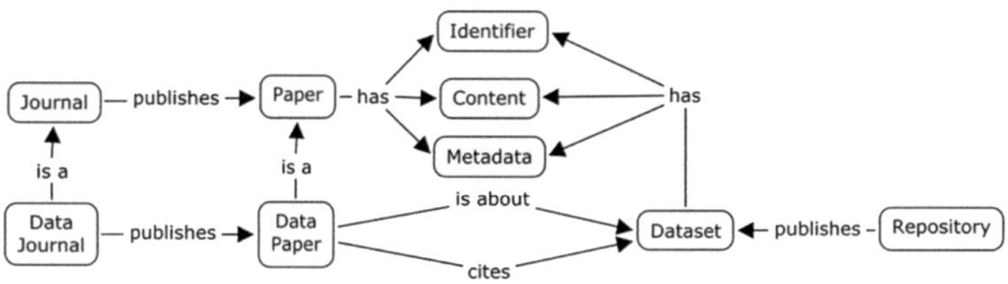

[Figure 4.2] Data Papers in an UML view by Candela et al. (2015)

The critique that DPs are a concept not worthy of further development has already been raised. In 2013, Callaghan defended the DP against accusations such as their being a "soon-to-be-obsolete stepping stone to something better." In light of the overview of different goals and functions of DPs, it is now possible to assess this critique better.

First, the original argument, that DPs lack conceptual standardization, misses the whole point. Social embeddings and context-aware technical flexibility are the most important aspects, conceptually opposed to the idea of formal consistency and strictness. With this priority, the concept of DPs became successful after many other approaches putting a technological model first have failed to create impact. The existence and success of Data Papers is a testimony of this failure.

Secondly, the misunderstanding of the context of DPs leads to a confusing model of DPs. The point is not only that a formal model of DPs has little to offer. In fact, the inclusion of two link relations does offer little compared to the written evaluation of the last paragraphs. It conceals the whole metaphorical meaning of these links, not just linking texts with data but in the end also stakeholders, communities, and knowledge cultures.

Correspondingly, Parsons and Fox (2013) ask: "Is Data Publication the Right Metaphor?" They argue that the term data publication does not well represent the distinct ways in which research communities perceive and use data. The different ways, however, in which DPs are implemented and which are indicated in greater detail below, show that this variety has its place within existing DPs. It is specifically not something that had to be overcome.

Third, the critique of a lack of innovation is misleading because DPs seek to establish practices of innovation instead of presenting ideas that express a high level of innovative thought. Data Papers are significantly more successful than other digital publishing concepts. Accordingly, Assante et al. write in their conclusion that:

> ... data journals are now an established phenomenon in the scientific literature. In fact, the number of published data papers and data journals is rapidly growing; 23.5% of the existing data papers were published in 2013. (Assante et al. 2015, 1760)

However, it is not only the number of publication channels for DPs giving evidence of their success. The fact that also stakeholders like *Thomson Reuters* make heavy use of DPs to feed their Data Citation Index (Force et al. 2016), as well as the number of different disciplines in which the concept of DPs is adopted support this judgment.

Additionally, there are very innovative DPs in the sense that is used by Candela et al. (2005). The Biodiversity Data Journal, for instance, uses filled out metadata templates to generate written parts in a manuscript on the fly, (Smith et al. 2013; Robertson et al. 2014) thereby automatizing the writing process. The semantic tagging of entities in the paper, similar to SPs, is semi-automatically taking place within the authoring environment provided by the publisher Pensoft. Information is finally extracted from the DP once it is published and exposed as data on its own (Smith et al. 2013, 8). Thereby, this specific example of a DP comprises a whole sequence of integrated and highly sophisticated innovations, going from datasets to articles to processed standardized meta-data. Although it is not the purpose of DPs to comply with this notion of innovation, it is not true that DPs cannot provide it if it fits in with the respective publishing environment.

A Family Resemblance Between Different Implementations

The last argument draws attention to another facet of DPs. As mentioned previously, DPs are not meant to establish a new fixed standard publication format. Obviously, this means that there are many different DP implementations. While the aforementioned Biodiversity Journal complies with many ideas from the field of e-Science, the other examples mentioned above suggest different preferences. In fact, DPs are used by stakeholders to promote a variety of ideas depending on the stakeholders' priorities.

In Rees' working paper, the relatively simple definition of DPs is followed by a very detailed list of recommendations. These recommendations suggest using open standards for a formal description of DPs, and putting particular emphasis on licensing of datasets in the public domain. As a member of Creative Commons, this focus is a reasonable step. Other publishers of DPs show less interest in this specific issue.

The DP concept presented by Newman and Corke (2009) includes the publication of DPs as printed articles. Mostly, DPs are published online, and many take a hybrid approach. The Biodiversity Data Journal print-, PDF-, and xml-versions are all offered at once. The connection between datasets and articles may similarly look very different. Some DPs even embed chunks of the dataset they describe, others are automatically updated when relevant chunks of the corresponding dataset are updated. Most often, there is a link with a persistent PID which leads to the dataset, but sometimes DPs policies do not require this, either. Some DPs additionally experiment with new types of reviewing, more precisely the open peer review approach[25]. Many of the differences of DP implementations are summarized by Candela et al. (2015).

Data Papers as Boundary Objects

Instead of creating isolated reference implementations, DPs provoke innovation from within the existing publishing ecologies.

The summary of aspects and functions of DPs has made clear how much the concept is committed to the idea of enabling innovation in scholarly publishing instead of just presenting an innovative idea. These are two different motivational needs which need to be distinguished clearly.

25 Open peer review is a set of alternative propositions in order to make the peer review process more transparent. Open peer review may include among other things that the review process happens online, that the reviews are published together with the publication, or that authors have the ability to interact with reviewers.

Otherwise, the assessment of DPs is not able to grasp their most valuable features. This is the problem of the evaluation by Candela et al. (2015). If the key aspect of DPs is the provision of a link, as the authors suggest, then this link connects far more than a text resource with a data resource.

Data Papers link stakeholders to stakeholders, different ways of perceiving and using data, data with metadata, different ambitions, and of course also different ideas of how publishing will change. Regarding this final aspect it is not surprising that it is possible to find key features of other publication concepts in one or the other instance of DPs. In this section, SPs, like tagging, the existence of DPs across different formats as in HPs, and the automatization of its creation process as in APs was mentioned explicitly. Weilenmann (2014) furthermore discusses DPs in terms of new forms of information units as well, which is reminiscent of the argument of MAs. Data Papers are indeed a hybrid concept. They are not aimed at imposing a standard but at creating better conditions for standardization in digital publishing. Thus, it misses the point to demand a more standardized version of DPs as has been done by Candela et al. (2015).

In the end, DPs also do connect the past of publishing with the future. By virtue of being a hybrid concept, they function like a boundary object[26] of which different stakeholders and research communities can be a part. Therefore, it does not surprise that different authors define a different period for the emergence of DPs. It also fits well in this context that Rees (2010) encourages writing DPs about datasets that were created in the past and are not available in digital form.

Like HPs, DPs stand out by the strong emphasis they put on cultural and social aspects of publishing. The difference is that DPs as boundary objects are still a hybrid concept. It is a concept used to mobilize the community around scholarly publishing. In the case of HPs, things are the other way around. Hybrid Publishing is an attempt to mobilize the community so that new sustainable forms of publishing might be forged.

26 The concept of boundary objects, stemming from sociology and information science, is an object that is both flexible enough to adapt to the specific situation of different socio-cultural contexts and stable enough to share an identifiable idea across these contexts. As such, it is an object that is perfectly suited for linking different communities together. For further details on the concept refer to Star and Griesemer (1989).

Self-Contained Publications

The final concept in the current history of digital publication formats could be called Self-Contained Publications (hereafter referred to as SCPs). At the beginning of the second decade of the new millennium, the ongoing success of the PDF format, despite all efforts to establish new publication formats, led to a systematic evaluation of its strengths. According to Pettifer et al. (2011, 213) around eighty percent of digital publications were still in PDF format.

A comprehensive overview of strengths is offered by Attwood et al. (2010), Pettifer et al. (2011), and Willinsky, Garnett, and Pan Wong (2012). According to them, PDFs are reliably resistant to legal and technological changes, as well as changes of the content itself. They can be used personally, on a local machine, and offline by researchers. They are built on top of a mature technology associated with a plethora of tools for their creation and consumption. The presentation of the content is most often carefully designed in terms of layout rules benefiting from a long history of reading experiences. Relatively standardized workflows exist for the creation of PDFs in the publishing process between researcher and publisher. According to Willinsky, Garnett, and Pan Wong (2012, sec. Conclusion), this is not the case for other publication formats, especially SPs.

In an attempt to explain the success of the PDF, Pettifer et al. (2011) discuss the state of the discourse on digital publishing in relation to the image *Ceci n´est pas une pipe*[27] by René Magritte. In the same way in which the image title seeks to highlight the difference between an object and a certain representation, people should not confuse publications as real objects and publications as abstract concepts. The authors distinguish between works, expressions of such works, and their manifestations. A work is an abstract entity which may have several expressions. Each expression is realized while having distinct goals in mind.

The above listed benefits of PDFs address specific usage patterns and publishing requirements. Other formats address different patterns and requirements. The main claim of the paper is that no technical format as such should be confused with the concept of a publication. Digital publishing in particular offers and requires expressions of publications that aim at very different usage scenarios. The lack of success of new publication formats is due to their goal of replacing the PDF and to the devaluation of specific advantages of the PDF over other formats.

27 "This is not a pipe" (author's translation)

Putting it more concisely, this line of argument is similar to the approach of HPs. The consequences are very different, however. According to Attwood et al. (2010, 569), many of the aforementioned benefits result from the fact that a PDF is a "self-contained" document. All its components, information what to do with them, and how to render and present them are part of the same object or more precisely the same file. A PDF packages all these things in a way that is very hard to modify. In fact, PDFs are even capable of storing computer code. It is not hard to see that these characteristics fundamentally oppose main principles of SPs, ROs, and LPs among others. However, as Willinsky, Garnett, and Pan Wong put it:

> If we were being cynical, we could easily suggest that it is exactly PDF's stodgy inflexibility that has borne out its success, and we will for that matter always have some need for a stodgy, inflexible document. (Willinsky, Garnett, and Pan Wong 2012, sec. Conclusion)

Contributions in this section therefore all build upon the idea of Self-Contained Publications.

Self-Containedness and Emulation

Pettifer et al. (2011) insist that data should be stored in the PDF and not just referenced there. Under names such as *Utopia Documents* (Attwood et al. 2010), or *interactive PDFs* (Labtiva Inc. 2015), PDF-like publications are created that try to implement some of the features proposed in other publication formats within the PDF framework. These initiatives mostly start by making changes on the application level (reading software and authoring tools) and then on the format level. Significantly, approaches like the one by Willinsky, Garnett, and Pan Wong (2012) even try to show how a certain progress can be achieved just by using the existing potentials of PDFs differently and without any change to the format.

The two main points behind the line of argument by Pettifer et al. have some weaknesses. On the one hand, a PDF is not really self-contained. It still needs software to be presented. On the other hand, the point of embracing multiple expressions of publications instead of pushing a specific expression is not completely consistent with extending the scope of PDFs themselves.

However, the use of the term self-containedness, as introduced by the authors, is problematic itself. It is hard to imagine any digital publication that does not need some type of additional software environment in order to function. Self-Contained Publications are thus not really self-contained, but focus on the development of publications that allow a much higher degree of self-containedness. Regarding the diversity of expressions, it needs to be said that the authors just use this argument to strengthen a publication format which had become the symbol of what needs to be overcome.

The enhancement of PDFs, furthermore, is not a complete refutation of the diversity argument. As opposed to all other formats, the PDF became a standard because it builds much more upon the long history of print publications. There are fewer elements in this history which other formats can refer back to, and thus also fewer existing supportive mechanisms and organizational means for these formats to benefit from. Its very maturity and level of adoption compared to other solutions (see below) are the reasons why the authors have chosen it.

Scientific Publication Packages, ROs, and related formats had already integrated software as a key resource into the publication. Building upon the idea of linked open data, they nonetheless do not include software in a self-contained manner. Yet in 2012, Zhao et al. (2012) present a survey which shows that at that time, eighty percent of ROs from the myExperiment portal could not be used any longer because the computational environment in which they had been created was not reproducible. Meng and Thain (2017, 705) also refer to this issue as the "workflow decay." Boettiger (2015, 72) similarly remarks that reproducible research, despite all these attempts, is not realized due to issues like unmaintained software, lack of documentation, and "barriers to adoption and reuse in existing solutions."

Such experiences also initiated a development process of SCPs in e-Science domains. Most of these formats make use of so-called *emulation*. Put simply, emulation is the ability of an operating system to emulate a specific software environment within itself, such as another operating system.[28] With some technological assistance it is possible at any point in time to save the state of an entire operating system to a file. This file is most often called an image. When image files are opened on a computer capable of emulation, the user is presented with the very same operating system in the state in which it was saved on the original computer.

28 The term emulation is not used in the strict way that complies with the subtle distinctions between this concept and comparable concepts like virtualization and containerization among others from the field of computer science. Here it is used instead as an umbrella concept for all these approaches in order to prevent the reader from having to deal with difficulties that are not crucial for the present work's line of argument.

Publications as images do not only allow publishing of content, but also of what is required to open, render, or execute the content. Of course, a program to open and run the image itself is still needed. The issue nevertheless shifts to a higher level of abstraction, as has been noted before. The publication is self-contained, because it puts all resources, and also all applications, programming libraries, and compilers among other things into one file in order to interact with the resources. Additionally, it could be argued that this higher level of technological abstraction reduces technical heterogeneity.

The shift to emulation and the results from the survey confirm from an opposite point of view what Willinsky, Garnett, and Pan Wong (2012) said about the inflexibility of the PDF. A certain degree of inflexibility, or better stability, appears necessary for publication formats to meet their requirements. Often, earlier projects have tried to achieve this stability by attempting to propose technological or semantic standards for the structure of publications. The proliferation of publication formats described in this work, together with insights like the one by Zhao et al. (2012, see also above), suggest that the predicted standardization process has not adequately taken place. Liew et al. (2016, 66:1) see the SCP approach as a response to "the complexity and diversity of applications, the diversity of analysis goals, the heterogeneity of computing platforms, and the volume and distribution of data."

Besides maturity and self-containedness, there is another interesting facet of SCPs. In the same way Pettifer et al. (2011) highlight the merits of PDFs in contrast to approaches appearing more digitally native, the authors stress the necessity of narrative form and illustrative content in publications. Their critique is explicitly directed at Mons' considerations on NPs, but addresses any initiative that privileges computational features of digital publications. They elegantly turn the argument upside down that these elements only compensate the absence of data and experiments in historical publications. They point out that only the worst programmers leave code uncommented. This is so because code itself is hard to read and understand even for the people who wrote it. Thus, code, data, text, and illustrations among others should not just be perceived as serving a purpose in their own right. They should be taken as different means to serve one and the same purpose — transmitting scientific results and truths — and therefore combined as such.

In fact, such an integrated global model exists since the early eighties even in computer science. This model is called *literate programming* (Knuth 1984).

While early models of literate programming mainly addressed the issue of code documentation, later adoptions extended it to a unique way of computing and for the creation of digital publications. In so-called *electronic notebooks*, executable code alternates with layouted text, diagrams, and rich media with equal rights and in a narrative linear way. These notebooks are used heavily both in computer science and by researchers who use computation in research.

The popularity of projects like the *jupyter notebook* (see figure 4.3; Perez and Granger 2013), the *beaker notebook*[29], but also projects like *knitr*[30] give evidence about the success of this approach.

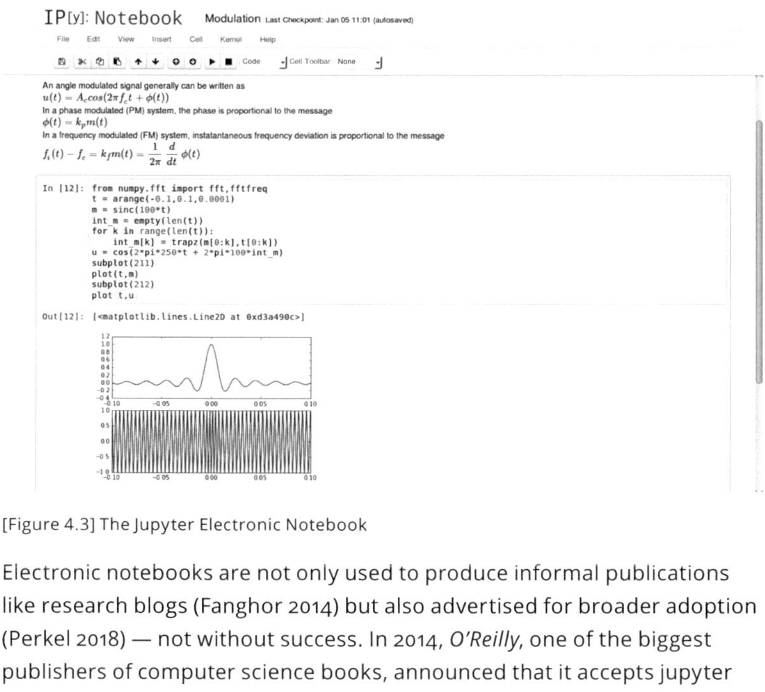

[Figure 4.3] The Jupyter Electronic Notebook

Electronic notebooks are not only used to produce informal publications like research blogs (Fanghor 2014) but also advertised for broader adoption (Perkel 2018) — not without success. In 2014, *O'Reilly*, one of the biggest publishers of computer science books, announced that it accepts jupyter notebooks from authors as templates for books to print (Odewahn, Kelley, and Madsen 2014; Odewahn 2015). Additionally, the authoring platform *Authorea*[31] which enables direct submission of authored publications to publishers from earth sciences, life sciences and astronomy permits embedding jupyter notebooks into the manuscript. Thereby jupyter

29 http://beakernotebook.com/
30 https://yihui.name/knitr/
31 https://www.authorea.com/

notebooks are part of publishing workflows "at each of the top 100 research universities worldwide" (jupytercon 2017).

Curiously enough, the jupyter notebook was also originally invented to provide "an open source framework for interactive, collaborative, and reproducible scientific computing and education" (Perez and Granger 2013; Wittek 2014; Thomas et al. 2016). Nevertheless, instead of separating articles from data and software the jupyter notebook attempts to achieve this goal by tying all these elements more closely together.

However, this digression to electronic notebooks was not just intended to demonstrate that arguments similar to those provided by Pettifer et al. exist in e-Science, too. In fact, electronic notebooks have recently become SCPs in their own right. Originally, they did not include the software libraries required by the code in the notebook in order to function. They provided an environment that can make use of such libraries if they exist on a computer in order to execute parts of code in place, or more precisely inside the notebook. In this scenario, electronic notebooks may run into the same problems outlined by Zhao et al. (2012) and others.

To prevent this, projects using electronic notebooks for publishing similarly recommend emulation strategies. O'Reilly, accordingly, proposes a so-called *Docker*[32] container which does not only contain the electronic notebook, but also the whole computational environment used by the notebook in order to create a "self-contained" environment (Cito et al. 2017, 323). A comparable path is taken by the project *Binder*[33].

On the one hand, electronic notebooks have become SCPs. On the other hand, SCP projects which originally had nothing to do with the approach of electronic notebooks use literate programming concepts to circumscribe their key features. Therefore, SCPs do not only tone down the distinction between the content of publications and its carrier, but also the hierarchy between different modes of representation. It could even be said that SCPs implicitly use some of the arguments of TPs. This is important because electronic notebooks and emulation are deeply linked to e-Science and computer science, where, as was shown already, text has been widely treated as documentation. Accordingly, Welch et al. stress:

> The preservation community could benefit from widening its collecting scope to include complex objects such at scientific desktops, databases, machines running networked business processes or

32 https://www.docker.com/

33 http://mybinder.org

> computers .... Such objects are not just interesting in their own right but also have the potential to provide a more immersive and contextually rich experience than simpler digital object. (Welch et al. 2012)

Up to this point, two different strategies (PDF and emulation) to achieve the goal of self-containedness have been introduced. Other strategies could be described which try to achieve similar goals. However, it is a comparison between the different types of emulation techniques that offers most meaningful insights into the most recent state of digital publications. Formally, such differences could be split into two groups: differences pertaining to the questions of at which point self-containedness begins, and those of applying different mechanisms to produce self-containing objects. Santana-Perez et al. (2017) and Nüst et al. (2017) also provide an overview of scholarly publications using emulation, but one that is less systematic than is intended for the next section.

What Is a Self-Contained Object?

The question concerning the nature of self-contained objects is a question of scope as well as of content type. What does a publication need to include in order to not significantly depend on resources out of its control? Definitions vary between extremely simple and highly sophisticated. In the first category, there are contributions like the one by Pebesma, Nüst, and Bivand (2012), who propose to use the concept of a *dependency tree* coming from software package management in the UNIX world. Put simply, a dependency tree is a description of software packages that need to be available in a software environment so that another software can be executed. A formal description of the additional software installed during the process of installing the original piece of software can be read by another system in order to reproduce the necessary environment for the presentation[34] of a publication on another computer.

A list of names and version numbers of required software is a simple thing. The other side regarding scope is represented by approaches like *Paper Mâché* (Brammer et al. 2011) and *SHARE* (Mazanek 2011; van Gorp and Mazanek 2011). The underlying strategy behind these projects has already been discussed. These projects create images of so-called virtual machines which contain the "frozen" version of a whole computer system, providing it

34 Here presentation includes both running computational experiments as well as making data sensually perceptible, for instance, by showing a page or visualization on the screen.

as a transferable and copyable file. The approach is accordingly often called full virtualization[35].

Dependency trees and virtual machine images could be understood as the two poles of the scope in which it is reasonably possible to discuss the theme of self-containedness. However, it is the inclusion of other concepts such as *sandboxes* and *containers* through which this discussion gains theoretical value. The benefit of sandboxes for SCPs is highlighted by Meng et al. (2015). In principle, sandboxes are working spaces on a computer which are gradually isolated and independent from the underlying operating system. As such, they have their own disk space and configuration, but may still use core services and software of the operating system. One use-case for sandboxes is software development, where it is used to produce an environment important for the software project that does however not affect the operating system. It is possible, for instance, that a software project needs another version of a software library than the operating system. Sandboxes allow use of a specific version in the development process without the need to remove the version on which the operating system depends.

Sandboxes can be reproduced on another operating system. The things they are not able to reproduce are the components of the operating system that the sandbox requires in order to function. Following Meng et al. (2015), this is the point where containers come into play. Containers do not contain a whole operating system but only those software components crucial in order to run the main applications in the container. Accordingly, this approach is called para-virtualization. Regarding SCPs, Pham et al. (2015) call containers a lightweight virtualization approach. Containers recently became a very successful approach in many areas in computer science. Besides the authors mentioned above, Odewahn (2015), Cito, Ferme, and Gall (2016), and Boettiger (2015) propose containers as part of the concept of SCPs.

The term lightweight indicates one of the reasons that led to a reasonable shift to containers instead of virtual machine images. All authors highlight that virtualization is expensive, meaning it needs a lot of disk space and computational resources. Consequently, this issue poses the question of

35 The reader should remember that this study, for the purpose of simplicity, refrains from making all the subtle distinctions behind some of the concepts in this field of research. Here, it is possible to equate virtualization with emulation. Full virtualization refers to the fact that what is virtualized really is an entire operating system.

what exactly is necessary for a reproducible publication. This question is in turn just another way to ask what self-containedness is.

Correspondingly, Zheng and Thain (2015) describe four different scenarios for containerization in which the boundaries of each container are set differently. Terminologically interesting is the fact that boundary is defined by the term's *isolation* and *consistency*. Although these terms have domain specific meaning in computer science, such meaning is easily transferable to a theoretical discussion on what it means to create a self-contained object. Finally, the authors measure the "costs," i.e. the necessary efforts to produce SCPs, for each container type.

Indeed, in recent years the discussion on self-containedness turned theoretical within the SCPs community itself. Cranmer et al. (2015), who evaluate different containerization strategies for the *ATLAS*[36] archive, introduce the difference between reproducibility and replicability. The latter addresses a strategy in which the underlying technologies of a publication are constantly updated and not conserved. The goal is to not reproduce the same software environment, but to assure that the supposed key aspects of a publication can be presented in an always up-to-date software environment. With this distinction, the question of the identity of publications completely shifts away from the publication as a physical — in the sense of being stored on a hard drive — object to publications as ideal things.

Likewise, Meng et al. (2015, 139) discuss the distinction between repeatability and reproducibility. While the first term describes the capacity to regenerate the same results again and again, the second concept emphasizes the capability of changing parameters within the same set-up that was originally published. Arguing that such set-ups are the real outputs of a research process, the question of what the core of the publication really is once more put into a new context. Welch et al. conclude their contribution with questions such as:

> What exactly comprises the object which is to be preserved authentically? Are the numerous operations to reduce the original disk image size identity transformations? Could the preservation of the integrity of the preservation target's content be proven in an automated way? How much change of the original image on the block level is acceptable? (Welch et al. 2012, 278)

36 https://atlas.cern/

How to Obtain Self-Containedness

In consequence to different definitions of self-containedness, different strategies exist for identifying all necessary components. On a general level, such strategies distinguish between imaging, tracking, and describing. Additionally, strategies could be further categorized into imperative and declarative approaches.[37]

Imaging approaches were discussed at the beginning of this section (see also Welch et al. 2012). Automation strategies try to track computational research processes in a computational manner. A piece of software that monitors a given research process is supposed to identify and record any of its involved elements. As the boundaries of SCPs vary, so does the monitoring software. Some approaches include the development of software specifically designed for creating SCPs (Pham et al. 2015), others use proven standard software such as the UNIX tool *ptrace* (Meng et al. 2015).

Descriptive strategies create SCPs in a manual fashion. Boettiger (2015), for instance, outlines the usage of the Docker containerization software for reproducible research. He highlights that for the creation of such containers, all that is needed is a small *shell script*.[38]

Assembling a list of commands to create a container is one approach. Obviously, it depends on a specific computational environment such as Docker to be functional. Another approach is to use so-called declarative semantics. These semantics describe the features of the expected output environment, not the steps required to get that environment. Accordingly, different technological environments can interpret such descriptions in their own way. Boettiger (2015, 73) points out that the "black box" virtualization is seen as a challenge to the ideas of transparency in science by its critics, anyway. Declarative descriptions help to overcome this situation.

The use of declarative semantics for the description of computer environments is detailed by Santana-Perez et al. (2014) and Santana-Perez et al. (2017). The authors remark that there is a plethora of virtualization and containerization software already, and that therefore a standardized model is necessary to be able to negotiate between projects. Furthermore, the articles demonstrate how the use of such models in research can enable

37 For a different type of classification see Nüst et al. (2017)

38 A shell script is basically a small computer program using a UNIX shell environment. In this context it contains a sequence of commands written by the author of the publication and parsed by a computer to create the container environment.

purely descriptive, reproducible digital publications. Purely descriptive here means that the software and other resources are not part of the resulting publications any longer. In the context of this work, it is possible to say that such publications are extended versions of ROs. They do not only contain a description of a workflow and its resources, but also of the environment in which this workflow takes place. Although this approach addresses virtualization, it just remains a description. Therefore, it is not really an SCP anymore. It nevertheless it is one outcome of the path of SCPs.

Nüst et al. (2016) and Nüst et al. (2017) present an approach that is more of a hybrid. The concept of *Executable Research Compendiums* (also referred to as ERC) is still a container, but a container which follows a standardized model (also referred to as ERM) of what SCPs should look like.

The designs of various scopes of SCPs, as well different approaches for their creation, demonstrate that this publication concept reintroduces the idea of sound authoring of monolithic objects, instead of aggregating information units. The creation of containers in this approach is a process of decision making and design, carried out by a human creator in the first place. Even if automated processes put the container together at the end, many design decisions in terms of what is required, and how the required things are gathered to obtain self-containedness, must be made in advance. This observation becomes clearer if one looks at four of five major issues that turn up during the creation of containerized SCPs, highlighted by Meng et al. (2015, 138–39). These issues deal with the aspects of dependencies, configuration, selectivity, and volatility in the process of authoring SCPs.

The idea of authoring as a human, decision-driven design process became extremely marginal in many publication concepts in the last chapter. OLBs and ROs were aimed at unfiltered mediation of the research process. The implementation of ROs subsequently showed that it is not only the workflow, but also the environment of the workflow that needs to be tracked. In a final step, it became clear that the environment cannot just be tracked, but depends on authoring tasks. This means that while the act of authoring seemed illegitimate at the beginning, it is conceived of as unavoidable years later. To push things further, it might even be possible to argue that SCPs today "author" different modes of authoring strategies, such as imaging, tracking, and describing.

From Artifacts to Aggregations to Artifacts

Self-Contained Publications are comparable to DPs in precisely one aspect. Like DPs, the concept of SCPs is an open and inclusive concept. Most approaches to SCPs do not prescribe the exact content of a publication. It would, for instance, be easily possible to turn a TP into a SCP. In fact, this could even provide a solution to the preservation issue of TPs raised by Ball and Eyman (2015). The difference between DPs and SCPs is the property by which such inclusiveness is achieved. While DPs offer a flexible and open concept, SCPs enable technological flexibility. In contrast, this means that DPs are criticized as in need of technological improvement (see section on DPs), while only stakeholders with a high level of technological understanding are even capable of authoring SCPs.

As described at the beginning of this section, emulation strategies in SCPs were also the result of issues with publication concepts such as ROs, which put a strong emphasis on reproducibility. Another goal of ROs was to build publications on top of a distributed network of resources linked together in a specific way in each publication. Self-Contained Publications built on the argument that distribution is not a feasible way of organizing publication content. Studies from within the research field of SCPs have presented a lot of evidence in order to support this claim. Emulation and packaging are the opposite approach to the ideas of LOD, but it is considered necessary for achieving more reproducibility.

The consequence of this decision is a discussion about the right scope, the necessary elements, and reliable authoring strategies in order to really achieve self-containedness. This discussion has highly theoretical implications, and sometimes even makes use of poetical phrases, such as in Welch et al. (2012, 79), stressing that the creation of SCPs need "a certain 'cooperation' of the original operating system." The theoretical dimension of such discussions of cause also challenges the theoretical foundations behind other publication types, even, or especially, when, the context is to just solve concrete technological problems. This dimension, more precisely, questions the scope of the impact of notions like the aggregative nature of publications, or the possibility to formalize reproducibility.

The fact that this discussion is carried on by computer scientists, and thus within the same community in which such concepts were born in the first place, supports this observation further. It was Herbert Van de Sompel who coined the phrase "From Artifacts to Aggregations," and who significantly influenced a whole set of digital publications by developing the OAI-ORE model. Yet, with the emergence of SCPs, the notion of artifacts is re-introduced, and the term re-appears with positive connotation by authors such as Welch et al. (2012).

Although SCPs solve some problems of conceptual and technological heterogeneity, they also produce their own type of heterogeneity. This heterogeneity is actively addressed by Santana-Perez et al. (2017), and regretted by Nüst et al. (2016). It drives a new attempt to define formal semantics for the description of computational environments (Santana-Perez et al. 2014; Santana-Perez et al. 2017), or for the components that scientific publications as containers should provide.

In light of the last paragraph, SCPs remain a concept authentically residing in the field of computer science. The suggestion of an ontology in order to describe computational environments in a standardized way, without preserving these environments, again tries to find a technological solution to a problem that concepts such as HPs and DPs predominantly treat as a social issue.

An interesting aspect of SCPs is the fact that a certain sensibility towards social issues of publication concepts emerges in a completely different area. The argument behind the development of "light-weight" container solutions instead of operating-system images has been the inefficient amount of resources (disk space among others) these images require. In other contributions, the term "costs" is used. Zheng and Thain (2015) offer a comprehensive evaluation of different cost types for distinct approaches to SCPs.

Although this term is not meant monetarily in the first place, it effectively addresses monetary issues. Computational resources consist of hardware and energy used by this hardware. Both must be bought in the same way as time resources equate to salaries. Hence, the recurring theme of costs in SCPs corresponds with an awareness of what could be called the social weight of digital publication formats, that is, the perceivable efforts necessary to treat these publication concepts as a future standard. Similar quantifications of efforts cannot be found for other publication concepts in such detail as in Zheng and Thain (2015).

These efforts are concrete and countable, compared to the more abstract references to necessary efforts in concepts like SPs. Self-contained publications might make sense for such issues, due to the key decision to not make a formal distinction between form and content of a publication, the allegedly contingent social aspects, and the technologically pure parts of a digital publication.

Putting Digital Publications into Context

The period described in this chapter marks a significant change in the development of digital publications.

Sometimes openly, but in most cases implicitly, the four concepts in this chapter relativize many of the paradigms advocated in earlier projects. Hence, in HPs the discourse of open access was put into perspective, but not abandoned. Instead, a strategy of "subsequent monetization" was proposed that accepts certain social dependencies. Hybrid Publications, at the same time, tone down the judgmental distinctions between new and old publication formats. They do so by arguing that different publication formats serve different needs. The idea that "old" needs disappear, just because digital technologies are able to also serve other needs, appears as an unnecessary simplification.

SCPs raised similar critiques. However, their counter-approach to the modularization of publications and their abolishment of the content/form distinction are clearly more important aspects of this concept. Although OpenAIRE did not abolish the theme of standardization, its approach is nevertheless clearly different from the way former projects pursued this goal. The project supported a gradual approach to standardization, in which the responsibility for its achievement was in parts moved to a high-level infrastructure and to the project itself.

Such an approach, in which harmonization is pursued by acts of curation, has also been taken by Overlay Journals and, later on, DPs, concepts that intentionally make use of historical publication formats. The concept of DPs also took account of epistemological issues when Parsons and Fox ask: "Is Data Publication the Right Metaphor" (see above). Emphasizing what data means, and how interaction with data takes place, and how this differs between domains, means undermining the line of argument of concepts in e-Science, in which data-driven science has one face and one only.

The support for the article form in DPs could also be understood as a support of linear narrativity as a unique means to adequately contextualize empirical research beyond just metadata (see also Gil and Garijo 2017). The success of electronic notebooks in research fields that make heavy use of computation gives reason to expect a re-evaluation of the affordances of linear narrativity in e-Science on a more general level within the next years. Correspondingly, Kery et al. (2018, 17:1) in "The Story in the Notebook: Exploratory Data Science Using a Literate Programming Tool" quotes the computer scientist Knuth who once called for "considering programs to be works of literature."

The ongoing rejection of great parts of scholarly stakeholders, connected with the scholarly domain, of which the complaints in the introduction give evidence as well, furthermore, demanded finding new ways of engaging with these stakeholders. The position that agents who do not want to adapt to the alleged necessity of progress "go to the wall," as Cameron Neylon put it, was not maintainable any longer — especially not for the sake of advancing digital publications.

If just going back is neither desirable nor possible, and continuing to propose new innovations not sustainable, an alternative strategy is to look out for possibilities to better include stakeholders (see also Holtermann 2017). The focus needs to shift to social issues. Significantly, during the advent of DPs, Rees emphasized its role as a "social management function."

Each of the concepts in this chapter reflects this turn towards a more socially acceptable notion of digital publications in its own unique way. Hybrid Publishing gives the most prominent example in the sense that it literally puts all stakeholders (McPherson) and publishing environments (Hall), each with equal rights, at the center of all progress in digital publishing. Data Papers deliver a mechanism of conceptually and politically addressing publishing concepts, and are significantly different in terms of technology as well as goals. That way they redefine the fragmented and heterogeneous landscape of digital publications such that it is possible to perceive all these activities as part of the same process.

Self-Contained Publications do the same thing that DPs do conceptually, but in a technology-driven way. It is true that due to their vast technological requirements, SCPs cannot be used by everyone. However, they allow the development of consistent solutions for problems such as long-term preservation and access across very different digital publications formats. Hence, the need to standardize form and content of digital publications as containers is minimized. Creators of such publications are less forced to think about technological consequences of their publication model.

OpenAIRE is a special case because the project shifted into two different directions. On the one hand, the concept of SCIs seems to accept a publication landscape that remains at a certain level of heterogeneity, on the other hand the scaled approach of OpenAIRE and its interventions reveals a top-down standardization strategy. Such minor contradictions, however, also appeared within the publication concepts mentioned earlier. The idea of Single-Source Publishing proposed by Burkhardt (2015), for instance, contradicts the notion of continuous remediation outlined by Gary Hall in the context of HPs. Likewise, there is a tension between self-containedness as a solution to semantic heterogeneity and the later attempt to semantically standardize containers in SCPs.

This chapter demonstrated that over the last years a significant shift took place in digital publishing. This shift significantly complicates the analysis of the development of digital publications. Before, development was driven by strong ideas that offered orientation for personal engagement and commitment. The relativization of such ideas partially takes this orientation away. Hence, the inconsistencies observed in the last paragraph are not surprising. The fact that almost every aspect of digital publications since the ACM publishing plan is now put into context makes "rewiring publishing" a challenging task that has just begun.

[5]

Post-Digital …

A Less Random Definition of the Digital

After the first decade of the new millennium, fields like media-studies, cultural studies, and the arts were attracted by a new concept: *post-digitality.* In a first attempt to grasp an overlapping core behind the varying applications of the term, Cramer writes:

> More pragmatically, the term "post-digital" can be used to describe either a contemporary disenchantment with digital information systems and media gadgets, or a period in which our fascination with these systems and gadgets has become historical — just like the dot-com age ultimately became historical in the 2013 novels of Thomas Pynchon and Dave Eggers. (Cramer 2014)

The last chapter's title suggested that the development of the field of digital publishing can be observed in a similar way. However, it might not be clear immediately in which way or up to which extend this is the case. Obviously, the field of digital publishing can by definition not act as disenchantment from digital information systems. The second part of the quote seems to be applicable more easily here, however. It has been argued that projects discussed in the above chapter relativize former key ideas of digital publishing, each in their own way.

Even where such ideas are still going strong, as the case with OpenAIRE, their status changes from being seen as imperatives to providing points of reference to aspire to, up to the extent possible within a given situation. The concept of SCIs as a unifying layer of abstraction is useful only because the ideals of digital publishing are not expected to become manifest in colloquial scholarly publishing soon. Thus, it is the OpenAIRE infrastructure, and only that, which sustains such ideals.

The discourse around concepts such as ROs and LPs presumed that corresponding ideals adhere to an inner logic of computation, which in consequence drives a transparent historical development of science and scholarly publishing (e-Science and open science). In contrast, the experiences that led to the conceptualization of SCIs give testimony of doubts about the inherent necessity by which such ideals will be adopted. By doing so, OpenAIRE transfers the conceived logics of a historical process into infrastructure that creates social necessities.

In the same way it would be wrong to say that DPs are completely detached from key ideas of digital publishing. Nevertheless, if such ideas constitute what is "fancy" about digital publishing, then the most important aspect of DPs is the fact that they are significantly less driven by fascination about them, compared to earlier publication concepts. SCPs, in contrast, often do follow a strong computational logic and are also partially linked to the e-Science research model. Still, it has been shown that the way they do so completely rearranges the conceptual matrix of digital publications. They also provide a solution which is not only valuable for this specific research model alone. Emulation strategies can be used to solve problems with TPs in the same way as with computational workflows.

The case of HPs needs less explanation. As described at the beginning of the last chapter, HPs by definition include a critique of certain aspects and claims behind digital publications. In fact, both terms — Hybrid Publishing and post-digitality — are mentioned together in Ludovico (2015).

The quote from the beginning of this chapter suggests that post-digitality, as a scientific term, refers to a certain kind of social behavior towards digital technologies. Indeed, the term itself does not come from the scientific domain, but from performative arts. It was first used by Cascone (2000) and Andrews (2002) to outline the agenda for post-digital art and music. Genuine scientific studies on post-digitality took place in closely connected disciplines. Accordingly, Hayward (2013) wrote a contribution about post-digital cinema in a Routledge Handbook.

While according to Cramer the early post-digital movements seek to reject ideas of progress and perfection associated with digital technologies, the systematic scientific appropriation of the concept begins with the remark that while this complete:

> ... withdrawal may seem a tempting option for many, it is fundamentally a naive position, particularly in an age when even the availability of natural resources depends on global computational logistics, and intelligence agencies such as the NSA intercept paper mail as well as digital communications. (Cramer 2014, sec. Revival of "old" media)

In this light the growing phenomena of rejection, disenchantment, or decreasing fascination provoked a more systematic evaluation of this phenomenon, as well as the concept of post-digitality itself. Moreover, it provokes rethinking of the concept of digitality in the first place.

Cramer conducts such an evaluation as part of a broader research group. This group published its findings on post-digitality in a special issue of the APRJA online-journal (Andersen, Cox, and Papadopoulos 2014). He responds to the leading question: "What is 'Post-Digital'?" by separately discussing how the prefix "post" should be understood and what is addressed by digitality.

According to Cramer, "post" in post-digital is not meant in the sense of the "post-histoire" that is "the end of history" as Francis Fukuyama put it (Fukuyama 2006). It is not intended to mark a clearly different new time period that most fundamentally undermines all aspects by which former temporal periods could even be identified as such. In contrast, the author argues that the prefix functions like in post-feminism or post-colonialism. More precisely, it functions as a marker for a "critically revised continuation" of what is prefixed. In the same way and within a more problematic context, the term post-colonial does not assume the end of colonialism but the transformation of colonialist relationships into more subtle, more complex, and more diverse variations of this relationships.

Cramer selected these two examples well, because they indicate the ambiguity of "post" in post-digitality. On the one hand, there is a positive connotation in which a progressive concept undergoes a revision with the intent to sustain it. On the other hand, it shows the negatively connoted indication that a certain power structure may last, even if the political system around it has changed. In both cases, the goal is not to argue that a certain phenomenon no longer exists, but that this phenomenon has changed so much that reflection on it has to find new viewpoints:

> "Post-digital" describes a perspective on digital information technology which no longer focuses on technical innovation or improvement, but instead rejects the kind of techno-positivist innovation narratives

> exemplified by media such as Wired magazine, Ray Kurzweil's Google-sponsored "singularity" movement, and of course Silicon Valley. (Cramer 2014, sec. Post-digital = hybrids of "old" and "new" media)

It was argued at the beginning of this chapter that most recent publication concepts are somewhat aimed at such a development in an unconscious way, full of inconsistencies as a consequence of the transitory moment in which they emerged. However, at this point an analysis that turns the observation of a post-digital moment into a theoretical foundation for digital publications is lacking. Such a foundation might help to develop a more strategic idea of post-digital publications. A good starting point for this task is again Cramer's discussion of the term "digital" in "post-digital."

This discussion consists of nothing more than a clarification of what people actually talk about when they talk about digitality. This clarification shows that the distinction between digital and analogue is far less clear than is often assumed. For instance, Cramer gives the example of analogue computers that function with water and measuring cups to compute key mathematical operations. In contrast, a "digital" computer works on the basis of analogue processes, more precisely voltage-ranges, that are artificially divided into ones and zeros. The screen functions through pixels that are clearly separated from each other, but the pixels themselves work within ranges of light intensity. Cramer therefore calls the computer screen a "hybrid digital-analogue."

The meaning of digital and analogue underlying this line of argument stresses that:

> "Digital" simply means that something is divided into discrete, countable unit — countable using whatever system one chooses, whether zeroes and ones, decimal numbers, tally marks on a scrap of paper, or the fingers (digits) of one's hand — which is where the word "digital" comes from in the first place; in French, for example, the word is "numérique." Consequently, the Roman alphabet is a digital system; (Cramer 2014, sec. Digression: what is digital, what is analog?)

Analogue, in contrast, refers to something that has not been made or rendered discrete and which therefore:

> ... consists of one or more signals which vary on a continuous scale, such as a sound wave, a light wave, a magnetic field (for example on an audio tape, but also on a computer hard disk), ... (Cramer 2014, sec. Analog ≠ undivided; analog non-computational)

In this respect, the distinction between digital and analogue is neither a result of the invention of the *Turing Machine* (see below), nor are digital technologies today purely digital machinery. This argument has already been discussed in a more philosophical context by Buckley (2011).[1] However, it is the fuzzy application of such terms that stimulates among other things the aforementioned "techno-positivist innovation narratives," and that has also been found behind a variety of digital publication concepts. As will become clear later on, this critique can be applied to both e-Science related publication concepts as well as to concepts such as TPs, HPs, and UBs. The reason why this is the case is better understood when looking at the consequences of such terminological clarification. Cramer continues:

> Consequently, there is no such thing as digital media, only digital or digitized information: chopped-up numbers, letters, symbols and any other abstracted units, as opposed to continuous, wave-like signals such as physical sounds and visible light. Most "digital media" devices are in fact analog-to-digital-to-analog converters. (Cramer 2014, sec. Technically, there is no such thing as "digital media" or "digital aesthetics")

Thus, if digital technologies do not just quantify but convert between different modes of representation, and are also conflations of digital and analogue components themselves, then it becomes highly problematic to demand "true digital publications." The only true thing about digital publications in this point of view is a tremendous potential to turn different types and forms of research input into multiple output formats, undefined in number. In fact, this is exactly what the last chapters have shown, a wide variety of publication concepts often referred to within the field as heterogeneous.

Such concepts appeared so very different not just because different opinions exist about what they should look like and what the impact of digital technologies[2] is. They appeared so different because these technologies, by virtue of their capabilities to convert, provide significant

1 Buckley shows very well that the distinction is at the heart of a philosophical question going back to the third aporia of Zenon of Melea about the possibility of perceiving movement.

2 In the light of the arguments above, it would be more appropriate to use another term such as computational technologies. The term "digital technologies", however, has become part of colloquial language when referring to technological innovation that took place in the second half of the twentieth century. It will therefore be used in the missing part of the present inquiry as well. This seems less problematic together with the clarifications in the last few paragraphs.

support to giving technological shape to these opinions. This observation marks a clear contrast to arguments in e-Science or open science, arguing that digital technologies have a clearly defined and predictable impact on scientific methodology, as well as on the form of scholarly publications. This point will be developed in greater detail in the next sections.

Furthermore, it could be argued that ideas about the true digital format or the true digital method further stimulate the proliferation of publication formats. It definitely motivates focusing on one's own format and spending resources on its development, instead of relating formats to each other and building a digital publishing environment.

However, it is important to emphasize again that the argument is not that what is called digital technologies does not have a significant impact on science and publishing. The whole discussion is not about the level of impact at all. The critique of the "techno-positivistic innovation narrative" concerns the confusion between such innovation and specific types of conversion. It is part and parcel of this confusion to furthermore think that the success of digital technologies includes their always being appropriate and it being efficient to always mediate everything by them. Thus, even the notion of "digital" publications somehow distorts the whole picture. It follows that:

> "Post-digital" refers to a state in which the disruption brought upon by digital information technology has already occurred. (Cramer 2014, sec. Post-digital = anti-"new media")

The question of new versus old formats turns into a question of the best fit within different publication scenarios. Accordingly, the rare cases of research in post-digitality which draw attention on the topic of publishing highlight strength and weaknesses of publishing formats, regardless of their relationship to digital technologies. The fact that such choices have to be made is the very outcome of the success of digital technologies, and would be impossible without them.

In the present work, contributions in the area of HPs have weighed in most significantly in this respect. Especially Gary Hall, Joanna Zylinska, and Janneke Adema supported the idea of publishing in formats that convene with the specific needs of peculiar publishing situations, instead of hunting the one new format. The contingent list of publication formats gathered by Worthington and Furter (2014) in the so-called publication taxonomy explicitly references the term post-digitality. In fact, the taxonomy is presented as a reaction to the "parallel usage of different media-types" and the "proliferation of tools" for production, in consequence of the "post-digital condition" (Worthington and Furter 2014).

While supporting the idea of equal rights for different approaches, the quotes by Worthington do not completely open up a view of the consequences of the aforementioned line of argument in all its dimensions. Following Cramer's clarification of the digital and the analogue, it cannot just be the parallel use of different media-types which distinguishes post-digital publishing, but also different formattings of one media-type provoked by other media-types[3].

This point was also the core of Pettifer et al. (2011) argument in favor of the PDF. More precisely, the fact that the PDF is a format that is partially designed by applying principles of paper articles and monographs is a weak argument against it from a post-digital point of view. The Photomediations project is another illustrating example of the more subtle dimension of post-digitality in publishing, although the online version of Photomediations includes many components that exist because of digital technologies. It also emphasizes the concept of binding which, as Hall has stressed, belongs to the monograph world and is by no means necessary for the online version. In reverse, the online version controls the production cycle and content generation of the printed versions of Photomediations.

Such examples illustrate well how these intersections and interdependencies[4] become invisible if one analyses publishing in the light of a common understanding of the digital. More precisely, such a careless definition of the digital only makes sense as long as convincing visions for digital publications exist, visions which make it possible to trivialize the impact of such interdependencies. The previous chapter showed that such visions have lost plausibility even in the field of digital publications itself. In consequence, the imposed separation between both worlds — the digital and the analogue — becomes problematic and even hindering. In a more general perspective, Berry therefore proposes:

3 The term media-type needs a clarification here. In the context of the taxonomy in which Worthington makes the quote, it refers mostly to what has been called publication concept in the study at hand. Nonetheless, the term lacks precise definition within the taxonomy. What is meant in this sentence is the fact that new formats also pickup properties of existing formats or redefine their properties.

4 For further explanations and examples of these phenomena in the context of publishing in a broader perspective refer to Ludovico (2013) and Ludovico (2015).

> Thus, the post-digital is represented by and indicative of a moment when the computational has become hegemonic. ... We might no longer talk about digital versus analogue, but instead modulations of the digital or different intensities of the computational. We should therefore critically analyze the way in which cadences of the computational are made and materialized. (Berry 2013)

The critique of the discourse on digital technology complied with three logical steps. First, it was clearly defined what should be considered digital and what analogue. Second, it was illustrated that this distinction as such is not altered by digital technologies. More generally it does not equate to the distinction between digital technologies and other technologies. Finally, it was deduced that this means that there is no even more digital world to come, but that digital technologies have already happened, and innovation takes place elsewhere.

The quote by David Berry, however, mixes up two things, which, as has been shown before, do not categorically belong together in the first place: digitality and computation. Obviously, they appear together in this quote because the equation between digitality and computation is part of the discourse on digital technologies. There are rare environments in which this fact is easier to observe than in the field of digital scholarly publications. Everything, from making publications more machine-readable, to breaking down the scope of publication to data, up to the publication of algorithms in computation workflows, is a process of adapting publications to a supposed computational paradigm. All these modifications were additionally framed in distinct ideological contexts. From the end of theory up to open science, it is argued that the way knowledge is produced, and functions will significantly change due to computation. In fact, in a kind of circular reasoning it was estimated that computation will be the dominant paradigm and argued that because of this, publications should resemble computational properties.

Topological, Typological and Mathematical Knowledge

In the cases in which digital publications explicitly refer to computation, they in fact mean mathematical evaluation. It is a question outside the scope of the current research if this equation between computation and mathematics is actually valid. It is however worth considering in this context that both a purely mathematical description — the *λ-calculus* by

Alonzo Church — as well as a mathematical and technological description — the Turing Machine by Alan Turing — mark the perceived beginning of what is called digital technologies today. But even if computation were to basically mean operationalizing mathematics itself, and the equation were to turn out to be valid, it is possible to challenge the consequences drawn on top of this equation. Since in digital publications, the phenomenon of computation is used to make claims about how truth and evidence is best represented and discovered, it seems a reasonable next step to try and clarify which type of knowledge mathematics engenders.

Among many other researchers, Jay Lemke has carried out this task by comparing it in a sophisticated way to other types of knowledge. What this means will become clearer in the next paragraphs. His contribution "Mathematics in the Middle" (Lemke 2003) fits well into the current context because he actively links his evaluations to discussions of the difference between digital and analogue. Lemke elaborates his answer to the question of which type of knowledge is produced by mathematics from a so-called *social semiotic* point of view. Social semiotics is a subfield of linguistics introduced by Michael Halliday in the seventies (1978; 1985). In order to understand Lemke's analysis of mathematics, it is important to understand some basic ideas of social semiotics.

Halliday's approach to language completely rejects the idea of speaking as an application of language as it had been introduced by the founding father of linguistics, Ferdinand de Saussure (Saussure 1959). Saussure considered a categorical difference between the use of language by people in a specific situation (parole) and the language system of a culture this person belongs to (langue). In his view the relation between the language of the speaker and the act of speaking is always one of application. The system of language exists beforehand. Furthermore, Saussure assumes the existence of a layer of rules — langage — which restricts and enables the creation of concrete languages such as English or German.

For Saussure, the core of language is langage, a timeless abstract formal system that conditions the possibilities of concrete languages. In contrast, Halliday provides a pragmatical definition of language, intended to work completely from the bottom up (O'Halloran and Lim Fei 2014, chap. Analysis). More precisely, he claims that when people communicate, they want to do three basic things. First, they want to refer to something or some state in the outside world. Language is about something. Second, they want to engage with the outer, yet social world. People want to tell somebody something. Finally, language is built up as a composition of signs, words, or sentences. These elements of language refer to each other in some way. Halliday calls these three functions *ideational*, *interpersonal*, and *textual* functions. The bottom line of Halliday's argument is that everything that is capable of developing ideational, interpersonal, and textual functions can potentially serve as means for communication.

Consequently, there exists no realm of language outside of its usage. Language emerges within certain practices. Things belong to language when they fit these basic needs and not because they are recognizable or part of a formally grasped language system being always there beforehand. Language — where observable as a system, as a cognitive structure, or in form of the experience that we understand each other — is always embedded in concrete situations, which at the same time change it (Halliday and Martin 1996, 122–25; Eggins 1994, 81–83).

Pushing this line of argument forward, vocal sounds or letters in an alphabet are also not derived from an underlying system of language to which they both belong. They are signs referring to different resources for sign making — voice and writing — which were historically related to each other. On the whole, signs are neither preconditioned nor ultimately defined. They are created out of appropriate material through the practice of people who want to communicate. To put it more formally, signs are entities rendered in the process of *semiosis* (Kress 2010), or *signing* (Kress 2013), the technical term that defines the historical process of sign making. Signs may come and go, and accordingly it is possible to really study them in terms of "their life within society" as Saussure had originally planned to do.

On the basis of social semiotics, Lemke is able to actually ask the question of what kind of knowledge mathematics provide and how mathematics relate to the type of knowledge that is language. Because of social semiotics, mathematics does not appear as something completely different from language. It is the outcome of the same human process to produce meaning and tell something that engendered language. Social semiotics similarly suggests carrying out such a comparison not by means of looking at the different types of symbols and notations in mathematics and in language, but by analyzing how both developed historically, the purposes of their application, and which facts are easily representable and which are not.

Lemke (2003, sec. 2.1) highlights that unique mathematical symbols developed much later than mathematics itself. They were originally derived from Greek words. A lot of mathematics existed in rhetoric form, and approaches to mathematics like geometry refrain from using algebraic symbols. It is therefore misleading to put a categorial difference between mathematics and language at the starting point of a comparison of its relationship. Instead, Lemke claims that mathematics has evolved historically as an extension to language and out of language in order to represent things that could not be well represented in language. He remarks that the first historical evidence of what is considered mathematics in research are lists of descriptions to solve specific problems "with no theory" (sec. 2.1):

> I want to argue that they (mathematical meanings, author's note) have evolved historically to allow us to integrate two fundamentally different kinds of meaning-making: meaning-by-kind and meaning-by-degree. Mathematical meaning enables us to mix and to move smoothly back and forth between meaning-by-kind, in which natural language specializes, and which I will call categorial or "typological" meaning, and meaning-by-degree, which is more easily presented by means of motor gestures or visual figures — the meaning of continuous variation or "topological" meaning (connoting the topology of the real numbers). (Lemke 2003, sec. 3)

The description of typological and topological knowledge is reminiscent of the distinction between digital and analogue. Although it is not Lemke's primary intention to relate these two topics, he mentions their similarity. In the current research, their relationship can be described as follows: while the terms digital and analogue tend to address material and technological aspects, topological and typological refer to two different ways of perceiving and representing something. On one hand, bits are mechanisms in a computer that can be on or off, and a thermometer varies continuously on a scale. On the other hand, it is possible to give different names to the color of the sky on different days, or to create a diagram that draws these differences on a scale.

It is important to distinguish between those two perspectives, because this distinction is at the very heart of discussions about the epistemological consequences of digital technologies. As no digital technology is fundamentally digital, no phenomenon enforces a topological or typological representation of itself. Instead, its representation depends to a great extent on the type of meaning people want to produce and the social practices in which it is involved.

According to Lemke, mathematics, just like "motor gestures or visual figures" (above), is better at describing topological knowledge compared to language. However, to prevent another simplification, it is important to remark that language and mathematics do not exclusively represent typological and topological meaning. Both domains provide examples for both types of meaning. Both, nevertheless, developed their particular strengths in one of these two knowledge domains and are therefore better suited to one or the other. Although language, for instance, is capable of representing much more than the fact that some thing is something, it is quite hard to precisely describe nuances, such as in color or temperature, with words.

The question now is, what does mathematics do differently from other topological knowledge representation systems such as graphs. The difference is that mathematics describes such relationships in a completely different way than graphs and other topological knowledge systems do. Mathematics, more precisely, uses "quasi-linguistic" elements which denote discrete things to represent continuous phenomena without boundaries (Lemke 2003, sec. 3). According to Lemke, this key strength of mathematics is best represented in fractions and functions:

> Nevertheless, in a fraction such quantitative-meanings are represented quasi-linguistically by two numbers, each of which can be regarded as a discrete counting type or category (the integers as cardinals), and by the instruction to consider some relation between them (ratio, or multiple of a part, to be evaluated by the algorithm of division). All of these elements are typological, but the meanings which fractions represent as ratios are topological. If I give you a set of fractions: 13/19, 11/17, 4/6, 9/13; you know that there is no simple way to tell from these typological representations even what the order of sizes of these ratios is, without performing calculations. But if I presented these same ratios visually, you would have a much better idea of their relationships. (Lemke 2003, sec. 3)

In the same way, functions are an algebraic and quasi-linguistic way to describe continuous and sometimes unbounded covariance "in terms of typological operations on typological variables." Consequently, most parts of mathematics are hybrids in the sense that their meaning is topological, but their tactics and means are typological. This is what the title of Lemke's article "Mathematics in the Middle" is intended to address. By doing so, mathematics is able to represent topological knowledge more precisely than language, but gives more control over such knowledge than for example graphs do.

A second question now is if mathematics and its development have the power to fundamentally change the role and relationship between typological and topological knowledge systems. Is it able to undermine key aspects of, for instance, language, so that the use of language becomes arbitrary in the context of scientific knowledge? Or the other way around, does mathematics have the potential to minimize the value of topological representations? The last two sentences indicate already that this is not the case. Mathematics will never be able to communicate topological knowledge in such a direct and clear way as for instance graphs do. This is not due to missing developments in mathematics, but because it was developed towards a different strategy to represent. It can describe topological knowledge, but hardly communicate topological knowledge. This is not only the reason why visual communication became such an integral part in computational research today — take the jupyter notebook as an example — it is also the reason why complicated algorithms are explained and understood best by diagrammatic explanations.[5]

Lemke argues further that even our topological understanding of parts of mathematics can be most convincingly understood by topological dimensions in using mathematics than by its categorial content. The feeling for the meaning of numbers accordingly is a consequence of the time that passes while counting, by the length of the line of numbers while writing down a sequence of numbers, or by an image of twelve apples in a bowl. The more complicated matters are, and the more mathematical expressions abstract from topological representations, the more its understanding refers to the understanding of other expressions of mathematics itself (see the example of fractions).

Similarly, only language offers the necessary means to evaluate the gap between mathematics and its application in a concrete situation as well as between the result of a mathematical operations and its interpretation.

After all of this, mathematics derives its own domain of application from the distinction of topological and typological knowledge, a distinction which historically became an issue with the advent of language and its codification. In as much as such codification broadened the gap between these two types of knowledge, better mediation between them became a major challenge. Mathematics, according to Lemke, is the attempt to create the means for this mediation.

5 Illustrating examples for this can be found in the documentation of the machine learning programing library scikit-learn http://scikit-learn.org/stable/modules/clustering.html or in one of the countless examples of algorithm tutorials on YouTube.

The discussion of this issue was carried out in such great detail because of the extent up to which advocates of certain publication formats make references to themes such as the end of theory, the fourth paradigm, big data, massive computation, and the sufficiency of statistical correlation. In the light of Lemke's research on mathematics, it can be argued that massive computation on the grounds of big data will never be able to replace textual and narrative publications, as argued by De Roure and others. This incapacity resides in the categorial difference between what mathematics and language were developed for. Articles and monographs are therefore not just supplements of computational research that humans need for easier understanding. They offer their own type of access to what they describe, an access that creates its own type of understanding, which might be influenced by mathematics, but which also influences the application of mathematics.

The notion that big data allows empirical analysis of the whole domain of a problem, whereby theoretical descriptions become obsolete (see De Roure and Andersen) cannot change the fact that the definition of the whole — in terms of its boundaries as well as of its parts — remains a theoretical issue. The same applies to decisions about the appropriate mathematical model and algorithm best describing the problem domain as well as to what a resulting correlation denotes.

The argument of the fourth paradigm is slightly more interesting in the current context. It does acknowledge that computation deals with the relationship between two types of knowledge such as those specified by Lemke. However, as far as computation is concerned with mathematics, this relationship is not new in a paradigmatic way, it was introduced by mathematics.

Up to this point it is possible to summarize the extended discussion of a post-digital perspective on scholarly publishing by emphasizing that:

- digital technologies are not only digital, and analogue technologies have digital aspects;
- computation is not a process by which everything becomes digital. It is about transformations between analogue and digital as well as vice versa. This becomes most obvious in areas like 3D printing, nano-technology, robotics, and bio-engineering;
- correspondingly, mathematics and computation are not replacements for language in order to eliminate the flaws of the former. They are strategies that provide the unique possibility to

mediate between two different representation strategies, each with its own unique advantages and flaws.

Still, the question remains why certain innovations within the technological landscape created such a dominant and ubiquitous discourse of digital technologies. Research in post-digitality does not deny that the impact of such innovations is fundamental. Post-digital research, however, does not need to respond to this question because it reacts to the fact that the discourse about digitality and the term digital technology is already ubiquitous[6]. By challenging the premises of this discourse, post-digitality reacts to a social truth, which is then toned down, qualified, and put into context. In consequence, the majority of post-digital research follows two different types of analysis. The first one analyses the simultaneous usage of objects that are considered digital and those that are not. The second type of analysis investigates how such objects influence each other (see the Photomediations example above).

Another argument that is made by more critical research on digital technologies claims that it is the act of asking alone which keeps alive both the discourse on new technologies as well as the dynamics of technological innovation (Treusch-Dieter 2001). Accordingly, every historical episode of innovation functions like a self-fulfilling prophecy, which is literally stimulated by occult powers (Andriopoulos 2003). However, even if every period of technological innovation were rooted in quasi-prophetic dynamics, intervening with such dynamics within a specific period of innovation would require knowing how such dynamics work internally. In the end, it could be argued that such critiques are part of the dynamics of innovation in digital technologies themselves, even if claiming to question technology as such. By trying to react to the impact of digital technologies in a way that addresses technology as such, the authors are drawn into esoteric arguments and styles of writing which repeat the characteristics they attribute to their research objects.

The argument can thereby also be turned upside down. That means it is important to strive towards a precise understanding of the structure of a specific self-fulfilling prophecy in order to deal with what seems to

6 A random query for the term "digital age" in a research literature search engine brings up titles from "Government in the Digital Age" (Gosling 1997) to "The Role of the Postal and Delivery Sector in a Digital Age" (Crew and Brennan 2014) up to "Learning Queer Identity in the Digital Age" (Siebler 2016; first page of results in LIMO 14.03.2017 http://limo.libis.be/). The example shows how each sector in society is reflecting itself based on an epochal change, constituting this change with its reflection at the same time.

be problematic for the authors, by referring to it in terms of prophecy and occultism. The critique or, in the context of post-digitality less harsh: qualification, has to come from within. Thus, both the meta-technological reflections on digital technologies, as well as the post-digital reflections, cannot explain the emergence of a problematic but ubiquitous discourse on digital technologies or digital publications. They only provide different means of highlighting its problematic facets.

The present study claims that only further attempts to define digital technologies are able to tone down the problematic consequences of the discourse on digital technologies, despite the fact that these new definitions will again be lacking. It is precisely because discourse matters why neither the "deconstruction" of discourse nor ignoring it suffice. A set of conflicting definitions that take themselves seriously is therefore preferable to ongoing attempts to show that it is hardly possible to speak of digital technologies. Similarly, computational ubiquity does not mean that the surface of publications is structured by computational principles, as it is often suggested (see the beginning of this section). The remaining sections in this chapter will therefore try to develop a definition of digital technologies that is derived from the issues found in the discussion of digital publications. It is a definition driven by the attempt to explain such issues on the grounds of the line of thought that was rolled out by the field of digital publications itself.

Representation Strategies, Intermediality and Their Relationships

It has been argued that one of the main motors of the dynamics of digital publishing is the claim that digital technologies change all fields of research in an epistemological way. The above digression on Lemke demonstrated that the way this change is perceived in many areas can be easily challenged. Therefore, the question of what digital technologies are in terms of digital publications must now be substantiated in a way that explains why certain technological innovations have produced the impression of a change in the epistemological environment of scholarly publications. In the same way as this explanation rejects the claims of certain authors, it also has to leave open the possibility of epistemological changes.

In "Textualität, Visualität und Episteme"[7] Sybille Krämer (2003) closely analyses how the formalization of the mathematical system of signs, and the creation of new mathematical objects, makes use of and depends on sensory aspects of writing and text. This analysis is carried out against a certain historical notion that, according to Krämer, perceives writing primarily as a cognitive activity. Text in this respect belongs to the inner eye of the mind, which is genuinely blind in terms of the things the eyes of the body may see. It abstracts from what the physical eye might see.

Within mathematics, zero is given as a paradigmatic example, insofar, as it is an entity with equal rights to other numbers, but one which cannot be experienced in the same way as the others. Similar claims are possible about infinity. Krämer argues that the *infinitesimal calculus* introduced by Leibniz was successful, particularly because it separated its mathematical efficiency from the metaphysical nature of the question of what infinity is and how our experience relates us to infinity.

> Der Witz der Kalkülisierung ist es also, das Operieren mit Zahlen zurückzuführen auf ein Operieren mit Zeichen für die Zahlen, und zwar nach Regeln, die nicht mehr auf die mathematischen Referenzobjekte der Zeichen, sondern nur noch auf deren syntaktische Gestalt Bezug nehmen.[8] (Krämer 2003, 18)

In this respect the mathematical sign for infinity and the fact that it is possible to operate with it in a grammatic-mathematical sign system constructs infinity as a concrete entity. Both the re-introduction of zero into mathematics in Europe, as well as the definition of infinity within numeric operations went together with the formalization of mathematical signs and their grammatical relationships.

If this process consists of rationalizing mathematical objects and streamlining mathematical calculations, the question arises how exactly sensory aspects play a key role in it. Krämer emphasizes that this process is part of a general cultural practice of calculation[9]. The cultural practice of calculation in the context of mathematics is a practice which seeks to better

7 "Textuality, Visuality, and Episteme" (author's translation)

8 It is the key aspect of Calculus to equate operations with numbers to operations with signs for numbers, while the rules for such operations now merely reference the syntactic content of such signs and no longer what these signs refer to (author's translation).

9 In German language, the philosophical meaning of the term calculation is used more often than the mathematical one, for which there is another term, "rechnen". In this context, the meaning of calculation refers to a way of acting strictly purposefully and functionally. Hence the distinction between calculating as dealing with numbers

control the process of mathematical calculation, i.e. to make it easier, more reliable, and more efficient. Krämer shows that in the fifteenth century this meant turning the "implicit knowledge and ingenious knowing how" of solving an equation into "Zeichenmanipulationsregeln bzw. Mustertransformationsregeln"[10] (Krämer 2003, 18). The calculated use of textuality as a resource for mathematics engendered a technical application of language which allows doing complicated things in a relatively simple way. In this respect, Krämer calls text a "symbolic machine" (19) — symbolic because it creates its own mathematical signs to take the place of something to be counted, and mechanic because it rationalizes the process of counting.

At the point of writing, the two main sensory aspects behind the formalization of mathematics into text only need to be made explicit because they were implicit already within its description. While writing is conceived of as a cognitive process, and text as an abstraction from what is described, they take place on a two-dimensional plane — mostly a sheet of paper — that connects with a body, with eyes, and the hand that holds the pen. The goals of calculating activity behind the formalization of mathematical language can only be achieved because such manipulation and transformation rules have layout and spatial relationships at its disposal. The integrity of purely theoretical objects like infinity or zero depends fundamentally on its visual persistence across situations. Their meaning is the effect of the operations and the rules of these operations in which they are operationalized. However, these rules, as mentioned above, are also spatial relationships, in which a writing hand has to move back and forth in a rule-based manner. By bringing abstract phenomena to the eye, and operational rules to the hand, the cultural practice of calculation also transforms mathematics into a new type of essential body experience.

> Tatsächlich ist die Wissenschaftsentwicklung nicht umstandslos dem Schema einer Austreibung der Sinnlichkeit ihrer Gegenstände subsumierbar. Vielmehr verdankt sich die Dynamik der Wissenschaft gerade dem Umstand, das kognitiv Unsichtbare, also abstrakte Gegenstände und theoretische Entitäten, dem Register der Sichtbarkeit zuzuführen, sie in sinnlich wahrnehmbaren Zeichen unserer Anschauung vorstellig zu machen.[11] (Krämer 2003, 25–26)

and doing something in a calculated way is stronger than in the English language. Calculating with numbers is an example of calculatory practice.

10 "rules to manipulate signs and to transform models." (author's translation)

11 "In fact, it is not possible to simply subsume the development of science under the theme of an expulsion of sensuality from its objects of interest. The dynamics of innovation in science more likely are a result of the strategy to transfer abstract

Hence, the described process has two facets. On the one hand, it is a process of rationalization and abstraction, in which certain engagements with the world are transferred to a system of self-referential rules which cut most of the experiential relationship of this engagement with the world. On the other hand, this process requires experienceable resources and makes use of them in a new way. It introduces a new sensory and experiential realm that takes the place of the former. Both the strategies to refer to the world as well as the way it refers to us shift.

These examinations provide enough insights to develop a hypothesis for the epistemological impact of digital technologies. In modern mathematics — sign systems as described by Krämer — an epistemological impact occurs on two levels. The most obvious impact is caused by its ability to give operational reality to phenomena like infinity, of which reality is neither philosophically nor empirically certain. It is a truth effect that exist only due to the way modern mathematical sign systems work technically.

The second epistemological impact underlies the first one, but is more subtle. Krämer's critique of perceiving the formalization of the mathematical sign system only as a process of rationalization made one thing clear: different strategies of representing phenomena in the world (iconic and discursive among others) are not becoming more or less important in technologically mediated developments. Instead, they just change place within our cultural and epistemological environment. Since such strategies provide the means of how to refer to or interact with the world, as well as how the world refers back, changes within this epistemological environment fundamentally affect people's perception and experience of it. Consequently, Krämer asks:

> Könnte es sein, daß nahezu alle epistemischen Effekte, die mit Medieninnovationen verbunden sind, sich bei genauerem Hinsehen als ein Surplus erweisen, das entsteht, wenn ein Medium einem anderen Medium inkorporiert, in ein anderes Medium übertragen wird? Und könnte es des weiteren sein, daß Medien immer schon genuin hybride Bildungen sind, so daß also die Idee des Einzelmediums sich "nur" einem Akt der theoretischen Stilisierung verdankt? Eine Stilisierung, die vielleicht genau in dem Augenblick möglich wird, wo ein Medium zum

things and theoretical entities into the domain of the visual, i.e. into signs that can be perceived visually" (author's translation).

> Inhalt eines anderen Mediums wird und dadurch überhaupt erst als eine bestimmte Form zutage tritt?[12] (Krämer 2003, 26)

As explained by Krämer above, innovation in writing took place by virtue of a reconfiguration of the visual or iconic dimension of writing for the sake of counting and calculation. This however also means that the role of using visual capacities in the context of mathematics shifts. Krämer demonstrates these types of shifts by highlighting how the Roman abacus compensated the impossibility of the Roman sign system to serve as an instrument for counting (18). Hence, people had to literally look somewhere else — into the world or to a tool — and visual strategies in mathematics functioned differently. The same shift underlies Krämer's observation that scientific progress substantially relies on making abstract phenomena visually experienceable, instead of just abstracting from what is experienced visually.

The important insight for the sake of the current inquiry is Krämer's observation that there is no linear history of progress in which one medium supersedes the other. Instead, there are relocations of the usages and positions of certain modes of experiencing the world, i.e. capacities to represent the world. This is important to keep in mind while evaluating phrases such as "show, don't tell" and critiques of the textual organization of truth, common in the field of digital publications. The hypothesis of Krämer may, however, explain very well how media innovations such as those of digital technologies disintegrate a certain epistemic environment, together with their known and trusted practices of creating and verifying knowledge. It is then not surprising that, as shown by the previous chapters, digital publications look like a potpourri of experiments for the sake of finding convincing modes of creating and verifying knowledge in the "digital age."

Krämer's final quote also contains a hypothesis that can explain why, in the field of digital publications, claims about different media tend to overstress certain changes such as those outlined in the sections on post-digitality and mathematical knowledge. More precisely, it is possible to take the theme of "epistemological effects" and put it into the context

12 "Could it be, that all the epistemological effects which emerge out of changes in media are in fact a surplus of the incorporation of one medium into another? Could it furthermore be the case that media are always already hybrid constructions, such that the idea of unique media is just the consequence of theoretical conventionalization, a conventionalization that seems possible at the very moment in which one medium becomes the topic of another medium, so that it has the possibility to appear as a specific form of media in the first place?" (author's translation)

of the discourse on digital publications today. Epistemological effects are created where certain capacities of representing the world engage with each other in new ways, due to innovation in media and media-technology. In the author's illustration, this engagement is the iconic restructuring of a medium that has been perceived as a mostly discursive medium before. In the field of digital publications, the same processes are indicated by phrases like the fourth paradigm or the end of theory. Surplus is not just the process of reorientation within a new epistemic environment (see above paragraph). It is the act of constructing and re-defining two media — the old and the new — in order to gain orientation within an epistemologically fragile situation. It is an idealization, because for the purpose of orientation it stresses features that help to separate media and medialities within this situation.

In Krämer's analysis, this idealization takes the form of a disregarding attitude towards the visual in former evaluations of the history of science. Hence, the iconic condition within this history remained hidden for a certain period. However, there are also examples of a positive idealization. One example is given by Bernard Stiegler in his revision of Platon's critique of written text compared to spoken language (Stiegler 2006). According to Stiegler, Plato conceived of written text as an artificial memory which builds on a technical relationship with language. Spoken language for Plato is in contrast not based on a technical relationship with language, which privileges it for the task of philosophical truth seeking.

By making significant use of the work of Derrida (1982) on the relationship between spoken language and written text, Stiegler illustrates, however, that Plato's description of language fundamentally presupposes a technical use of vocality, which is the same he attributes to text. Thus, the distinction between written text and spoken language appears fuzzier than considered by Plato. Using the words of Krämer, the emerging text-based culture in Athens created a "surplus" when reflecting on spoken and written language.

The idea of surplus makes it possible to qualify some of the claims about epistemological changes provoked by digital technology, like those about the end of theory or the transgression of binaries that belong to the "restrictive" culture of textuality. At the same time, it gives evidence of the fact that changes in representational strategies take place in times of media innovation, and that these changes require re-orientation and intervention, as will be discussed now.

Representing in Times of Calculated Calculation

The Computer as a Calculatedly Calculating Machine

Krämer (2003, 21) describes innovation in the usage of textuality, leading to what she calls, "operational script." It remains an open question how Krämer's line of argument makes it possible to identify something specific about the intermedial situation of digital technologies today. From her point of view, the usage of calculation (see above) is responsible for the development of operational script. A revision of this use of calculation thus might also help to gain insights about today's intermedial situation.

As has been described above, the author defines calculation as a goal-oriented, functional, and efficient process. This definition is substantiated by the explanation that such a calculated process is one in which *knowing how* and *knowing that* diverge:

> Das Wissen, wie wir eine Rechenoperation durchzuführen haben, trennt sich vom Wissen womit wir dabei eigentlich umgehen und warum diese Operation tatsächlich aufgeht.[13] (Krämer 2003, 21)

This divergence also underlies Krämer's comparison between the Roman and the modern mathematical sign system. While the former focused on the representation of mathematical entities, the latter focus on facilitating counting. The first depicts entities, the second depicts its relationship to other mathematical symbols. For Krämer, such divergence is crucial for any kind of calculative practice requiring a technological relationship to its object of application. This again clarifies the application of the term "machine" in her definition of mathematical text as a symbolic machine (above; Krämer 2003, 19).

The term "machine" indicates the relationship to the topic of computation, since modern computation is fundamentally a result of calculatory practice. The Turing Machine, the theoretical of modern computation, was a response to the so-called *Hilbert Program*. It aimed at proving or rejecting the "Entscheidbarkeit" (decidability) of a calculus. In simple terms, this means that it tries to prove that any mathematical statement, build upon logical axioms, will conclude in a finite number of steps. In the context of computers this means the question of whether a computer will halt so that

13 "The knowledge about the procedure and steps which we have to take in order to carry out a mathematical calculation is isolated from knowledge about the issue we are dealing with, as well as why this procedure actually leads to a correct result." (author's translation)

in computer science terminology the Turing Machine is concerned with the *Halting Problem*.

As in the scenario described by Krämer, the result of this calculatory practice decouples a type of knowing-how from its corresponding knowing-that. Knowing how to manipulate or program a computer and wait for it to "halt" does not require knowledge about what mathematical decidability means. Furthermore, it is possible to argue that using the terminology of Krämer, rules to manipulate signs turn into rules to manipulate a machine. In the early years of computation this was quite a mechanical matter.

However, there is a significant difference between the outcome of calculatory practice in the creation of lists for problem solving (Lemke), or operational writing (Krämer), and the Turing Machine. With the Turing Machine, for the first time calculatory practice is fully concerned with itself and thus self-reflective. Lists facilitate the reproduction of steps in order to solve problems. Operational writing facilitates counting in order to enable its colloquially ubiquitous application. Only in the Turing Machine does calculatory practice evaluate itself. It is not just a machine, but a machine in symbolizing machinery. Likewise, what is operationalized with the Turing Machine is operationality itself. Operationalized operationality, finally, is nothing else than automation.

Once again, it must be highlighted that what is worth emphasizing about the impact of computation is not what it does to mathematics, or how it changes our relationship to mathematics, as it is argued in e-Science, but the way it significantly alters the state and role of calculatory practice. Stressing the issue of automation as a universalization of calculatory practice makes it furthermore difficult to maintain the claim that mathematics, or a familiar though not identical thing like programming, is at the very heart of digital publications. Mathematics is not the goal but the means for generalizing this practice. Automation means benefiting from mathematics without the need to do math, just like operational script means benefiting from counting without deeper knowledge about mathematical rules. The benefit is to have some input and get some output, precisely without having to understand what lies in between. In a very different context, this observation is a repetition and confirmation of Cramer's remark that if anything, digital technologies are technologies of transformation.

Universalizing Symbolization Conversions

It is now possible to phrase the question about the intermedial situation of digital technologies in a more precise way: the question is how automation does — the ability of a machine that calculatedly calculates — affect people's relationship with the world in terms of representing and knowing it. Making use of the insights gained by the inquiry of Krämer, this question splits into two parts: first, how does automation reorganize the relationship between certain representation strategies, and second, how does it change the environment in which these strategies are applied.

In fact, possible answers, derived from observations about the field of digital publications, offer some indications already. These indications can very well be related to some of the conclusions from the current chapter. Regarding the first question, examples showed that the usage of different ways to communicate something meaningful such as text, images, or in TPs also sound, were more and more treated as equal. Representation strategies were used for a variety of purposes and for a similar purpose different representation strategies were mobilized.

This phenomenon confirms the prospect that social semiotics laid out for the making and use of signs. The epitome of this development is what the research field of *multimodal analysis* calls a process of increasing *grammatization* of means to represent other than by language. Multimodal analysis (hereafter referred to as MuA) is a set of research fields that emerged out of the program of social semiotics (Jewitt 2011; O'Halloran and Smith 2011; O'Halloran 2011; Jewitt 2014). While social semiotics predominantly carried out analysis of language, MuA uses Halliday's conceptual tools to analyze the use and status of different, i.e. multimodal, means of representing in a very systematic way. Concepts such as semiotic resource, multimodality, and grammatization are part of the outcome of this attempt.

In this process, the term grammatization refers to two things. First, it addresses the process itself, in which more and more resources are used in everyday communication in order to produce meaning and to represent something, i.e. to become semiotic resources. Secondly, it refers to the observation that the type of use of these semiotic resources, on their own and in combination with each other, engenders certain rules that are similar to grammatical rules in language (O'Halloran 2011, 126). From this point of view, things like images, space, sound, color, and gesture among other things become *semiotic resources* within a multimodal discursive practice (O'Halloran 2011, 120–21). Building upon such observation, MuA tries to analyze these grammatical structures, their development, their application in colloquial communication, and translations of meaning between semiotic resources.

One does not need to agree with the claim that each semiotic resource can develop the same level of grammatization or is equally suitable for discourse. It is furthermore possible to challenge the idea that there is a historical drive towards ever increasing grammatization, as is sometimes suggested (Stiegler 2010; Tinnell 2015). However, such criticisms do not invalidate the observation that the evaluation of the capabilities of different means to represent something, and the parallel use of different strategies, have significantly increased in the context of digital publications and its corresponding discourse on digital technologies.

Both phenomena, the increased use of resources as semiotic resources, as well as a process of grammatization for many of these resources, can be explicated via the definition of digital technologies and computation in this chapter. Cramer's observation that computers mostly convert between signals, for instance analogue signals into digital signals, is just another description of the same phenomenon, a conversion of something into a representation of the same thing. The same applies to the issue of grammatization. The cultural practice of calculation formalized, not to say, grammatized the iconography of mathematical symbols and the layout of the paper on which they are written or printed. It therefore goes without saying that a machine which mimics the idea of calculatory practice itself has a lot to offer for converting between different modalities in a calculatory way or using such modalities purposefully.

It does not surprise, then, that in MuA the phenomenon of multimodal representation and communication is expected to grow significantly as a direct consequence of digital technologies. For O'Halloran (2008), the unique aspect of digital technologies is the fact that they introduce what she calls a *universal symbolism*, i.e. a mechanism for omnipotent representation. Regardless of the question if it is really a universal symbolism that the computer introduces, or if it is better described as the universalization of practices of representation and symbolic conversions as in this study, the crucial point remains the same: the increasing capability of using many different semiotic resources in order to represent and to communicate is so fundamentally entangled with digital technologies that, in the eyes of MuA, it makes sense to call such practices a "digital literacy" (Rowsell 2013).

As has been indicated already, it is possible to observe the impact of this universalization of symbolic practice in many digital publications described in the preceding chapters. It underlies the inclusion of different types of media with equal rights proposed by publication concepts as different as RIPs, UBs, or TPs. The case of TPs stands out most in this respect because they aim at the same universal level on which O'Halloran's characterization of digital technologies is located. Indeed, the peculiarity of TPs is the proposition to not only add different media types to a publication, but to create something that is more than its parts: a transmedial, which in this context could be translated to universal, mode of producing meaning.

An argument against this characterization is the alleged primacy of data, advocated in e-Science approaches to digital publications, in order to support more "data-like" publications. However, this argument only looks like a counter-argument. There are two reasons for this claim. First, where such approaches advocate the publication of data, this data is normally addressed in a way that is far from being data in the strictest sense. A *csv* file for the representation of tabular data, for instance, is a textual representation of the concept of sequenced lists of information in the first place. The same applies to SPs, in which more than binary data is produced and published as texts, including certain grammatical extensions useful for the computer. They are not published as binary files but as text files, and for good reason, because as binary files they would be hard to use in their respective environments.

The confusing point about the term data and its usage is the fact that rather than referring to certain properties of the thing, it denotes what people want to do with it. What the ideal of data really advocates is not the primacy of a certain type of representation above all others, but of programing as the ultimate form of inquiry. What distinguishes the two examples is a certain level of formal structure, but this does not oppose it completely to text, which itself has formal structure in terms of grammar, style conventions and layout.

It could however be argued that it has a specific type and degree of formal structure that makes computation more efficient. Accordingly, something becomes data when it is highly structured and organized. In recorded data such as the music files in the Executable Music Documents project (De Roure 2014a) and other sensory data, it becomes clear that this distinction does not hold either. There is very little structure in such data, considering the way structure is understood above. In this context, people might speak of raw data. Nevertheless, nothing stops those same music files from being heard by someone through the means of an audio player that computes, meaning it converts the file into sound waves, or from being processed by a data analyst through programming. It could just as easily be defined as a piece of music as raw data.

The issue of formality and structure, again, refers more to the computational model by which a certain resource is processed and to specific computational capacities at a certain point of time, than to properties of the resource itself. The need for structure in data varies, as such models and capacities vary.

Having said all this, it is not reasonable to aim at more "data-like" publications, since it is wrong to interpret the corresponding discourse about data as counterargument against the claim of an expansion of the capabilities of symbolic or semiotic practices. Everything without any exception is digital data if turned into a representation that consists of bits in a computer. However, this data is nothing more than a self-description of the computer as a machine. No one, especially not in the context of science, engages directly with this representation. They engage with it as a binary representation of a representation of a text-documents — for instance TEI-XML — or as a binary representation of a representation of a music file such as *RIFF WAVE*. Consequently, data is a representation which evokes representations. This, however, is exactly what was argued about the consequences of the idea of a calculatedly-calculating machine for the status of representation above. As machines of conversions, digital technologies universalize the practice of symbolization, meaning the representational use of different resources or modalities and the perception of what representations are.

The Difference between Representation and Intervention

The implementation of a universal symbolic system and the simultaneous use of different modalities for different semiotic purposes is only one horizon of the calculatedly-calculating machine. Another one can be derived from Krämer's observations that the calculatory practice of operational script turns abstract and theoretical entities into entities that can be sensed and experienced. In Krämer's example, it is the eye that sees mathematical symbols on a paper and the hand that touches this paper while writing on it. Thus, there is not just an extension of symbolic means, but also a reconfiguration of the role sensing. Krämer emphasized this aspect because it is often forgotten, so that now the question to be answered is: what is being overlooked in the picture above?

Up to this point, it is not clear how digital technologies reconfigure the realm of things to be experienced. They appeared as technologies creating new means of what can be sensed only, just like the transformation of topological into typological knowledge, or the conversion of analogue phenomena into digital. Nonetheless, some indications in the work of Cramer suggest that this is only part of the issue. In fact, universalized conversion in the light of the calculatedly-calculating machine does not just mean *analogue to digital* or *digital to analogue* but ... *to analogue to digital to analogue to* .... It addresses the ability to sequence such conversions in an instant without leaving the machine itself, i.e. without anyone's participation.

Looking from the viewpoint of representing something, this sequence of conversions addresses the capability of digital technologies to completely detach from the representational context and the motivation that started the sequence in the first place. That means it can produce discrete objects for which, theoretically, it is no longer reproducible what they represent and that they represent. In consequence, such objects have to be experienced and sensed not as a means to interpret or decode them, but to open up any possibility for decoding and interpretation in the first place.

In principle, a simulation is a first step in this direction because the transformation steps between the description of a phenomenon and the simulation are complex to such an extent that a simulation is sensed more than it is read. In fact, it often is the very purpose of certain types of simulations to provoke sensing and affection (Licastro 2017). Nevertheless, a simulation is still associated with the domain of digital technologies, that means likely to be understood as representation of something, rather than being something of its own, because it remains the screen on which the phenomenon was both described and turned into a simulation. The point becomes clearer when the example of the 3D printer is taken, because a 3D printer produces objects out of representations that are not only meant to be sensed, but which are also completely detached from the technological apparatus. It is a new autonomous "living" object which is able to relocate in time and space and thereby begins to speak for itself.

Within this description, representation in digital technologies would be better understood as intervening. The transgression of this frontier is articulated very clearly where it is applied as a scientific methodology. Accordingly, Sayers et al. (2015, 4) quote Neil Gershenfeld in "Between Bits and Atoms," a contribution for the *New Companion to Digital Humanities* (Schreibman, Siemens, and Unsworth 2016), when they refer to this frontier in terms of "'the programmability of the digital worlds we've invented' applied 'to the physical world we inhabit'". This methodology consists of "creating a conversation between the physical world and the virtual world of the computer" which is "the conversion of one form of energy into another" (7).

The constructive and truth-creating act Krämer describes in the context of the infinite and the zero in mathematics needs therefore to be understood more literally for the case of the calculatedly-calculating machine. What is constructed are objects that fully become part of what is called the real world and hence exist literally.

A set of extreme examples for this interventionist dimension is given by bio-engineering, nano-technology, and robotics, among other disciplines — disciplines which quite literally "write" reality. Representation does thus not only turn more easily into an intervention in the represented context, but also into an entire transformation of this context. In a metaphoric way, people like Bernard Stiegler coined the term "Science Fiction" in comparison to "Science" in order to emphasize the qualitative shift that digital technologies carry out on the practice of representing (Stiegler 2011; Abbinnett 2017, 56). In the area of digital publishing, phrases like "Show Don't Tell" or the abundant evaluations of the status of text in digital publications gave testimony of this uncertainty about the status of the practice of representation as such. In a firm plea to open up the field of digital scholarly publications, Stephen Ramsay and Geoffrey Rockwell also use the term "thing knowledge" as a new type of epistemology, and proclaim that "according to this view, we should be open to communicating scholarship through artifacts, whether digital or not" (Ramsay and Rockwell 2012).

Again, and in a more theoretical context, a constellation that can be reproduced by a technology that supposedly delivers perfect conditions for representation, is opposed by a use of this technology that undermines representation as such. Only this time, it is not about the concept of aggregation as the perfect representation of publications, and the artifactual is not represented by SCPs, but by the concept of reality itself.
In summary, the impact of the calculatedly-calculating machine for the practice of representing is not just a significant extension of its means, but also a closer entanglement with other practices that are called interventional or transformative.

The Three Epistemological Effects of Calculated Calculation

The Omnipotence and Crisis of Representation

After analyzing the changes that digital technologies caused for the practice of representation in the light of Krämer's concepts, it is now possible to have a closer look at what she called epistemological effects in the epistemic environment of an intermedial situation. As has been indicated, the term "epistemological effect" is intended to denote the irritating impact that changes within this environment have on people's strategies when conceiving of, representing, and understanding the world, as well as the ways in which this world unfolds for people.

Concerning the issue of universalized representation, two effects can be identified regarding the idea of a calculatedly-calculatory machine. One of these effects can be derived from an analysis of the logical end of the idea of multimodal and universal representation, the other focuses on the consequences of multimodal representation practices for systems of representation.

The allegedly universal ability to use different semiotic resources in order to represent certain issues, to use semiotic researches in different ways, and to use them at the same time in a hybrid and complex representation suggests the idea of a perfect representation. Where such an idea is disqualified due to philosophical reasons, it still introduces criteria of representation quality in terms of multimodal density, complexity, or plurality. Publications in journals such as Vectors, Kairos, or other TPs are very often built around such a notion.

The second effect is based on the possibility of a contrasting perspective of the aforementioned ability. The advancement of these abilities can similarly be evaluated as an increase of heterogeneity, contingency, and unsteadiness in the domain of representation. Representational disorientation is a possible outcome here. Krämer's discussion indicated already that in the past, specific resources tend to have specific functions in particular contexts. Not all potentially semiotic resources were used in a semiotic way. This was also part of certain technologically mediated limitations in the use of resources for the sake of representation. In this sense, she highlighted the correspondence between iconographic aspects of Roman numbers and things that could be called countable by the eye. She also showed that such functions may change, as they changed in the shift of the visual focus from things that are counted to visual aids to support the process of counting. Epistemological effects were also defined as an irritation produced by this shift, meaning the defamiliarization of familiar usages of a certain resource in a specific strategy of representing the world.

A more insightful and systematic description of this issue in the context of digital technologies can be found by referring to the concept of *mode* and its development in MuA. If multimodality is the general possibility of using different resources for representation, and grammatization indicates the development of rules within such usages, the question is how to identify rule-based multimodal representation. Multimodal analysis discusses this issue under the concept of mode. Accordingly, part of MuA is to ask the question: “What is Mode?” (Kress 2013), or better, when is multimodal communication creating certain modes that each share recognizable application patterns across situations? Chapter six will provide an in-depth analysis of mode that goes beyond the remarks in the following lines.

There are analytical and pragmatic answers to this question. Gunther Kress, who prefers the term mode to the term resource, defines it as an entanglement between media, semiotic logics, and social actions (Kress 2013, 61). Media, sometimes called technology or device, means physical material or device involved in meaning production, such as paper or computer screens. Semiotic logics are concerned with syntactical limitations and potentials of media. Instruments or speakers, for instance, cannot make use of elements of color, but of time and pitch. Additionally, modes are socio-culturally encoded. A medium such as a book is most often a socio-cultural artifact. The usage patterns of semiotic logics and the situations in which a mode is used are more or less socio-culturally defined.

In other words, specific technologies conflate with certain modalities and corresponding semiotic logics. These are organized in a historical process by virtue of cultural norms and practices, in order to form a relatively stable entanglement. The relative stability and thereby transparency of this entanglement exists for members of a socio-cultural environment over a certain period of time. With some fuzziness left, it could be argued that Krämer describes a process in which a specific mode of representation — that of mathematical writing and arithmetic books — develops, except that Krämer’s perspective focuses on a specific process and describes this process from within, while mode is a top-down conceptual framework that seeks to be applicable across specific examples.

However, it has just been argued that digital technologies can take the form of many devices and to mediate between devices in different ways.

The aspect of automation, furthermore, puts much more control over the process of organizing modalities in the hands of domains and individuals. In the light of the aforementioned heterogeneity and the variety of the abundance of digital publication formats, it could therefore be argued that in times of digital technologies, there is a constant tension between the processes towards establishing social conventions for the usage of modalities and their arrangement for the sake of specific situations or contexts.

The comparison between Krämer's analysis and the concept of mode allows a closer look at how discussions of the status of mode reveal the shape of epistemological effects caused by digital technologies. Within MuA itself, the whole issue is analyzed in a very precise way, which benefits from the analytical instruments described above. Thus, Boeriis and Johannessen (2015) argue that the whole concept of mode becomes problematic, due to digital technologies. They assert that:

> ... as a result of new technologies, logogenetic action-perception cycles in multimodal articulation happen at an ever-increasing rate, which causes both ontogenetic growth and phylogenetic conventionalization dynamics to speed up as well. (Boeriis and Johannessen 2015, 13)

In simpler terms, digital technologies undermine the conditions that are necessary for modes to emerge. Already in 2005, Lemke observed that the concept of multimodal genre, a term that has a great similarity to mode, does not hold any longer (Lemke 2005). Lemke states that due to the proliferation of modal and semiotic options, and the dissociation between specific devices and the use of semiotic resources, the idea of genre is substituted by so-called "traversals." Within traversals, the link between modalities and semiotic aspects of such modalities does not exist independently from a specific situation, controlled very often by only a few individuals. Hence, there is no "grammatical" relationship beyond the "cohesive chain" of elements.

It has been said that epistemological effects in an intermedial situation consist of irritations to the common strategies of representing and referring to the world. Such irritations can also be found today. A good example for illustrating the shifts and the irritations they often provoke is given by Mersch (2004). In his examination, Mersch tries to specify the uniqueness of iconographic descriptions of the world compared to those in language. At the same time, however, he regrets that this uniqueness is slowly disappearing in contemporary usages of images, which themselves start to work like language. He offers the example of images in science, which, according to the author, are used as arguments in something he denotes as an iconographic discourse. Mersch regrets these changes because he interprets it as a loss of a particular mode of making sense of the world. This regret can be considered a good example of one of the epistemic effects of intermediality. Additionally, the example supports the claim that the relationship between certain modalities and what they mediate depends less on a specific logic of this modality, and more on the practices in which they are embedded, as well as the ways people conceive of them.

How then can the epistemic effects derived from the universalization of symbolic practices be summarized? The first approach, as has been argued at the beginning of this section, welcomes the freedom and flexibility by which semiotic resources can now be used for representation purposes. It celebrates multimodal complexity as a goal in itself. The second, however, indicates that this flexibility might also come with the loss of certain semiotic capabilities, of use and play with conventions and the emergence of genre norms.

To push this point further, the availability of the aforementioned universalization, and the concurrency of multiple representational modes as well as multiple usage patterns for modalities, may likewise be conceived of as a crisis of the strategic practice of representing as such. Examples for such perception today are given above. This is not surprising, since from an ontological point of view a perfect representation turns into the thing itself, so that any type of representational relationship disappears.

The same crisis can be observed from the opposite side. A hypothetical traversal, in which the use of semiotic resources is governed solely by the situation of use, could not be considered part of a collective representational system any longer. It would become difficult to identify the semiotic use of resources as such, because, as social semiotics has argued, being a sign is already a social convention. For this reason, a subfield of MuA emphasizes that one should not distinguish between acts of representation and other actions any longer. In this research field, called *Multimodal Interaction Analysis* (hereafter referred to as MIA), everything is an action (Norris 2011), and representation as a practice by itself vanishes.

Omnipotence and Crisis Beyond Representation

The concept of action resembles the notion of intervention used before. While the first term focuses on the relationship between an agent and an action, the second addresses the relationship between an action and its effect on its environment. In the light of this second relationship, another important epistemological effect can be identified: the more representation and intervention conflate with each other, the more the distinction between the concepts of nature and culture becomes inappropriate.

In a certain way, Krämer's digression on the constructivist facet of operational script demonstrates that such a distinction was always problematic. Nonetheless, the extent to which it appears problematic in the context of the calculatedly-calculating machine seems to pose new challenges. Once again, it helps to remember that this machine does not just cause a new set of entities to appear as operational script did in mathematics. Neither did it just cause a shift in the relationship between nature and culture. It seeks to control the relationship itself.

A variety of theoretical discussions exist which give evidence of the impact of the resulting epistemological effect. These discussions are attempts to arrange a new epistemic setup under the aforementioned conditions. One of these discussions is addressed by the term *Anthropocene*, a concept that raised much attention across various scientific domains in the last fifteen years. It is most often associated with geological and climate-related phenomena. All of these phenomena, like for instance climate change, indicate the impact of people on processes of the earth's environment (Waters et al. 2016). Hence, it addresses a setup in which no aspect of what is called nature can be considered out of the reach of people. Likewise, the epochal wording of this setup as a phase in the history of the earth reflects that the change is conceived of as fundamental. Accordingly, Bethany Nowviskie states in "Digital Humanities and the Anthropocene" that "it is a geological age of our own making" (Nowviskie 2015, 6), using a quote by Andrew Revkin. Another quote that is often re-used in this debate is that of Vladimir Vernadskij, who in a much earlier attempt to address the same issue states:

> We study the influence of the scientific thought as a geological force, and in this case often the thought and will of a separate person may suddenly change natural processes and manifest itself through this change. (Vernadskij 1997)

On a more fine-grained level, the distinction between culture and nature equates with the distinction between human and non-human. Consequently, contributions exist which also highlight the fragility of this distinction in the light of digital technologies. In this respect, Bradley (2011) argues in *Originary Technicity* that today's technology, more than anything else, reveals the technicity of the idea of the human. Promoting the concept of the "post-human," he offers a philosophical generalization of ideas that have been introduced already by Haraway (1991) in her work on *Simians, Cyborgs, and Women: The Reinvention of Nature*. In the opposite direction, David Gunkel calls for an ethic beyond human rights, which include artificial intelligence and robots (Gunkel 2007; Gunkel 2012).

The point here is not to evaluate the correctness of all these contributions. The point is that the epistemological effects of digital technologies are such that a significant number of researchers from all scientific domains feel obliged to question the distinction between culture and nature, the system of representation, and what is being represented.

The relevance for the topic of digital publications is demonstrated by the fact that publication formats, which tend to belong to the field of e-Science, are defined with comparable ideas in mind. Accordingly, an epistemological setup in which correlation supersedes representation, and empirical data substitutes theoretical inquiry resembles a situation in which there is an identity between the world and its representation.

In the light of this section, however, this claim must be put into context correctly. The one crucial aspect it suppresses is the fact that an epistemological setup, in which technology "makes obsolete a scientific method" (Anderson 2008) to theorize people's relationship with the world is also a world in which the celebrated benefits of empirical knowledge disappear. After the examples given before, and again from an ontological point of view, such empirical knowledge would just correlate with people's theorizations about possible worlds. In the final analysis, this is another possible interpretation of Stiegler's claim that science has become science fiction.

Crisis and Surplus

In consideration of Krämer's remarks on intermediality, a third epistemological effect needs to be discussed. This effect builds upon the phenomenon translated from Krämer's work with the term "surplus." Surplus denotes the insight that in an intermedial situation, properties of old and new media are defined in a simplifying and contrasting manner, to achieve a better grasp on the changes that take place in this situation. The creation of surplus gives orientation and obscures at the same time.

With the inquiry into digital technologies in mind, the area of surplus is indicated by the characterization of such technologies as calculatedly-calculating technologies, and the corresponding notion of automation. As has been outlined previously, digital technologies only represent the idea of generalizing calculation as automation. They are pretty successful representations of this idea, but remain representations nonetheless. This fact is unambiguously presented by the halting problem that has been discussed previously. The status of the halting problem produces an irritating space. It is the problem of a machine that represents automation so well in everyday life that automation turns into a general principle, but, remaining a representation, produces its own quotidian life situations in which people cannot be sure of the impact of this problem.[14]

The consequences described in the previous two sections thus only describe the mindset produced by the conceptual framework of digital technologies, as those technologies that trivialize the theoretical revolve around the calculatedly-calculating machine. They are the result of over-stressing and ontologizing certain ideas and concepts of this machine. Such an ontological point of view was, however, necessary, because digital publication concepts, as shown throughout the current study, were driven by the same tendencies. It had to be shown that thinking one's way to the end of this laid out path leads to contradictions, and that these contradictions are a crucial component of the field of digital publications.

The real epistemological irritation now is a consequence of the uncertain status of surplus. On the one hand, it is necessary to identify the properties of a changing epistemological landscape within an intermedial situation, because this landscape is changing. On the other hand, it is only possible to identify directions of these changes by creating a surplus. The extent and the value of this surplus can, however, not be known, because the reflections on it are in motion, as is the process of the transformation instigated by digital technologies.

To put it differently, the issue is not that the two types of effects described above are completely wrong. It is more the uncertainty that exists concerning what they conceal, and in which situations this has a liberating impact and where it poses new problems. To take the example of the fourth paradigm, the impact of digital technologies might still be such that the opposition between empiricism and hermeneutics becomes if not obsolete, then at least less important in some circumstances. In other words, it might be more useful not to pay attention to this opposition than to emphasize

14 For examples of the relevance of the halting problem for colloquial issues in computer science, please refer to the wonderful explanation at https://cs.stackexchange.com/questions/32845/why-really-is-the-halting-problem-so-important.

it. In the same way, the conflation of culture and nature suggested by the discourse on the Anthropocene does not actually make a philosophical claim, but argues that in the perception of certain problems, it would help to leave the opposition behind in order to deal with current problems of the environment. In short, if the starting point is the perception of a changing epistemological landscape, as addressed by many discussions around publication concepts, then the issue of surplus clearly expresses that it is not possible to anticipate where the epistemological setup might stabilize.

Publications Beyond Cold Technology and Pure Theory

At this point, the purely theoretical discussion of aspects of digital publishing, which is sorely missing in literature on digital publications concepts themselves, demands looking out for a new starting point for the engagement with digital publications. The theoretical discussion of certain leitmotifs from the discourse on digital publications fulfilled the task of showing that a focus on alleged intrinsic capabilities of digital technologies leads to an uncertain and even contradictory position. Due to the results of the theoretical analysis of digital technologies, such an analysis, however, did not lay the groundwork for this new starting point either, at least not explicitly. This starting point needs to come from another source. In fact, the last phase of the genealogy of digital publications already pointed into a certain direction, a direction that highlighted the need to reconsider digital publications as social objects. The final part of this chapter will demonstrate how this need can be derived from the line of arguments in the sections above.

The following discussion of key ideas in different approaches to digital publishing showed their intrinsic logical aporia. In the case of the "end of theory," this contradiction consists of the fact that a world that has no need for theoretical representation is likewise unable to host empirical knowledge. Since it is hardly possible to think this thought outside of the realm of logical reasoning and the issue of surplus, the social realm is the only place where the distinction between one or the other is constantly negotiated and continuously modified.

The same discussion, furthermore, showed that a world in which every resource is considered a resource for creating and communicating meaning in a multimodal way, the concept of meaning itself is at risk of becoming meaningless.

In a hypothetical scenario, the perfect multimodal representation becomes the thing itself. The relationships between such objects, which are both representations of themselves and themselves, do not have any typological differences anymore. They are just inter-operating, as it is sometimes written in the context of *Object-Oriented-Ontology* (Bogost 2012, 38), within a one-dimensional space. This space of objects that do not relate to each other in other ways than by interaction is then another possible way to describe the perspective of the social world.

The second reason behind the demand to adopt a more socially oriented point of view turns the perspective of the first one upside down. Here, the question is not what happens if certain claims are radically thought through. The issue is to remember the fact that this end only exists in theory. As it has become clear in the course of the entire chapter, none of the key features of digital technologies are exclusive to digital technologies, and neither have they only become crucial by the advent of digital technologies. The opposition between digital and analogue, the transformation of practice into calculations, and the expansion of symbolic means have all been key aspects in the cultural history of humankind for hundreds of years, as Cramer, Lemke, Krämer, and Halliday have argued.

Likewise, it needs to be emphasized that although the idea of calculated calculation is on the conceptual level qualitatively different, digital technologies will never embody this idea completely. The reason for this situation was discussed as the halting problem. Curiously enough, in mathematics the halting problem has been converted from being a theoretical problem into a probabilistic problem by Gregory Chaitin and others (Raatikainen 2001). In simple words, the theoretical issue that a computer may not halt with certain computations is transformed into a concrete problem in which the probability that a computer may not halt is calculated for a defined computation. It makes a theoretical concept useful, because its risks and potentials can be evaluated for a task in each situation. In the same way, it could be argued that the usefulness of ideas of digital publications depends on the level on which it is possible to evaluate them in light of concrete social situations and not as values as such. The challenge that arises is to create better conditions for mediating, and synchronizing between processes of technological innovation and social organization, as both have equal rights.

Finally, an evaluation of technology itself suggests refraining from any perspective that distinguishes between the engagement into specific technological innovations and the social environment in which this engagement takes place. While the last paragraphs dealt with the imaginary part of the idea of digital technologies, the following arguments address the imaginary aspects of technology as such.

Lemke as well as Krämer described the development of technologies as efficient problem-solving strategies. Both, the development of technologies as well as their implementation in a peculiar situation, are motivated by solving a problem efficiently. The efficiency of such strategies can be jeopardized in two ways if the element of time is considered, in which both the development of technology as well as its application take place.

On the side of development and implementation of technology, this means that a situation in which a defined technological solution appears to be most appropriate is not the same anymore at the precise moment in which this solution is implemented, or ready at hand. The conditions might have changed, or new technologies might have been made available which relativize the efficiency of the initial approach. Hence, the efficiency of technological design is at risk if non-technological developments are not included.

On the site of application, the situation is similar. At the very moment a technological solution is available, it automatically relates to much more than to the original problem. This means that it may be used in unintended ways, but also that it causes unforeseeable changes to the whole environment in which the original problem resides. Both angles address the social adoption and impact of technology, and are comprehensively analyzed in research fields like *Social Construction of Technology* (Bijker 2009, also referred to as SCOT). Thus, the powerful decision in technology-making to isolate a problem-solution relationship becomes its most vulnerable aspect, if there is no sensibility for the fact that the process of making and its result also do not exist in isolation.

At first glance, these arguments might appear trivial and familiar. Nonetheless, the summary of their relevance for digital publications, discussed in the next section, will demonstrate their significance. Additionally, they become less trivial when they are re-evaluated in the context of the calculatedly-calculating machine, i.e. a machine of ubiquitous and automated conversion. Here, such conversion capabilities dramatically increase the impact of the aforementioned phenomena, both in the environment in which technological development takes place, as well as for the effects of its results. This means that the social environment becomes potentially more dynamic and volatile, and the means of appropriation by persons and agents increase. Consequently, it seems necessary to also reconsider the way in which social aspects are addressed for the design of digital publications.

The broader inspection of theoretical aspects of digital technologies, as they appear in digital publishing, have revealed the extent to which they have to be relativized as socially embedded technologies. In doing so, theory mostly led to the same conclusions as in the field of post-digitality, by densifying observations like the partial failure of claims about digital technology, or the increasing use of digital and non-digital media at the same time.

One of the benefits of this inspection is the fact that now, the imaginative part of digital technologies can be deduced and not only asserted on the grounds of the aforementioned observations. Having in mind the epistemological effects of intermedial situations, a certain necessity for such imagination exists. This necessity is justified by the tension between the current impact technology has on the relationship between people and environment, and its unnegotiated scope in the future. Since this tension needs negotiation, neither the attempt to stick to the imaginative part of digital technologies as in e-Science, nor the support of hybrid approaches as such, as in post-digitality, UBs, TPs, or HPs is enough.

The process of negotiating the aforementioned tension is a social process, and cannot be shaped without intervention. The discussion in this section offered some clues in order to get a better idea of how such interventions should look and how technology and the social are connected. Such clues will be elaborated further in the remaining part of the present study.

At this point it should be clear that the:

> … messy state of media, arts and design *after* their digitization (or at least the digitization of crucial aspects of the channels through which they are communicated). (Cramer 2014)

similarly is an appropriate description for the situation the scientific domain, or at least crucial aspects of the channels through which it communicates its knowledge. Therefore, a productive approach could be the one sketched by Berry:

> We might no longer talk about digital versus analogue, but instead modulations of the digital or different intensities of the computational. We should therefore critically analyze the way in which cadences of the computational are made and materialized. (Berry 2013)

These differences happen within the social appropriation and application of technologies, which the next chapter will move on to.

[6]

… Publishing

Concepts of Social Aspects in Digital Publications and What They Miss

The turn to post-digitality and the theoretical arguments it provoked within the preceding sections followed a shift in digital publication projects towards new ways to confront the social dimension of publications. Now that the background, the function, and, even more important, the need for this shift has become clear by virtue of theoretical discussion, a discussion which rarely took place in most publishing initiatives, it is necessary to evaluate the concept of social aspects within such initiatives more systematically.

Three different outcomes of this evaluation are possible. First, the issues already indicated in chapter four and five will be substantiated. It will be shown that publication formats which react differently to social issues of publications are not reflecting on such issues in all their dimensions. Second, certain patterns of ruling out social aspects of publications against a technological background will arise. Finally, such patterns will provide a first step towards bringing order into the "messy state of publications after digitization."

From Technology as a Social Phenomenon to the Social as a Technological Feature

The first pattern of neglect of social issues of publications consists of implicitly or explicitly creating a hierarchical relationship between technology and the social dimension of technology. In this hierarchy, social tensions of digital publications are projected onto a technological framework, so that the framework itself remains untouched by such tensions.

The most obvious example of this strategy are certain approaches of NPs, more precisely Kuhn's attempt to make digital publications a type of "publishing without publishers" (Kuhn et al. 2015). It has been described in the chapter before that this attempt tries to convert stakeholders, who carry out necessary social functions in publishing, such as quality control, into functions of technological infrastructure.

The anti-socialization process has two dimensions. The approach is developed because of frustration about publishers' rejection of new forms of publishing. The aforementioned conversion implies that there are no arguments for this rejection, apart from the stakeholders' will to secure their social position. Consequently, the attempt refrains from solving or negotiating a social conflict in order to create a solution away from any zone of ongoing conflict. Additionally, the approach taken by NPs implies that social practices associated with scholarly publications are addressed sufficiently by simply modelling their workflow, i.e. without requiring their own social agents in form of institutions or curators. In other words, issues such as quality control are sufficiently dealt with by providing rating functionality. Kuhn and others apply this approach not just to the example of quality control, but develop it as a general strategy.

The established hierarchy is such that the existence of social stakeholders, who deal with certain practices around publishing, is treated as a historical contingency. Accordingly, there are no serious obstacles to replacing such stakeholders by technology.

Another strategy to embed social issues into technology, in order to avoid the analysis of how technology is embedded in the social realm, is the creation of certain linear narratives of progress. In light of the question discussed in this section, such narratives provide the means to put stakeholders with different technological setups or different understandings of technology on different steps of a ladder that leads to an overarching known technological setup.

The present work has presented several narratives which were used this way. They were created most prominently in the context of e-Science and open science, which could be understood as meta-narratives. Its most outstanding example is probably De Roure's outlook on the "future of scholarly communications" (De Roure 2014b). In this work, the development of the whole field of scholarly publications is perceived in a two-dimensional coordinate system defined by increasing automation and increasing collaboration. The degree of innovation of publication formats can then be compared by calculating their distance from the furthest point of the top right quadrant. The strategic advantage of this approach is also well expressed in rhetoric decisions made by De Roure. He describes the current situation in past tense and adopts the role of a historian looking back to the present from the future.

The reformulation of conflicts between different perceptions of digital publications into issues of different positions of stakeholders on a ladder to progress has a second effect. It often leads to an extremely simplified, but also sometimes lofty, concept of the social. This phenomenon is comparable to the one that has been exemplified by NPs. In this case, however, it is motivated not by frustration of stakeholders' behavior but by fascination with technological capacities.

In fact, De Roure and other authors very much address the topic of social aspects in digital publications. De Roure uses terms like "social machines" (De Roure 2014b, 237), or "scientific social objects" (De Roure, Bechhofer, and Goble 2011). The question is thus what image of the social realm is projected behind the use of the term. A social machine is defined as "processes in which the people do the creative work and the machine does the administration" (237). According to De Roure, machine-readable publications are necessary in order to allow this scenario to happen. Machine-readable publications are publications which follow their own concept of scientific social objects. The whole setup of publications and corresponding infrastructure results in an interaction between humans and machines that turns the computer into a social agent.

There are several reasons for why such a use of the term social is problematic. First, the definition of a social machine adds nothing to the definition of computation as calculated calculatory practice. Hence, every type of computation is social in the sense that it has an input and an output that relates to humans. Second, it should be recalled once again that the argument builds upon a simplistic definition of machine-readability, which tautologically defines computation as the type of computation addressed by scientific social objects.[1] Accordingly, computers do not only become social agents by following De Roure's approach to computation. Instead,

1 Obviously, text mining algorithms do not read a plain text article any less than a SPARQL query which "reads" the formally annotated entities exposed as RDF. However, it does so differently with different outcomes and purposes.

they are always social agents, but agents with a whole gamut of relationships to humans that existed and will continue to exist side by side.

The fact that social activity is only perceived as such if it takes place within a technological frame that itself is no longer a social issue results in a purely quantitative measure of what is social activity. More precisely, the more interactivity is measurable among the highest possible number of agents, the more social activity takes place. In De Roure's terms, this means "how big is computation," and "how dense is a network." In contrast, the absence of interaction is not considered a social relationship itself. It is just perceived as less social activity. In other words, missing measurable interaction is not considered an action itself, and what is measurable is defined by the one who measures. The idea that such absence could address crucial issues of the social dimension of digital publications therefore becomes impossible. Consequently, the whole problem of the absence of researchers and stakeholders from digital publication concepts is turned into an awareness problem when Matthews et al. (2013, chap. 6) writes that:

> ... many researchers, data practitioners, publishers and policy makers are unaware of the potential of Research Objects as intellectual entities.

It has been said that e-Science and open science are meta-narratives. Accordingly, the anti-socialization of digital publications by means of narratives of progress are not just strategical means. Indeed, they propagate a set of antisocial elements in the theoretical setup of open science itself. One should keep in mind the definition of openness, as given by the Open Knowledge Foundation: "Open means anyone can freely access, use, modify, and share for any purpose" (Open Knowledge Foundation 2015). This definition leads to an ethical claim, made by most advocates of openness and precisely articulated by Brown: "Open science is the philosophical perspective that sharing is good and that barriers to sharing should be lowered as much as possible" (2016). Since this principle is rarely toned down within the open science community, and is presented as a philosophical and not an empirical argument, some of its antisocial components can be addressed quickly:

- It neglects the case where the conditions under which a resource is opened up are such that crucial aspects of the resource cannot be opened up with it. This might relate to the layers of presentation, to metadata, but also to qualitative aspects of a resource that need more context than a given environment can offer. In this situation, opening up a resource with the explicit intent of letting it circulate across contexts in fact has a negative social impact.

- It neglects that a resource usually represents only part of a theme or a specific viewpoint of the theme, and that this type of openness in isolation can violate the ethical goals of open science itself. In other words, openness does not automatically agglomerate positive impact on the social or scientific goods, it creates time dependent impulses for a specific social setup, in which the effects of this impulse are potentially unique. Boyd (2017) gathers a bunch of examples of the negative impact of open data resources, even in cases where the bias of such resources is minimal.
- It neglects the factual inequality of different social agents who create resources that can be made open under a normative definition of openness. This inequality does not mean technological capacity only, it relates as well to the social position and context of agents that might give them time, resources, public attention, professional liberty, or even the option to work digitally in order to create open resources.
- Similarly, different social agents possess different capacities of actually making use of open resources for the very same reasons. The question of how fast and how efficient different people and stakeholders are able to extract value from open resources must be answered differently for different stakeholders. This difference, however, has a huge impact on the status of the openness of the outcome, as well as for the structure of the field of science as such and beyond.
- Finally, the open circulation of resources across contexts, as envisioned by open science, ignores any perspective of how the whole social field of production and exchange of scholarly resources changes when a resource circulates from context a to context b. In conjunction with the last point, this could actually mean the overall conditions of openness decrease because of openness. More precisely, high-potential agents may benefit from the availability of open resources, while not publishing derivates under open or socially beneficial principles. Some examples for these Issues were gathered by Jeffrey Beall (Beall 2013; Beall 2017).

Beyond the examples, these arguments are theoretical possibilities. However, since the original claim by Titus Brown and other authors in the field of digital publishing is most often only theoretical, nothing more is required at this point. The lines of arguments reveal a simplified concept of the social within open science that, as has been stated before, treats social aspects only in terms of the level of connectivity, without consistently reflecting either on the specific position of these agents in the network, nor on how the realization and use of specific connections change the balance of a network. In short, this means that the more connectivity, the better, and the more an agent supports connectivity, the more she is positively seen to serve the greater good. Little research has actually been carried out to confirm or qualify these judgements, especially not in the field of digital publications with connections to the open science domain. While this observation supports the present critique, the first studies from peripheral open science topics such open access monograph publishing (Milloy and Collins 2016; Ferwerda, Pinter, and Stern 2017) have recently indicated that things are often more complicated. Levin and Leonelli (2017, 286), accordingly, conclude in a sociological field study on the implementation of open science principles that:

> ... whether openness leads to increased transparency and accountability depends on how, by whom, and for which purposes openness is enacted. ... specific instantiations of openness can foster attitudes that many would regard as alien to open science mandates ... . Thus, we argue that current scientific and political discussions should focus on what parts of research should be open, how, when, and for which purposes. The variability of situations in which openness is enacted, and the related need to evaluate its implementation on a case-by-case basis, needs to be taken into account by open science policies.

As much as the emergence of more subtle perspectives in the periphery of open science and open access — such as the one above — must be welcomed, its strong absence from digital publication concepts from the open science domain needs to be stressed. An even more problematic aspect of the asocial attitudes in open science is the ethos that as long as there are no immediate reasons against the open publication of resource, the most open option should be chosen. In this context, empirical proof for potential risks are demanded, while their own line of argument often refrains from including comprehensive empirical data on the aforementioned issues.

The anti-socialization of the topic of digital publications by means of narratives of progress, and its corresponding limited concepts of the social field, literally turn into asocial behavior where the tensions that such narratives create is explicitly addressed. In this respect, the phrases by Cameron Neylon that have already been quoted need to be re-interpreted.

The transformation of social conflict into heterogeneity

After several examples, where aspects of the social dimension of technology were converted to social facets within peculiar technologies, another transformation of social issues requires attention. This is the transformation of social conflicts into issues of heterogeneity. What is meant by this terminological substitution is the implicit or explicit idea that differences never exclude each other, but can always be harmonized or may exist side by side. Additionally, it means the idea that a harmonized set-up is always the preferable option.

One example for such a transformation is the idea of Scholarly Communication Infrastructures and the OpenAIRE approach. Different from former approaches, OpenAIRE accepts the state of heterogeneity in the field of digital publications. However, the scaled approach of OpenAIRE showed that this acceptance is only preliminary. The goal of this infrastructure is to gradually implement policy seeking in order to unify scholarly publishing, and at the same time maintain the idea that the harmonization of domain specific publication environment is a desirable and achievable goal.

Furthermore, domain repositories as science 2.0 repositories build on the idea of heterogeneity as a gradual deviation from the norm, perceived of as generic, a deviation that as such can then be included and exist side by side with others. Consequently, the OpenAIRE project defines *Enhanced Publication Meta-Models* from which so-called "domain-specific" *Enhanced Publications Data Models* can be derived, using the *Enhanced Publications Data Model Definition Language* (Bardi and Manghi 2015a). In a next step, an *Enhanced Publication Domain Specific Manipulation Language* assures the mapping between concrete EPs in a domain and its domain-specific data model.

What is most notable when regarding this chain of steps is the conviction of a seamless integration of differences. The possibility that the meta-model might not suffice, or is just not meaningful enough to describe specific publication types, does not occur. The relationships between different publication formats are therefore a hierarchy of `subclass` and `sameAs` relations.

The OpenAIRE project was already a reaction to the experience that harmonization of crucial areas around digital publications had not occurred automatically, or as a result of a bottom up approach pursued for SPs, and in the field of the semantic web in general. As in the OpenAIRE context, SPs advocate the idea that the use of shared semantics in order to structure a publication is desirable and useful for any type of publication. Likewise, it is built on the idea that the provision of sufficient means (technological or organizational) will assure that such semantics will appear. There furthermore is a similarity between the hierarchical ordering of the landscape of publications and the taxonomic logics in the core model, as well as spirit of the semantic web.[2] Therefore, it can be understood as an earlier version of an understanding of social differences in terms of heterogeneity, instead of tension or conflict.

A significant property and necessary consequence of this line of thought is the way in which existing differences are analyzed. Bourne, Buckingham Shum, et al. (2012) summarize:

> The software developers who build the current research informatics infrastructure are also very aware of the shortfalls and hindrances generated by today's fragmented development efforts. The problems here can be attributed to a number of elements. First, heterogeneous technologies and designs, and the lack (or sometimes the superfluity!) of standards, cause unnecessary technical difficulties and directly affect integration costs. … Third, research software developers typically work in a competitive environment, either academic or commercial, where innovation is rewarded much more highly than evolutionary and collaborative software reuse. This is especially true in a funding environment driven by the need for intensive innovation, where reusing other peoples" code is a likely source of criticism. … The impact of these tools is, far too often, solely based on how immediately useful they will be to researchers themselves, with no thought for the wider community.

Thus, the heterogeneity is described as unnecessary in the first place. Although social reasons are given initially, the following lines turn this

2 It is true that in the semantic web, many non-taxonomic models exist to formally describe semantic relationships, like for instance rule-based or thesaurus-like models. Nevertheless, the core model RDFS is taxonomic. More importantly, the modelling culture around specific domain semantics often inherits a taxonomic way of thinking. A paradigmatic example for this situation can be found in the way the W3C Web Annotation Data Model treats its property motivation. The terms which can be used for this property are modelled by using relationships of a thesaurus. Web Annotation allows adding and relating domain specific motivations terms to these terms. In contrast to the complex relationships that are possible by using relationships of a thesaurus, Web Annotation demands treating the given terms as generic terms allowing only specification. That means the formal potential to relate to a model in complex ways is turned into taxonomic practice.

explanation into a personal issue of fear of critique and asocial behavior. By including not only developers but stakeholders of digital publications in general, Goble, De Roure, and Bechhofer (2012, 14) bring it more to the point when they use the title "Open Knowledge Flow: The Common Good vs. Self-Interest."

The main point behind the critique of transformation of differences into deviation is not to say that any kind of difference is necessary and needs to be respected. The point is that this transformation results in the very opposite. It treats any kind of difference as potentially unnecessary in the first place. This fact is also represented by the use of the term generic to describe the goals of modelling, used by many authors. For instance, Shotton et al. (2015, 7) call the Documents Components Model (DoCO) "a generic model harmonizing all these aspects." In contrast, the goal of modelling could also be described as finding a stable model, or a model that represents a functional "contact zone" (Dallas 2016) between stakeholders. The difference is that such orientations create a higher sensitivity to questions such as: what is the right layer of abstraction a model addresses? what is an efficient scope for the model? and finally, what is the role of modelling in a specific publication context? These questions are addressed by taking into account the social environment in which modelling practices take place and responding to them differently in each situation.

In contrast, genericity and harmonization have privileged an attitude in which individuals are made responsible for the burden of tremendously ambitious modelling goals. Hence, the lack of respect for social structure and state of a domain turns into the image of asocial agents driven by self-interest. In this respect, the irony is significant that the section on SPs showed that the attempt to harmonize semantics created new heterogeneity. In contrast, Assante et al. (2016, 7) remark, still within the logical structure of OpenAIRE, that generic solutions are often also not very useful solutions. Unfortunately, the authors do not think their way to the end of the entire set of consequences of this observation.

A Theatrical Concept of Social Aspects

As has just been noted, generic solutions may of course exist in one or the other situation. They may also be desirable and supportive in others. With that, another pattern of anti-socialization arises, stemming from a point of view opposing the one in the last section. While in the last section authors underestimated the qualitative dimension of differences, it is as possible to overemphasize this dimension. The result could be called a theatrical concept of the social dimension of publications. In this concept, theatrical means that each difference is equally important, and that each element that appears in consequence of observable differences has the same value for scholarly publications. In consequence, there is a lack of design of publishing concepts, a fact that creates its own set problems.

The areas in which this pattern is observable concern the forms of representation in publications, different strategies of publishing publications, the social impact of publications, and finally the components of publications.

The approach of TPs is the one approach in digital publishing that is most notably built on the extension of symbolic practices provoked by digital technologies. Single-Resource Publications are somewhat a part of the same development, because they are supposed to represent research in its own right. The first achieves multimodal publications as a combination of different semiotic resources within one publication, the second does the same by treating each semiotic resource as an equally useful publication environment.

Although these examples are the most significant ones, it became clear in the history of digital publications that semiotic resources other than text also got significant attention in concepts like SPs or EPs. While this short compilation emphasizes a shared principle, a significant difference still exists. It is important to distinguish between attempting to support the growing influence of a variety of semiotic resources and aiming at the highest level of multimodality in publications themselves.

The section on TPs and similar lines of arguments showed that multimodal complexity becomes a value in itself. Nevertheless, there is an important gap between the theoretical insight that "there is no such thing as a perfect interface that shows everything" (Adema 2014), and to intentionally push towards multimodality. This push is a reaction to the preceding observation, which does not follow automatically, but requires another step of interpretation and decision making. The fact that a combination of semiotic resources — within or across publications — might "show" more does not mean that any semiotic resource or a great level of multimodal complexity is automatically useful.

In multiple places in this inquiry it became clear that the value of publications much depends on issues such as the archivability of publication formats, and the implementability as well as maintainability of technological and organizational infrastructure necessary to realize it.

Following the goal to "show" much, it also depends on the capability of consumers to process and understand that much. In other terms, representations need to be read, not just viewed. A dense multimodal description says nothing about its readability and efficiency.

All of the aforementioned issues address certain capabilities of digital publications and their stakeholders. They hence describe the social constitution of this field, which has, as was highlighted by many authors, limited resources of the material and abstract kind. In contrast, the main argument on which the goal of maximal multimodal complexity is based is purely theoretical. Chapter three presented a set of problems which do indeed reflect this tension discussed among authors such as Diender (2010), or Ball and Eyman (2015). Accordingly, not everything that enters the social sphere of publishing is socially sustainable. Even if it will eventually, becoming such furthermore requires qualifying the idea in correspondence with the social constraints of a given situation. Significantly, McPherson (2010), as an exception to this line of research, voted in favor of multimodal templates, after having worked with TPs.

The idea of templates leads to another problematic notion of social aspects in digital publishing. In principle, this model is just a repetition of the issue discussed in the last paragraphs, but on the level of publication formats. While transmediality showed a tendency to not differentiate the value of different modes of representation, this notion often denies a distinction between being publicly available and being a publication. This distinction has indeed become problematic, as the abundance of digital publication formats examined here has demonstrated. Once again, there is a difference, however, between observing and respecting this process, and ignoring this difference entirely. Similarly, acknowledging that there is no "one-size-fits-all" approach does not directly lead to the idea that what makes a publication can only be defined "on a project-to-project basis," as Hall, Kuc, and Zylinska (2015) suggest.

The approach that everything that is publicly available should be considered a publication appeared in most publication formats in different slants. One of those, which is of particular importance in this section, is to refrain from distinguishing between scholarly publications based on the social environment in which a resource is available. OLBs and HPs, for instance, promoted the use of Google spreadsheets, images from Flickr, or infrastructure such as GoDaddy or 1&1. Some UBs have been published using commercial services such as PBworks. The question of how far commercial services or proprietary formats comply with the requirements of academic publishing did not affect their inclusion into approaches to publishing.

While in the case of OLBs this decision was pragmatic, it appears strategic in HPs. The makers of HPs want to transfer the right of deciding what a publication is to the research project and to researchers. Correspondingly, what a publication actually is would no longer be the result of a consensus between agents in the social sphere of publishing. Each agent gets the right to define something as a publication, and thus everything that is publicly available can be potentially considered a publication. As before, the social aspect is no longer the sphere in which the status and context of publications is negotiated.

This line of thought is also well reflected in the so-called publication taxonomy mentioned earlier. Apart from the fact that it contains "publications" ranging from e-mail to *rapid SMS*, it does not have a taxonomic structure. A taxonomy organizes terms in a hierarchical structure, i.e. it prioritizes on the grounds of organizing principles. The publication taxonomy just contains two lists. It refrains from organizing in order to index.

Hybrid Publications build on the idea of the post-digital. The aforementioned list appears to analyze publishing in the light of the "post-digital condition." As has been outlined, a key aspect of the post-digital condition is the importance of context in order to decide what is most suitable out of a set of options in a hybrid environment. Notably, publishing itself is not explicitly addressed in these examples as a social context, a frame that creates its own set of criteria in order to distinguish between suitable and unsuitable formats.

Cramer concludes that "the term 'post-digital'" in its simplest sense describes the messy state of media, arts, and design *after* their digitization" (Cramer 2014). He thereby confirms the results of chapter five, namely that the creation of messiness is an effect, although not a necessary one, of the introduction of what is called digital technologies. Similarly, Adema (2015, 6) refers to the issue of messiness but in a different way when she writes about her attempt of:

> … reimagining a different, more ethical humanities, albeit a humanities that is messy and processual, contingent, unbound and unfinished. (Adema 2015, 6)

What some authors, thus, try to do is to multiply the effects of digital technologies instead of building a social environment around such effects.

Without seeing it that way, these authors probably act much more in line with the logics of digital technologies than with a process that socializes these technologies.

As is clear from the last quote, some of the authors behind this type of anti-socialization follow a certain type of ethic. Quoting Alan O'Shea, Adema argues that publishing is a practice that "constitute[s] us as particular kinds of subjects and exclude[s] other kinds. The more routinised our practices, the more powerfully this closure works" (Adema 2015, 26). A publication, and the historical monograph in particular, then, is the nexus that orchestrates and stabilizes such practices.

A complete discussion of such ethics is outside of the scope of the present study. Nevertheless, it is necessary to quickly highlight in which way such ethics might contain a simplistic notion of the social domain. This necessity derives not only from its impact on the design of many publications, but also from the fact that it will reveal familiarity with some issues of openness.

The first of Adema's two quotes showed that here, her main critique is directed against any kind of fixation. The second quote shows that publications — historically the monographs — appear to be the key fixations of academia. The unethical dimension of fixations is the fact that they introduce bipolar distinctions. A scholarly publication defines what is considered science and what is not. Related practices and the environment in which they take place divide stakeholders into those who are able to participate in science, and those who are not. The critical concern with bipolar distinctions has been similarly highlighted in Tara McPherson's comments on the mediation between binaries.

Accordingly, approaches following this line of argument to publications pretend to design publication formats that avoid fixations. Most notably, this idea is manifests in great parts of UBs. Its intended incompleteness has been coined as a measure against dogmatization. Similarly, its crowd-sourced and author-less production form is understood as social inclusiveness. In *Posthumanities: The Dark Side of "The Dark Side of the Digital"* Adema and Hall (2016 sec. Disruptive Humanities) UBs are presented as the means for:

> ... affirmatively disrupting the humanities by seeing the threat to humanism and the human associated with the emergence of these new "posthuman" technologies as offering us a chance ... .

What remains unreflected in such designs, however, is the extend up to which they create their own fixations, especially that of unboundness. To put it differently, such designs do not only represent the volatile and contingent facet of people's worlds that the format tries to respect, they also have a multiplying effect on it. Whether this effect is necessarily good, understood ethically, is not discussed anywhere. Apart from any response to this question, this format, following its own line of argument, becomes a force that produces what it represents, and in this respect does not distinguish from what it criticizes.

In correspondence with the main theme of this section, this ambivalence is based on a selective awareness of the social dimension of publications. They are selective insofar as they do not include agent's capacity to play with bipolar distinctions themselves, and to subvert them by using them. It furthermore ignores aspects of empowerment that are mediated by fixations and distinctions, aspects that were visible throughout the whole discussion on calculatory practice.[3] To put it differently, fixations are not just mechanisms of exclusion. They also offer a more trans-subjective point of orientation for the excluded, to at least becoming aware about what needs to be included, a source that at its best can also denote a resource that can be used in order to legally demand inclusion. In short, this type of critique of bipolar distinctions introduces a new bipolar distinction in the social domain, that between inclusiveness and exclusiveness.[4]

Adema herself remarks that O'Shea warns against attributing too much power to the aforementioned practices and the fixations on which they rely. She also conducts a complex discussion on what is critique in this respect. However, as follows from the last paragraphs, such relativizations remain without consequences for corresponding formats of publications and statements like the ones above. These formats, thus, are those which intend to disturb the allegedly intrinsic logic of the social space of publishing towards victimization and dogmatization, and which celebrate the "messiness" to which these formats seem willing to contribute. Although framed in an intellectually more sophisticated theory, these formats produce a deterministic model of victims and dogmas, instead of social agents and pragmas in the field of publishing.

3 The issue is not that the relationship between power and empowerment is not addressed within the theoretical background of these publications, but that when it comes to the design of publication formats, the ambivalence is neglected.

4 The problematic dimension of this issue is very often discussed in the context of debates on the theoretical school of constructivism (see Collin 2008).

Likewise, few examples exist in which the social impact — repressive as well as progressive — of concrete distinctions made in historical and new publication formats are evaluated in the context of such approaches. There are only few attempts of real design of new publications that organize the field of post-digital publishing — besides the ambiguous single-source approach — using new, old, and modified fixations. The publication is conceived of as a channel instead of as an object, regardless of the fact that a channel is also provided by an object, i.e. the application. It is a matter of perspective: the perspective presented in this section attempts to bring the interactions of a social field (science), organized around and through publications, into the publications in order to "hypercyberdemocrize" (Adema 2015, 164) this field. This relationship shows that these formats, despite their critique of the regulatory effect of publications, have a strong intent to regulate and control. It could furthermore be argued that by trying to relocate social interactions around publications into publications, this aspect is strengthened. Again, it is argued that this attempt "is not one that should be conceptualized as a project or a model" (ibid.). A model nevertheless it is, insofar as it makes a point and creates projects like Liquid-, Living-, and other types of Books that are a product of its argument. As much as corresponding authors deny this tension, they discursively refer to a structure in the social space of publishing that ceases to exist. This structure increasingly turns into an avatar, a situation in which it becomes more and more difficult to react to new social patterns in the field.

This problem is notably reflected by the fact that many Living Books are not living at all. The role of the author is reproduced by the fact that few actors contribute to them, so that the initiator of the project becomes a traditional author without intent. Similarly, the formally unbounded book becomes effectively bound by the scarcity of updates after being put online. An exception worth mentioning was the AiME project. It has been highlighted, however, that the main difference between this project and other UBs is the enormous effort it puts into the design, organization, and sustainability of the social space around the AiME Unbound Book. The aforementioned ethics discourage such a degree of intended organization and control used in a tactical manner. Once again, the irony lies in the fact that the AiME Unbound Book became effectively inclusive, instead of just enabling inclusiveness.

It has been written that some overlap exists between the ethics of this section and the topic of openness. Obviously, open science is an ethic. More important is the fact that both ethics are ethics maintaining the same idea of inclusion. In the same way, as one seeks to address an abstract anyone (agents), the other aims at including an abstract everything (resources). It is important to emphasize this similarity, because it shows that otherwise completely disconnected publication formats are part of a comparable ethical development, a development that appears closely related to the effects of digital technologies themselves. It shows that in a certain perspective there is indeed a common ground behind publication formats like UBs on the one hand and SCPs on the other.

Self-Contained Publications carry the same ethics towards the research process as UBs apply to social agents. They seek to prevent any exclusion of digital elements in the design of their format, in order support a likewise abstract idea of reproducibility. Curiously, similar experiences are made in this area of research as were addressed by the AiME project. Tremendous effort is necessary to turn such formats into real, i.e. socially effective, publications. Such efforts question the original idea. The reason is not only the dimension of the costs. The costs for realizing SCPs have been discussed in depth. The reason is rather that these efforts contradict the original idea. In the case of AiME, this is the case because the intensive design of workflows, the definition of roles such as for moderators able to approve and reject content is exactly what Adema problematizes in the context of the book. In the case of SCPs, the discussion showed that the more radically reproducibility is pursued, the more it requires making decisions that could have been made otherwise while producing a reproducible publication.

Three different types of de-socialization of the field of digital publications have been discussed. The first showed how social issues are translated into issues framed by peculiar technologies, and how this translation obscures the reflection on the social status of such technologies themselves. The second described approaches which perceive social process as processes of standardization and harmonization only. The last type addressed an all-inclusive idea of social aspects and the contradictions they run into.

The evaluation of such types of anti-socialization permits arguing that different approaches are linked in different ways to these three types. On a more general level, it is even possible to claim that approaches driven by disciplines from the arts and humanities relate to them differently than approaches driven by the sciences. For obvious reasons, examples for type one and two are often publication formats from the sciences, while type three, with some exceptions, is showcased by formats from the humanities.

As in the case of epistemological claims, the attitude towards social aspects in publication formats can be interpreted in the context of the epistemological effects of digital technologies and their surplus. Thus, it is not difficult to relate the second type to the supposed conflation between representation and intervention. Claims concerning the end of theory, and data as the only and ubiquitous mode of representation that is no longer representation, permit the belief that there are few sources of epistemological conflict left. Data is conceived of as precise, and its form of production is necessary. In consequence, differences have to be differences of misunderstanding, a judgment quoted several times in part one. This means that it is an issue that can be solved incrementally. In the same way elements of the third type of de-socialization can, and have been, related to the idea of a universal symbolism.

However, it is the notion of a surplus of digital technologies which explains why a general negation of certain aspects of the social life around publications undermines the social integrity of such publications, as indicated by some of the examples in this chapter. In accordance with the concept of epistemological effects and post-digitality, it would also be wrong to argue that these three negations come without reason. Instead, the interesting relationship between type one and two on the one side, and type three on the other, reveals the real problem. While the first two try to control and engineer the social space too much, the last tries to be as little of an influence as possible. The question of digital publications therefore is also the question of the type of social relationships that need to be designed to let digital publications be sustained and become valuable.

The Ambiguous Issue of Heterogeneity

The present inquiry into digital publications was driven by the motivation to explain the conjunction between efforts in creating digital publications and complaints about their impact. It was claimed that such an explanation is necessary because this conjunction appears to be more stable and profound than expected in the dynamics of innovation. Far from being abandoned, as Denning and Rous (1995, 72) have predicted for the case of failing adaptation, scientific publishing carried its alleged breakdown until today and extended it into something that has simply been called its messy state after digitization.

Such messiness, moreover, might appear to be a product of the very same process that in most cases is meant to solve it. There are at least two indicators that justify continuing an analysis in this direction. The first indicator is a quantitative measure, the second one is qualitative, to be discussed further below. The degree of activity around the creation of new publication formats and its increase over time offer no reason to believe that it has contributed to the stabilization of the publishing landscape. This first measure alone depends on interpretation; one possibility was offered within the outline of part one, structuring these activities in its own narrative, supporting the aforementioned hypothesis. It will furthermore become transparent throughout the rest of the study how the results of these measures reflect the problematic relationship between digital publications and their social environment.

Quantitative Indicators for the Lack of Sustainability of Digital Publications

A quantitative measure of research activity on digital publications is represented in figure 6.1. It shows the amount of research publications concerned with digital publication formats (y-axis) and thereby its distribution within the timespan of analysis (x-axis). The selection of research publications mostly matches the approach to the topic of digital publications in this inquiry (see Introduction).

Accordingly, two types of publications were considered. The first type describes the design or implementation of peculiar formats envisioned or implemented by the authors themselves. The second type consists of publications in which authors describe formats described by others. These publications promote a particular publication format in a certain field, or argue in favor of doing so. In other words, they attempt to position a format in a field or research domain. Another necessary criterion for the inclusion into the measured corpus, also highlighted already, is the condition that the publication explicitly needs to reference the overarching theme of digital publications.

The resulting dataset contains 413 research publications on digital publication formats. The research publications were all published between 1995 and 2017 and can be seen as a comprehensive selection for this period. As has been discussed in the introduction, there are quite a few reasons to define 1995 as a starting point for the topic of digital publications. Most of these publications, although not all of them, are mentioned and discussed throughout this investigation.

The diagram shows an increase in the overall number of publications until 1998, followed by a period of stagnation that rapidly ends around 2008. The most active year in terms of publications about digital publication formats so far was 2014. The curve corresponds in great detail with the sequencing of corresponding research into the phases in part one. According to this, the topic was generally introduced until the millennium, followed by a period of investment into social and technological infrastructure. This infrastructure gave rise to an immense dynamic of activities that yet again slow down over the last three years. Figure 6.2 makes this pattern clearer by applying a *kernel density estimation* (also referred to as KDE) with gaussian kernel to the same data as was used for the figure above.

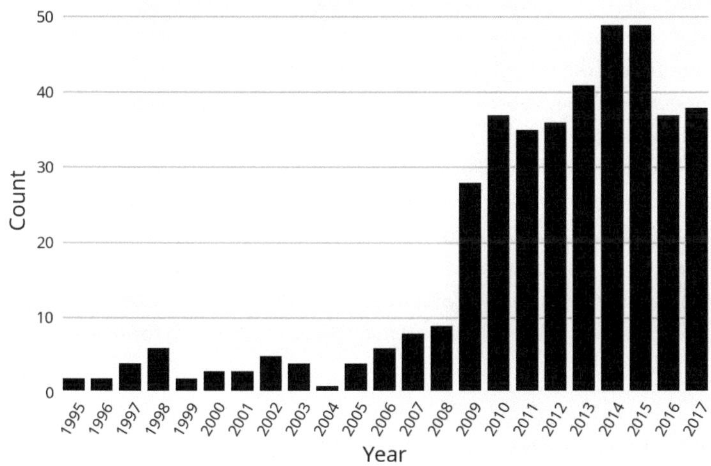

[Figure 6.1] Research literature about digital publication formats between 1995 and 2017

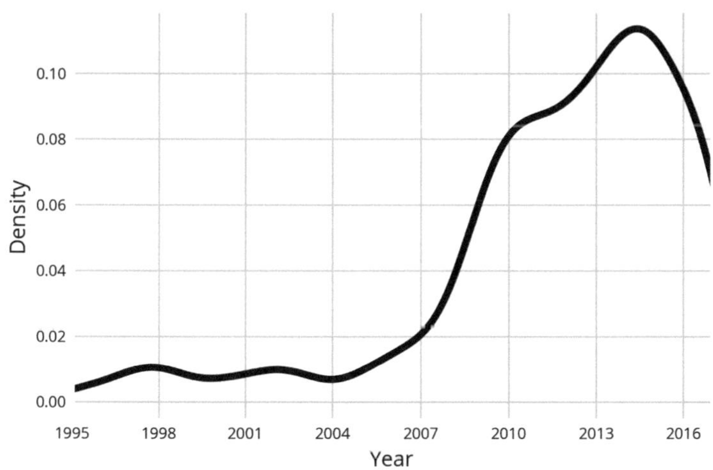

[Figure 6.2] KDE applied to the data used in figure 6.1

Two interpretations of the diagrams are generally possible. The first one would be to read the increase of publications as a sign of their success. Accordingly, the diagrams would give testimony of the fact that more is invested into the development of digital publication formats until 2014 because they are becoming a part of scholarly publishing.

However, such interpretation would interpret in a biased way what the publications in the collection represent. As was just mentioned, publications were chosen that represent activities of design, implementation, and promotion of digital publication formats. Hence the increase of activity does not automatically represent the stabilization and settling of digital publications, but only the increase of efforts.[5] It shows that more and more is invested with the aim of arriving at a stable digital publishing field. Additionally, it is problematic to interpret the small decrease after 2014 in favor of such stabilization. The introduction and chapter four suggested that it more likely reflects the disillusion of digital publication advocates and, accordingly, the slowdown of new engagements. In any case it is important to remember of what such activities exactly stand for in each of the four phases.

Qualitative Indicators for the Lack of Sustainability of Digital Publications

Overwhelming evidence for the claim that the increase of effort does not correspond with a stabilization of the field emerges when attempting to group activities around comparable approaches. Different approaches to digital publications have been the key aspect of part one. The violin plot in figure 6.3 gathers all the approaches that have been discussed (y-axis) and aligns them on a time axis (x-axis). This alignment is again made by referring to the publication dates of publications that cite a certain approach within the above collection. The width of each violin represents the number of publications of a corresponding publication format at a specific point in time. This being said, disappearance does not necessarily mean that the approaches are abandoned. However, in most cases, such as MAs, it may be interpreted this way.

5 In order to validate the former, it would be necessary to evaluate the usage of formats itself. In order to obtain comprehensive results, such analysis would of course require not only counting the number of publications for each format but also finding qualitative criteria for each implementation. Such an effort is outside the scope of the present inquiry. However, it is also not necessary, due to the complaints about the lack of adoption related stakeholders themselves express. Additionally, the lack of adoption was illustrated more closely across the entire text wherever possible.

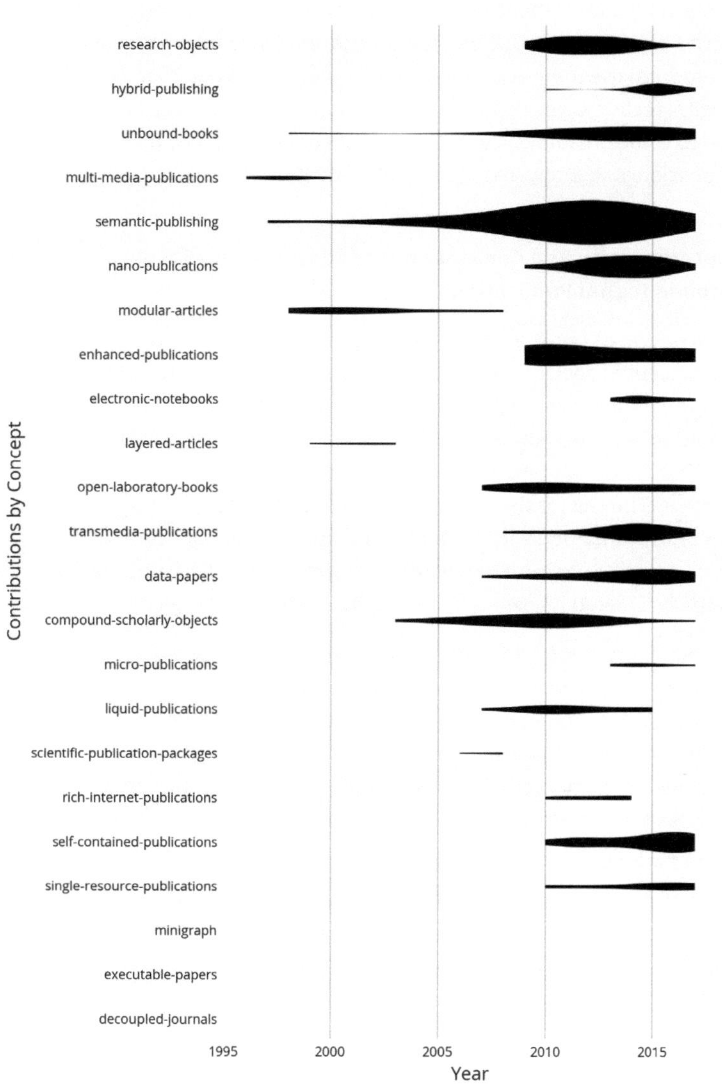

[Figure 6.3] Research literature on digital publication formats ordered by format and time

What is shown in the diagram is doubtlessly a good measure for the proliferation in the field of digital publications, which appeared all over and up to the recent past, as described in the present inquiry. In fact, its increase seems to correlate with the increase of efforts carried out in order to decrease it. This reflection on the heterogeneity of digital publications is not something merely mentioned or conceived of by the corresponding research field. By doing so, it offers empirical evidence for what is to be expected from the theoretical discussion of digital technologies. It confirms that digital technologies do not force a certain path for the digital publication to come. Instead, as technologies of conversion, they multiply the set of possible paths towards digital publications.

Heterogeneity as a Consequence of Contradictory Patterns around Digital Publications

The description of publication formats in part one, as well as the sections on the concept of social aspects within these formats, were full of examples for the paradoxical pattern rendered in an empirical manner above. The creation of better conditions for formal semantics, combined with higher efforts for standardization, led to formal semantic heterogeneity in many areas. The call for deconstructing publications into "atomic" information units, combined with better technological conditions for such deconstructions, sparked a variety of such approaches. Each approach, additionally, created its own type of "atomic" information unit.

Nonetheless, there are two scenarios that illustrate this paradox in a paradigmatic way. The first scenario has only appeared incidentally as one motivation behind many formats: the data deluge. The other scenario was introduced as a significant paradox, but has not been systematized further until now. This scenario is provided by the observation that recent approaches such as emulation and self-containedness oppose the early theme of decomposability and modularity.

In 2001, Keller presented the results of a survey of the impact of digital publications on the field of scholarly publishing. The study itself was conducted in 1999. One of the key results was the claim that digital publications have the potential, if not to solve, then at least to alleviate the serial crisis. Similar claims had been made in the ACM Electronic Publishing Plan. As Adema (2015, 135) points out, the serial crisis is a monograph crisis as well.

As it turns out in the genealogy of digital publications, this crisis is far from over. Authors reference it even today. Furthermore, the problem permutates and transforms into new versions, versions which correspond with concepts of the environments of new publication formats. Accordingly, the serial crisis spreads into an "age of information overload" (Shotton et al. 2009, 13), where information is the unit of choice. It became the "data deluge" that predicated the e-Science program (De Roure 2011, 10).

Hence, it could be argued that instead of making step-by-step progress in the process of solving this issue, the issue re-appears in a way that fits the steps' most important characteristics. As before, it is possible to observe a dynamic in which the attempts to solve certain problems of digital publications go hand in hand with their production.

The issue of SCPs offers an even more illustrative example for the paradoxical situation of heterogeneity in the development of digital publication formats. Chapter four concluded by drawing attention to the paradoxical fact that a development that started with the idea of modularity engenders the theme of self-containedness at its preliminary end. It was indicated that a faction within this field of research has recently started to work on the formal description of the structure of SCPs. Up to this point, no further attention was paid to this new twist.

A closer look reveals the dynamics of digital technologies around the topic of heterogeneity — if no social viewpoint is added that qualifies and interrupts this logic. The point is that both approaches, the infrastructural and the semantic approach to harmonization and standardization, are not merely coexisting. At least for the case of digital publications, they react to each other. Modularization — in this context the use of formal vocabulary in order to isolate components or connect resources of an object of interest — appeared as a reaction to earlier, so-called electronic publications. These existed in form of digitized images of publications or, at their best, as plain text. In the eyes of modularization, these "monolithic" articles were a major source of heterogeneity in publishing, a heterogeneity of objects and language with allegedly redundant information (see sections on NPs). Technological innovation permitted the semantic markup of elements, or their relationships in publications, in cases where they had already been published independently. The harmonizing of heterogeneity was supposed to be achieved by aligning or re-using elements in a connected publication space.

Self-Contained Publications, again, were among other things a reaction to the heterogeneity produced by the aforementioned process. SCPs respond to a new type of heterogeneity of modules and semantics, by offering a technical platform, the container, that allows to abstract from the issue of modules and semantics and provides a unifying layer around any type of heterogeneity. Especially the approach of emulation makes it possible to ignore the question of what the elements of a publication are that are formally described, and what means are used in order to describe them. After this succession of shifts, it is not surprising that this approach, once more, creates its own type of heterogeneity, that of emulation techniques, which is promised to be solved by developing technological means to "semantically" abstract from such heterogeneity of techniques (Santana-Perez et al. 2017). This, however, is a shift back to the formal-descriptive approach that was already offered by modularity.

Each turn tries to apply a technical solution to a technical problem, instead of addressing its social status. It neglects the fact that digital technologies can be the means of a solution, but never the solution themselves. In consequence, the problem of heterogeneity cascades upstream.

Publication Formats as Domain Driven Discourse Objects

Confronted with the dynamics of heterogeneity around digital publications, the question arises whether such heterogeneity has a certain structure that goes beyond the pattern found in the last section. In other words, is this structure in fact contingent, or does a pattern exist that would allow to see in it not heterogeneity, but more of a configuration?

Since approaches to digital publications maintain a simple view of heterogeneity, this task has not really been carried out yet. As has been argued on several occasions, attempts to analyze the heterogeneity of digital publications look for a generic core within this heterogeneity (EPs, LPs, ROs and others), or they take a nearly all-inclusive direction (TPs, HPs, DPs and others).

Since the limited evaluation of heterogeneity is based on a narrow concept of social aspects, it appears consistent to start the process of structuring by analyzing the dependency between social domains and the creation of digital publications that begins in figure 6.4.

Contributions of Research Domains to Digital Publication Concepts

In the case of science, using research domains as a key unit to analyze science's social structure is a likely idea. On various occasions throughout the study at hand, particular research domains, furthermore, seem to have played a crucial role in the development of publication formats. In order to create an overview of the impact of specific research domains, self-descriptions by authors in the collection used above were extracted from the papers. These self-descriptions mostly consist in their institutional affiliations as mentioned in the front or back of a paper. If the publications use a specific showcase or target group, the domain names of such showcases and groups were also taken into account.

Domain information often addresses different levels of granularity and contains subject related overlaps, for instance for the case between terms such as atmospheric research and climate science. Some authors refer to their research domain as biology, others prefer a more precise description of their field, such as biodiversity. As this happens in many fields, the overall result is a participation of fifty-six domains, sub-domains and research areas contributing to research literature on digital publication formats. Figure 6.4 shows the fifteen most mentioned disciplines ordered by the number of their appearances in research publications about digital publication formats.

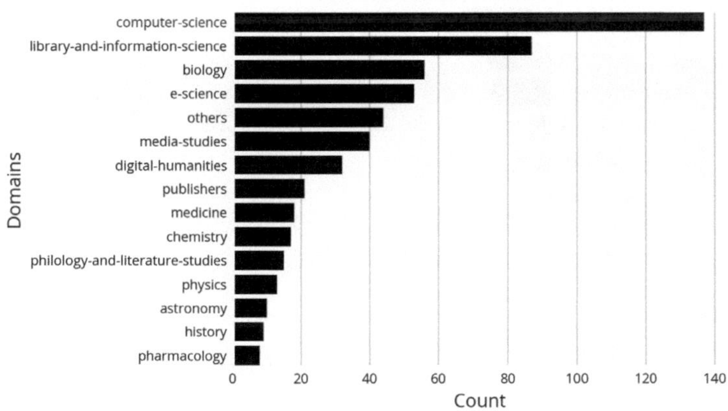

[Figure 6.4] The top fifteen disciplines involved in research literature about digital publication formats

In order to increase compatibility and consistency, these terms were then aligned in a two-dimensional taxonomy. This taxonomy is based on the *Dewey Decimal Classification* scheme[6] (also referred to as DDC). However, some modifications to the DDC approach were also made, so that the data is more suitable to the subject of the current inquiry. The most outstanding change consist in the introduction of the class *e-Research* at the first level of the hierarchy. E-Research has the two subclasses e-Science and digital humanities. In contrast, terms such as *bioinformatics* were merged with their area of application (biology).

6 https://www.oclc.org/dewey.en.html

Another significant difference to DDC is the way the dataset handles the field of information science. Information science, as well as computer science, are subclassed under a newly introduced domain group called *information-and-technology*. This seems reasonable, since only a fraction of information science is involved in the design of digital publication formats, and this fraction is heavily leaning towards designing technological infrastructure. Examples include the work of Herbert Van de Sompel (2010), or the DRIVER project (Sierman, Schmidt, and Ludwig 2009).

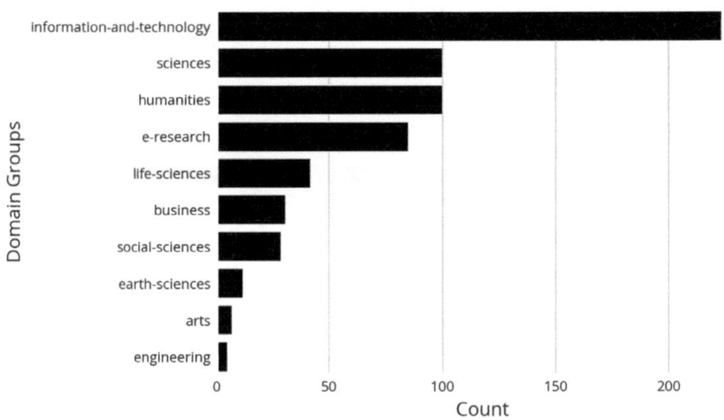

[Figure 6.5] Domain groups in the dataset on digital publication formats

The domain group which by far dominates research literature on new publication formats, even with the aforementioned modifications made to the DDC scheme, is the domain group information-and-technology (see figure 6.5). This dominance increases further if the domain of e-Research is added. This means that the research field of digital publications is most notably shaped by disciplines which do not just apply technology to scholarly publications but of which its primary research interest is technology.

At a first glance the humanities seem to be equally represented as science. However, there is a significant predominance of mostly empirical domains. Similarly, social sciences are less represented.

One way to interpret this result is to follow the model of a linear history of the digitization of research, as outlined at the beginning of this chapter. In this case, it would just reflect the delay by which some domains integrate digital technologies. In this view, computer science represents the path of progress itself, while certain disciplines can adopt the principles of this progress more easily than others. The "end of theory" debate would provide the explanatory background for such an argument. Accordingly, theory-based disciplines need more time to adapt to a world without theory than empirical disciplines.

As has been discussed in the last chapter, this assumption would, however, misinterpret the concept of digital technologies by equating such technologies with a specific practice and a specific application model of such technologies. Similarly, the results from the data do not relate to the fact that there always must be computer scientists to implement a publication format. In most of the literature on the conceptualization of digital publications, as in the case of HPs or TPs, computer scientists do not appear as authors at all. Additionally, computer scientists often appear together with authors from non-computer-science domains. Disciplines that only appear as showcases without being represented as authors have furthermore been included as has been mentioned. The dominance of information-and-technology domains can thus not be deduced from the way the present study defines digital publications. What this situation means exactly will become clearer when domains are related to publication formats below.

Another observation can be made that likewise discourages the afore-mentioned explanation. The by far most outstanding discipline from the science domain is biology. If one were to add the intersection between biology and life sciences or biology and chemistry, the share would become even more dominant. Such a high number shows that in the sciences as well there are areas which engage significantly differently with the topic of digital publications than others do. This observation precludes just explaining the results within the simplifying framework of empirical sciences, theoretical sciences and technology.

The Relationship Between Scientific Domains and Digital Publication Concepts

The whole picture becomes clearer when different concepts of digital publications are taken into account. Figure 6.6 shows the participation of research domains in ten publication formats. These formats are:

- Hybrid Publications (hp)
- Electronic Notebooks (en)
- Unbound Books (ub)
- Open Laboratory Books (olb)
- Data Papers (dp)
- Transmedia Publications (tp)

- Enhanced Publications (ep)
- Research Objects (ro)
- Nano Publications (np)
- Semantic Publications (sp)

One diagram corresponds with one domain group. The y-axis on each diagram shows the number of contributions for each format.

One aspect which shows up immediately is the dominance of humanities disciplines in HPs, TPs and UBs while their influence is low or completely absent in other formats. The arts — not generally well represented — contribute most to TPs. While not dominating SPs, business is most present in SPs. Science disciplines dominate OLBs while e-Research is the most prominent domain in ROs. Information-and-technology finally shapes the approach of EPs. If one looks deeper into the disciplines behind the domain contributions it will show that science in NPs is almost exclusively represented by the discipline of biology. In the case of OLBs it is chemistry. Similarly, around eighty-five percent of information-and-technology disciplines behind EPs refers to information science. In the case of ROs it is the other way around. In this approach seventy-nine percent of this domain comes from the field of computer science.

It is therefore possible to summarize that in most cases identifiable domain clusters exist which tend to contribute to one format over another. A first attempt to explain this situation can be made by reviewing what each format stands for.

The biggest share of library and information science exists in EPs and SPs. Both formats are organized around the concept of information resources and information. Accordingly, they are shaped by an abstract entity constitutive to this specific domain. Enhanced Publications with its underlying concept of aggregations inherit the idea of collections as constitutive elements in research from this domain. The preference for the intensive use of highly formalized semantics resembles the practice of cataloguing and the creation of tools such as authority files.

Computer science, in contrast, dominates the RO concept. Research Objects are self-described as formal descriptions of computational workflows, using digital resources in a way that is "native" to the web architecture. Such a description defines which resources, such as data or software, are used, by identifying them with URIs. Afterwards, it defines how they are linked together by representing how and when they were processed to generate a research result. The goal of Research Objects is

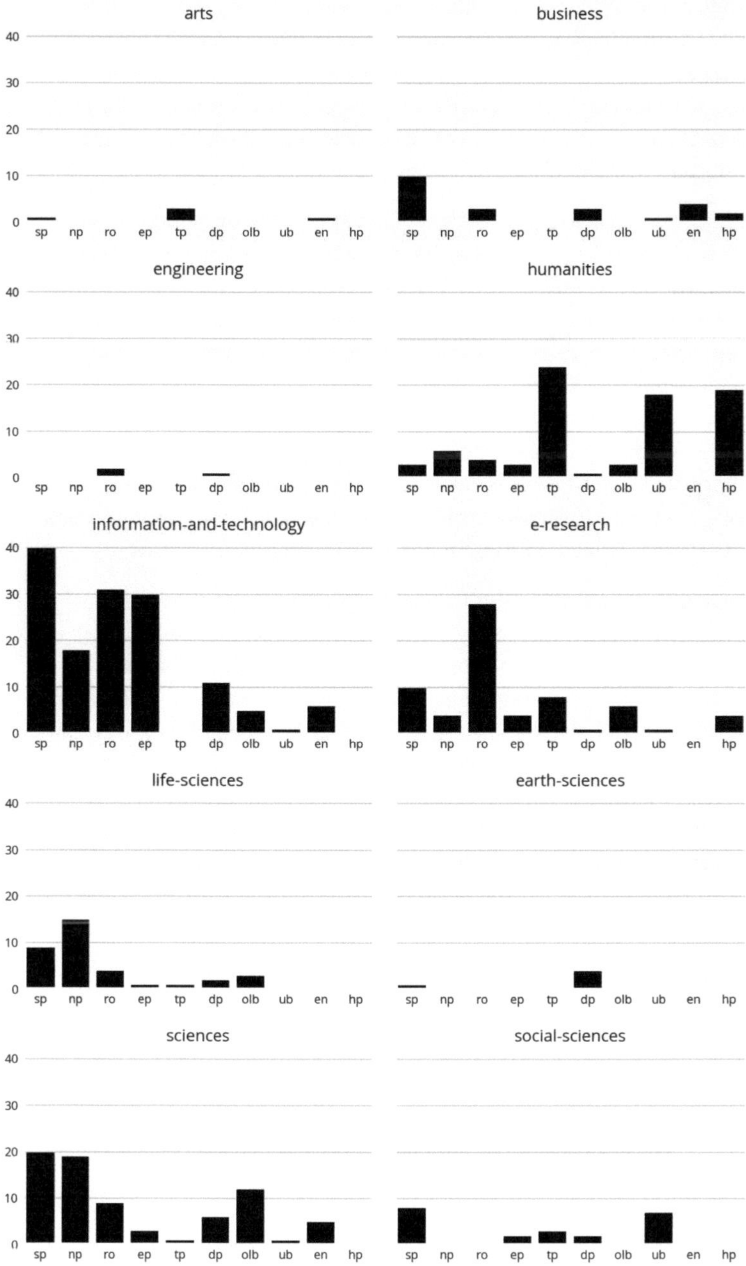

[Figure 6.6] The influence of different domains in specific publication formats

to enable automated reproducible experimentation and automation of science. The theme of automation and the networked nature of Research Objects as living in the web directly reproduces key topics in computer science. The ideological framework of e-Science translates such principles into aspects of science. For instance, it equates reproducibility with the input-output model of computation.

Nano Publications are largely designed and influenced by biology and the life sciences, in particular pharmacology, medicine, and research on proteins. The two key features of NPs are the central theme of assertions, and the way they organize evidence. They build upon a specific conflation of three aspects, which adequately describes the situation of the aforementioned research cluster. The first two aspects address the centrality of factual knowledge, both for representing research results and organizing the research domain. The example of ROs demonstrates that this is not necessarily true for all environments with a strong empirical research context. The third aspect reflects the actual availability of many databases which contain factual data about many similar things, i.e. proteins.

Indeed, examples given for NPs from such fields center around pieces of knowledge such as that protein X has property Y (Chichester et al. 2014), or substance X interacts with substance Y (Schneider, Ciccarese, et al. 2014). The point is not to say that other disciplines do not work with factual knowledge. The point is that the share of factual knowledge, as well as the usefulness of its representation as assertions, is specific to a field which collects information about thousands of protein chains and other substances. The corresponding research literature also gives evidence of the situation of how the availability of a few clearly definable research objects (proteins, pharmaceutical substances, etc.) facilitates the availability of many databases containing such data. Finally, the descriptions of medical use cases of NPs accentuate the specialized demands of some disciplines promoting NPs. Accordingly, Rodriguez-Gonzalez et al. (2014) outline the usage of NPs in decision making processes in medicine. In those processes, the reuse of parts of experiments that led to factual knowledge as targeted by ROs is not meaningful. Instead, there is a demand to quickly have an overview of how much research favors one or the other assertion, so that a quick decision can be made. Consequently, NPs focus not on facts and assertions, but on a specific practice of using facts and assertions that seems to be inherent in the research domains supporting NPs.

Transmedia Publications are an outstanding example of strong interest in the issues of representation and mediation of the entanglement between representation and socio-cultural processes. Since such questions are key questions of the humanities, it does not surprise that humanities disciplines largely sustain this publication concept. Moreover, it is the one approach where disciplines from the arts contribute most. These disciplines are based around different notions of design. Thus, it does not surprise that they relate to the one format by which they "might formally be brought into academic knowledge systems in the actual modalities of their practice" (Ball 2016, 53).

Business is not dominating in SPs, yet there are convincing arguments why it engages most into this format. SPs do not aim at altering the existing format of articles substantially. They extend it by adding annotations to the file of the article, by means of formal semantics in the markup, or microdata format. These annotations make articles easily machine-readable. They thereby facilitate the implementation of additional services, which need to process the article as data. For business stakeholders, these qualities entail that they are able to maintain their product form while being supported in the creation of new products (see chap. 3). Although there is no research object or scientific methodology guiding these stakeholders, their goals, key interests instead, carry a certain logic comparable to those disciplinary logics discussed above. The question of how to maximize profit is no different from the question of how to best support discovery in this respect.

A closer look at the heterogeneity of publication formats revealed that it is not just defined by contingency. On the contrary, the patterns and their explanations suggest that the field of digital publishing, instead of fostering a new ecology of digital publications, is a stage for ongoing debate about the nature of scientific truth and the presupposed essence of digital technologies. It is a stage on which "epistemic cultures" (Knorr-Cetina 1999) and cultures of technologies meet and continue to advocate their convictions, not only by argument, but more importantly by design. The publication design becomes the argument.

The possibility of doing so is one of the most fundamental consequences of digital technology for the field of scholarly publishing. It is a consequence of the fact that digital technologies are technologies of conversion, and not technologies in favor of particular ideas. In this context, conversion means that digital technologies do not privilege a specific format. Instead, they facilitate the design of formatting options as semiotic resources for creation of meaning in concrete publications. On several occasions, authors have argued that digital technologies reconfigure the relationship between form and content. At this point, it seems appropriate to argue that such reconfiguration is not so much a clearer separation between form and content as it is a discontinuation of the distinction itself.

Accepting and Challenging Heterogeneity

In the light of this conflation, the heterogeneity in digital publishing appears to be consistent and unrevertable. Nevertheless, there are two factors which multiply its dimensions. As has been argued, the epistemic effects of digital technologies require a reconfiguration of the epistemic setup. Publications belong to this setup and are means of reconfiguring it. Since such reconfiguration is not predefined, broad experimentation is not just obvious, but also necessary in order to gain insights into the new situation. Likewise, it will be necessary to step back from experimentation to let reconfiguration take place. Thus, the first factors are the transitional phase of epistemic irritation and the attempts to find appropriate means for reconfiguration.

The second factor is the lack of awareness of social dimensions of scholarly publications, discussed in several places. In the context of the current section, this problem shows up as a mismatch between the awareness of the design context of a peculiar publication format and its intended target groups. This was the result of the empirical analysis above: that formats are strongly linked to research domains, and researchers as designers of publication concepts propagate the universality of their formats. Bechhofer et al. (2012, 2) accordingly argue that ROs are suited for "scientists from virtually any discipline." Sometimes, domain specific demands are explicitly mentioned. De Roure (2014b, 235) defines the ability of publications to function across disciplines as a key factor of publications. However, such demands never invalidate the format itself. Instead, they are considered modifiers of minor aspects within the format, such as the terms that are used to markup content in MAs and SPs.

Such attitudes multiply heterogeneity, because they hinder the negotiation and situation of formats. They lead to demonstrations of how a specific format is generally capable of representing research from uninvolved disciplines, instead of comparing different practices of representing research and using research results. The consequence is a situation with many "generic" formats, instead of fewer, but sustainable and maintainable, formats.

Arguing Science Through Designing Publications

It was said in the last section that the field of digital publishing is an ongoing argument about technology and the production of scientific truth, carried out by means of design. If this is the case, then the question arises what the elements of this argument are by which these conflicting opinions are represented. In other words, what are the bases on which different hypothesizes are built? As far as publication formats represent an entire line of argument, they are not suitable for this kind of analysis. As a trigger for variation, these aspects need to be aspects appearing in any format, but handled differently across formats. The description of publication formats within chapter one already gave a first impression of these aspects, but comparisons were made from a genealogical angle and not in a systematic way. Accordingly, the aspects which are of interest at this point are a more systematic extraction of comparable features. The following list contains a selection of those aspects. It outlines the most fundamental areas of debate, as well as the whole scope of the ongoing argument as such. It comprises the publications:

- scale
- architectural integrity
- logical cohesion
- secularization
- attitude towards research
- intended residence time
- synchronization with research
- structural rigor
- modal complexity
- intermodal relationship types

The aspects in this list are not completely isolated from each other in the sense that any kind of combination is possible. Sometimes, a choice for one aspect restricts possible choices for another aspect. Additionally, choices for two aspects may link to the same feature in a publication format, because this feature represents several ways to look at publications. The exact meaning of this will become more obvious after these aspects have been described in greater detail over the next paragraphs.

The aspect of *scale* addresses the portion of the research process isolated from this process in order to form a publication in a specific format. In single-resource publishing, the scale can be extremely coarse-grained and often contains only the output of a particular action, such as a diagram. In OLBs, the publication mostly represents a logical step within the research process. Research Objects, SPPs, or EPs bundle entire research processes, while LPs consist of repositories that grow and change with a researcher or research group, beyond research projects. The question at stake is: what is a meaningful independent unit of research?

The term *architectural integrity* comprises concepts which describe how producers and consumers are linked by the publication. Most formats belong to one of *platform*, *channel*, or *object*. When a publication is a platform, as in the case of UBs, it does not distinguish between producers and consumers outside of the publication itself. Instead, agents connect to the publication to become producers and consumers. Channel-publications such as OLBs design a fixed producer-consumer relationship in which the publication establishes a potentially ongoing connection between both. Object-publications are publications in a historical sense. They do not bind producers to consumers, but float independently between them. Architectural integrity models the distance between producer and consumer roles. It makes a statement about which model best represents the idea of knowledge creation as a result of the circulation of existing knowledge.

Logic cohesion addresses the key idea that links the elements in a publication format. In ROs, the cohesion is given by the workflow idea. Hybrid Publications create cohesion by the concept of translation. To put it differently, a HP is an abstract, ideational publication that references different expressions, or rather materializations. These materializations are indeed materializations, because their creation is perceived as a translation of the abstract publication. Nano Publications create cohesion on the grounds of the concept of evidence. Elements in NPs are grouped by the property of containing proof for one and the same claim. In TPs, it is the idea of modal quality of elements that joins and organizes them into publications. Thus, in TPs, cohesion is created by meaning potentials. In Self-Contained Publications, the goal to maintain the integrity of publications is the uttermost aspect of cohesion. In a certain way, SCPs represent the theme of cohesion itself.

The aspect of *secularization* is a consequence of the form-content debate. In relation to what has been argued throughout the entire second chapter, this aspect obviously does not describe how much content and form are separated from each other. Instead, it represents how meaningful and crucial the distinction is for the design of the format. While in TPs, and with some restrictions also in SCPs, this difference is not made at all, in single-source publishing it takes its most radical form. Likewise, it is a key element of SPs.

The aspect *attitude towards research* defines the functional relationship between research as a process of knowledge production and a publication. For instance, the primary attitude of Living Books is qualification in the name of democratization. The format ensures that whatever is published out of a peculiar research process can only be published in a way in which the structure of the format automatically presents this process as one besides others. It undermines finality and dogmatization of research processes. This holds true even if other research processes do not contribute, because it is the format that frames research in this respect. Research Objects' primary functional relationship is that of recording the research process. The main functional relationship of historical articles may in contrast be described as systematization, at least some authors in digital publishing understand it this way (Bradley et al. 2010). Those publications summarize, contextualize, and generalize the research process. They distinguish between significant and insignificant parts of it. Open Laboratory Books take a documentary attitude, while SPs' attitude and the scaled approach of OpenAIRE is that of harmonization. In two different ways, the last two formats relate to the research process in a way that favors those properties of research that are shared with others. Obviously, publication formats have more than one functional relationship. Nonetheless, it is possible in most cases to identify, by the format itself, or by the way the authors present it, one relationship that is more important than others.

Digital publications started to conceive of the *residence time* of a publication, meaning the time span a publication should be available, as one of its designable elements. Accordingly, SPPs and LPs discussed the possibility of a "decay" factor. HPs take up a more pragmatical but nevertheless highly decisive approach. Since in times of digital technologies, "remixing" and transforming publications between formats is a frequent phenomenon, taking care of long-term availability of publications becomes less important than before. "All publishing becomes vanity publishing" (Hall 2013, 497; see also McPherson 2010, 4).

Similarly linked to the issues of time are different approaches to the *synchronization* between research process and publication. The corresponding question is the question about the right moment to externalize research into publications. Open Laboratory Books carry out an approach that can be called *parallel-successive*. The publication process advances in parallel to the research process by publishing parts, which combined in turn form the entire publication. Living and Unbound Books synchronize with research in a *parallel-* or *trans-incremental* way. This means publishing is a process which adds, deletes, or modifies the content of a publication. This process is arranged parallel to research processes or across research processes, but belongs to a shared research endeavor. Finally, the publication of ROs, SPPs, or SCPs tends to mark the end of a research process.

Structural rigor is another aspect by which publication formats can be distinguished. In fact, MAs introduced a new level of formal and structural rigor to publications, by defining exactly which components of publications should be clearly separable from each other and how they relate to each other. Structural rigor does not include the *level of formality* and *formal complexity* of the underlying technological model. It only addresses the question of how detailed, precise, and complex a publication concept prescribes components of publications and their interplay, regardless of their technological implementation. NPs and MPs, for instance, have a higher level of rigor than EPs. They are significantly more restrictive and precise in terms of the question of what a publication is allowed to contain and what it is not. The case of SCPs is interesting insofar, as, similar to TPs and HPs, they try to minimize structural rigor. They turn the discussion of structural rigor upside down.

Modal complexity and *types of intermodal relationships* address the question of how many different resources for representation like text, diagrams, photos, and video-audio are combined by a format, and how their modal qualities are addressed. An image can explain a textual narrative, as is often the case in DPs. It can also be intended to create meaning, together with text that cannot be reduced to one or the other. This is the case for TPs. Finally, an image can be stored for computational analysis without ever looking at it. It might also be packaged with other resources in order to offer optional supplemental material, as it is called in ROs.[7]

As has been mentioned above, this list of aspects or ideas is just a selection. It contains aspects which intend to clarify the extend up to which the design of publication formats is part of a scientific discourse about science and technology. Similar patterns could also be described for aspects that are much simpler, for instance the role and use of layout. Such analysis is carried out on broad terms in multimodal analysis, for instance by Guo (2006). While specific technological means of publication concepts cannot be related to particular opinions on the aforementioned aspects as such, they nonetheless tend to support specific opinions better than others. More important is the fact, however, that part one showed that the development of these means is in any case closely linked to certain

7 Rowsell (2013) offers a comprehensive overview of relationships of meaning between different types of resources for meaning production.

opinions. Both sides have influenced each other while not determining each other, and this entanglement is exactly what is intended to be demonstrated throughout this inquiry.

Many attitudes towards the majority of aspects of digital publications listed above can be distributed on an axis between two extremes. In other words, possible choices relating to one aspect are most often organized around a bipolar structure. The two examples in table 6.1 and table 6.2 illustrate this dimension.

action		step	project	cluster
SRPs	OLBs, UBs	SPs	ROs, SPPs, EPs	LPs, LBs

[Table 6.1] Axis for the scale aspect of digital publications

Different attitudes towards scale are ordered along an axis between one action in a research process and a cluster of research processes. This polarity allocates other attitudes in the order: step and process.

determined			contingent
NPs, ROs	EPs	OLBs, DPs	HPs, TPs

[Table 6.2] Progression of the aspect of structural rigor in digital publications

The polarity that forms the shape of attitudes towards structural rigor can be described as a polarity between full determination and structural contingency. Although distinctions on such axes resemble distinctions between information, information units, and complex information units in MAs, an important difference exists. They are not meant to play a normative role, but to offer orientation between different formats. Their main function is to give evidence of the fact that they exist as influential axes in digital publication concepts. They are not intended to precisely define what each segment looks like, as MAs try to do with neurological arguments. The distinctions are of a relational nature and if necessary, could be defined by comparison, as has been done for the arrangements in the tables.

Furthermore, the allocation of approaches on such axes are approximations. Part one has shown that there is always variation around specific approaches. For instance, DPs exist which are completely determined. Nevertheless, it has also been argued that this variation does not make it impossible to speak of unique approaches. All in all, Data Papers show very different approaches to the issue of structural rigor. It is the consistency of these differences that make it blind to the issue of structural rigor and not question how many DPs exist that are determined in comparison to those that are not.

Some aspects cannot be rendered on axes like those above because they are more categorial in nature. Of the aspects discussed, these are logic cohesion and attitude towards research. The few examples given for such aspects show that they reference a complex space of possibilities that is potentially open.

Since digital technologies are technologies of conversion, they do not enforce any peculiar decision on certain options for aspects. In fact, the individuality of paths taken by different formats is another indication of the level of impact of this claim. This, and the plurality of publication formats that have been created on top of it, started a process in which any such aspects are already automatically interpreted as a statement about technology or about science. There are no better examples for this fact than the different notions towards narrativity that have been outlined in part one. As much as narrativity becomes less necessary by means of technology, publication concepts reconsider its overall necessity. As far as this reconsideration leads to a continuation of the extensive use of narrativity, it is automatically perceived of as a statement. This holds true regardless of the fact of whether this statement is really made or not, because it is the environment that has changed in such a way that it constitutes a statement. The critique by Candela et al. (2015) that DPs are not sufficiently data-like is a good example for this fact.

Contradictory Patterns in the Development of Digital Publications

As mentioned previously, the extremes and ranges of aspect do not exist as such and thus are not static. This remark was made not only to prevent new simplifications comparable to those that were made in MAs.[8] The fact that the extent of such ranges, and the exact choices they offer, is the outcome of a historical process, draws the attention to particular facets of that history. As in the example of the relationship between infrastructural and descriptive approaches to deal with heterogeneity, developments around digital publication aspects go into different directions at the same time. These developments create the space of possible choices within bipolar

8 Modular Articles randomly referenced physics and neuroscience in order to empirically define differences between information, information units, and composed information units on a non-theoretical information complexity vector that cannot take into account the context-dependency of what forms a composition and what forms a whole.

ranges of aspects of publications in the first place. Activities that take part in the field of digital publishing often share common goals, but the strategies chosen to get there frequently oppose each other. It shows that the geneaology of digital publications reveals an aporetic core structure. This structure is best demonstrated by the general observation that all projects try to define the future publication, but each contribution adds new features that in parts contrast those of other activities.

Part one contains many such contradictions, and the ranges above can all be read as opposites. Contradictions appear all over digital publications: some abstract as much as possible from modes of representation, and some are combinations of all kinds of representation strategies; they are atomic information units, but also containers that contain any resource used in research; they are meant to be aggregations and images for emulation as well; they should contain an internal formal structure (microdata), but also be built out of an external formal structure (OAI-ORE); they change with the flow of time, but are recorded or designed versions of timeflows at the same time; they are conceived of as a derivation of a publication meta-model, but emphasize a historical state of publishing, in which it is allegedly no longer reasonable to think about publishing as a model-based approach at all (see next section).

The notion of contradictions radicalizes the discussion of heterogeneity around digital publications. It shows that digital publications have not just produced a lot of heterogeneity instead of harmonizing it, but that this production is systematic. Digital publications systematically produce representations for any option that can be perceived of as a feature of publications today. From the angle of the two debates on truth-making and technology, this means two things. First, within the development of digital publications, any scientific knowledge culture tries to be represented in the form of publication formats. Second, this development is one in which convertibility as the dominant feature of digital technologies is realized by comprehensively testing conversions between scientific actions and multimodal representations and vice versa. Using the terminology of MAs, these two angles can be combined by saying that both are contributions to a process in which more and more resources are turned into semiotic material, i.e. material that becomes suitable for the creation of meaning and the representation of knowledge for digital publications. This description, however, also means that more than designing new scholarly publications, former developments have only prepared the ground for such publications.

The notion of contradictions came to light when the different developments behind digital publications were subsumed under the common goal of creating the future scholarly publication. This viewpoint eliminates the temporal dynamic of the phenomenon, in order to highlight its fictional vanishing point. When the development itself is perceived of as such, the contradiction turns into a dialectic process. More precisely, when the development of digital publications is observed while keeping in mind the general phenomenon of contradiction, this development reveals dialectical patterns such as the relationship between modeling and engineering in digital publishing, highlighted in the section heterogeneity. It is the pattern of semantic solutions to infrastructural issues which engender problems that in turn require infrastructural solutions and so forth. Likewise, the containerization and emulation approach to publications did not just develop in parallel to others. It got attention in reaction to modularization and atomization approaches. Such approaches first received the technological infrastructure necessary for its realization[9], but by doing so created a new set of problems[10]. In the same fashion, explorations into multimodal strategies of representation and the volatile nature of the format aspect of publications temporally appear as a response to the advancements of approaches that focus on technology and information. This response is even spoken of explicitly by Adema (2015, sec. 1.1.2), when she outlines the necessity to highlight "genealogical modes" of digital publications against the success of "teleological schemes."

Fundamental Tensions between Publication and Communication

If digital publications until today mainly semiotize the environment of publications, i.e. comprehensively prepare the space of options, for new types of scholarly publications, the question is how this situation affects the notion of publications as such. In order to evaluate this question, it seems promising to have a closer look at the overarching leitmotif in the research on digital publications: communication.

9 RDFa and OAI-ORE among others.

10 The effort to represent a publication in a modular way as a set of atomic parts, maintaining the integrity of a publications the parts of which exist in a distributed environment.

Communication, the Leitmotif of Digital Publications

The by far dominant frame in which digital publications are discussed across contexts, time, and concepts concerns its function in scholarly communication. The vast majority of authors regard the issue of publications as that of research communication. When the question is raised how to make use of digital technology in the context of publications, it is generally interpreted to be asking how to improve scholarly communication.

Obviously, publications have more functions than the enabling of communication in academia. The few exceptions to this norm, as well as issues discussed in passing, bear witness to this argument. Adema (2015) discusses publications as an organizational means for structuring the social field of academia. The publishing toolkit by Pensoft, which used DPs in a way that enabled distribution of the efforts necessary for their creation among different stakeholders, was also introduced. Self-Contained Publications showed that the question of publications is not just one of "more effective scholarly communication" (Bourne, Shotton, et al. 2012, 46), but also one of effective resource management. Transmedia Publications raised the issue of appropriate representations. McPherson (2010, 10–11) offers the most comprehensive overview of functions publications must carry out in order work properly.

These facets and their discussion, nevertheless, do by no means match the attention the general theme of research communication receives, especially where the discussion reflects digital publications on a broader and sometimes theoretical scale. Accordingly, Candela et al. (2015, 1748) call publications "custodians, yet they need to reconsider their mission in modern scientific communication." Even McPherson subsumes her overview under the basic theme of "Thoughts on the Future of Scholarly Communication." For Hall (2013), writing an article is the act of "performing scholarly communication." He also emphasizes that the historical article did in fact not really accomplish communication, and that this failure is a consequence of the print environment. The key point behind this and related descriptions is always the same: digital technologies have initiated a progression towards scholarly publications that are more communication-like than before. As such, they promise to fulfill a goal of publications that had always been their primary aim, but one that could not be supported properly due to technological restrictions, which are now outdated.

Still, the development from publications to digital publications is a development "from scholarly publication to scholarly communication" (Hogenaar 2009), a transformation in which publications are "about to be replaced by what has been coined research communications" (Nentwich 2003, 304), to form "the future of scholarly communications" (De Roure 2014b). Evidently, the term communications replaces the term publication on many occasions (Bourne, Shotton, et al. 2012; Clark, Ciccarese, and Goble 2014) in order to comply with the "revolutionized scholarly communication paradigm" (Van de Sompel and Lagoze 2007, 1).

The publication-format point of view indicates that the paradigm of communication is less defined by concrete specification, but more, indirectly, by removing as much as possible of whatever is conceived of as technologically conditioned constraints of historical forms of publishing. To push things further, focusing on the theme of communication leads to the phenomenon of historical constraints being nearly always only discussed as technologically motivated constraints. Other possible sources for constraining publications rarely appear as explanations. Aiming for digital publications that are worthy of scholarly communication means removing constraints from publications.

The overarching theme of communication in the research field of digital publications does not add much to a general definition of scholarly publications after the introduction of digital technologies. From this perspective, publications are just "units of communication" (Van de Sompel and Lagoze 2007, 1). More than being something, they are what remains after a purely formal distinction has been made — which is necessary in order to be able to talk about communication: obviously no communication can take place when there is nothing to communicate. What the phrase allows, however, is to talk about communication without the need to specify further what this something is, or at least how much specification[11] it requires.

The impression that the use of the term communication in the majority of cases simply signals the urge to develop an all-inclusive and less-restrictive notion of publication is made explicit when Hogenaar (2009, para. 5) remarks that "science is flourishing thanks to communication, a much broader concept than publishing," and Candela et al. (2015, 1761) claim that "it is a responsibility of scientists to assist the rest of the scientific communication realm to remove the barriers affecting it."

11 It is true that the contribution quoted here introduces the OAI-ORE model. However, this model is only a technical one. Its content by definition states that it is nothing more than "aggregates of multiple distinct components" (Van de Sompel and Lagoze 2007, 2).

And once again, there is a paradoxical situation in the research into digital publications. This time, it consists of the observation that its main entity — the publication — is only addressed implicitly and in a negative way. Digital publications appear as those publications that need to be defined less as publications compared to communication. This is the setup, at least since Kircz put the issue of digital publications under Garvey's claim that communication is the essence of science.

Authenticity and Presence: How Digital Publications Conceive of Communication

Another interesting question is whether such barriers have something more in common than being barriers and, correspondingly, if this urge, emphasized so much in the discussion of the communication theme, aims at something that could be made more specific. Hence, what are such barriers in the first place? Candela et al. (2015, 1761) are relatively clear in their answer on this question. From their point of view, common publications are "no, slow, incomplete, inaccurate, or unmodifiable communication." Bourne, Shotton, et al. (2012) add to these four properties the property of "outdated communication" (47), and "expensive communication" (54), which addresses similar issues as efficient communication.

No, incomplete, and inaccurate communication describes different scenarios in which information considered to be relevant is missing. Slow communication addresses the time lapse between the creation of the content of a publication by a researcher and its consumption by another researcher. Expensive communication does indeed mean both financial costs of publications and the efforts necessary to create them. Consequently, these costs can block or again delay communication.

From this perspective, the theme of communication is indeed the key driver for the vast majority of publication formats. This is so because most issues that creators of digital publications highlight and seek to solve with new formats were and can be expressed as a form of restricted communication. The whole aspect of information redundancy and efficiency is part of the narrative of incomplete, inaccurate, or ineffective communication.

As discussed in the abovementioned section and elsewhere, communication is conceived of as restricted by redundancy on the grounds of the claim that it is evident what the information is, that it is the same information as in other publications. It is conceived of thus, because it is considered possible and desirable to give formal representations of that information for any kind of knowledge. With those claims, certain aspects of historical publications, such as their narrative structure, become an obstacle. Several arguments, among them the end of theory debate or the references to Gärdenfors, have shown that the formalization of structure and information in approaches like MAs, SPs, MPs, NPs, and so forth is not meant to be a concretization or a negotiation about the content of publications. Instead, it is conceived of as coming to the real thing. Consequently, the step from publications to communication is the step of leaving behind anything allegedly contingent. Seeking communication within this narrative thus does not roll out a different strategy for scholarly communication, but pretends to eliminate the distinction between information and representation. It targets the direct and unfiltered availability of meaning.

Immediate availability of meaning is one side of the end-of-theory argument. As mentioned previously, the other one is immediate access to truth. As much as truth is conceived of as something to which direct access exists, the burden of publishing and acquiring research results counts more than the effort of doing research. At least this is what the accelerationist motif behind many digital publications suggests. For Goble, De Roure, and Bechhofer (2012), "accelerating scientists' knowledge turns" is the primary goal of the ROs format. Similarly, De Roure et al. (2009, 2336) seek to "accelerate the time to discovery of new research results" by introducing digital publications. In 2005, Marcondes (2005, 119) already wanted to bring "information technology in[to] the scientific communication process in order to accelerate the embodying of new research results." This conflation between publishing of research results and doing research as scholarly communication stands out most in Kuhn (2015) and Sofronijević (2012). In such approaches, "real-time publications" (Kuhn 2015, 1) prepare the ground for communication of autonomous algorithms, which then immediately carry out further research. In summary, communication means accelerating the production of publications up to the point of real-time, in which the notion of research results vanishes, because the distinction between discovery and publication, marked by the concept of research results, conflates into undisturbed, ongoing communication.

Communication in the form of real-time publications indicates that acceleration of research obviously similarly builds on the acceleration of publishing, up to the point of no-time-at-all: "communication becomes instantaneous" (Bourne, Shotton, et al. 2012, 44). Several barriers exist for instantaneous communication, and the aspect of time is only an aspect in which such barriers become visible. Bourne et al. also highlight that they become instantaneous "across geographic boundaries." Consequently, the use of the term communication for digital publications seeks to invalidate the category place for the design of publication formats. This is more than saying that publications bridge geographical boundaries. In the light of communication, such boundaries cease to exist.

A radicalization of this aspect is the intent of ROs, OLBs, and, with some exceptions, SCPs to entirely reproduce the original research process. They try to break down the barrier of different ranges of experience between the creation of publications and their consumption. In this context, the turn from publications in science to scholarly communication means putting the consumer in the same position as if she had gone to the lab (OLBs), or as if she had experienced the experiment in person (ROs). Direct availability of shared spaces of experience is likewise pursued by approaches which apply the term communication to collaboration practices (see see beginning of this section). Accordingly, "the future of scholarly communications" is a future of "hybrid physical-digital sociotechnical systems" (De Roure 2014b, 1). The idea of such systems, therefore, is the idea of experiences that are shared, as well as shared experiences.

An entirely quantitative and less radical variation of the idea that communication means the delivery of the full research experience is the demand that anything produced during research should be considered worthy of publishing. Bourne (2010, 2) supports this claim by arguing:

> Some would say that much of what is published today should not be, so why add more superfluous information to the record of science? The response is that one person's trash is another person's treasure.

Likewise, Castelli, Manghi, and Thanos (2013) argue that current communication infrastructure is infrastructure where all results from the research process form publications interlinked in many different ways. Disregarding such standards would lead to "knowledge burying" (De Roure et al. 2009, 10) in a "digital dark age" (Choudhury et al. 2008, 21). In this context, the term communication marks the shift from a time where publications were curated to a vision of absolute transparency beyond any curational filter or intervention.

A much more abstract and therefore more profound barrier for communication was introduced by Hall's critique on the form aspect of the book. For Hall, form is the materialization of any type of reification, may it be triggered by semantic, political, economic, or social processes.

Communication, in contrast to the book, refers to the attempt to allow any play with meaning and content in a multiplicity of "channels" without disturbances. If the high number of references to Derrida made in research literature on Liquid Books, UBs, and others are serious, those approaches have to be aware that content only comes by form. Some remarks in the work of Hall and Adema give evidence of this assumption. However, for these authors, form has and should have situational meaning only. The application of theme of communication, accordingly, aims at deconstructing form by pushing the utmost plurality of forms. It is thus not wrong to argue that despite the acknowledgment of the form, dependency of meaning, and communication, theme of communication is used to establish the ideal of formless publishing.

It was furthermore described that the background of this ideal is political in the first place. Formless publishing, similarly, addresses the elimination of uneven narratives, disparate social positions of participants in research, and asynchronous information flows. The theme of communication therefore also represents the ethics of direct contact between people, unfiltered by social institutions or relations such as hierarchies conceived of as damaging to society and research alike. It is the model of colleagues with equal rights, doing research together, instead of an institutionalized organizational body of stakeholders with specific roles and a particular relationship in the system of science, that those approaches try to advocate.

A final, and indeed, extremely simple variation of the notion of presence is the already discussed phenomenon that putting something online is often conceived of as making a publication out of it. Worthington and Furter (2014), accordingly, argue that putting an item online is enough to consider it a publication. The taxonomy includes "conventional" and "unconventional" publications. In fact, for most unconventional publications this just means that they are somewhere available online. The environment, and the context of such an online presence, is of no further importance. Similarly, a certain number of RIPs and Webtexts are just HTML websites, uploaded on some server in the web. Often, the web itself is considered a publication environment, so that anything on it automatically becomes a publication.

This viewpoint corresponds with familiar and more general thoughts on the status of the web. Authors like Stiegler (2012), for instance, define the whole "digital technical system" as a "global and contributory publication and editorialization system" (4). Similarly, resources that are put on a website without any additional restriction are considered publications in OLBs. Meeks (2012) carries out a broader analysis of this equation between putting something online and considering it a publication.

The description of goals behind the theme of communication, as given in the last section, is therefore incomplete, as it focuses only on the removal of barriers. The emphasis which is put on terminology and discourse, next to certain arguments, reveals a much stronger aim. In a plethora of cases, this aim corresponds with the notion to not only remove concrete barriers, but to invalidate entire distinctions that make room for possible barriers. In conclusion, it seems more meaningful to argue that digital publications are not so much about publications than about the transfer of alleged properties of communication — presence, purity, immediacy, and authenticity — into digital environments of academia. They are about communicating digitally.

What Lies Beyond: Exclusion and Persistence

If most of the attention is given to the aforementioned aspects, it is urged in this chapter to look for elements and topics that are quite difficult to include here. What are these elements, how are they discussed, and in which state are they? In the context of digital publication formats, these questions address two things. The notion of authenticity and presence in digital publications derives from the fact that such publication formats, each with its own strategy, seek to extract and host parts of the research process, instead of only representing it. If the term presence is defined as the presence of authentic research — as thought of by the particular logic of the format — then exclusion refers to those parts of research and the research process that do not appear in such a logic. The second angle addresses the gap between a publication as an object and all potential situations in which such an object should count, without having happened yet. De Roure (2014b, 235) and others remark that the key criterion of success of the article format was its capacity "to cross boundaries of time, place, and discipline." In this respect, the second angle focus on the way by which publication formats address, anticipate, and treat the issue of their own persistence within these dimensions.

A comparison between different publication formats and their respective strategies to keep the research process present in publications shows that it is not enough to just identify differences between them. Such differences have a more complex relationship with each other. For OLBs, for instance, the presence of the research process means temporal synchronicity between the moment in which certain results are made and the moment they are published. The format stresses that the authenticity of the research process is replicated in the publication by suppressing any possibility for finality on the level of the format. In contrast, ROs, in terms of replayability and repeatability, aim at this authenticity by retrieving the whole research setup that led to results. In order to achieve this, ROs require a start- and an endpoint. It is not possible to replay a workflow that has no beginning and will never have an end. Hence, one concept of presence renders the other one impossible.

The relationship between OLBs on the one hand and UBs and LPs on the other is a similar one. Unbound Books and LPs allow continuous modifications towards a presupposed whole of a publication, while OLBs prescribe continuous additions. Such additions are steps which lay out a path, instead of working on an object. Both approaches problematize the statefulness of publications as well as of research, and attempt to constantly be up to date. While UBs and LPs try to resemble something that could be — and in some cases indeed was — called the state of the art, OLBs try to resemble movement of scientific progress. Modifications make the modified element disappear, while additions pile up.

In the same way, SPs' attempt to perpetuate the factual content of research processes, apart from their distorting representation in textual publications, is incompatible with the extension of modal means in TPs. Both approaches seek to preserve "the real thing." Whereas SPs do so by reducing representational means to formal structures, TPs multiply these means in order to prevent the represented thing from reification. Both strategies have opposing notions of presence and authenticity towards the research object and, consequently, choose different options from the set available, in order to design digital publications. The decision in favor of one strategy automatically challenges the other, and vice versa.

There are many other examples following the same pattern as those above. In order to keep certain aspects of the research process alive, others need to be cut out of the publication format. Authenticity and exclusion in publication formats depend on each other. While digital technologies improve mediation of the presence of certain aspects of the research process, they are everything but technologies of presence and authenticity. To research, publications remain just interfaces. The design decisions that need to be made in order to create these interfaces are far more numerous than they were before, and it is the necessity of these decisions that make a publication concept an interface besides others.

In the light of communication as pure presence this logic is rarely reflected openly in the discourse on digital publications, as summarized in this inquiry. In consequence, the leitmotif of scholarly communication makes the impression that the adventure of digital publications is about more authenticity and less exclusion while it could be argued that it is about more (granular) decisions of inclusion and exclusion.

The second angle was called persistence. It addresses the form in which digital publication formats confront the issue of time, place, and discipline. There are two dimensions of this aspect. The first dimension is the form in which designers of digital publication concepts perceive and describe issues of time, place, and discipline for publications. The second dimension is the relationship between this perception and the status of these issues for implementation and existing digital publications. As shown, designers of digital publication formats have a great amount of freedom to make decisions about these issues. It is possible to decide, for instance, how long the lifecycle of publications is expected to last, or in which contexts it is supposed to appear. The type of implementation, and the technology used, significantly influenced when publications of its kind are present and where they are absent. The level of persistence relates choices that can be made by concept designers. Jane Hunter's proposition, to think about a decay factor for SPPs, is an example of choice regarding the time dimension.

Despite the tremendous growth of means for the purpose of defining and modelling the behavior of publications across the aforementioned boundaries, each concrete publication still remains an autonomous instantiation of models. Hence, while digital technologies allow more fine-grained decisions about how a specific publication of its kind should deal with such boundaries, it is still possible — and in the context of the current analysis absolutely necessary — to analyze to what extent principles of publication concepts and the situation of concrete publications match.

Having said that on the level of the format, publication formats are able to choose their level of relative stability, it is highly significant that few reflected choices such as the one by Hunter et al. have been made in this respect. From Kircz in the early years up to De Roure in recent years, the notion of absolute stability is the dominant goal of digital publications. Accordingly, De Roure (2014b, 235) argues that the capability of historical publications to cross time, place, and disciplines is the one feature that should be transferred to digital publications without any modification. In fact, he conceives of this feature as a kind of transcendental core of publications. It was written that on the level of discipline, which can be interpreted as a more socially grounded way to refer to place and time, the same absoluteness of such goals prevailed. It was outlined how terms such as "knowledge burying" or "digital dark age" furthermore call for a state of emergency to archive everything. Considerations like the decay factor, for instance, were left as ideas. This issue was thoroughly reflected and discussed for HPs, but not made part of a decision-making process on the level of the format.

In line with De Roure, Kircz (2001a, 271) remarks:

> The conclusion of the above discussion is that the scientific article will change its form considerably but that, in its new more composite form as an ensemble of various textual and non-textual components, it will retain the cultural and scientific demands with regard to editorial, quality and integrity.

All three properties are properties of reliability and thus stability. While the first concerns the social perception and status of the publication, the last one more clearly represents the consistency of the publication as an object across different types of boundaries. The list of ten demands that Kircz provides confirms this equation. It contains demands such as long-term-preservation, persistence, authenticity, public availability, permanence, and similar. Consequently, what Kircz argued for in the early years of digital publications, and De Roure et al. re-confirm in recent times, is that for aspects of stability, nothing should change, while everything else should.

The paradoxical situation of digital publications, more drastically, is the fact that discourse demands adaptation of nearly all properties of publications to the situational and eventful facets of research, with the one exception being the status of concrete publications in space and time. While every aspect of publications is considered a question of design, this one is not. If publications should be designed around the notion that scientists' knowledge turns accelerate (Goble, De Roure, and Bechhofer 2012), as ROs demand, why then is a less stable publication not likewise acceptable? It could be argued that if digital publications are approached as units in scholarly communication, the notion of communication has not been developed radically enough. Thus, a unit in communication may not only look very different, it may also behave very differently. It goes without saying that the goal of this and other, previously mentioned arguments is not to give up on stability and persistence. Instead, the whole process makes it plausible to reflect on different types of stability that correspond with the way communication is rendered in specific formats. Since the field of digital publications has not provided a coherent definition of publications in the aforementioned logic of communication, and publications as mere "units" of communication do not go beyond a pure formalism, the way this fields deals with the issue of stability is likewise in more of an abstract or idealistic way.

Stability and Sustainability as Infrastructure

This has consequences for the actual stability of concrete digital publications and their infrastructure. The highly problematic state of the integrity of digital publications is an issue which has accompanied the field up to now. As shown in the respective sections, it is mentioned in the context of EPs, RO, SCPs, TPs (Webtexts), and others. Similar observations prove to be right, even where they are not discussed openly. Accordingly, the integrity of Scalar TPs depends heavily on the Scalar web platform, because not all the information that constitutes a Scalar publication as a transmedia object is exportable into the RDF based representation. Sufficient integrity of publications in new publication formats therefore remains a fundamental issue, even in relative terms.

There are other issues which follow the same pattern. Credit and reward are two of those. They regard necessary conditions for the social stability of digital publication formats, i.e. the degree to which such formats are accepted and respected within the research community. Obviously, their acceptance depends on the fact that an author can expect acknowledgment of a used format, an acknowledgment which is supported by a shared value system that corresponds with this format. As early as 2010, Bechhofer, Ainsworth, et al. (2010) remark in the context of ROs that a credit and reward system is a key factor for the success of ROs. This remark, however, remained just that and is still an open issue today. Nüst et al. (2017), currently, refer to the same issues as having to be dealt with in the future. Although it seems that awareness exists for these issues in the ROs community, they mostly conceive of them as issues that will be solved by others. This attitude makes it easy to let the publication format focus on technical or epistemological aspects, and treat issues of stability as something pertaining solely to the environment and the surrounding infrastructure.

Beyond problems such as those above, there are other issues regarding the stability of digital publications that are rarely mentioned, for which no empirical basis exists (Jankowski et al. 2012), or for which existing insights are seldom considered in the design of publication formats. The persistent identification of digital publications, parts of digital publications, and micro-contributions of different types of contributors (Stäcker et al. 2016, sec 2.1), for example, is not just a technical issue. It is also a question of the social valuing and of efficient citing practices. The question is if each of the new types of citations and giving of credit support a functional and sustainable citing culture. An ethos that, in the spirit of presence and authenticity, focuses on granularity and preciseness, misses significant facets of citing.

The same could be said about the question of how published data in data-centric digital publications is really used. In other words, do the data-usage patterns that formats assume match with the usage-patterns by which consumers of digital publications engage with such publications? The ambiguity of the concept of data-centric form in digital publications has already been discussed elsewhere. This ambiguity would, however, have remained more of a theoretical issue if digital publication designers had related their designing process to analysis about existing data practices (Key Perspectives 2010; Dodds 2013), instead of building on one specific empiricist data practice (e-Science). The principle of authenticity is only applied to the relationship between research situations and publications, but not to the relationship between real-world publications and their dissemination in specific research domains. This brought forth publications that express the abstract idea of data, but have a hard time sustaining and promoting data-driven research practices. Theoretically, they are stable across place, time, and discipline, because they are indeed generic. Unfortunately, this has not made them more stable across the time that has passed in the history of digital publications.

On a more abstract level, this issue also includes questions about the interfaces of digital publications in general. Here, the term interface defines different things, such as visual and technological interfaces, but also logical interfaces with the research process. The question is what type of interactions are suggested on all these levels, and do they prove themselves when publication formats become operational. Few examples exist where such perspectives go hand in hand with the development of digital publications formats. Such examples, however, illustrate well how a development model, which develops concrete strategies for the stability of digital publications instead of just referring to it in an abstract way, may look like. In the context of EPs, Adriaansen and Hooft (2010) and Jankowski et al. (2012) tried to implement such a strategy for issues such as authoring tools and user interfaces. Pensoft's approach to DPs also shows well how the design of new interaction models between publishing stakeholders by means of formats can emerge gradually, out of established and ongoing publishing practices. The Scalar project developed its platform, an authoring software at its core, as a nexus for all its other engagements in digital publishing.

Hence, it is possible to develop digital publication formats in setups that mediate very differently between the layers of format, technology, and their social environment. If an integrative approach seems too resource-intensive, the obvious prioritization still does not need to be in favor of the model, or of technology. As written in the introduction and throughout the whole study, the impact of digital publication formats in terms of use and acceptance is limited. Many digital publication formats remained experiments and did not succeed in becoming established components of scholarly publishing until today. An interesting observation can, however, be made about those efforts that are successful in one way or another. This observation illustrates that projects in digital publishing might have underestimated the complexity of the dynamics, possibly leading to stable publication formats.

For the sake of this discussion, impact is understood as projects in digital publishing which:

- engendered publications that constitute significant contributions in their research domain;
- gave testimony of a significant degree of institutionalization beyond the project phase;
- created a high level of participation.

Looking at the examples of the Pensoft Writing Toolkit and the GBIF Integrated Publishing Toolkit, the Scalar platform, and finally the AiME project, which succeeded in one or more of these criteria, one common aspect stands out. All three projects invested tremendous resources in assuring the success of its approaches to publishing. Additionally, a great deal of these resources was spent on means and technologies applied to mobilizing stakeholders. In contrast to ROs or OLBs, which perceive publications as recordings or documentations, these projects adopt a curational approach to content.

Accordingly, the toolchain associated with Pensoft organizes new relationships between stakeholders and orchestrates workflows, in order to support the emergence of DPs. Counting the Vectors Journal and the Scalar project together, Scalar took around ten years to gradually and strategically form a community. Within this process, this community participated in the design of the process itself. Finally, the AiME project created an extremely sophisticated workflow in order to stimulate, maintain, and channel content creation for its UBs. It invested into technology which mediated this workflow, and into human resources that controlled the process.

Obviously not all digital publication initiatives were able to acquire resources on this scale. However, it is also necessary to understand the issue of digital publications as a problem that in fact needs those resources in order to become more successful. This is especially true for time resources. The last paragraphs, but also the complaints and problems that appeared throughout this study, showed that often, resources, but more importantly the way they are strategically used, do not match the goal of absolute stability of publications across space and time. Thus, the underestimation of the scope of related problems and the type of intervention they deem necessary for the stability of digital publications resembles the misconception of social dimensions discussed in the respective chapter.

Looking at the entire section, it was argued that the relationship between issues subsumed under terms of authenticity, presence, exclusion and persistence are not generally well balanced. The fact that often only those aspects of research that can now be made present in new formats appear in the discourse, but not those that have to be excluded as part of the same process, suggests such an imbalance. The way in which the stability and persistence of publications across time, space, and social boundaries is dealt with theoretically confirmed this impression.

It has been addressed that, if so many authors of digital publications aim at accelerating science up to the point of instant discovery, then this has to mean also that research and resources representing this research lose value more quickly. Similarly, the fact that the formats of digital publications are deeply entangled with the disciplinary discourse rolled out in publication formats easily questions the need for placing such formats into a transdisciplinary scope.

These tensions, between publications' loyalty to the moment of discovery and the demanded provision of eternal accountability, between the publication format's methodological concretization and the goal of transdisciplinary dissemination, superposes all the others that have been discussed in the context of digital publication. Using the terms that are used respectively in the discourse of digital publications themselves, this means there is a tension between what is meant by communication and what is addressed when the term publication is used. The engagement with issues in the first perspective is very concrete, while those in the second are discussed in a formal or abstract way, if at all.

Against this background, it is also possible to argue that the whole issue of information overload and data deluge is less of a technical problem but more a result of a misconception between different aspirations and ideas in the discourse on digital publications. The issue of data deluge and information overload might thus result from the fact that publication formats not only differ in what they present and how they are structured, but that they are not also distinguished in terms of how much they are part of a concept of publication that is never really specified — or not, as it were. Robertson (2013 sec. Kindergarten and the arrival of the newborn child) similarly notes in a more theoretical contribution that "when every potential publication is actually published, publication itself no longer has value." In short, the data deluge and information overload might result from the fact that people in certain areas have similar expectations of different things, and that the proclamation of a data deluge problem derives from the fact that different issues, some of which might not be issues at all, are merged into one big challenge.

A concise theoretical definition of publications rarely exists across projects. As a unit of units in communication, publications are mostly defined as publications by appearing in communications. The term unit offers no further detail. Summarizing all insights that came to light up to this point of the present inquiry, a clear concept for publications after the advent of digital technologies is missing, because of:

- the attempt to use digital publications for the comprehensive exploration and implementation of possibilities of digital technologies;
- the attempt to use publication formats in order to as perfectly as possible mirror the shape of specific scientific methodologies and research topics;
- the fact that the discourse on digital publication formats is primarily structured by notions of authenticity, purity, and presence, among others.

No definition arises from these aspects because:

- digital technologies are conversion technologies, and thus only lead to the representation of heterogeneous ideas, instead of revealing a common ground, based on which it might be possible to conceive of them as part of the same concept;
- despite any claims made in the research field of digital publications, digital technologies do not dissolve general epistemological distinctions, such as between theoretical and empirical knowledge, or typological and topological knowledge;

- the conceptual frame of speaking about digital publications in terms of communication is not sufficient to derive any general definition of scholarly publications. Especially, it is not enough to just call publishing a unique type of communication. What set of properties constitutes this uniqueness?

The question of whether it is still necessary to define publications in digital publishing, however, is not discussed explicitly, either. Publications and publishing are still the most used terms in the field, even though their purpose is to posit the topic of communication. Only from an angle that is able to treat publications as something different from, or as a defined case of communication in the first place, it is possible to discuss the eventuality of getting rid of the concept. Regardless of the intent to foster or dismiss the notion of publications, a grasp of how it is possible to talk about it while looking at it through the lens of communication is needed.

Publications in Terms of Communication

Since the theme of communication is at the center of the discussion of digital publications, but within it any overarching, thought-provoking sense of the term publication is missing, the question arises of whether a communication-oriented approach exists elsewhere that can provide such a meaning in a systematic manner? It would also be desirable for such an approach to offer further insights into the tensions between what has been called elements of authenticity, presence, exclusion and persistence. In concrete terms, this includes the attempt to let the research process stay alive as much as possible in the publication format, to treat sustainability of publications and publication formats as an absolute value, or to develop strategies for such sustainability as a formal issue.

The methodological framework of MuA has been used on several occasions already. It has proven useful in some places, because it allows the insight that the heterogeneity in digital publications, still today perceived as "a fragmented hybrid publication landscape" (Richards 2018, 37), is an integral part of the development of digital technologies. In fact, it similarly anchors this heterogeneity of the production of sense and meaning in the topic of communication as well. It therefore seems reasonable enough to deepen the understanding of this field of research, and to discuss some concepts that may prove useful for these two tasks.

Framing

One of the key concepts in MuA — and probably also the most fundamental, according to Kress (2013) — is the concept of *framing*. Framing basically describes how the creation of something meaningful in communication depends on the creation of demarcations made on different levels. Meaning can exist only with such demarcations, because the demarcation creates a seclusion that is necessary in order to interpret something as meaningful. Written language is a good illustration in this situation. Only the use of spaces as *framing devices* for word boundaries creates words, by including and excluding letters. Likewise, the full stop is a framing device that introduces the possibility of a new type of meaning, in which words create meaning by relating to each other and not to others. As in the case of words, the logic of framing is such that in order to create the possibility of something meaningful, it is necessary "to draw a line" that includes something and excludes something else, which then can create meaning on its own.

This relationship between framing and meaning is the same across all resources which might become resources for communication purposes. Accordingly, Kress explains how things like pitch and intonation work as framing devices in speech, and how breaks form and separate rhythm patterns in music. The process of framing does not stop at the fine-grained level from which these examples were taken. Certain spatial compositions constitute another type of information unit in text: the paragraph. Margins that create text blocks and columns are frames. The binding of a book that bundles papers together is a frame that enforces us to interpret its content as belonging to a connected discourse, topic, or a more complex semiotic entity that could be called a monograph. Accordingly, different framing devices (Kress 2013) usually exist side by side: a sheet of paper, certain aspects of layout, punctuation, and markings among other things. In conclusion, a book works just as much as a frame as a dot does, although the book combines several framing devices.[12] Consequently, Kress (2000, 134) understands "text as a complex sign." Accordingly, publication formats can be understood as frames which draw together a certain set of framings and frame devices, and reject others. This process of excluding and including is a precondition for the creation of complex meaning, and creates what van Leeuwen (2005, 4) calls *semiotic meaning potential* of a specific type.

12 Gary Hall's remarks about the monograph were not so different from what is discussed here, though the concept of frames and framing highlights the necessity and the empowering aspects of frames such as a binding.

The key element of the concept of framing for the purpose of this inquiry is the structural dependency of what is communicated on the way communication resources are structured. In other words, no intrinsic nature of meaning exists that enforces a certain structure of complex signs such as publication formats, and no other logic of communication exists beyond the creation and delivery of syntactical units of different kinds in consequence of framing. The restrictions of framing devices and their applications are hence tightly coupled with people's notions of and familiarity with the structure of knowledge. Such notions do not precede them (van Leeuwen 2005, 3).

Consequently, the boundaries of atomic units of information that are presented to the human brain by approaches like MAs are in fact more a consequence of the use of certain framing devices that underlie complex signs. In MuA, the term information unit actually also exists, but only to refer to syntactical boundaries that exist due to framing (Kress 2013), and not in terms of any type of meaningful content.

Similar things can be said about the emphasis put on the dynamic facets of knowledge by authors behind UBs, LPs, OLBs, and others. Again, the logic of framing suggests rejecting the idea that such formats come closer to the true nature of knowledge, which is described as being dynamic and ephemeral. Digital technologies provide complex new means that allow technological and social framing of the temporal dimension of communication in different ways. By doing so, however, it also re-frames our perception of knowledge. The claim that knowledge is dynamic cannot be separated from the introduction of new framing devices which create information units of a new kind, but framing devices they remain. They also force communication into a certain temporal logic, from which they cannot escape without using a different format that frames time differently. On the one hand, Hall's critique of the enforcement of binding is confusing, insofar as binding as an example of framing is constitutive of meaning, and thus of communication as such. On the other hand, Hall's emphasis of the dynamic nature of knowledge happens at the same time as technologies appear which allow decisions about its constancy.

All things considered, the application of the concept of framing to the topic of digital publications forces emphasis on the following points:

- By introducing the notion of the complex sign, it is a first step to developing a concept of publications out of a theory of communication. Accordingly, it meets the requirements of a situation in which the distinction between the form and the content of publications gradually disintegrates, because digital technologies provide more direct access to more framing devices.

- It will not lead to sustainable publication formats if the design of such formats, understood as a process of framing, primarily looks for the perfect relationship between the research process and its notion of truth on the one hand, and the format of a publication on the other. This is true not only because research methodologies are different. It is true, because each frame — configured in order to provide a resource and used to represent something from the research process — in most cases leads to the exclusion of other options. It thus brings with it the preconditions for different opinions on the issue, if the configuration of this specific framing device better suits its purpose, or excluded ones might be better. It also causes the question of whether the excluded devices refer to something crucial in a research process that is less accessible to the framing devices used in a certain format. These issues cause the definition of new formats in consequence of the definition of formats, as long as their appropriateness for the representation of the research process and their notion of truth is the primary criterion in the definition and interpretation of digital publications. That does not mean that certain frames and framing devices may be more appropriate for a specific notion of research process. It only means that this aspect cannot be central for the design of publication formats.
- The same is also true for those formats which more consciously reflect these dynamics, but try to define formats that minimize their effects by minimizing the timespan in which certain frames are set, notably OLBs, LPs, LBs, and UBs. These formats intend to undermine the logics of frames. The issue with such formats, however, is the fact that they do so by violently configuring framing devices for the temporal dimension of publications. As has been demonstrated, this dimension is a valid resource for the production of meaning in digital publications. The corresponding approaches thus operate outside of the logics of frames as suggested by them.
- In this sense the concept of frames and framing devices illuminate the fact that certain opposing facets of communication form part of the same process. They may help to tone down some of the aforementioned tensions in the field of digital publications that relate to them.

The discussion of the concept of frames therefore suggests that the field of digital publications needs to emancipate itself from overemphasizing the epistemological functions and, in the case of UBs and of some notions of open science, the ethical implications of publications.

Mode

The example of the book as a complex sign was given in order to describe how framing is a practice across different levels of granularity in communication. It might thus provide a good tool in order to avoid some of the problematic perceptions that have driven the design of digital publication formats. It does, however, not suffice for obtaining a supportive concept of digital publications. To approach such a concept, it is necessary to refer again to the three aspects of communication in MuA that have been summarized in the discussion of topological and typological knowledge.

These functions comprise the ideational, the interpersonal, and the textual, or maybe better structural, function of signs. This means that when people communicate, what is communicated refers to something, that is to say, it represents something they wish to communicate to others, which means communication is directed. It also means that the means of communication possess a certain internal structure: communication is composed of elements and these elements relate to each other in a certain important way.

In fact, Halliday introduces such aspects not primarily in order to understand how language alone works, but in order to understand the nature of signs and the change of sign systems. As mentioned, this opens up the perspective of the analysis of semiotic structures outside of language, a perspective that has been used intensively in the present inquiry. But it obviously also provides the means to analyze concrete acts of communication in language and other forms of communication. O'Toole (2006), for instance, by following this strategy, offers an impressive example of the multimodal interpretation of the Sydney opera house as an object that carries a certain discourse. Looking at how a phenomenon, analyzed as an act of communication, embodies these three functions, one obtains an interface to the meaning it engenders. Kress (2013) lists the same three angles in order to explain concrete discourse rolled out by people writing diaries. Here, the three functions are analytical lenses, allowing a deeper sense of the meaning produced in a specific situation. This type of research, that uses the foundations of Halliday, is called *Multimodal Discourse Analysis* (Kress and van Leeuwen 2001; O'Halloran 2011).

It would be possible to describe both angles, the creation of means to produce meaning, as well as the production of meaning in such a way, as an act of framing. The usage of space in order to create the unit of words is a framing process, as is the creation of the Sydney opera house, or the writing of a diary. The opera is not just a functional building, but it is designed to have a message. The issue of the publication cannot be compared to the organization of resources in order to build a whole meaning system such as language. It is however also not comparable to the writing process of a particular diary or monograph. The specification of a type of publication, such as the monograph, could be described, by referring to a point from McPherson, as a "template."[13] Consequently, in all of these angles, framing takes place, but it is the framing of a peculiar type that needs to be described. In order to do so, it is necessary to discuss another concept of MuA: mode.

Kress defines mode as an entanglement of media, semiotic logics — sometimes also referred to as ontology —, and social practices (Kress 2013, 61). In this context, the term media would be best understood as a technological device or material means. Thus, again, at the heart of mode lies the trias of perspectives on communication, but in this case not as functions alone. Instead, mode addresses, and more importantly is the outcome of, the application of "organizing principles" (Kress 2010) within these three areas. Consequently, "definitions of mode are dependent on what are counted as well-acknowledged regularities within any one community" Mavers and Gibson (2012, para. 2).

The acknowledgment of a community is a social issue, and compared to other concepts in MuA, mode puts significantly more emphasis on communication as a social phenomenon, and on those elements of it that are shared across people and situations. It is derived from the fact that these regularities can be observed — sometimes more and sometimes less — when people communicate. Monographs and diaries, but also for instance architecture, are socially highly codified configurations creating "frameworks" (O'Halloran 2004) in which the production of meaning as well as communication can take place, and which serve as a reference system for specific acts of communication. Hence, the concept of mode is built on the claim that a significant part of the understanding of communication

13 The reader might have the impression that at this point the notion of form and content that was qualified before is used again. Although these angles address the same issue, it will become clear during the rest of this section that the proposed framework uses these angles slightly differently and that it adds a significant twist to the form-content debate in the field of digital publications and beyond.

remains hidden if the issue of social organizational principles is not addressed independently. This is not to say that any aspect of communication is governed by such configurations, but that it is a crucial angle of communication.

Accordingly, the more framing is concerned with or aims at supporting the regularities in communication, the more it is part of the level of mode as the angle of stability in communication. Since this mode is located within the social semiotic notion of communication, the effectiveness is determined by how well the three facets are served all in all. As a socially driven process, mode is where actions resemble practices, agents are supported by institutions, arrangements of means overlap with grammatical relationships, and material means have become accepted tools. "Mode is typically seen as a stable backdrop for multimodal communication" (Boeriis and Johannessen 2015, 8).

Examples of modes often given are books or computer screens. Both include certain technologies of production and consumption, the use of specific visual means for representation, and the support of established practices like writing, in order to form a functional mode of communication within a certain social community. Burn (2013, 2) speaks of theatre as a mode, where, again, material means, such as the stage, enable the use of gaze, movement, and the voice among others in a culturally encoded and institutionalized environment. However, the author also introduces the term *kineiconic mode* — his main object of interest — of which he remarks that it partially incorporates the theatrical mode at the early stage of moving image media. Movement and voice are furthermore treated as "supportive" and "embodied" modes (6) throughout the book. Consequently, the concept of mode can become very fuzzy, and the interplay between the three perspectives on communication is not always clear or balanced. Kress and van Leeuwen (2002) even speak of color as a semiotic mode. This introduces a level of abstraction where specific social or techno-material aspects can hardly be analyzed productively.

It is thus not surprising that the concept of mode is challenged vigorously, even within certain branches of MuA itself. From the multimodal interaction analysis point of view, Norris (2009) criticizes that mode is only a heuristic category that does not exist empirically. With the intent to analyze multimodal meaning production in micro situations, she furthermore argues that the macro perspective of mode neglects the contingency by which each such situation undermines the concept of mode. In other words, if communication is only analyzed as the use and application of mode, which she accuses Multimodal Discourse Analysis of doing, significant parts of the produced meaning remain hidden. In contrast, Stöckl (2013, 276) criticizes that "the term 'mode' ... represents a rather heterogeneous concept, as various notions converge in it."

Both claims, the one addressing mode as only a heuristic concept, and the other one stressing inconsistencies in the use of the term, are argued well and cannot be invalidated. However, this is not necessary in order to maintain the key element that still assures its integrity and usefulness. First, there are indications that neither Kress nor Leeuwen consider modes to exist effectively, a fact that will become more transparent below — there are just different research interests. Kress and Leeuwen are interested in evaluating the existence and the effect of socio-cultural conditions of communication, while Norris and her school of MIA try to analyze how multimodal means are appropriated by specific people in temporally limited situations. Second, although the concept of mode refers to many different things, a certain perspective is applied when the term is used. This perspective refers to the referenced phenomenon as one which is in some way organized, and by this characteristic facilitates communication. The present study therefore argues that the key element of mode as a concept is not so much defining exactly what properties need to be found in order to be able to speak of mode. It also argues that it is not necessary to treat concrete communication as a subclass of mode. It is a specific aspect of communication, revealing that socially motivated regulation of communication happens, and that this type of regulation is a source of a specific type of meaning that depends on this regulation process. In the words of Burn (2013, 376), mode is the outcome of a process of orchestration, "the overarching framing systems in space and time."

The research field of digital publications can benefit in multiple ways from the inclusion of the perspective of mode into its conceptual framework. It builds on the notion that stable structures in communication are an issue that is not external to the logics of communication, but a part of it. Communication is the output of a socio-cultural endeavor. Communication happens because people communicate, and where people communicate with each other, regularities emerge and where regularities become recognizable, means to support them are built. The whole of this process, starting from individual motivations and reaching to communication systems, is formed by the conflation of social, technological, and ontological angles — or, in a different context, interpersonal, textual, and ideational functions. Mode, as framing, thus provides the framework to discuss issues of stability and sustainability of digital publications within the same theoretical context, and not as separate issues.

The stability and sustainability of publications, then, refers to the concept of mode. It allows re-use of the form-content distinction, but in a way that prevents the artificial and simplifying distinctions in parts of the field of digital publications, and that protects from the problems of that field caused by this. The distinction is one that does not originate in any technological or semiotic logic. It is an outcome of social practices by people and institutions who start to refer to certain sets of frames as the stable backdrop used to give one's own communication purposes a form. It is the act of referring that constitutes mode. The concept of mode thereby explains why different form-content distinctions emerged in the field of digital publications, why this is a reasonable and useful dynamic, and that this research field should support selected versions of these distinctions, instead of clinging to the idea of one meta-logical form of them. The form-content distinction and the existence of modes of communication is a framing process itself, not ontologically different from the separation of words by spaces.

Where the enabling and empowering aspects of making this distinction are highlighted — aspects depending on the availability of such backdrops — the concept of mode also shows that any kind of backdrop requires building upon some sense of regularity and its enforcement. The concept of mode, thus, also makes clear that sustainability of the field of digital publications can likewise not emerge from a general acceptance of its immense heterogeneity, or from its politically motivated positive re-interpretation, but only by applying "organizational principles."

Finally, and probably most importantly of all, mode makes transparent what is necessary to gain more or less stable digital publication formats and a sustainable publishing environment, of which digital publications are a part. By building on the three functional requirements of signs, mode shows that digital publications can emerge only out of setups in which material and technological means, social practices and bodies, and, last but not least, semiotic logics and ontological premises, mutually support each other, each with equal rights. It was shown throughout the whole of the study at hand that this was not the case in most circumstances. Not only were some of these areas not included in the design of digital publications or corresponding tasks postponed; equal rights mean that any of these areas have to be given the right to overrule demands of other areas, for the overall goal of creating sustainable publications. This perspective — with few exceptions — can hardly be found in any of the analyzed initiatives.

Semiosis

It was indicated before that critique comparable to the one by Norris also arises from a completely different point of view. Several authors have argued during the last ten to fifteen years that digital technologies, sometimes called multimedia technologies, have made the appearance of modes unlikely (Lemke 2005; Jewitt 2013; Boeriis and Johannessen 2015). Thus, these authors do not challenge the concept of mode in general. What they question is its relevance for communication today. More precisely, they argue that the means of communication today do not produce the necessary conditions for new modes to appear. The inquiry into digital technologies this study has carried out indeed also offers some results supporting this observation. It will not deny that the conditions for mode have changed. It nonetheless argues that its complete rejection both misunderstands the concept of mode and exaggerates the impact of digital technologies on communication. In order to do so, this section will conclude with a discussion of MuA's concept of semiosis.

In short, semiosis is defined as the historical process in which semiotic resources — means of communication — appear as such and change over time (Kress 2010; MODE 2012; Newfield 2013). It was mentioned several times now that the unique element of Halliday's view on language is the extent to which he discusses language as a socially created project. The transfer of Halliday's premises to phenomena other than language by MuA are at the foundation for the concept of semiotic resources, for modes as well as for the analysis of digital publications in the study at hand.

While in the present study the term semiotic resource was primarily used in order to refer to the situational availability of resources other than language, for the purpose of concrete acts of communication, mode and specifically semiosis open up the perspective for a holistic analysis of how semiotic resources emerge and change as socially shared and codified phenomena. The concept of mode encompasses semiotic resources insofar, as their use is shared within social communities of a certain size that make it reasonable to speak of them as social phenomena. Semiosis substantiates the centrality of the social dimension of communication, by offering a viewpoint for understanding the place of modes in the overall socio-historical project of engendering communication.

It could be argued that the concept of semiosis is a necessary consequence of the claim that signs do not exist as such, but are socio-historically constructed. As constructed entities, they may not only change, but, of course, also disappear. In other words, there is no other realm in which signs, modes, and meaning reside than in practice. Halliday's approach then suggests conceptualizing some logic behind the coming, the change, and the going of sign systems and communicative means that originates with this school of thought.

The two components of this logic are given by the terms *chain of semiosis* and *punctuation of semiosis*. These terms give names to the statements that signs and sign systems are constructed and emerge historically, as well as the fact that this aspect makes them dependent on actual use. In principle, the chain of semiosis refers to the process of semiosis itself, as it was described above. The specification of this process as a chain, however, adds an important aspect. A process of semiosis could have provoked the idea that, if not specific signs and modes, then at least semiosis as such — the need to create signs and modes — is an autonomous and self-supporting phenomenon. The illustration of this process as a chain emphasizes that no such self-supporting dynamic of semiosis exists. It encourages looking out for the means by which this process is mediated and driven: the punctuations which create the chain.

On the abstract and formal level, which is the one taken in semiosis, punctuations are phenomena "of relative stasis and stability" (Kress 2010, 121; see also Kress 1996) within communication, i.e. the process of semiosis. The dependency between semiosis and its punctuations is twofold:

1. Punctuations are the only manifestations of signs and sign systems. Concrete objects or acts of communication such as particular monographs, dialogues, performances, movies, buildings, diagrams, and paintings among others are the only form by which it is possible to say that signs and sign systems exist. Punctuations thereby provide the only points of reference, or starting points for future punctuations, to use and modify signs and sign systems. Only due to this process of reproduction and actualization, meaning the memorization and anticipation of past and future punctuations, can signs become part of a socio-historical sign system, i.e. the process of semiosis in which a specific phenomenon is conceived of as a monograph or a movie, among others.
2. Consequently, only the angle of semiosis provides the necessary means to conceive of something as a sign or a semiotics resource, in short, something that has meaning. It becomes a punctuation,

> because it reveals itself as something that beyond being itself is a link in a chain that is the chain of semiosis. It is this link, the relational structure people put around such phenomena, that makes a punctuation "readable," and that indicates the realm of mode.

Corresponding with these two interdependencies, Kress (2010) remarks that punctuations of semiosis have two dimensions. The first is the material dimension and the second is the abstract dimension.

The concepts of the chain of semiosis and its punctuations specifically address the issue of stability and organization in communication, as highlighted in the quote by Gunther Kress already. Punctuations are the only things that can be regarded as stable enough to sustain semiosis, and the projected stability of an ongoing process of semiosis is the only notion that enables communication. In contrast, both dimensions have their ephemeral aspects. Books are forgotten or get lost, they are re-edited into new versions. Dialogues and performances end, sometimes they are recorded. Paintings yellow with age and all of these punctuations are continuously replaced or re-represented by new ones. Semiosis, consequently, is always in motion and change, and has always been. Therefore, semiosis is about "relative stasis and stability," and mode is exactly the one concept that provokes substantiation of the notion of relativity, instead of referring to it in a purely theoretical or formal sense.

It could be argued that mode is also a punctuation of semiosis, but one of a specific type. This seems to be partially inconsistent with what has been said so far. The notion of mode is neither a concrete act nor an object of communication. Additionally, it was mentioned above that a particular branch of MuA criticizes mode for being too inflexible to grasp peculiarities and contingencies of concrete acts of communication.

The inconsistency, however, is less critical when reconsidering Kress' remark that punctuations possess two dimensions, an abstract and a material one. Having said that, mode is at the center of two constructivist processes. Where the concept of mode is affirmed and analyzed, it substantiates the idea of an abstract semiotic context (semiosis). The necessity to assume this context turns into the definition of concrete means and practices combined by mode that allow an understanding of certain facets of concrete communicative acts. Where mode is criticized, it is used as a delimiter, in order to posit a level of meaning that is more subtle than the meaning that would have been derived solely from an understanding of a certain definition of mode. By declaring that certain semiotic choices in an analysis situation do not correspond with common usage patterns, defined in modes, such an analysis similarly defines what is not characteristic in most cases. The characteristic gains much of its meaning here by having a contrasting relationship to the general rules of mode. The first perspective approaches mode within the "abstract dimension," as a condition for concrete acts of communication of a certain type. The second perspective approaches it from the "material dimension" of a concrete use of semiotic resources, which in confrontation reveals itself as richer than any abstraction can express.

For both perspectives, the assumption of a layer addressed by the concept of mode is indispensable. It is this indispensability by which mode becomes a phenomenon in itself, and by which it could be said to exist. As such, it can be analyzed and addressed within its own logic. It does in fact become a punctuation of semiosis on its own, a punctuation of a type that tries to give concrete answers to the question of how necessary it is to analyze and to aim at the social organization of communicative means at any given point in time, so that concrete acts of communication create value.

In the context of digital publications, the issue of semiosis indeed substantiates the claim that the questions of how far it is reasonable to assume the emergence of stable publication setups, and what form stability will take in this respect, are more important than the discussion of specific formats. It has been shown that in the overall discourse on digital publications, an unbalanced relationship between the notions of communication and publication prevents a serious discussion of this issue. While certain ideals of persistence and maturity of publications remain untouched, everything that connects to a more flexible, dynamic, context aware, or precise notion of communication is celebrated, without putting it into any context. It is then not surprising that those formats that address the issue of stability and sustainability of formats as such explicitly tend to define the one new format that will supersede the older ones (EPs, SPs), or are likely to give up on any notion of persistence of organized structures in publishing (HPs). Mode is without doubt a heuristic. As a necessary heuristic between the process of semiosis and its punctuations, it demands a response to the question of the conditions and needs for the organization of persistent, sustainable setups in scholarly communication, specifically in any new period and situation.

Having said this, the design of publications as sustainable scholarly publication setups appears to be an issue of a social practice of a particular type. This type of practice does not equate stability with a static formal definition of something (see below). It furthermore does not strive for any accelerationist visions — semiosis does not move towards ends, it saturates the here and now — though such visions may become true along the way. It is a relational-social practice evaluating the possibilities of new publications on the grounds of three conditions, again, representing the three meta-functions of signs following Halliday, i.e. how may publications exist and look like:

1. when confronted with semiotic resources and established representational strategies at our disposal;
2. in order to be understandable, consumable, and processable;
3. in order to be socialized, sustained, institutionalized, or patronized.

The first condition asks questions such as what does the combination of semiotic resources in the design of a digital publication look like? How do such designs interoperate with each other? How are they embedded in a notion about the state of semiosis in scholarly communication, and finally which communicative purpose is embodied by a particular design in comparison with others, possibly with their own designs? The second condition looks at issues like how much the semiotic material used can be considered to be easily understandable or efficiently readable.[14] It analyses patterns of practices by which target audiences interact with publications, and the situations in which this happens. This does not in fact necessarily mean reproducing existing patterns, but that it is necessary to know and consider them. The last condition is more obvious and concerns the fact that publications require financial, institutional, personal, and temporal resources among others, in order to become and remain persistent, accessible, and socially valuable. The likeliness with which such resources can be produced in a long-term perspective depends on the organizational shape both of the publication concept and the state of the scholarly (communication) environment.

While in this paragraph, and in the section on mode, these angles provide the means to successfully build publication setups, their application in the context of semiosis is different. Here, they provide aid for making concrete responses to the question of the conditions and needs for the organization of persistent, sustainable setups in scholarly communication, earlier found to be necessary. In other words, they provide the means to identify and frame an area within the broad social space of science in which first, it seems useful and necessary to organize communication around specific

14 A simple and good example are the elements and types of diagrammatic communication, but also the state of use for specific semiotic resources in specific fields. Sequential and discursive organization of resources, for instance, are variously part of different fields of research, as has been shown before.

publication designs, and second, where such an intervention meets the necessary requirements. In its entire equivocalness one could say that semiosis allows to ask within which social boundaries publication formats make sense, but without questioning the formatting of communication as such.

Some of the publication concepts discussed before could actually be described in this respect. It has been argued that Nano-Publications, for instance, make sense within the well-defined boundaries of certain areas in the bio- and life-sciences. Accordingly, it could be that some things might look similar in a research field on new scholarly publications informed by arguments such as those made in the current research. The point is that such engagements would have different goals, would make different strategic decisions, intervene differently into the scholarly community, would relate their work in a more sensible way to other initiatives, and the outcome, regardless of how similar or different it would look to current formats, would be an outcome of maturation and not definition.

Together with such clarifications, it is necessary to specify further what the adjective "relative" might denote, in order to prevent issues such as those discussed in the field of digital publications. The horizon of semiosis is temporal. Projecting the future of semiosis means thinking about new forms of communication that have not been rendered in punctuations yet. The dependency between the chain of semiosis and its punctuations, together with the notion of relative stability, means that punctuations are only stable insofar as they neither just duplicate existing punctuations, nor focus on realizing the imaginative horizon of semiosis lying ahead (the accelerationist viewpoint). They exist in time, that means they are embedded in the process of semiosis. They are not solely oriented towards the two ends of the horizon of semiosis. This does not mean that the latter are not punctuations of semiosis, but that it is necessary to think differently about the scope and quality of its stability. Just like publication formats should mature instead of being defined, initiatives in the field of digital publications should understand their work as an intervention, instead of foundational or avant-garde. The crucial question is then what an intervention might look like that is most efficient in a given context, in a given time period, and under the considerations of the three angles identified above. Such an intervention can provide foundational work, but it can also mean positing and promoting a very fuzzy term such as Data Papers.

A second misunderstanding is the one that could arise from the centrality of the concept of framing, when seen in conjunction with punctuations of semiosis. It has been noted that any communicative act is an act of framing in multiple ways and on multiple levels. Since punctuations of semiosis are effectively communicative acts, the issue of framing needs to be dealt with here, too. Burn's specification of the act of orchestration, and the framing of the appropriate social space for an intervention, has indicated this already. The aforementioned misunderstanding would consist of claiming that the higher the degree of consciously and intentionally set frames, the more stable the punctuations. The relative stability of punctuations does not correspond with the quantity of explicitly defined frame boundaries observable across the same period of relative stasis and stability. The concept of framing allows analysis of, or intervention into, the inner structure of punctuations of semiosis, not judgment about, or prediction of, its role within semiosis.[15]. It would however also be wrong to assume that there is no relationship between these concepts. It is just not a fixed relationship. Instead, it depends on the specific situation in semiosis.

Evaluating stability in the context of semiosis does not mean aiming at an abstract or fixed notion of stability, or at the highest degree of stability seemingly possible. It means looking out for a reasonable way to influence the process of semiosis and shaping punctuations of semiosis in a sustainable way, so that each supports the other within their constitutive relationship before the backdrop of a given state of affairs.

With this emphasized, it appears necessary to briefly re-approach the critique of several branches of MuA regarding the impossibility of modes — i.e. the relative stability of the structure of certain ways of communication — in the light of digital technologies leading to the discussion of semiosis. This is even more relevant considering the background that this claim is supported by the heterogeneity and volatility of new publication formats, and the insight that no notion of stability in communication exists as such. Two paths can be taken in reaction to this critique. One is to revise and clarify what is meant by using the term stability as a point of reference within this topic. The other is to qualify the critique and to put supporting observations into context.

It has been indicated several times already that the concept of semiosis does not permit assuming any general idea of stability. Consequently, there is only more or less stability in relation to other conceived or quantified dynamics. Modular Articles were obviously a less stable concept than the

15 The difference is comparable to the difference between clarity and usefulness, which has been analyzed in depth in philosophy of language, especially in Wittgenstein (2006).

monograph, and maybe even the notion of a module will be. The pace of innovation in the era of digital technologies is often conceived of as too unstable to match the expectations of stability of digital publications and publication environments. Accordingly, the concept of stability as seen in semiosis seeks to define setups of relative stability. Precisely such qualification distinguishes the leitmotif of stability, as it is suggested here, from abstract and absolute notions of stability. The issue of stability for scholarly publications is neither represented well within the foundational thinking of infrastructure projects such as OpenAIRE, nor within the narratives of "forced bindings." To aim at relative stability means opening up, concretizing, and using the possibilities to promote stability in scholarly communication, without idealizing them by assuming any kind of inherent logic towards a certain type of maturity. The observation that the conditions for modes of communication as representations of relative stability in communication have changed does thus not impose stopping to reach for new and more appropriate modes. Such attempts will, nonetheless, have to take into account much more flexible notions of stability than those presupposed in many attempts to establish new publication formats.

This argument is already leading to the critiques of the concept of mode in MuA and corresponding insights presented in part one. Although it has been confirmed that digital technologies do change the conditions for stable patterns in scholarly communication that would engender scholarly publication modes, it is of crucial importance to note that very few attempts have been made to more broadly evaluate current conditions for stable communicative modes. From the implementation level of concrete projects, through the conceptual level of publication formats up to the theoretical level in parts of MuA[16], research activities have primarily focused on showcasing, representing, and analyzing the pluralization of resources and strategies in scholarly communication instigated by digital technologies. Stöckl's critique, that the concept of mode is fuzzy and inconsistent, can also be interpreted against this background: since much analysis in MuA is done for the purpose of describing new and complex multimodal setups in communication under the label of mode, the concept's main issue, which as has been argued is the issue of stability, sustainability, and persistence in communication, gets lost from view.

Norris, by declaring that mode is a heuristic concept obscuring the subtle meanings of today's communication, is also not willing or able to

16 Significant examples for this type of research include Doloughan (2011), Smith et al. (2011), Rowsell (2013), Ferdig and Pytash (2014).

substantially analyze the concrete dimension of this tension, due to the methodological focus of her research agenda. It leaves open what kind of an impact the application or the abolishment of such heuristics itself has on their usefulness. An analysis is not just an observation but at the same time an intervention that changes the state of the analyzed object. In short, not only do few activities function in the spirit of a sophisticated concept of mode, some of these activities even persistently undermine any possibility of new modes. It is therefore highly double-edged to argue that the heuristic of mode is of no use, or to complain from the opposite point of view that digital publications have never gone beyond the "lumpen pdf." Judgments on the possibilities of new forms of publishing, finally, also have to take into account what has been called issues of epistemological shifting. To put it differently, claims that are made about the impossibility of modes in times of digital technologies cannot be judged independently from the fact that intermedial situations of high dynamic provoke simplifications of the nature of ongoing changes, in order to regain epistemological confidence on lost grounds.

In fact, the discussion of mode as a mediating concept seems appropriate for also mediating between the emphasis of the plurality of present-day communication caused by unbalanced notions of authenticity and presence, and the abstract demands for absolute sustainability and persistence that do not stop despite such emphasis. Mode is a concept that raises awareness of the fact that the important question is not whether sustainable configurations in scholarly communication are still possible. It allows to ask where stable patterns in all these new experiments and explorations in digitally mediated scholarly communication might be conceivable, and what would be needed in order to support these areas.

Intervening in Communication: Designing Scholarly Publication Modes

After analyses of the concept of framing, mode, and semiosis, and their partial application to the issues of new publication formats, the attempt will now be made to briefly indicate what interventions into scholarly communication, like the ones discussed in this work, could look like when shaped by the arguments made. It goes without saying that even the intent to sit down and pretend to define and design the new format for publishing within a specific scholarly environment "at once" — as some of the projects have done — contrasts with the aforementioned framework. It might, nonetheless, be a useful exercise in order to put some of the points back into a well-known context and thereby support the process of familiarization with them. The outline of this intervention will remain an outline, as its primary goal is to communicate a certain spirit. It was, after all, claimed that it is the spirit that prevented the field from making further progress on the goals it sought to achieve, not specific elements or a particular type of inventions.

For the purpose of this exercise, the notion of mode is simplified, in order to represent what was discussed as the publication format in many of the preceding approaches. The illustrating task thus is to start with a design approach to the creation of a mode of scholarly communication, meaning a socially, technically, and structurally more saturated and reliable form of communication. Candela et al. (2015), has criticized DPs as "slow communication." By intentionally misusing this phrase, one could say that publications by definition always belong to slow communication in a certain sense. They are slow because they are organized via demands which exceed those that are immediately transparent and comprehensible in the communicative situation itself.

As modes, the three constitutive dimensions for publications equate to the three meta-functions of communication. It is possible to apply a functional approach to the design of publication concepts as well, which is then seen as a communicative act. As said before, the three dimensions are represented by three questions in Halliday's and successive works. Applied to the goal-oriented design of publication concepts and related projects, these points can be translated into questions by asking:

1. How should the structure of knowledge be modified? Which new semiotic resources and regulations should be promoted, and which methodological commitments for the creation of accountability of research should be supported?
2. What does the network of stakeholders look like that should be shaped by the publication concept? Which stakeholders are there, and how do they interoperate with each other? Where is institutional support desired and where does institutionalization have to take place?
3. What is the technological and infrastructural environment that it tries to sustain or introduce?

The phrasing of these questions reflects the intention of the intervention to introduce changes and reach goals. The last sections above suggest that it is supportive of the design process to relate the answers to these questions with each other, instead of responding to them in isolation. That does not necessarily mean that answers need to be perfectly fitted to each other. Since each dimension brings with it its own specific logic, this is hardly possible in any case. Becoming aware of the relationships and maybe rearranging them here and there, however, is something different. An intervention, furthermore, changes the given situation, which is more than a zero point of future modes of communication. It is a situation under construction, partially satisfactory and partially not. There is something to lose and something to gain. Addressing this situation, Halliday's meta-functions can therefore be similarly re-phrased in order to make more than a zero point out of them. Accordingly:

1. What are conventional strategies for organizing knowledge, and what semiotic resources are used how in order to do so?
2. What practices between which agents support such strategies?
3. What does the infrastructure and technology look like that embodies and sustains these strategies and practices?

While the first version of the questions takes a strategic point of view, the second version has more of an analytical angle.

Any new publication format or intervention into the landscape of scholarly publications takes up a position, first within the matrix of possible answers to the strategical set of questions, and secondly by creating a specific connection between the strategic angle and the retrospective one. This position is marked by a variety of decisions. For the first set of questions, such decisions may reveal different levels of attention to or interest in one of three dimensions. In-between the strategical and the analytical set of questions, decisions may appear *conservative*, *generative*, *adaptive*, or *creative*.

A conservative decision follows established ways of doing things. It is important to mention that the term conservative does not include any type of judgment. The PDF takes a conservative stand in terms of structuring and presenting knowledge, as the majority of advocates of digital publications have highlighted so well. It does so because it tries to resemble the presentational and organizational knowledge in paper articles or monographs. A creative decision is a decision that leads to the introduction of a completely new idea of how things should change in one of the three areas. Collections and ROs, accordingly, staged the use of the OAI-ORE technology as a key technology of digital publications. Open Laboratory Books posited the idea of open-endedness as an organizational paradigm for publications and so forth. Adaptive decisions transfer ideas of change that might be known or operative in other scholarly environments into environments where this is not the case. The Open Notebook Humanities project outlined earlier is a project and a concept which tried to implement ideas of OLBs and of NPs, and which has already been implemented in other domains of the humanities. Generative decisions, finally, are decisions leading to concept sand implementations that facilitate changes in the direction of concepts, and implementations that are more difficult to realize directly. These decisions are not identical with the original goals, but stimulate changes to reach such goals. Many decisions behind DPs are of a generative nature, and it has been argued in this work that generative decisions, at least after the period of digital publications, are potentially those with the greatest impact.

This does not mean that only generative decisions create the ideal type of intervention as such, it depends on the overarching purpose of an intervention nor a new publication format design. If the attempt is to create a beacon project, generative decisions are not a good fit. It goes without saying that a beacon project may be a valuable contribution, for instance in order to show alternative paths in a deadlock situation. This contribution nonetheless has to be evaluated and identified between the strategical and analytical angle and its three dimensions. The important aspect is to adapt any following design decision to the general decision about what such an intervention or such contributions should represent and communicate. A beacon project does not require infrastructure development, and a serious attempt to introduce changes to the landscape of scholarly publications should probably avoid building on the most creative concepts and technologies. The analysis of publication concepts in part one suggests that few efforts have been made to clearly evaluate and define what these concepts could become and what they should become in the scope of the projects that pushed them forward.

Applied to the example of the Unbound Book, the following answers to the first set of questions can be formulated:

1. The UB understands knowledge as an uncentred, inconsistent phenomenon. Thus, the publication should reflect the plurality of viewpoints and the diversity of modes of representing knowledge.
2. The UB wants to democratize the political economy of knowledge production in the context of critical relationships with concepts of power and hierarchy in academia.
3. Technology has to be accessible and must allow participation of as many stakeholders as possible, but there is no original technical goal.

In consequence to these responses, the following design decisions on aspects and resources were made. Most of these aspects were discussed in the section on UBs already.

The answers to the strategical versions of the three questions illustrate the intent of UBs to introduce changes, mostly in the areas of social practice. The most innovation is introduced within the second dimension, and even the first dimension is interpreted in a way that relates to the second dimension. Another step reveals the relationship between the responses and the design decisions, summarized in the table above. The portal decision, for instance, clearly links to the second questions. Neither a channel nor an object could engender the level of participatory curation of content. The scale of the information unit rendered within UBs also refers to the second question. In contrast, issues like the intermodal relationship type and modal complexity more strongly reflect the first question. The moderate way in which they make use of this approach reflects the aforementioned relationship between dimension one and two. The technological serialization shows very well that technological decisions are driven by the first two questions, and not so much by goals that are genuinely technological. This is very different from many other publishing concepts that have been introduced.

resource	decision	resource	decision
architectural integrity	portal	intermodal relationship type	inter-medial
scale	the whole of a research track	cohesion	given by the social network of agents
secularization	none	residence time	defined by contributions
synchronist	parallel-incremental	structural rigor	moderate
modal complexity	moderate	technological serialization	contingent (different proprietary software solutions)

[Table 6.3] Design decisions behind the Unbound Book concept

By using these terms in order to describe the relationship between the different angles behind the two sets of questions, further specifications are possible. The choices by which UBs implement the goal of allowing additional media resources in a publication can be described as generative, even conservative, when compared with the use of different media in anthologies and monographs. Only the appearance of videos in one or the other distinguishes them, while TPs' role is really to be creative in this respect. The second goal can be defined as creative, or at least adaptive. A non-restricted collaborative and continuous authoring of books was a very new approach at a time when projects presented in this work implemented UBs. The adaptive to conservative decision regarding technological goals is represented by the way UBs are technologically serialized.

The importance of the modelling of the example lies not so much in correctness, it is probably possible to argue about one or the other aspect, and the description is far from being complete. The importance lies in the creation of references in order to enable a design process which is more environmentally aware. In an ecological approach towards innovation for scholarly publications, every contribution is a contribution situated between stabilizing and destabilizing effects, a contribution which attracts and rejects. One way to interpret the lack of success of digital publishing concepts, diagnosed by their advocates, would be to argue that often, the potentially destabilizing effects on the existing landscape of digital publications outrank the attraction they create. Yet again, it is important to not idealize this landscape as the de facto stable backdrop. It goes without saying that the analysis of the existing landscape can reveal a very unstable state calling for innovative impulses. In semiosis, as it was highlighted in the last section, there is no general stability, and any intervention into the landscape of scholarly publications, conceived in the context of semiosis, can be described as a "design of social relations" (Kress 2010, 143).

In an ecological perspective such as the one above, the many ways in which a new concept requires adjustment to the existing landscape may appear too expensive. This is especially true if the number of concepts that demand adjustment is that high. Once again, such adjustments can be described in terms of the three constitutive dimensions of communication. Hence, they require technological and infrastructural adjustments, adjustments of social practices and institutions, as well as adjustments on the level of semiotic practices and symbolic values (Bourdieu 2010). It is possible to model these issues in terms of a cost-benefit calculation. Specifications like those exemplified above can help to gain an understanding of the complexity and extent of such costs. Additionally, they may allow more strategic and thus more effective handling of costs, meaning the distinct efforts necessary to establish a certain type of publication. Thinking about them as abstract, in terms of cost, may also allow thinking about the exchange of costs in one dimension with resources available in another dimension. This is exactly the strategy that NPs adopted when trying to solve social issues of publications with technological means. It was an attempt that did not work out well, because NPs neglected the fact that such means must become socially acceptable in order to really function. Nonetheless, such strategies of value-exchange between implementation and construction work, social engagement, and other type of tasks do not need to be wrong in general when applied in a more sensible way.

When talking about scholarly publication formats as modes of communication that saturate and stabilize over time, and about generative interventions, the inclusion a time-oriented angle into the design perspective of publication concepts seems natural. It makes a lot of sense to conceive of design as an iterative process, in which the design of the publication format becomes more and more concrete over multiple iterations. In each iteration, the intervention takes a position between the analytical and the strategic perspective. However, each iteration also brings with it the adaption of the analysis to the changes that took place since the last iteration, as well as possible modifications to the strategic goals. The iterative process, consequently, is not just a stepwise procedure towards fixed goals, but a course of action that, by using information technology terms, could be defined as an agile process. The term was also used by the LPs project in order to describe the “more natural” procedure by which publications can be created within the LPs framework. The irony is that this principle, emphasized as more appropriate for grasping how research works, was not applied to the research on the LPs format.

In the final analysis, an approach conceiving of publications as modes establishing themselves within a process of semiosis needs to consider seven tasks:

1. the definition of communicative goals,
2. the evaluation of semiotic, socio-cultural, and technological resources,
3. the evaluation of stabilities and instabilities in the existing publication landscape,
4. the definition of certain social boundaries that permit reasonably carrying out task two and three,
5. the type of intervention (beacon project, solving a problem, establishing a new format etc.),
6. the composition of one or more interventions, each conceptually situated somewhere between the analytical (3) and the strategical (2) angle,
7. optionally, the organization of an iterative process.

This last section of the study at hand has shown how concepts from the field of MuA can re-arrange key motifs in the field of digital publications in a way that tones down the tensions highlighted in the preceding sections. The relationship between technological and social issues, the status of heterogeneity and the data deluge, the mediation between different desires regarding the representational capacity, and the sustainability of publications — all these and other issues can be described by such concepts in a form that accentuates their interplay instead of positing false hierarchies. They thereby help to avoid unproductive expectations, unreasonable resource allocation, and, last but not least, emotional frustration, such as outlined in the introduction, based on selective or controversial conceptions. The analysis presented publications as modes in communication, and thus as the issue of organizing communication. This does not mean that communication is not always organized in one way or the other. It means, as has been emphasized before, that mode, and thus publications as modes, evaluate the stabilizing organization of communicative resources over time as a semiotic resource itself. In other words: to what extent does this type of organization create "meaning potentials" that would not exist without it, and to what extent is this possible and desirable within a defined social context and within a specific period? This viewpoint opened up a distinct area of publications under the theme of communication. It turns this concept into more than an empty placeholder — a unit of communication — because it has its own logic that can be made methodical use of. The illustration at the end is far from providing such a complete methodology, but it should suffice to convince that such a methodology is possible and empowering.

Conclusion

In the introduction, the topic of digital publications was presented via the early work of Owen as one of the first authors who tried to raise the question of the impact of digital technologies on scholarly publications, in a way that would go beyond programmatic excitement or categorical skepticism. Much of the analysis can be situated between perspectives of articulated expectations, reasonable expectations, misled expectations, expectations that came true and those that did not, all framed by discourses on a coming revolution, a failed revolution, or a revolution that would never happen. It therefore stands to reason that in his concluding sections, Owen tries to develop his own theoretical model of change, one that would go beyond the empirical results, showing significantly fewer modifications of publication formats and related scholarly communication practices.

This model of change derives from what he refers to as the *evolutionary model* or *selection theory*. According to Owen (2006, 198), selection theory brings about progress on the basis of three types of steps: innovation, selection, and reproduction. Innovations in technology provide new possibilities and new options. Selection is a step carried out by agents who decide to make use of some of these options and reject others. Another aspect of selection is the liberty to choose in which way the selected options are used. This appropriation can vary significantly from the intentions that led to the introduction of said innovations. Reproduction addresses the need for individual selections to turn into common practices, in order to provoke real changes. While this model is still quite linear and progress-oriented, it includes significant differences compared to the progress-oriented narratives in the field of digital publications. In selection theory, subsequent steps are not determined by earlier ones. It cannot be assumed that the introduction of new options equates with the selection of such options, or defines how they are appropriated. No selection by any agents causes a change of cultural norms and common practices. The reason for this is that each step adds its own assessment criteria and modifications, changing what appears to be beneficial and useful overall. Following from this is that:

> … the outcome of evolutionary development processes such as that studied here is emergent and contingent. It is emergent in the sense that the outcome of a change process cannot be deduced from the pressures that bear on it, however relevant these pressures are to the outcome. And it is contingent in the sense that the outcomes can be expected to fit the pragmatic context of the actors (e.g. scientists)

> rather than any theoretical or ideological model. When closure has happened, the process and its outcomes can be described in a logical fashion. But as the result of a highly complicated process with a multitude of pressures bearing on the path towards closure, the outcome, however logical once it has been achieved, cannot be predicted from the beginning. (Owen 2006, 200)

As mentioned above, Owen's research led him to the conclusion that in 2006, digital technologies have not changed publications and related scholarly communication practices in any way that revolutionaries, or, as he calls them, change agents, presupposed. In his view, these agents, and with them a certain notion of progress, oversimplify the meaning of progress as a sequence of steps. They treat technology as the main agent, while it is merely the agent that delivers possibilities. This reductionism then causes a "battle against more conservative and ignorant forces" (211) that is inherent in the revolutionary point of view.

Owen continues that, due to the abovementioned logic, change agents have overlooked a significant tension preventing digital technologies from becoming originary technologies of scholarly communication. Drawing on the results of his empirical analysis of properties of digital publications, he notes that digital technologies appear to favor changes supporting ephemeral aspects and subjectivation. In line with his change model, he concludes that digital technologies are more open to being shaped than they are shaping technologies themselves (212). This, however, constitutes a fundamental incompatibility with what he calls the "objectifying function" and the requirement of persistence of publications. These two aspects are, in his view, aspects of publications that are beyond cultural or technological change (223). Consequently, Owen claims that no fundamental changes could be expected any longer, and that the revolutionary excitement driven by digital technologies has little further basis.

It is indeed astonishing just how much many of the results of the present study are reminiscent of observations made by Owen. The emphasis that is put on social appropriation of technology, the insight that digital technologies go hand in hand with the accentuation of ephemeral aspects in publishing, and the description of a quasi post-digital situation all had counterparts in the last chapters. This insight, however, causes a problem. The study at hand divided the history of digital publications into four phases. Owen worked on his research during the second phase, which was shaped by a decrease in the production of innovative scholarly publications. His observations thus match the characteristics of this phase.

How then should it be interpreted that immediately after the publication of his book, a second, much more vibrant, phase of innovative publication formats started that not only renewed the revolutionary discourse but even surpassed the earlier one? This observation apparently not only challenges Owen's claims: it must also be understood as a challenge to the ones in the present study, insofar as these claims resemble Owen's. There is, nonetheless, no doubt that, again, this new outburst of initiatives has calmed and turned into a less active phase in recent years. It appears that there is a pattern in which reasons that fuel the revolutionary's excitement and those that support general skepticism seem to alternate.

This alternation suggests looking for differences between the first and the second iteration; first, in terms of differences between claims in this study and those by Owen, and second, between the two "revolutionary" phases and the quieter phases.

Although this study shares a certain tendency in the evaluation of the field of digital publications, there are two significant differences. On the one hand, Owen, as described above, builds his claim about the impact of digital technologies on scholarly publishing around the same fundamental distinction between "ephemeral" aspects of digital publications and the requirement of an abstract notion of stability. The only point at which he differs from digital publications advocates is his judgement on the feasibility of integrating both facets into new publication formats. On the other hand, his judgement often refers to the topic of scholarly publications as a more or less homogeneous issue. This means that he evaluates change in terms of changes that are applied to the article format, while it has been mostly argued in the present study that change strives towards additional formats and plurality of communication practices. The perceptible change is more of a diversification than a replacement. Again, this orientation towards a mostly homogeneous scholarly publication landscape is a similarity between Owen and many — not all — of the projects discussed before. Thus, in parts his line of arguments remains attached to what he criticizes.

Inasmuch as Owen's conclusions are still shaped by the two abovementioned bipolarities, he might not have been able to predict how much the following phase would be driven by the vast possibilities offered by digital technologies to fill the space between the two poles respectively, i.e. the space for possible publication formats in different domains and different methodologies, and the space between communication and publication. Furthermore, phase three and four are obviously more than just repetitions of phase one and two. Looking at initiatives such SPARC, the open access declaration, Science Commons, OAI-ORE, and linked open data in general, the second phase is shaped by initiatives intending to change foundational conditions for intellectual, legal, and technological aspects of publishing. In contrast, the fourth phase produced initiatives like the Alliance for Networking Visual Culture and boundary objects such as Data Papers, attempting to relate stakeholders to the form of publications and to embed as well as adapt existing standards and technologies, respectively. The second phase is foundational, while the fourth phase starts to be relational. Similarly, the first phase comprises initiatives which very much focus on concrete journals such as the Living Review of Relativity or The *IMEJ of Computer-Enhanced Learning*. In the third phase, those initiatives promote innovations that are widely independent of specific journals or other types of established communication channels. Approaches such as ROs, NPs, and with some restriction even SPs were defined as a concept before, or at least in parallel to, their application in concrete publishing environments. It was furthermore described how much the third phase applied technological standards, where few standardization processes existed in the first phase.

Having said this, the fourth phase might be similar to the second phase in terms of the slowing development around new publication formats. Yet, there is a difference when it comes to the situation the fourth phase responds to, as well as the type of response. As mentioned at the beginning of the last paragraph and argued in chapter five and six, the third phase has demonstrated that it is not feasible to innovate scholarly publishing under the theme of digital technologies while at the same time maintaining a holistic view on publishing as well as a "transcendental" core of absolute values of publications. In 1997, Eason et al. (1997, sec. 7.4) had already argued that "it is our belief that progress across the entire academic community will depend upon recognizing the differences." At least another fifteen to twenty years had to pass until it was possible to estimate what such differences would include. Initiatives of the third phase would likely have had more impact — less disappointment for sure — if they had reflected more on this background. Heterogeneity today is not just the surrounding circumstance of a transformative process, there is something constitutive within heterogeneity for today's state of affairs. It has nonetheless also been discussed that accepting this situation equates to the celebration of "messiness." "Recognizing the differences" means acknowledging different options between the ephemeral and the persistent, it means to stop debating whether there will be digital publications or not.

In all these respects, the conclusions of the present study, albeit resembling those of Owen, are quite different. They reflect a different state of affairs. The goal, as said in the introduction, was to present a way of perceiving digital publications that avoids the distinction between the revolutionary and the skeptic view. The result is an approach that simply puts differences in their place as one distinction, and a very basic model that makes recognizing these differences more of a systematic endeavor than a basic attitude. For obvious reasons, this study had to call this approach "post-digital" at a certain point in time. Post-digital, as Cramer (2014) puts it, is "a term that sucks but is useful."

Another conclusion of the present research is that such engagements will not stop, as some skeptics might eventually think. Section 5 showed that the author acknowledges that the introduction of what is referred to as digital logics, and what has been analyzed under the theme of the calculatedly-calculating machine, is disruptive in many aspects. The difference is that this disruption is less the result of what digital technologies allegedly prescribe, but precisely a consequence of what they do not prescribe. They introduce uncountable new options and possibilities of referring to or engaging with the world, without suggesting any specific form of application. They qualify and question options and possibilities of the past, without bringing experiences and arrangements of the future along.

How then should engagements with forms of scholarly publications be different from those with digital publications? They would differ insofar as they reject the implementation of supposedly most innovative technological innovations, most appropriate types of representation, or the greatest extent of freedom. They are informed by all these developments and prospects, they reflect and consider them in one way or another, but they do not act on their behalf. Accordingly, such engagements with scholarly publishing are probably always a disappointment. They reference a field and a discourse of exciting promises, but seem to not take such promises seriously. They do so in order to facilitate the realization of some of these promises, but at a time where these do not appear exciting any longer.

They are, however, more radical when it comes to another aspect of digital publishing. Nothing has been emphasized more strongly in the discourse on digital publications than that scholarly publishing is about scholarly communication. It turned out that this motif was not taken seriously enough. The radicalization of this thought under the theme of semiosis revealed a more systematic and balanced description of facets necessary for communication in order to function well.

Such facets were of material-technological, socio-cultural, as well as semiotic-epistemological nature. The history of digital publications brought to light publication concepts focusing on one or two of these areas while neglecting the other: new "units of information," a more appropriate representation of knowledge, a more efficient mediator of progress, a more democratic catalyst of knowledge creation processes, less costly forms of distribution, and many more. New publication formats will have to do a better job of considering all three areas within the same design process at the same time in order to become significant.

While the abovementioned three areas are constitutive for any type of communication, it was shown in the sections on mode and semiosis that their belonging together is of even greater significance when it comes to the development of more organized configurations in communication, configurations desired in the field of digital publishing itself, but which the same field has partially undermined as well.

Accordingly, hybrid publishing strategies cannot invalidate technological issues of standardization and interoperability in publishing today. Embracing HPs without taking care of such issues, as is done in some of the examples, risks arbitrary publishing without much of a strategic aspect left. TPs, comparably, emphasize the representational function of publications but neglect socio-cultural issues of dissemination, readability, and the feasibility of long-term-preservation. The engagement into socio-cultural issues in ROs only makes an initial difference. Even though it is true that authors like David De Roure talk a lot about the social dimension of publications, it has been shown that when it comes to the impact of this dimension on the design of the format, social aspects are only respected in as much as they fit in. Research Objects are not in fact social objects within the current socio-cultural horizon.

In contrast, promising examples also exist, giving an idea of facets of engagements into scholarly publishing after the digital. They can be derived from Scalar, DPs, video-essays, the Guide to Open and Hybrid Publishing, the Journal of Digital Humanities, OLBs, SPPs, and others. Accordingly, it was shown how the Scalar project uses the Alliance for Visual Networking Culture to create an innovation process driven by stakeholder integration, not only for the question of how to realize goals, but more importantly to set the goals in the first place. Scalar, furthermore, offers an exceptional example of innovation planned to be a long and incremental process instead of a one-time intervention. Together with its predecessor Vectors, Scalar publications look back at a history of nearly fifteen years. With its agency in the Critical Commons initiatives and the contract-based association with contributing digital archives, Scalar, finally, offers very subtle insights into the limitations of purely formal approaches to inter-operability and openness, so common in the context of digital publications. Data Papers demonstrated how success and impact might be the product, not of precisely and formally defined publication concepts, but of the right level of fuzziness and flexibility that makes this concept accessible enough for a broad range of stakeholders, but also decisive enough to guide a directed innovation process. The format of the video-essay is a great example of how innovations in publishing that are accepted and that have impact can be created by considering and mobilizing existing capacities and regard within a defined environment. The Guide to Open and Hybrid Publishing is interesting because, despite its discussed limitations, it at least suggests establishing strategic relationships between forms of publishing, instead of pursuing a new form of publishing. The Journal of Digital Humanities and some activities in the area of OLBs are worth mentioning, with their attempt to lift ongoing online communications into more elaborated publication environments, instead of trying to change the original communication environment. Yet again, Hunter's SPPs have to be named for the opposite point of view. The decay factor of SPPs, in conjunction with the notion of situationally lifting existing informal communication into more organized publication environments, is a convincing first setup for dealing with today's fluent transition between publication and communication.

Engagements and experiments in publishing may become convincing insofar as they are willing to build upon strategically set boundaries or frames, whereby strategic refers to frames that support the cohesion of the three constitutives of communication within a defined publishing environment. A cohesive frame is a frame that has a supportive, or at least non-breaking, relationship with frames within the other two constitutive areas of communication. Accordingly, engagements into scholarly publishing should be conceived of as something that is often called an ecological approach. The tension between cohesion and innovation might be one of the main reasons for the frustration described in the introduction, because cohesion must always restrict possible innovations in one of the constitutives, due to the affordances of the other two.

Similarly, there need no longer be attempts to create generic approaches, a term that is often used in information technology environments, but stabilizing approaches.[1] The different notions of interoperability referenced above reflect the same issue. Future scholarly publishing will greatly benefit from a socio-culturally motivated misappropriation and reinterpretation of technological concepts. The same could however also be stated in the opposite way: future scholarly publishing will greatly benefit from technological substantiation of socio-culturally motivated approaches to new forms of publishing, which often treated technological implementation as a negligible aspect.

Design questions that follow the cohesion principle may ask, for instance, what type and level of volatility of continuously updatable publications still meet the requirements of efficient citing practices; which degree of multimodality and multimedia in publications can be sustained by preservation infrastructure and remain accessible for consumers; in which ways should publications share data and computations, considering that there are different notions of the nature of data and computation?

How to interlace principles of methodological "openness" and accessibility in terms of copyright with the political economy of researcher careers and the uneven relationship between public and private research?[2]

Building on the principle of cohesion, many initiatives in the first and third phase of the digital publication history were not engineering the new scholarly publishing landscape. They mostly just outlined the elements and components that an emergent publishing landscape might refer to. This is not to say that such contributions are not important or necessary, but it put a different light on corresponding expectations and desires, the analysis of which was one of the primary goals of this study. The mismatch between the type of engagement these contributions choose to carry out and the type of engagement they proclaimed to follow can be found without doubt in all situations in which frustration and disappointment went hand in hand with the design of digital publications as presented in the introduction. To, therefore, qualify these engagements can hopefully also lead to a better

1 Dallas (2016), in the context of modelling, calls a comparable difference the difference between the "wild frontier" approach and the "contact zone" approach. The first approach seeks harmonization in a top-down fashion, while the latter emphasizes negotiation and agreements between relevant stakeholders.

2 In this context, the new initiative by Herb and Schöpfel (2018) to establish a domain of critical open access studies for the support of open access values has to be very much welcomed.

valorization of the gains that they actually made, especially by those skeptic of changes of scholarly publications.

The term cohesion and the discussion of design decisions that support cohesion refers to the description of scholarly publications as modes of communication that were developed at the end of the final chapter. The introduction mentioned that a certain notion of scholarly publications needs to be developed in order to re-configure the discourse on digital publications, and mode is the cautious response to this need. It furthermore became clear why this notion has to remain cautious: although the phenomena of mode and stability in communication are crucial issues for the purpose of communication in general, resources are now available for the realization of situational communicative goals which formerly shaped the possibility of communicating as such.

It was said that more than ever, form is hardly separable from content. This is just another way of phrasing Owen's remark that digital technologies are technologies that are formed instead of forming technologies. It is therefore not reasonable to assume, nor to strive for, the one new publication format, not even for the fewest imaginable numbers of formats. Heterogeneity of publication formats is and will be a fact of publishing after the digital. To realize and to accept this may significantly help to overcome great parts of the frustration in the field. It is therefore necessary to refrain from overambitious ideas of defining contemporary scholarly publishing, an idea which, for instance, drives the fields of SPs, EPs, ROs, and others.

This does not mean, on the other hand, that publishing formats should be arbitrary, a direction that can be observed in some arguments of TPs and HPs. If the ongoing success of the PDF is to be interpreted, then it is both, the incapacity of the digital publishing field to deal with the extent of different and conflicting demands articulated in the field, as well as the unsystematized or welcomed randomness of options for "going digital" in publishing. No new type of scholarly publication, but neither no typing at all, that is the space in which scholarly publishing finds itself today. This is the situation of publications in terms of communication.

The example of the chain of developments from SPs to NPs to MPs, as well as the coexistence of professionally operated research blogs next to monograph publications, show very well how, in defined social environments, demands for different levels of publishing exist in parallel. Accordingly, certain formats might become publishing modes across different social environments, and in each environment, there will probably be more than one publishing mode. A systematic description and development of this ecology, in contrast to the often isolated or strongly focused contributions in the past, is a task for further research on scholarly publishing.

Concerning the analysis of the effects of digital technologies on the semiotic landscape, it seems appropriate indeed to conceive of publishing from a standpoint of communication. In contrast to the way of doing so in the field of digital publishing, in which the meaning of the concept of publishing remains widely unrelated, publishing is an organizational intervention into communication. As such, the two are neither the same nor opposites. Publications in form of communication create a continuum, in which due to digital technologies transitions have become extremely fluent and are marked by different communicative goals.

It would in any case offer great support to research on new forms of scholarly publishing to evaluate and systematize the backgrounds and goals of acts of scholarly communication, and relate them to possible formats. The argument of Pettifer's et al. (2011) observations on the success of the PDF has emphasized this already. This study has also taken a first step in this respect, even if it only made epistemological goals and goals in innovation transparent. It should be obvious from the arguments given that communication goals mean so much more than this.

The description of publications as “currency” for the curricula of academics, the dissemination of knowledge, or the provision of accountability for truth are all aspects that, of course, are not false, but far too abstract for understanding the entire context of different communications today. Variation refers to questions such as: dissemination to whom, what kind of knowledge, which step, what part of the curriculum, and many more.

The abovementioned continuum of stability of new forms of scholarly publications brings to mind, again, the positive mention of the Journal for Digital Humanities and the OLBs, for their effort to “lift” certain communications to more formal forms of communication. Scholarly publishing after the digital is indeed an activity that defines certain organizational stages in this continuum. Such stages correspond to clearly defined communication strategies, with environments able to sustain them. They do not exist just because it is possible to imagine them. Accordingly, it is not necessary to generally treat a tweet or a twitter dump as a publication, like the publication taxonomy suggests (Worthington and Furter 2014). Nevertheless, communication goals may exist that make it worth transforming such tweets or dumps into publications, by lifting them into a context that has another organizational stage and adds structure. In this respect, the Debates in the Digital Humanities series provides another insightful example. These anthologies publish, among other things, texts which have been written and published as blog posts already. Accordingly, they pull content out of a more day-to-day and ephemeral publication context and stage it in a publishing environment with greater social, infrastructural, and symbolic support. Following such examples, publishing after the digital can also be defined as staging communication. The task for an accompanying research field would then be to take care of popular or promising stages. For each publication mode to arise it is hence also necessary to ask how far staging, in terms of intended organizational complexity, has to go.

The answers to this and other, aforementioned, questions that attempt to describe the attitude towards scholarly publishing after the digital have to come from an autonomous conceptual space of publications. This space is rendered by the potential to design more than ephemeral formations between techno-materiality, socio-culture, and epistemologico-semiology, but indeed also less stable ones than required for the ultimate resource of "objectivation," as Owen has put it. It must refrain from objectifying the objectivation function of publications itself. These abovementioned formations do not just emerge along the way. This is what the experiences of the first and third period of digital publishing can teach. Neither only a fascination for new ways to represent, nor ethical drives to restructure the political economy of knowledge production and dissemination, and certainly not the implementation of technological principles will be able to help saturate the landscape of scholarly publishing. Instead, publishing modes will emerge in spaces where costs, motivations, and benefits in such areas are able to accommodate each other. And there is still a long way to go for this to happen.

According to the arguments presented in the last sections, the key question of a research field of scholarly publishing today actually is: when is it, and should it be, publishing? This is a question calling for concrete answers in concrete contexts. The notion of a revolution to come and its counter-claim that no substantial changes will actually take place, that, as shown in the introduction, so much drive the engagement into the field of publications today, require some final, general answers. To the revolutionaries, a suitable response alludes to a title by UB advocate Bruno Latour (1993). Just like he tries to convince that "we have never been modern," it could be argued that there never have been digital publications and there will never be any.

A response to the skeptics would be to emphasize that the discourse on digital technologies, and the drive towards digital publications has disrupted scholarly publishing too much already. Whether such realities emerged under questionable circumstances or not is of secondary concern. It could even be argued that it is not so much about how convincing these circumstances are, but about how much the historical configuration of scholarly publications dealt with its own questionable circumstances, heterogeneity, and imaginary drivers. It thereby might have caused the drive towards digital publications in the first place, long before digital technologies gave it form. In any case, the important task now is to make sense of these realities. The present study has tried to contribute to this task, by providing the means to see and build some patterns where there is so much regret about heterogeneity, or celebration of messiness.

APPENDIX

Acronyms

ACM Association for Computing Machinery
AIDA Atomic, Independent, Declarative, Absolute
ANVC Alliance for Networking Visual Culture
API Application Programming Interface
APs Automated Publications
CRIS Current Research Information Systems
CSS Cascading Style Sheets
CWA Concept Web Alliance
DDC Dewey Decimal Classification
DH Digital Humanities
DIDL Digital Item Declaration Language
DOI Digital Object Identifier
DP Data Paper
DPO Digital Publishing Organizations
DRIVER Digital Repository Infrastructure Vision for European Research
EP Enhanced Publication
EPMS Enhanced Publications Management Systems
ERC Executable Research Compendiums
FORCE The Future of Research Communications and e-Scholarship
FRBR Functional Requirements for Bibliographic Records
GBIF Global Biodiversity Information Facility
HP Hybrid Publication
HTML Hypertext Markup Language
IMEJ (IMMJ) Interactive Multimedia Electronic Journals
IMRaD Introduction, Methods, Results and Discussion
JDH Journal for Digital Humanities
JSON JavaScript Object Notation
JSTOR Journal STORage
KISS Keep it simple, stupid
LB Living Book
LOD Linked Open Data
LORE Literature Object Re-use and Exchange
LP Liquid Publication
LaP Layered Article
MA Modular Article
MIA Multimodal Interaction Analysis
MP Micro Publication
MuA Multimodal Analysis
NP Nano Publication
OA Open Access
OAI Open Archives Initiative
OAI-ORE Open Archives Initiative Object Reuse and Exchange
OAI-PMH Open Archives Initiative Protocol for Metadata Harvesting
OCR Optical Character Recognition
OLB Open Laboratory Book, sometimes also referred to as Open Notebook Science
OWL Web Ontology Language
PDF Portable Document Format
PID Persistent Identifier
PLOS Public Library of Science
RDF Resource Description Framework

RDFS	Resource Description Framework Schema
RIDE	Review Journal for Scholarly Digital Editions
RIP	Rich Internet Publication
RO	Research Object
RSS	Really Simple Syndication
SALT	Semantically Annotated LaTeX
SCI	Scholarly Communication Infrastructure
SCOPE	Scientific Compound Object Publishing
SCP	Self-Contained Publication
SGML	Standard Generalized Markup Language
SKO	Scientific Knowledge Object Pattern
SP	Semantic Publication
SPARC	Scholarly Publishing and Academic Resources Coalition
SPARQL	SPARQL Protocol and RDF Query Language
SPP	Scientific Publication Package
SPRO	Semantic Publishing and Referencing Ontologies
SW	Semantic Web
SWAN	Semantic Web Applications in Neuromedicine
TEI	Text Encoding Initiative
TP	Transmedia Publication
UB	Unbound Book
UML	Unified Modelling Language
UMLS	Unified Medical Language System
UNIX	Uniplexed Information and Computing Service
URI	Uniform Resource Identifier
URL	Uniform Resource Locator
VCS	Version Control System
WYSIWIG	What you see is what you get
WYSIWYM	What you see is what you mean
XML	Extensible Markup Language

References

Aalbersberg, Ijsbrand Jan, Sophia Atzeni, Hylke Koers, Beate Specker, and Elena Zudilova-Seinstra. 2014. "Bringing Digital Science Deep Inside the Scientific Article: The Elsevier Article of the Future Project." *Liber Quarterly* 23 (4): 274–99. doi:10.18352/lq.8446.

Abargues, Carlos, Carlos Granell, and Joaquín Huerta. 2010. "Describiendo colecciones de recursos para la Web de Datos." GeoInfo. http://www.geoinfo.uji.es/pubs/2010-jiide-GeoCollector.pdf.

Abbinnett, Ross. 2017. *The Thought of Bernard Stiegler: Capitalism, Technology and the Politics of Spirit*. London: Taylor & Francis.

Ackoff, Russell L. 1989. "From Data to Wisdom." *Journal of Applied Systems Analysis* 16 (1): 3–9.

Adema, Janneke. 2014. "Hybrid Publishing: Scalar and Watching Reading Write." *Open Reflections*. March 18. https://openreflections.wordpress.com/2014/03/18/hybrid-publishing-scalar-and-watching-reading-write/.

———. 2015. "Knowledge Production Beyond the Book? Performing the Scholarly Monograph in Contemporary Digital Culture." Coventry: Coventry University.

Adema, Janneke, and Gary Hall. 2016. "Posthumanities: The Dark Side of 'The Dark Side of the Digital'". *Journal of Electronic Publishing* 19 (2). doi:10.3998/3336451.0019.201.

Adriaansen, Dennis, and Jürgen Hooft. 2010. "Properties of Enhanced Publications and the Supporting Tools." http://www.cs.uu.nl/docs/vakken/mdic/papers/Adriaansen-fin.pdf.

Agosti, Maristella, Owen Conlan, Nicola Ferro, Cormac Hampson, and Gary Munnelly. 2013. "Interacting with Digital Cultural Heritage Collections via Annotations: The CULTURA Approach." In *Proceedings of the 2013 ACM Symposium on Document Engineering*, 13–22. New York: ACM. doi:10.1145/2494266.2494288.

Akers, Katherine. 2014. "A Growing List of Data Journals." *Data@MLibrary*. May 9T13:00:29+00:00. https://mlibrarydata.wordpress.com/2014/05/09/data-journals/.

Alsop, Graham, Chris Tompsett, and James Wisdom. 1997. "A Study of Human Communication Issues in Interactive Scholarly Electronic Journals: eLib Supporting Study." 35423. UKOLN, University of Bath. http://opus.bath.ac.uk/35423/.

Amerika, Mark. 2011a. "Remixthebook." http://www.remixthebook.com/.

———. 2011b. *Remixthebook*. Minneapolis: University of Minnesota Press.

Andersen, Christian Ulrik, Geoff Cox, and Georgios Papadopoulos, eds. 2014. "Post-Digital Research." *A Peer-Reviewed Journal About* 3 (1). http://www.aprja.net/?page_id=1291.

Anderson, Chris. 2008. "The End of Theory: The Data Deluge Makes the Scientific Method Obsolete." *Wired*, no. 16.07 (March). https://www.google.de/url?sa=t&rct=j&q=&esrc=s&source=web&cd=1&cad=rja&uact=8&ved=0ahUKEwi2v4iKKzaAhWGb1AKHdoQCKwQFggrMAA&url=https%3A%2F%2Fwww.wired.com%2F2008%2F06%2Fpb-theory%2F&usg=AOvVaw0e06Sdy3GcTRtNvbdyn0AG.

Anderson, Nicholas R., Peter Tarczy-Hornoch, and Roger E. Bumgarner. 2006. "On the Persistence of Supplementary Resources in Biomedical Publications." *BMC Bioinformatics* 7 (1). doi:10.1186/1471-2105-7-260.

Andrews, Ian. 2002. "Post-Digital Aesthetics and the Return to Modernism." Presented at the MAP-Uts Lecture. http://www.ian-andrews.org/texts/postdig.html.

Andriopoulos, Stefan. 2003. "Okkulte und technische Television." In *Text und Wissen: technologische und anthropologische Aspekte*, edited by Renate Lachmann and Stefan Rieger, 105–26. Tübingen: Gunter Narr Verlag.

Assante, Massimiliano, Leonardo Candela, Donatella Castelli, and Alice Tani. 2016. "Are Scientific Data Repositories Coping with Research Data Publishing?" *Data Science Journal* 15 (April). doi:10.5334/dsj-2016-006.

Assante, Massimiliano, Leonardo Candela, Donatella Castelli, Paolo Manghi, and Pasquale Pagano. 2015. "Science 2.0 Repositories: Time for a Change in Scholarly Communication." *D-Lib Magazine* 21 (1): 4. doi:10.1045/january2015-assante.

Attwood, Teresa K., David Kell, Philip McDermott, James Marsh, and David Thorne. 2010. "Utopia Documents: Linking Scholarly Literature with Research Data." *Bioinformatics* 26 (18): i568–i574. doi:10.1093/bioinformatics/btq383.

Baez, Marcos, and Fabio Casati. 2010. "Liquid Journals: Knowledge Dissemination in the Web Era." DISI-10-028. University of Trento. http://eprints.biblio.unitn.it/archive/00001814/01/028.pdf.

Baez, Marcos, Aliaksandr Birukou, Fabio Casati, Maurizio Marchese, and Daniil Mirylenka. 2009. "Liquid Journals: Overcoming Information Overload in the Scientific Community." https://docs.google.com/document/edit?id=10spyCxs-G5jcUD7AhTr6TVRON9QTddCkUg00TO9tmK8&pli=1.

Ball, Cheryl E. 2016. "The Shifting Genres of Scholarly Multimedia: Webtexts As Innovation." *The Journal of Media Innovations* 3 (2): 52–71. doi:10.5617/jmi.v3i2.2548.

———. 2017. "Building a Scholarly Multimedia Publishing Infrastructure." *Journal of Scholarly Publishing* 48 (2): 99–115. doi:10.3138/jsp.48.2.99.

Ball, Cheryl E., and Douglas Eyman. 2015. "Editorial Workflows for Multimedia-Rich Scholarship." *The Journal of Electronic Publishing* 18 (4). doi:10.3998/3336451.0018.406.

Bardi, Alessia. 2014. "Scholarly Communication: What's Wrong with It?" https://rd-alliance.org/sites/default/files/attachment/AlessiaBardi.pdf.

Bardi, Alessia, and Paolo Manghi. 2014. "Enhanced Publications: Data Models and Information Systems." *Liber Quarterly* 23 (4): 240–73. doi:10.18352/lq.8445/.

———. 2015a. "A Framework Supporting the Shift from Traditional Digital Publications to Enhanced Publications." *D-Lib Magazine* 21 (1/2). doi:10.1045/january2015-bardi.

———. 2015b. "Enhanced Publication Management Systems: A Systemic Approach Towards Modern Scientific Communication." In *Proceedings of the 24th International Conference on World Wide Web Companion*, 1051–2. International World Wide Web Conferences Steering Committee. doi:10.1145/2740908.2742026.

Bartling, Sönke, and Sascha Friesike. 2014. "Towards Another Scientific Revolution." In *Opening Science*, edited by Sönke Bartling and Sascha Friesike, 3–15. Berlin, Heidelberg: Springer. doi:10.1007/978-3-319-00026-8_1.

Beall, Jeffrey. 2013. "Predatory Publishing Is Just One of the Consequences of Gold Open Access." *Learned Publishing* 26 (2): 79–84. doi:10.1087/20130203.

———. 2017. "Scholarly Open Access Critical Analysis of Scholarly Open-Access Publishing." January 11. https://web.archive.org/web/20170111172309/https://scholarlyoa.com/individual-journals/.

Bechhofer, Sean, John Ainsworth, Jiten Bhagat, Iain Buchan, Philip Couch, Don Cruickshank, Mark Delderfield, Ian Dunlop, Matthew Gamble, and Carole A. Goble. 2010. "Why Linked Data Is Not Enough for Scientists." In *2010 IEEE Sixth International Conference on E-Science (E-Science)*, 300–307. Brisbane: IEEE. doi:10.1109/eScience.2010.21.

Bechhofer, Sean, Khalid Belhajjame, Jun Zhao, Daniel Garijo, Kristina Hettne, Raul Palma, Óscar Corcho, José-Manuel Gómez-Pérez, Graham Klyne, and Carole A. Goble. 2014. "The Research Object Suite of Ontologies: Sharing and Exchanging Research Data and Methods on the Open Web." *ArXiv Preprint* 1401 (4307). https://arxiv.org/abs/1401.4307.

Bechhofer, Sean, Óscar Corcho, Daniel Garijo Verdejo, Khalid Belhajjame, Jun Zhao, Paolo Missier, David Newman, et al. 2012. "Workflow-Centric Research Objects: First Class Citizens in Scholarly Discourse." In *Proceedings of Workshop on the Semantic Publishing*. Vol. 994. Crete: CEUR.

Bechhofer, Sean, David De Roure, Matthew Gamble, Carole Goble, and Iain Buchan. 2010. "Research Objects: Towards Exchange and Reuse of Digital Knowledge." *Nature Precedings*, no. 713 (July). doi:10.1038/npre.2010.4626.1.

Becker, Gabriel, Cory Barr, Robert Gentleman, and Michael Lawrence. 2017. "Enhancing Reproducibility and Collaboration via Management of R Package Cohorts." *Journal of Statistical Software* 82 (1). doi:10.18637/jss.v082.i01.

Bekaert, Jeroen, Patrick Hochstenbach, and Herbert Van de Sompel. 2003. "Using MPEG-21 DIDL to Represent Complex Digital Objects in the Los Alamos National Laboratory Digital Library." *D-Lib Magazine* 9 (11). doi:10.1045/november2003-bekaert.

Berners-Lee, Tim. 2009. "Linked Data - Design Issues." http://www.w3.org/DesignIssues/LinkedData.html.

Berners-Lee, Tim, James Hendler, and Ora Lassila. 2001. "The Semantic Web A New Form of Web Content That Is Meaningful to Computers Will Unleash a Revolution of New Possibilities." *Scientific American* 284 (5): 34–43. doi:10.1038/scientificamerican0501-34.

Bernstein, Paula. 2016. "What Is a Video Essay? Creators Grapple with a Definition." *Filmmaker Magazine*. May 3. https://filmmakermagazine.com/98248-what-is-a-video-essay-creators-grapple-with-a-definition/.

Berry, David M. 2013. "Post-Digital Humanities." *Stunlaw*. October 17. http://stunlaw.blogspot.de/2013/10/post-digital-humanities.html.

Bijker, Wiebe E. 2009. "Social Construction of Technology." In *A Companion to the Philosophy of Technology*, edited by Stig Andur Pedersen, Vincent F. Hendricks, Jan Kyrre Berg Olsen, and Marc Vries, 1st ed., 88–94. Blackwell Companions to Philosophy 43. Chichester, UK: Wiley-Blackwell.

Birchall, Clare, and Gary Hall. 2006. *New Cultural Studies: Adventures in Theory*. Athens, Georgia: University of Georgia Press.

Bishop, Ann Peterson. 1999. "Document Structure and Digital Libraries: How Researchers Mobilize Information in Journal Articles." *Information Processing & Management* 35 (3): 255–79. doi:10.1016/S0306-4573(98)00061-2.

Bizer, Christian, Richard Cyganiak, and Tom Heath. 2007. "How to Publish Linked Data on the Web." http://wifo5-03.informatik.uni-mannheim.de/bizer/pub/LinkedDataTutorial/.

de Boer, Tim, and Kim Verkooij. 2011. "Interactive Visualization Toolkits for Rich Internet Publications." http://www.computerscience.nl/docs/vakken/mdic/papers/Verkooij-deBoer-fin.pdf.

Boeriis, Morten, and Christian Mosbaek Johannessen. 2015. "Semogenetic Perspectives on Conventionalization Dynamics." In *Conference Abstracts. Multimodality: Methodological Explorations*. London: University College London. https://multimodalmethodologies.files.wordpress.com/2014/07/mme-programme-and-abstracts.pdf.

Boettiger, Carl. 2015. "An Introduction to Docker for Reproducible Research, with Examples from the R Environment." *ACM SIGOPS Operating Systems Review* 49 (1): 71–79. doi:10.1145/2723872.2723882.

Bogost, Ian. 2012. *Alien Phenomenology, or What It's Like to Be a Thing*. Minneapolis: University of Minnesota Press.

Borgman, Christine L., Jillian C. Wallis, and Noel Enyedy. 2007. "Little Science Confronts the Data Deluge: Habitat Ecology, Embedded Sensor Networks, and Digital Libraries." *International Journal on Digital Libraries* 7 (1-2): 17–30. doi:10.1007/s00799-007-0022-9.

Bourdieu, Pierre. 2010. "The Forms of Capital." In *Cultural Theory: An Anthology*, edited by Imre Szeman and Timothy Kaposy, 81–93. Chichester: Wiley-Blackwell.

Bourne, Philip E. 2005. "Will a Biological Database Be Different from a Biological Journal?" *PLoS Computational Biology* 1 (3): 179–81. doi:10.1371/journal.pcbi.0010034.

———. 2010. "What Do I Want from the Publisher of the Future?" *PLoS Computational Biology* 6 (5). doi:10.1371/journal.pcbi.1000787.

———. 2011. "Digital Research/Analog Publishing One Scientist's View." *Serials* 24 (2): 119–22. doi:10.1629/24119.

Bourne, Philip E., Simon Buckingham Shum, Paolo Ciccarese, Bradley P. Allen, Aliaksandr Birukou, Judith A. Blake, Gully Burns, Leslie Chan, Olga Chiarcos, and Tim Clark. 2012. "Improving the Future of Research Communications and E-Scholarship." *Dagstuhl Manifestos*, 41–60. doi:10.4230/DagMan.1.1.41.

Bourne, Philip E., David Shotton, Ivan Herman, Anita de Waard, Timothy W. Clark, Robert Dale, and Eduard H. Hovy. 2012. "Improving the Future of Research Communications and E-Scholarship." *Dagstuhl Manifestos*. doi:10.4230/DagMan.1.1.41.

Boyd, Danah. 2017. "Toward Accountability Data, Fairness, Algorithms, Consequences." *Data & Society: Points*. April 13.

Bradley, Arthur. 2011. *Originary Technicity: The Theory of Technology from Marx to Derrida*. London, New York: Palgrave Macmillan.

Bradley, Jean-Claude. 2007. "Open Notebook Science Using Blogs and Wikis." *Nature Precedings*, no. 713 (June). doi:10.1038/npre.2007.39.1.

Bradley, Jean-Claude, and Kevin Owens. 2008. "Chemistry Crowdsourcing and Open Notebook Science." *Nature Precedings*, no. 713 (January). doi:10.1038/npre.2008.1505.1.

Bradley, Jean-Claude, Rajarshi Guha, Andrew Lang, Pierre Lindenbaum, Cameron Neylon, Antony Williams, and Egon L. Willighagen. 2010. "Beautifying Data in the Real World." *Nature Precedings*, no. 713 (September): 259–78. doi:10.1038/npre.2010.4918.1.

Brammer, Grant R., Ralph W. Crosby, Suzanne J. Matthews, and Tiffani L. Williams. 2011. "Paper Mâché: Creating Dynamic Reproducible Science." *Procedia Computer Science*, Proceedings of the International Conference on Computational Science, ICCS 2011, 4: 658–67. doi:10.1016/j.procs.2011.04.069.

Bresland, John. 2010. "On the Origin of the Video Essay." *Blackbird* 9 (1). https://blackbird.vcu.edu/v9n1/gallery/ve-bresland_j/ve-origin_page.shtml.

Breure, Leen. 2014. "Transforming a Research Paper into a Rich Internet Publication." *Information Services & Use* 34 (3–4): 335–44. doi:10.3233/ISU-140757.

Breure, Leen, Maarten Hoogerwerf, and René van Horik. 2014. "Xpos're: A Tool for Rich Internet Publications." *Digital Humanities Quarterly* 8 (2).

Breure, Leen, Hans Voorbij, and Maarten Hoogerwerf. 2011. "Rich Internet Publications: 'Show What You Tell'." *Journal of Digital Information* 12 (1).

Brooking, Charles, Stephen R. Shouldice, Gautier Robin, Bostjan Kobe, Jennifer L. Martin, and Jane Hunter. 2009. "Comparing METS and OAI-ORE for Encapsulating Scientific Data Products: A Protein Crystallography Case Study." In *E-Science'09. Fifth IEEE International Conference On*, 148–55. Oxford: IEEE. doi:10.1109/e-Science.2009.29.

Brown, Titus. 2016. "What Is Open Science?" *Living in an Ivory Basement Stochastic Thoughts on Science, Testing, and Programming*. October 22. http://ivory.idyll.org/blog/2016-what-is-open-science.html.

Brüggemann-Klein, Anne. 1995. "Wissenschaftliches Publizieren im Umbruch." *Informatik Forschung und Entwicklung* 10 (4): 171–79. doi:10.1007/s004500050025.

Brüggemann-Klein, Anne, Günther Cyranek, and Albert Endres. 1995. "Die fachlichen Informations- und Publikationsdienste der Zukunft Eine Initiative der Gesellschaft für Informatik." In *GISI 95*, edited by Friedbert Huber-Wäschle, Helmut Schauer, and Peter Widmayer, 2–12. Informatik aktuell. Berlin, Heidelberg: Springer.

Buckingham Shum, Simon, and Tim Clark. 2010. "Scientific Discourse on the Semantic Web: A Survey of Models and Enabling Technologies." *Semantic Web Journal: Interoperability, Usability, Applicability*. http://www.semantic-web-journal.net/content/scientific-discourse-semantic-web-survey-models-and-enabling-technologies.

Buckley, Jake. 2011. "Believing in the (Analogico-) Digital." *Culture Machine* 12. http://www.culturemachine.net/index.php/cm/article/viewDownloadInterstitial/432/463.

Burg, Jennifer, Yue-Ling Wong, Ching-Wan Yip, and Anne Boyle. 2000. "The State of the Art in Interactive Multimedia Journals for Academia." In *Proceedings of EdMedia: World Conference on Educational Media and Technology 2000*, 2: 37–42. Montréal: Association for the Advancement of Computing in Education. http://www.editlib.org/p/16036.

Burkhardt, Marcus. 2015. "Hybrid Publishing Lab. Wissenschaftliche Kommunikation Im Digitalen Zeitalter." Leuphana. https://www.leuphana.de/fileadmin/user_upload/portale/inkubator/download/1504_A01_HybridPublishing_DIN_lang_16s_de_RZ_lay.pdf.

Burn, Andrew. 2013. "The Kineiconic Mode. Towards a Multimodal Approach to Moving-Image Media." In *The Routledge Handbook of Multimodal Analysis*, edited by Carey Jewitt, 2nd ed., 375–85. Routledge.

Callaghan, Sarah. 2013. "Data Journals – as Soon-to-Be-Obsolete Stepping Stone to Something Better?" *Citing Bytes – Adventures in Data Citation*. January 29. http://citingbytes.blogspot.com/2013_01_01_archive.html.

Callaghan, Sarah, Fiona Hewer, Sam Pepler, Paul Hardaker, and Alan Gadian. 2009. "Overlay Journals and Data Publishing in the Meteorological Sciences." *Ariadne*, no. 60. http://www.ariadne.ac.uk/issue60/callaghan-et-al.

Candela, Leonardo, Donatella Castelli, and Pasquale Pagano. 2013. "Virtual Research Environments: An Overview and a Research Agenda." *Data Science Journal* 12: GRDI75–GRDI81. https://www.jstage.jst.go.jp/article/dsj/12/0/12_GRDI-013/_article/-char/ja/.

Candela, Leonardo, Donatella Castelli, Paolo Manghi, and Alice Tani. 2015. "Data Journals: A Survey." *Journal of the Association for Information Science & Technology* 66 (9): 1747–62. doi:10.1002/asi.23358.

Candela, Leonardo, Donatella Castelli, Pasquale Pagano, and Manuele Simi. 2005. "From Heterogeneous Information Spaces to Virtual Documents." In *Digital Libraries: Implementing Strategies and Sharing Experiences*, edited by Edward A. Fox, Erich J. Neuhold, Pimrumpai Premsmit, and Vilas Wuwongse, 11–22. Lecture Notes in Computer Science 3815. Berlin, Heidelberg: Springer.

Caracciolo, Caterina. 2003. "Towards Modular Access to Electronic Handbooks." *Journal of Digital Information* 3 (4). https://journals.tdl.org/jodi/index.php/jodi/article/view/86.

Carr, Les A., David De Roure, Wendy Hall, and Gary J. Hill. 1995. "The Distributed Link Service: A Tool for Publishers, Authors and Readers." Project Report. Southampton: University of Southampton. http://eprints.soton.ac.uk/250739/.

———. 1998. "Implementing an Open Link Service for the World Wide Web." *World Wide Web* 1 (2): 61–71. doi:10.1023/A:1019251328413.

Carter-Thomas, Shirley, and Elizabeth Rowley-Jolivet. 2017. "Open Science Notebooks: New Insights, New Affordances." *Journal of Pragmatics* 116 (July): 64–76. doi:10.1016/j.pragma.2016.12.003.

Casati, Fabio, Fausto Giunchiglia, and Maurizio Marchese. 2007. "Liquid Publications: Scientific Publications Meet the Web." Technical Report 07-073. Povo. http://eprints.biblio.unitn.it/1313/.

Casati, Fabio, Maurizio Marchese, Cristian Parra, Luca Cernuzzi, and Ralf Gerstner. 2011. "Liquid Book: Collaborative Reuse and Sharing of Multifaceted Content." In *Proceedings of 7th European Computer Science Summit*. Trento: University of Trento.

Cascone, Kim. 2000. "The Aesthetics of Failure: "Post-Digital" Tendencies in Contemporary Computer Music." *Computer Music Journal* 24 (4): 12–18.

Castelli, Donatella, and Pasquale Pagano. 2002. "OpenDLib: A Digital Library Service System." In *Research and Advanced Technology for Digital Libraries*, 292–308. Lecture Notes in Computer Science. Berlin, Heidelberg: Springer. doi:10.1007/3-540-45747-X_22.

Castelli, Donatella, Paolo Manghi, and Costantino Thanos. 2013. "A Vision Towards Scientific Communication Infrastructures." *International Journal on Digital Libraries* 13 (3-4): 155–69. doi:s00799-013-0106-7.

Chavan, Vishwas, and Lyubomir Penev. 2011. "The Data Paper: A Mechanism to Incentivize Data Publishing in Biodiversity Science." *BMC Bioinformatics* 12 (15): 1–12. doi:10.1186/1471-2105-12-S15-S2.

Chen, Ya-Ning. 2017. "An Analysis of Characteristics and Structures Embedded in Data Papers: A Preliminary Study." *Libellarium: Journal for the Research of Writing, Books, and Cultural Heritage Institutions* 9 (2). doi:10.15291/libellarium.v9i2.266.

Chichester, Christine, Pascale Gaudet, Oliver Karch, Paul Groth, Lydie Lane, Amos Bairoch, Barend Mons, and Antonis Loizou. 2014. "Querying NeXtProt Nanopublications and Their Value for Insights on Sequence Variants and Tissue Expression." *Web Semantics: Science, Services and Agents on the World Wide Web*, Life Science and e-Science, 29: 3–11. doi:10.1016/j.websem.2014.05.001.

Chichester, Christine, Oliver Karch, Pascale Gaudet, Lydie Lane, Barend Mons, and Amos Bairoch. 2015. "Converting NeXtProt into Linked Data and Nanopublications." *Semantic Web* 6 (2): 147–53. doi:10.3233/SW-140149.

Choudhury, Sayeed, Tim DiLauro, Alex Szalay, Ethan Vishniac, Robert Hanisch, Julie Steffen, Robert Milkey, Teresa Ehling, and Ray Plante. 2008. "Digital Data Preservation for Scholarly Publications in Astronomy." *International Journal of Digital Curation* 2 (2): 20–30. doi:10.2218/ijdc.v2i2.26.

Ciancarini, Paolo, Angelo Di Iorio, Andrea Giovanni Nuzzolese, Silvio Peroni, and Fabio Vitali. 2013. "Semantic Annotation of Scholarly Documents and Citations." In *AI*IA 2013: Advances in Artificial Intelligence*, 336–47. Berlin, Heidelberg: Springer. doi:10.1007/978-3-319-03524-6_29.

Ciccarese, Paolo, Marco Ocana, and Tim Clark. 2012. "Open Semantic Annotation of Scientific Publications Using DOMEO." *Journal of Biomedical Semantics* 3 (1). doi:10.1186/2041-1480-3-S1-S1.

Cito, Jürgen, Vincenzo Ferme, and Harald C. Gall. 2016. "Using Docker Containers to Improve Reproducibility in Software and Web Engineering Research." In *Web Engineering*, edited by Alessandro Bozzon, Philippe Cudre-Maroux, and Cesare Pautasso, 609–12. Lecture Notes in Computer Science 9671. Berlin: Springer. doi:10.1007/978-3-319-38791-8_58.

Cito, Jürgen, Gerald Schermann, John Erik Wittern, Philipp Leitner, Sali Zumberi, und Harald C. Gall. 2017. "An Empirical Analysis of the Docker Container Ecosystem on GitHub." In *Proceedings of the 14th International Conference on Mining Software Repositories*, 323–333. MSR '17. Piscataway: IEEE Press. doi:10.1109/MSR.2017.67.

Clark, Alex M., Antony J. Williams, and Sean Ekins. 2015. "Machines First, Humans Second: On the Importance of Algorithmic Interpretation of Open Chemistry Data." *Journal of Cheminformatics* 7 (March): 9. doi:10.1186/s13321-015-0057-7.

Clark, Tim. 2014. "Next Generation Scientific Publishing and the Web of Data." *Semantic Web Journal* 5 (4): 257–59. http://dl.acm.org/citation.cfm?id=2786113.2786114.

Clark, Tim, and Paolo Ciccarese. 2013. *Micropublications*. https://micropublications.googlecode.com/svn/tags/1.17/mp.owl.

Clark, Tim, Paolo Ciccarese, and Carole A. Goble. 2014. "Micropublications: A Semantic Model for Claims, Evidence, Arguments and Annotations in Biomedical Communications." *Journal of Biomedical Semantics* 5 (1): 28. doi:10.1186/2041-1480-5-28.

Clinio, Anne, and Sarita Albagli. 2017. "Open Notebook Science as an Emerging Epistemic Culture Within the Open Science Movement." *Revue Française des Sciences de L'information et de La Communication*, 11 (August). doi:10.4000/rfsic.3186.

Coleman, Anita S. 2002. "Scientific Models as Works." *Cataloging & Classification Quarterly* 33 (3-4): 129–59. doi:10.1300/J104v33n03_07.

Collin, Finn. 2008. *Konstruktivismus für Einsteiger*. Paderborn: Fink.

Collins, Ellen, Caren Milloy, and Graham Stone. 2015. "Guide to Open Access Monograph Publishing for Arts, Humanities and Social Science Researchers." Jisc Collections. doi:10.5920/oapen-uk/oaguide.

Concept Web Alliance. 2015. "Nanopublication Guidelines." February 19. http://nanopub.org/guidelines/working_draft/.

Cramer, Florian. 2014. "What Is 'Post-Digital'?" *A Peer-Reviewed Journal About* 3 (1). http://www.aprja.net/?p=1318.

Cranmer, Kyle, Lukas Heinrich, Roger Jones, and David M. South. 2015. "Analysis Preservation in ATLAS." *Journal of Physics: Conference Series* 664 (3): 032013. doi:10.1088/1742-6596/664/3/032013.

Creative Commons. 2005. "About Science Commons." *Science Commons*. http://sciencecommons.org/about/.

———. 2008. "Science Commons for Open Science." http://sciencecommons.org/resources/readingroom/principles-for-open-science/.

Crew, Michael A., and Timothy J. Brennan. 2014. *The Role of the Postal and Delivery Sector in a Digital Age*. Cheltenham: Edward Elgar.

Cribb, Julian, and Tjempaka Hari Hartomo. 2010. *Open Science: Sharing Knowledge in the Global Century*. Collingwood: Csiro.

Crick, Tom, Benjamin A. Hall, Samin Ishtiaq, and Kenji Takeda. 2014. "Share and Enjoy: Publishing Useful and Usable Scientific Models." In *Proceedings of the 2014 IEEE/ACM 7th International Conference on Utility and Cloud Computing*, 957–61. Washington: IEEE Computer Society. doi:10.1109/UCC.2014.156.

Critical Commons. 2016. "Critical Commons. For Fair & Critical Participation in Media Culture." http://www.criticalcommons.org/.

Cyganiak, Richard. 2015. "The Linking Open Data Cloud Diagram." http://lod-cloud.net/.

van Dalen, Arjen. 2012. "The Algorithms Behind the Headlines." *Journalism Practice* 6 (5-6): 648–58. doi:10.1080/17512786.2012.667268.

Dallas, Costis. 2016. "Digital Curation Beyond the 'Wild Frontier': A Pragmatic Approach." *Archival Science* 16 (4): 421–57. doi:10.1007/s10502-015-9252-6.

Darnton, Robert. 1999. "The New Age of the Book." *The New York Review of Books*. 46 (5): 5. http://www.nybooks.com/articles/archives/1999/mar/18/the-new-age-of-the-book/.

Davenport, Elisabeth, and Blaise Cronin. 1990. "Hypertext and the Conduct of Science." *Journal of Documentation* 46 (3): 175–92.

David, Paul A., Matthijs den Besten, and Ralph Schroeder. 2008. "Will E-Science Be Open Science?" In *World Wide Research*, edited by William H. Dutton and Paul W. Jeffreys, 299–316. Camebridge, MA: MIT Press.

De Roure, David. 2010. "E-Science and the Web." *IEEE Computer* 43 (5): 90–93. doi:10.1109/MC.2010.133.

———. 2011. "Machines, Methods and Music: On the Evolution of E-Research." In *2011 International Conference on High Performance Computing*, 8–13. Istanbul: IEEE. doi:10.1109/HPCSim.2011.5999801.

———. 2013. "Towards Computational Research Objects." In *Proceedings of the 1st International Workshop on Digital Preservation of Research Methods and Artefacts*, 16–19. DPRMA "13. New York: ACM. doi:10.1145/2499583.2499590.

———. 2014a. "Executable Music Documents." In *Proceedings of the 1st International Workshop on Digital Libraries for Musicology*, 1–3. DLfM "14. New York: ACM. doi:10.1145/2660168.2660183.

———. 2014b. "The Future of Scholarly Communications." *Insights: The UKSG Journal* 27 (3): 233–38. doi:10.1629/2048-7754.171.

De Roure, David, and Wendy Hall. 1997. "Distributed Multimedia Information Systems." *Multimedia, IEEE* 4 (4): 68–73.

De Roure, David, Sean Bechhofer, and Carole A. Goble. 2011. "Scientific Social Objects: The Social Objects and Multidimensional Network of the MyExperiment Website." In *Third International Conference on Social Computing (SocialCom)*, 1398–1402. Boston: IEEE. doi:10.1109/PASSAT/SocialCom.2011.245.

De Roure, David, Sean Bechhofer, Iain Buchan, Paolo Missier, John Ainsworth, Jiten Bhagat, Philip Couch, et al. 2013. "Why Linked Data Is Not Enough for Scientists." *Future Generation Computer Systems*, Special section: Recent Advances in e-Science, 29 (2): 599–611. doi:10.1016/j.future.2011.08.004.

De Roure, David, Khalid Belhajjame, Paolo Missier, José-Manuel Gómez-Pérez, Raúl Palma, José Enrique Ruiz, Kristina Hettne, et al. 2011. "Towards the Preservation of Scientific Workflows." In *Proc 8th International Conference on Preservation of Digital Objects*. Singapore: ACM.

De Roure, David, Carole A. Goble, Sergejs Aleksejevs, Sean Bechhofer, Jiten Bhagat, Don Cruickshank, Paul Fisher, et al. 2009. "Towards Open Science: The MyExperiment Approach." *Concurrency and Computation: Practice and Experience* 22 (17): 1–6. http://eprints.ecs.soton.ac.uk/17270/.

De Roure, David, Kevin R. Page, Benjamin Fields, Tim Crawford, J. Stephen Downie, and Ichiro Fujinaga. 2011. "An E-Research Approach to Web-Scale Music Analysis." *Philosophical Transactions of the Royal Society of London A: Mathematical, Physical and Engineering Sciences* 369 (1949): 3300–3317. doi:10.1098/rsta.2011.0171.

De Roure, David, Marco Roos, Kristina Hettne Soiland-Reyes, José Enrique Ruiz, Kevin R. Page, José-Manuel Gómez-Pérez, and Carole A. Goble. 2012. "Ro-Manager: A Tool for Creating and Manipulating Research Objects to Support Reproducibility and Reuse in Sciences." In *Proceedings of the Second International Workshop on Linked Science 2012*. Boston: CEUR.

Denning, Peter J., and Bernard Rous. 1995. "The ACM Electronic Publishing Plan." *Communications of the ACM* 38 (4): 97–109. doi:10.1145/205323.205348.

Derrida, Jacques. 1982. *Margins of Philosophy*. Chicago: University of Chicago Press.

Dewar, James A. 2000. "The Information Age and the Printing Press: Looking Backward to See Ahead." *Ubiquity* 2000 (August): 1–es. doi:10.1145/347634.348784.

Diender, Bas. 2010. "Enhanced Publications: An Enhanced Experience?" University of Utrecht. http://www.cs.uu.nl/docs/vakken/mdic/papers/Diender-fin.pdf.

Dodds, Leigh. 2013. "What Is a Dataset." *Lost Boy*. February 9. http://blog.ldodds.com/.

Doloughan, Fiona J. 2011. *Contemporary Narrative: Textual Production, Multimodality and Multiliteracies*. London: Continuum.

Doorenbosch, Paul, and Barbara Sierman. 2011. "Institutional Repositories, Long Term Preservation and the Changing Nature of Scholarly Publications." *Journal of Digital Information* 12 (2). http://journals.tdl.org/jodi/article/viewArticle/1764.

Dörr, Konstantin Nicholas. 2016. "Mapping the Field of Algorithmic Journalism." *Digital Journalism* 4 (6): 700–722.

Drees, Bastian, Angelina Kraft, and Thomas Koprucki. 2018. "Reproducible and Comprehensible Research Results Through Persistently Linked and Visualized Numerical Simulation Data." *Optical and Quantum Electronics* 50 (2): 59. doi:10.1007/s11082-018-1327-1.

Eason, Ken, Chris Carter, Susan Harker, and Sue Pomfrett. 1997. "A Comparative Analysis of the Role of Multi-Media Electronic Journals in Scholarly Disciplines." November. Loughborough: HUSAT Research Institute. http://www.ukoln.ac.uk/services/elib/papers/tavistock/eason/eason.pdf.

Eggins, Suzanne. 1994. *An Introduction to Systemic Functional Linguistics*. London: Pinter Publishers.

Elsevier. 2008. "Elsevier Article 2.0 Contest." http://article20.elsevier.com/contest/home.html.

———. 2011. "Article of the Future." http://www.articleofthefuture.com/.

Esposito, Joseph. 2013. "The Digital Publishing Revolution Is Over." *The Scholarly Kitchen*. March 4. https://scholarlykitchen.sspnet.org/2013/03/04/the-digital-publishing-revolution-is-over/.

Estellés-Arolas, Enrique, and Fernando González-Ladrón-de-Guevara. 2012. "Towards an Integrated Crowdsourcing Definition." *Journal of Information Science* 38 (2): 189–200. doi:10.1177/0165551512437638.

Eve, Martin Paul, and Caroline Edwards. 2015. "Opening the Open Library of Humanities." *Open Library of Humanities* 1 (1). http://eprints.bbk.ac.uk/13030.

Fanghor, Hans. 2014. "Blogging with the IPython Notebook." *Computational Modeling Blog*. April 22. http://www.southampton.ac.uk/~fangohr/blog/blogging-with-the-ipython-notebook.html.

Farace, Dominic, Jerry Frantzen, Christiane Stock, Laurents Sesink, and Debbie Rabina. 2012. "Linking Full-Text Grey Literature to Underlying Research and Post-Publication Data: An Enhanced Publications Project 2011-2012." *The Grey Journal* 8 (3): 181–89.

Fenner, Martin. 2010. "Beyond the PDF It Is Time for a Workshop." *Gobbledygook*. November 6. http://blogs.plos.org/mfenner/2010/11/06/beyond-the-pdf-it-is-time-for-a-workshop/.

Fenton, William. 2013. "Scalar." *PCMag UK*. May 30T15:47:00+00:00. http://uk.pcmag.com/scalar/2103/review/scalar.

Ferdig, Richard E., and Kristine E. Pytash. 2014. *Exploring Multimodal Composition and Digital Writing*. Hershey: IGI Global.

Ferwerda, Eelco, Frances Pinter, and Niels Stern. 2017. "A Landscape Study on Open Access and Monographs: Policies, Funding and Publishing in Eight European Countries." Zenodo. doi:10.5281/zenodo.815932.

Fink, J. Lynn, Pablo Fernicola, Rahul Chandran, Savas Parastatidis, Alex Wade, Oscar Naim, Gregory B. Quinn, and Philip E. Bourne. 2010. "Word Add-in for Ontology Recognition: Semantic Enrichment of Scientific Literature." *BMC Bioinformatics* 11 (1): 103–11. doi:10.1186/1471-2105-11-103.

Flusser, Vilém. 1994. *Gesten: Versuch einer Phänomenologie*. Frankfurt am Main: Fischer.

Force, Megan, Nigel Robinson, Mark Matthews, Daniel Auld, and Mariana Boletta. 2016. "Research Data in Journals and Repositories in the Web of Science: Developments and Recommendations." *TCDL Bulletin* 12 (1): 27–30. http://www.ieee-tcdl.org/Bulletin/current/papers/IEEE-TCDL-DC-2016_paper_3.pdf.

Foucault, Michel. 1982. *The Archaeology of Knowledge*. New York, NY: Pantheon Books.

Friend, Frederick. 1998. "Alternatives to Commercial Publishing for Scholarly Communication." *Serials* 11 (2). doi:10.1629/11163.

Fukuyama, Francis. 2006. *The End of History and the Last Man*. Reissue. New York: Free Press.

Gamble, Matthew, and Carole A. Goble. 2010. "Standing on the Shoulders of the Trusted Web: Trust, Scholarship and Linked Data." In *Web Science Conference 2010*. Vol. 2010. Raleigh: Journal of Web Science. doi:10.1.1.611.7967.

Gao, Yong, June Kinoshita, Elizabeth Wu, Eric Miller, Ryan Lee, Andy Seaborne, Steve Cayzer, and Tim Clark. 2006. "SWAN: A Distributed Knowledge Infrastructure for Alzheimer Disease Research." *Web Semantics: Science, Services and Agents on the World Wide Web*, Semantic Web for Life Sciences, 4 (3): 222–28. doi:10.1016/j.websem.2006.05.006.

Garcia, Alexander, Federico Lopez, Leyla Garcia, Olga Giraldo, Victor Bucheli, and Michel Dumontier. 2018. "Biotea: Semantics for Pubmed Central." *PeerJ* 6 (January). doi:10.7717/peerj.4201.

Garcia-Garcia, Alicia, Alexandre Lopez-Borrull, and Fernanda Peset. 2015. "Data journals: eclosión de nuevas revistas especializadas en datos." *El Profesional de la informacion* 24 (6): 845–54.

Gärdenfors, Peter. 2000. *Conceptual Spaces: The Geometry of Thought*. Cambridge: MIT Press.

Garvey, William D. 1979. *Communication the Essence of Science*. Oxford: Pergamon Press.

Gerber, Anna, and Jane Hunter. 2008. "LORE: A Compound Object Authoring and Publishing Tool for the Australian Literature Studies Community." In *Digital Libraries: Universal and Ubiquitous Access to Information*, 246–55. Lecture Notes in Computer Science. Berlin, Heidelberg: Springer. doi:10.1007/978-3-540-89533-6_25.

———. 2010. "Authoring, Editing and Visualizing Compound Objects for Literary Scholarship." *Journal of Digital Information* 11 (1).

Ghani, Norjihan bt Abdul, Suriawati Suparjoh, and Suraya Hamid. 2008. "A Framework for Online Publishing in the University of Malaya." Edited by Soliman, K.S. *Information Management in the Modern Organizations: Trends & Solutions* 1,2: 938–45.

Gibson, Andrew, Jesse van Dam, Erik Schultes, Marco Roos, and Barend Mons. 2012. "Towards Computational Evaluation of Evidence for Scientific Assertions with Nanopublications and Cardinal Assertions." In *Proceedings of the 5th International Workshop on Semantic Web Applications and Tools for Life Sciences*, 952:28–30. Paris: CEUR.

Gibson, Frank. 2007. "Do Scientists Really Believe in Open Science?" *We*. http://fgibson.com/2007/06/26/do-scientists-really-believe-in-open-science/.

Gielkens, Charley, and Jeroen Hulman. 2011. "Identifying Requirements for Enhanced Publications." University of Utrecht. http://www.charleygielkens.nl/wp-content/uploads/2012/10/Gielkens-Hulman-fin.pdf.

Gil, Yolanda, and Daniel Garijo. 2017. "Towards Automating Data Narratives." In *Proceedings of the 22Nd International Conference on Intelligent User Interfaces*, 565–76. IUI "17. New York, NY, USA: ACM. doi:10.1145/3025171.3025193.

GitHub. 2018. "About Gists." March 30. https://help.github.com/articles/about-gists/.

Giunchiglia, Fausto, Ronald Chenu, Hao Xu, Aliaksandr Birukou, and Enzo Maltese. 2010. "Design of the SKO Structural Model."

Giunchiglia, Fausto, Hao Xu, Aliaksandr Birukou, and Ronald Chenu. 2010. "Scientific Knowledge Object Patterns." In *Proceedings of the 15th European Conference on Pattern Languages of Programs*, 15:1–15:6. EuroPLoP "10. New York: ACM. doi:10.1145/2328909.2328928.

Goble, Carole. 2015. "Researchobject.Org." http://www.researchobject.org/.

Goble, Carole A., David De Roure, and Sean Bechhofer. 2012. "Accelerating Scientists" Knowledge Turns." *Communications in Computer and Information Science*, Communications in computer and information science, 348: 3–25. doi:10.1007/978-3-642-37186-8_1.

Gold, Matthew K. 2012. *Debates in the Digital Humanities*. 1st ed. Minneapolis: University of Minnesota Press.

———. 2016a. *Debates in the Digital Humanities*. Minneapolis: University of Minnesota Press. https://www.upress.umn.edu/book-division/books/debates-in-the-digital-humanities-2016.

———. 2016b. "Debates in the Digital Humanities. About." *Debates in the Digital Humanities*. http://dhdebates.gc.cuny.edu/about.

Golden, Patrick, and Ryan Shaw. 2015. "Period Assertion as Nanopublication: The PeriodO Period Gazetteer." In *Proceedings of the 24th International Conference on World Wide Web Companion*, 1013–8. International World Wide Web Conferences Steering Committee.

Gómez-Pérez, José-Manuel. 2013. "Wf4ever." http://www.wf4ever-project.org.

van Gorp, Pieter, and Steffen Mazanek. 2011. "SHARE: A Web Portal for Creating and Sharing Executable Research Papers." *Procedia Computer Science*, Proceedings of the International Conference on Computational Science, ICCS 2011, 4: 589–97. doi:10.1016/j.procs.2011.04.062.

Gosling, Paul. 1997. *Government in the Digital Age*. Work in the Digital Age. London: Bowerdean.

Gradmann, Stefan. 2010. "From Books to Xanadu to Semantic Publishing." presented at the Text and Literacy in the Digital Age, Den Haag, December 17. https://kulslide.com/download/from-books-to-xanadu-to-semantic-publishing-_59fd7ec8d64ab2f105a29592_pdf.

Grassano, Nicola, Daniele Rotolo, Joshua Hutton, Frédérique Lang, and Michael M. Hopkins. 2016. "Funding Data from Publication Acknowledgements: Coverage, Uses and Limitations." *Journal of the Association for Information Science & Technology* forthcoming. doi:10.2139/ssrn.2767348.

Groth, Paul, Andrew Gibson, and Jan Velterop. 2010. "The Anatomy of a Nanopublication." *Information Services and Use* 30 (1): 51–56.

Groza, Tudor. 2012. *Advances in Semantic Authoring and Publishing*. Vol. 13. Heidelberg: IOS Press.

Gunkel, David J. 2007. "Thinking Otherwise: Ethics, Technology and Other Subjects." *Ethics and Information Technology* 9 (3): 165–77.

———. 2012. *The Machine Question: Critical Perspectives on AI, Robots, and Ethics*. Cambridge, MA: MIT Press.

Guo, Libo. 2006. "Multimodality in a Biology Textbook." In *Multimodal Discourse Analysis: Systemic-Functional Perspectives*, edited by Kay O'Halloran, 196–219. London: Continuum.

Hall, Gary. 2008. *Digitize This Book!: The Politics of New Media, or Why We Need Open Access Now*. Minneapolis: University of Minnesota Press.

———. 2013. "The Unbound Book: Academic Publishing in the Age of the Infinite Archive." *Journal of Visual Culture* 12 (3): 490–507. doi:10.1177/1470412913502032.

———. 2015. "Culture Machine Liquid Books." http://liquidbooks.pbworks.com.

Hall, Gary, and Mark Amerika. 2011. "Force of Binding: On Liquid, Living Books (Version 2.0: Mark Amerika Mix)." *Remixthebook*. May. http://www.remixthebook.com/force-of-binding-on-liquid-living-books-version-2-0-mark-amerika-mix.

Hall, Gary, and Clare Birchall. 2009. "New Cultural Studies: The Liquid Theory Reader." *Culture Machine* 10.

Hall, Gary, Kamila Kuc, and Joanna Zylinska. 2015. "A Guide to Open and Hybrid Publishing." Europeana Space. https://drive.google.com/file/d/0B-OGUrkemSMiNoJQbldjNlNNUoU/view.

Hall, Gary, Joanna Zylinska, and Clare Birchall. 2011. "Living Books About Life Home." http://www.livingbooksaboutlife.org/.

Halliday, Michael. 1978. *Language as Social Semiotic: The Social Interpretation of Language and Meaning*. Baltimore: University Park Press.

Halliday, Michael, and Ruqaiya Hasan. 1985. *Language, Context, and Text: Aspects of Language in a Social-Semiotic Perspective*. Geelong, Victoria: Deakin University Press.

Halliday, Michael, and James R. Martin. 1996. *Writing Science Literacy and Discursive Power*. London: Falmer Press.

Hammond, Tony, Timo Hannay, and Ben Lund. 2004. "The Role of RSS in Science Publishing: Syndication and Annotation on the Web." *D-Lib Magazine* 10 (12): 1082–9873.

Haraway, Donna J. 1991. *Simians, Cyborgs, and Women: The Reinvention of Nature*. New York: Routledge.

Harmsze, Frédérique-Anne Pacifique. 2000. *A Modular Structure for Scientific Articles in an Electronic Environment*. Amsterdam: Self-published.

Harmsze, Frédérique-Anne Pacifique, and Joost G. Kircz. 1998. "Form and Content in the Electronic Age." In *Proceedings. Socioeconomic Dimensions of Electronic Publishing Workshop*, 43–49. Piscataway: IEEE. doi:10.1109/SEDEP.1998.730707.

Harmsze, Frédérique-Anne Pacifique, Maarten van der Tol, and Joost G. Kircz. 1999. "A Modular Structure for Electronic Scientific Articles." In *Conferentie Informatiewetenschap*

1999, 2–9. Amsterdam. http://www.science.uva.nl/projects/commphys/papers/infwet/infwet.html.

Hayward, Susan. 2013. "Digital Cinema/Post-Digital Cinema." In *Cinema Studies: The Key Concepts*, edited by Susan Hayward, 104–8. New York: Routledge.

Heath, Tom, and Christian Bizer. 2011. *Linked Data: Evolving the Web into a Global Data Space*. Edited by James Hendler. Vol. 1. 1. Williston: Morgan & Claypool.

Hendler, Jim. 2013. "Broad Data: Exploring the Emerging Web of Data." *Big Data* 1 (1): 18–20. doi:10.1089/big.2013.1506.

Herb, Ulrich. 2017. "Open Access Zwischen Revolution Und Goldesel." *Information – Wissenschaft & Praxis* 68 (1): 1–10. doi:10.1515/iwp-2017-0004.

Herb, Ulrich, and Joachim Schöpfel, eds. 2018. *Open Divide? Critical Studies on Open Access*. Sacramento: Litwin Books.

van den Heuvel, Henk, René van Horik, Eric Sanders, Stef Scagliola, and Paula Witkamp. 2010. "The VeteranTapes: Research Corpus, Fragment Processing Tool, and Enhanced Publications for the E-Humanities." In *Proceedings of the International Conference on Language Resources and Evaluation*, 2687–92. Valletta: European Language Resource Association. http://hdl.handle.net/2066/85921.

Hey, Tony, Stewart Tansley, and Kristin Tolle. 2009. *The Fourth Paradigm: Data-Intensive Scientific Discovery*. Redmond: Microsoft Research.

Hinsen, Konrad, Konstantin Läufer, and George K. Thiruvathukal. 2009. "Essential Tools: Version Control Systems." *Computing in Science & Engineering* 11 (6): 84–91. doi:10.1109/MCSE.2009.194.

Hitchcock, Steve M., Les A. Carr, and Wendy Hall. 1996. "A Survey of STM Online Journals 1990–95: The Calm Before the Storm." ELP2/35. London: JISC. http://eprints.soton.ac.uk/250742/1/survey.html.

Hogenaar, Arjan. 2009. "Enhancing Scientific Communication Through Aggregated Publications Environments." *Ariadne*, no. 61. http://www.ariadne.ac.uk/issue61/hogenaar.

Hogenaar, Arjan, and Maarten Hoogerwerf. 2009. "Sample Datasets and Demonstrator." In *Enhanced Publications. Linking Publications and Research Data in Digital Repositories*, edited by Marjan Vernooy-Gerritsen, 133–56. Amsterdam: Amsterdam University Press.

Holl, Andras. 2012. "Information Bulletin on Variable Stars and Novel Services for an Enhanced Publication." *D-Lib Magazine* 18 (5/6). doi:10.1045/may2012-holl.

Holtermann, Sabine. 2017. "Changing Books, Changing Roles: The Role of the Academic Book Publisher in the Digital Age." Master thesis, Leiden: Leiden University. https://openaccess.leidenuniv.nl/handle/1887/47746.

Hoogerwerf, Maarten. 2009. "Durable Enhanced Publications." In *Proceedings of the African Digital Scholarship Curation Conference*. Vol. 2009. Pretoria: University of Pretoria. http://www.ais.up.ac.za/digi/docs/hoogerwerf_paper.pdf.

Humphreys, Alex, Christina Spencer, Laura Brown, Matthew Loy, and Ronald Snyder. 2017. "Reimagining the Digital Monograph: Design Thinking to Build New Tools for Research." JSTOR Labs Report. JSTOR.

Hunter, Jane. 2006. "Scientific Models: A User-Oriented Approach to the Integration of Scientific Data and Digital Libraries." In *VALA2006*, 1–16. Melbourne.

———. 2008. "Scientific Publication Packages Selective Approach to the Communication and Archival of Scientific Output." *International Journal of Digital Curation* 1: 33–52. doi:10.2218/ijdc.v1i1.4.

Hunter, Jane, and Anna Gerber. 2009. "LORE: A Compound Object Authoring and Publishing Tool for Literary Scholars Based on the FRBR." In *4th International Conference on Open Repositories*. Georgia Institute of Technology. http://hdl.handle.net/1853/28466.

———. 2011. "The Aus-E-Lit Project: Advanced EResearch Services for Scholars of Australian Literature." In *VALA2010*. Melbourne.

Hunter, Jane, and Carl Lagoze. 2001. "Combining RDF and XML Schemas to Enhance Interoperability Between Metadata Application Profiles." In *Proceedings of the 10th International Conference on World Wide Web*, 457–66. New York: ACM. doi:10.1145/371920.372100.

Hunter, Jane, Kwok Cheung, Anna Lashtabeg, and John Drennan. 2008. "SCOPE: A Scientific Compound Object Publishing and Editing System." *International Journal of Digital Curation* 3 (2): 4–18. doi:10.2218/ijdc.v3i2.55.

Hunter, Philip. 2001. "The Management of Content: Universities and the Electronic Publishing Revolution." *Ariadne*, no. 28. http://www.ariadne.ac.uk/issue28/cms.

Hybrid Publishing Consortium. 2015. *A-Machine*. http://a-machine.net/.

Institute for the Future of the Book. 2008. "Mission." *Institute for the Future of the Book*. http://www.futureofthebook.org/mission.html.

Institute of Network Cultures. 2011. *The Unbound Book Conference Report*. Amsterdam: Hogeschool van Amsterdam. http://networkcultures.org/blog/publication/the-unbound-book-conference-report/.

———. 2017. "Postdigital Publishing." Amsterdam. http://hdl.handle.net/20.500.11884/388c0b99-f7a0-4246-a956-ff84925900df.

Ishizuka, Hidehiro. 1997. "Author-Friendly Electronic Submission to SGML-Based Academic Journal." In *Proceedings of International Symposium on Research, Development and Practice in Digital Libraries 1997: ISDL'97, November 18–21, 1997, Tsukuba, Ibaraki, Japan*, 209. University of Library and Information Science. http://www.dl.slis.tsukuba.ac.jp/ISDL97/proceedings/ishizuka/ishizuka.html.

Jackson, Korey. 2014. "More Than Gatekeeping Close-up on Open Access Evaluation in the Humanities." *College & Research Libraries News* 75 (10): 542–45. http://crln.acrl.org/content/75/10/542.

Jankowski, Nicholas W., and Steve Jones. 2013. "Scholarly Publishing and the Internet: A NM&S Themed Section." *New Media & Society* 15 (3): 345–58.

Jankowski, Nicholas W., Andrea Scharnhorst, Clifford Tatum, and Zuotian Tatum. 2012. "Enhancing Scholarly Publications: Developing Hybrid Monographs in the Humanities and Social Sciences." SSRN Scholarly Paper 1982380. Rochester, NY: Social Science Research Network.

Jansen, Bernard J., and Soo Young Rieh. 2010. "The Seventeen Theoretical Constructs of Information Searching and Information Retrieval." *Journal of the Association for Information Science & Technology* 61 (8): 1517–34.

Jewitt, Carey. 2011. "Different Approaches to Multimodality." In *The Routledge Handbook of Multimodal Analysis*, edited by Carey Jewitt, 31–43. London; New York: Routledge.

———. 2013. "What Next for Multimodality." In *The Routledge Handbook of Multimodal Analysis*, edited by Carey Jewitt, 450–55. London; New York: Routledge.

———. 2014. "Multimodal Approaches." In *Interactions, Images and Texts: A Reader in Multimodality*, edited by Sigrid Norris and Carmen Daniela Maier, 11:125–34. Boston: De Gruyter Mouton.

JISC. 2013. "Implementing a Virtual Research Environment (VRE)." https://www.jisc.ac.uk/guides/implementing-a-virtual-research-environment-vre.

Johnson, Rick. 2001. "Declaring Independence: A Guide to Creating Community-Controlled Science Journals." SPARC (the Scholarly Publishing & Academic Resources Coalition).

jupytercon. 2017. "Writing Professional Documents for the 21st Century with Authorea: JupyterCon, August 22 - 25, 2017, New York, NY." *Jupytercon*. https://conferences.oreilly.com/jupyter/jup-ny-2017/public/schedule/detail/63297.

Kaden, Ben, and Michael Kleineberg. 2017. "Zur Situation des digitalen geisteswissenschaftlichen Publizierens. Erfahrungen aus dem DFG-Projekt 'Future Publications in den Humanities'. " *Bibliothek Forschung und Praxis* 41 (1): 7–14.

Karisiddappa, C. R., and Lakshmana Moorthy. 1996. "Electronic Publishing: Impact and Implications on Library and Information Centres." In *Digital Libraries: Dynamic Storehouse of Digitized Information: Papers Presented at the SIS'96 15th Annual Convention and Conference 18–20 January, 1996 Bangalore*, 15:15. Taylor & Francis.

Keller, Alice. 2001. "Future Development of Electronic Journals: A Delphi Survey." *Electronic Library, The* 19 (6): 383–96. doi:10.1108/02640470110412008.

Kennedy, Eamonn. 2003. "A Framework for Academic Electronic Journal Publications." Dublin: Trinity College Dublin. http://hdl.handle.net/2262/839.

Kery, Mary Beth, Marissa Radensky, Mahima Arya, Bonnie E. John, and Brad A. Myers. 2018. "The Story in the Notebook: Exploratory Data Science Using a Literate Programming Tool." In *Proceedings CHI'2017: Human Factors in Computing Systems*. New York: ACM.

Key Perspectives. 2010. "Data Dimensions: Disciplinary Differences in Research Data Sharing, Reuse and Long Term Viability." Edinburgh: DCC. http://hdl.handle.net/1842/3364.

King, Ross D., Jem Rowland, Stephen G. Oliver, Michael Young, Wayne Aubrey, Emma Byrne, Maria Liakata, et al. 2009. "The Automation of Science." *Science* 324 (5923): 85–89. doi:10.1126/science.1165620.

Kircz, Joost G. 1998. "Modularity: The Next Form of Scientific Information Presentation?" *Journal of Documentation* 54 (2): 210–35. doi:10.1108/EUM0000000007185.

———. 2001a. "New Practices for Electronic Publishing: How to Maintain Quality and Guarantee Integrity." In *Proceedings of the Second ICSU/-UNESCO International Conference on Electronic Publishing in Science, París*, 19–23. Paris: UNESCO.

———. 2001b. "New Practices for Electronic Publishing 1: Will the Scientific Paper Keep Its Form?" *Learned Publishing* 14 (4): 265–72. doi:10.1087/095315101753141365.

———. 2002. "New Practices for Electronic Publishing 2: New Forms of the Scientific Paper." *Learned Publishing* 15 (1): 27–32. doi:10.1087/095315102753303652.

Kircz, Joost G., and Frédérique-Anne Pacifique Harmsze. 2000. "Modular Scenarios in the Electronic Age." In *Proceedings Conferentie Informatiewetenschap 2000*, 31–43. De Doelen.

Kitamura, Keiko, and John J. Leggett. 1996. "Representing Ancient Books for Human Science Research Based on a Hypermedia Model." In *Proceedings of HICSS-29: 29th Hawaii International Conference on System Sciences*, 2:147–54. Piscataway: IEEE. doi:10.1109/HICSS.1996.495393.

Knorr-Cetina, Karin. 1999. *Epistemic Cultures: How the Sciences Make Knowledge*. Cambridge: Harvard University Press.

Knuth, Donald E. 1984. "Literate Programming." *The Computer Journal* 27 (2): 97–111. doi:10.1093/comjnl/27.2.97.

Kobos, Mateusz, Lukasz Bolikowski, Marek Horst, Paolo Manghi, Natalia Manola, and Jochen Schirrwagen. 2014. "Information Inference in Scholarly Communication Infrastructures: The OpenAIREplus Project Experience." *Procedia Computer Science* 38: 92–99. doi:10.1016/j.procs.2014.10.016.

Koninklijke Bibliotheek. 2006. "DARE." https://www.kb.nl/en/organization/research-expertise/research-on-digitisation-and-digital-preservation/completed-projects/dare.

Koukounidou, Vasiliki. 2017. "OpenAIRE: Supporting the H2020 Open Access Mandate." In *Expanding Perspectives on Open Science: Communities, Cultures and Diversity in Concepts and Practices: Proceedings of the 21st International Conference on Electronic Publishing*, 56. IOS Press.

Krämer, Sybille. 2003. "Textualität, Visualität und Episteme. Über ihren Zusammenhang in der frühen Neuzeit." In *Text und Wissen: technologische und anthropologische Aspekte*, edited by Renate Lachmann, 17–27. Tübingen: Gunter Narr.

Kreitzberg, Charles B. 1989. "Designing the Electronic Book: Human Psychology and Information Structures for Hypermedia." In *Proceedings of the Third International Conference on Human-Computer Interaction on Designing and Using Human-Computer Interfaces and Knowledge Based Systems*, 457–464. Boston: Elsevier.

Kress, Gunther. 1996. *Before Writing: Rethinking the Paths to Literacy*. London: Taylor & Francis.

———. 2000. "Text as the Punctuation of Semiosis: Pulling at Some Threads." In *Intertextuality and the Media: From Genre to Everyday Life*, edited by Ulrike Hanna Meinhof and Jonathan Smith, 132–54. Manchester: Manchester University Press.

———. 2010. *Multimodality: A Social Semiotic Approach to Contemporary Communication*. London; New York: Routledge.

———. 2013. "What Is Mode?" In *The Routledge Handbook of Multimodal Analysis*, edited by Carey Jewitt, 2nd ed., 54–67. New York: Routledge.

Kress, Gunther, and Theo van Leeuwen. 2001. *Multimodal Discourse*. London; New York: Bloomsbury Academic.

———. 2002. "Colour as a Semiotic Mode: Notes for a Grammar of Colour." *Visual Communication* 1 (3): 343–68. doi:10.1177/147035720200100306.

Kuc, Kamila, and Joanna Zylinska. 2016. *Photoremediations: A Reader*. London: Open Humanities Press.

Kuhn, Tobias. 2013. "Nanobrowser." http://nanobrowser.inn.ac.

———. 2015. "Science Bots: A Model for the Future of Scientific Computation?" In *Proceedings of the 24th International Conference on World Wide Web Companion*, 1061–2. International World Wide Web Conferences Steering Committee.

Kuhn, Tobias, and Michel Dumontier. 2014. "Trusty URIs: Verifiable, Immutable, and Permanent Digital Artifacts for Linked Data." In *The Semantic Web: Trends and Challenges*, 8465:395–410. Lecture Notes in Computer Science. Heidelberg: Springer. doi:10.1007/978-3-319-07443-6_27.

Kuhn, Tobias, and Michael Krauthammer. 2012. "Underspecified Scientific Claims in Nanopublications." *ArXiv Preprint* 1209 (1483).

Kuhn, Tobias, Paolo Emilio Barbano, Mate Levente Nagy, and Michael Krauthammer. 2013. "Broadening the Scope of Nanopublications." In *The Semantic Web: Semantics and Big Data*, 487–501. Lecture Notes in Computer Science. Berlin, Heidelberg: Springer. doi:10.1007/978-3-642-38288-8_33.

Kuhn, Tobias, Christine Chichester, Michel Dumontier, and Michael Krauthammer. 2015. "Publishing Without Publishers: A Decentralized Approach to Dissemination, Retrieval, and Archiving of Data." In *The Semantic Web - ISWC 2015*, 656–72. Lecture Notes in Computer Science. Springer. doi:10.1007/978-3-319-25007-6_38.

La Manna, Manfredi, and Jean Young. 2002. "The Electronic Society for Social Scientists: From Journals as Documents to Journals as Knowledge Exchanges." *Interlending & Document Supply* 30 (4): 178–82. doi:10.1108/02641610210452475.

Labtiva Inc. 2015. "ReadCube Enhanced PDF." https://www.readcube.com/enhancedpdf.

Lagoze, Carl. 2009. "The OreChem Project: Integrating Chemistry Scholarship with the Semantic Web and Web 2.0." In *WebSci'09: Society On-Line*, 18–20. http://dsc.soic.indiana.edu/publications/The%20oreChem%20Project.pdf.

Lagoze, Carl, and Jane Hunter. 2006. "The ABC Ontology and Model." *Journal of Digital Information* 2 (2).

Lagoze, Carl, and Herbert Van de Sompel. 2007. "Compound Information Objects: The OAI-ORE Perspective." Open Archive Initiative.

Lagoze, Carl, Jane Hunter, and Dan Brickley. 2000. "An Event-Aware Model for Metadata Interoperability." In *Research and Advanced Technology for Digital Libraries*, 103–16. Berlin, Heidelberg: Springer. doi:10.1007/3-540-45268-0_10.

Lagoze, Carl, Herbert Van de Sompel, Michael Nelson, Simeon Warner, Robert Sanderson, and Pete Johnston. 2012. "A Web-Based Resource Model for Scholarship 2.0: Object Reuse & Exchange." *Concurrency and Computation: Practice and Experience* 24 (18): 2221–40. doi:10.1002/cpe.1594.

Larman, Craig. 2004. *Agile and Iterative Development: A Manager's Guide*. Agile Computer-Software Development Series. Boston, MA.: Addison-Wesley.

Latar, Noam Lemelshtrich. 2015. "The Robot Journalist in the Age of Social Physics: The End of Human Journalism?" In *The New World of Transitioned Media*, edited by Gali Einav, 65–80. The Economics of Information, Communication, and Entertainment. Berlin: Springer. doi:10.1007/978-3-319-09009-2_6.

Latour, Bruno. 1993. *We Have Never Been Modern*. New York, London: Harvester Wheatsheaf.

———. 2014. "An Inquiry into the Modes of Existence." *Modes of Existence*. http://www.modesofexistence.org.

Latour, Bruno, and Heather Davis. 2014. "The Amoderns: Thoughts on an Impossible Project." *Amodern*. October. http://amodern.net/article/amoderns-impossible-project/.

Leclercq, Christophe. 2011. "Summary of the AiME Project. An Inquiry into Modes of Existence." *Bruno-Latour.fr*. October 24. http://www.bruno-latour.fr/node/328.

van Leeuwen, Theo. 2005. *Introducing Social Semiotics*. London: Routledge.

Lemke, Jay. 2003. "Mathematics in the Middle: Measure, Picture, Gesture, Sign, and Word." In *Educational Perspectives on Mathematics as Semiosis: From Thinking to Interpreting to Knowing*, edited by Myrdene Anderson, 215–34. New Directions in the Teaching of Mathematics 1. Brooklyn: Legas.

———. 2005. "Multimedia Genres and Traversals." *Folia Linguistica* 39 (1–2): 45–56. doi:10.1515/flin.2005.39.1-2.45.

Levin, Nadine, and Sabina Leonelli. 2017. "How Does One "Open" Science? Questions of Value in Biological Research." *Science, Technology, & Human Values* 42 (2): 280–305. doi:10.1177/0162243916672071.

Li, Gangmin, Victoria Uren, Enrico Motta, Simon Buckingham Shum, and John Domingue. 2002. "ClaiMaker: Weaving a Semantic Web of Research Papers." In *The Semantic Web 2002*, edited by Ian Horrocks and James Hendler, 436–41. Lecture Notes in Computer Science. Berlin, Heidelberg: Springer. doi:10.1007/3-540-48005-6_37.

Licastro, Amanda. 2017. "Teaching Empathy Through Virtual Reality." In *Digital Humanities 2017 Book of Abstracts*, 504. Montréal, Canada: McGill University. https://dh2017.adho.org/abstracts/375/375.pdf.

Liew, Chee Sun, Malcolm P. Atkinson, Michelle Galea, Tan Fong Ang, Paul Martin, and Jano I. Van Hemert. 2016. "Scientific Workflows: Moving Across Paradigms." *ACM Computing Surveys* 49 (4): 66:1–66:39. doi:10.1145/3012429.

Liew, Chern Li, and Schubert Foo. 1999. "Derivation of Interaction Environment and Information Object Properties for Enhanced Integrated Access and Value-Adding to Electronic Documents." *Aslib Proceedings* 51 (8): 256–68. doi:10.1108/EUM0000000006985.

———. 2001. "Electronic Documents: What Lies Ahead." In *The Proceedings of the 4th International Conference of Asian Digital Libraries. Bangalore, IIIT-B*. Citeseer. doi:10.1.1.476.5934.

Liu, Lei, Rares Vernica, Tamir Hassan, Niranjan Damera Venkata, Yang Lei, Jian Fan, Jerry Liu, Steven J. Simske, and Shanchan Wu. 2016. "METIS: A Multi-Faceted Hybrid Book Learning Platform." In *Proceedings of the 2016 ACM Symposium on Document Engineering*, 31–34. DocEng "16. New York, NY, USA: ACM. doi:10.1145/2960811.2967155.

Lobe, Adrian. 2015. "Automatisierter Journalismus: Nehmen Roboter Journalisten den Job weg?" *Frankfurter Allgemeine Zeitung*, April 17. http://www.faz.net/aktuell/feuilleton/medien/automatisierter-journalismus-nehmen-roboter-allen-journalisten-den-job-weg-13542074.html.

Long, Do, and William Mobley. 2015. "Single Figure Publications: Towards a Novel Alternative Format for Scholarly Communication." *F1000Research*; London 4. doi:10.12688/f1000research.6742.1.

Lopes, Pedro, Pedro Sernadela, and José Luís Oliveira. 2013. "Exploring Nanopublishing with COEUS." In *Proceedings of the 6th International Workshop on Semantic Web Applications and Tools for Life Sciences*. Edinburgh: CEUR. http://ceur-ws.org/Vol-1114/.

Lord, Phillip, Simon Cockell, and Robert Stevens. 2012. "Three Steps to Heaven: Semantic Publishing in a Real World Workflow." *Future Internet* 4 (4): 1004–15. doi:10.3390/fi4041004.

Lourdi, Irene, Christos Papatheodorou, and Mara Nikolaidou. 2007. "A Multi-Layer Metadata Schema for Digital Folklore Collections." *Journal of Information Science* 33 (2): 197–213. doi:10.1177/0165551506070711.

Ludovico, Alessandro. 2013. *Post-Digital Print: The Mutation of Publishing Since 1894*. 2nd ed. Onomatopee; 77. Eindhoven: Onomatopee.

———. 2015. "Post-Digital Publishing." *Post-Digital Culture*. http://post-digital-culture.org/.

Lyon, Liz. 2009. "Open Science at Web-Scale: Optimising Participation and Predictive Potential." November. JISC.

Manghi, Paolo, Lukasz Bolikowski, Natalia Manola, Jochen Schirrwagen, and Tim Smith. 2012. "OpenAIREplus: The European Scholarly Communication Data Infrastructure." *D-Lib Magazine* 18 (9/10). doi:10.1045/september2012-manghi.

Manghi, Paolo, Nikos Houssos, Marko Mikulicic, and Brigitte Jörg. 2012. "The Data Model of the OpenAIRE Scientific Communication E-Infrastructure." In *Metadata and Semantics Research*, 168–80. Berlin, Heidelberg: Springer. doi:10.1007/978-3-642-35233-1_18.

Manghi, Paolo, Natalia Manola, Wolfram Horstmann, and Dale Peters. 2010. "An Infrastructure for Managing EC Funded Research Output. The OpenAIRE Project." *The Grey Journal* 6 (1): 31–41.

Marcondes, Carlos. 2005. "From Scientific Communication to Public Knowledge: The Scientific Article Web Published as a Knowledge Base." In *Proceedings of the 9th ICCC International Conference on Electronic Publishing*. Leuven: Peeters Publishing.

Marcondes, Carlos H., Luciana R. Malheiros, and Leonardo C. da Costa. 2014. "A Semantic Model for Scholarly Electronic Publishing in Biomedical Sciences." *Semantic Web Journal* 5 (4): 313–34.

Markowetz, Florian. 2015. "Five Selfish Reasons to Work Reproducibly." *Genome Biology* 16 (December): 274. doi:10.1186/s13059-015-0850-7.

Matthews, Brian, Vasily Bunakov, Catherine Jones, and Shirley Crompton. 2013. "Investigations as Research Objects Within Facilities Science." In *Theory and Practice of Digital Libraries 2013 Selected Workshops*, 127–40. Communications in Computer and Information Science. Berlin, Heidelberg: Springer. doi:10.1007/978-3-319-08425-1_12.

Mavers, Diane, and Will Gibson. 2012. "Mode." *Glossary of Multimodal Terms*. https://multimodalityglossary.wordpress.com/mode-2/.

Mazanek, Steffen. 2011. "Executable Papers with SHARE." https://sites.google.com/site/executablepaper/.

McAdams, Mindy, and Stephanie Berger. 2001. "Hypertext." *The Journal of Electronic Publishing* 6 (3). doi:10.3998/3336451.0006.301

McDonald, Fran, and Whitney Trettien. 2016. "Thresholds." http://openthresholds.tumblr.com.

McGann, Jerome. 1994. "The Complete Writings and Pictures of Dante Gabriel Rossetti: A Hypermedia Research Archive." *Text* 7: 95–105.

McGarry, Glenn, Peter Tolmie, Steve Benford, Chris Greenhalgh, and Alan Chamberlain. 2017. ""They're All Going Out to Something Weird": Workflow, Legacy and Metadata in the Music Production Process." In *Proceedings of the 2017 ACM Conference on Computer*

Supported Cooperative Work and Social Computing, 995–1008. CSCW "17. New York: ACM. doi:10.1145/2998181.2998325.

McIlroy, Malcom Douglas, Elliot Pinson, and Berk Tague. 1978. "Unix Time-Sharing System Forward." *The Bell System Technical Journal* 57 (6).

McLuhan, Marshall. 2002. *The Gutenberg Galaxy: The Making of Typographic Man*. Edited by Elena Lamberti and Dominique Scheffel-Dunand. Toronto: University of Toronto Press.

McPherson, Tara. 2008. "Introduction: Media Studies and the Digital Humanities." *Cinema Journal* 48 (2): 119–23. doi:10.1353/cj.0.0077.

———. 2010. "Scaling Vectors: Thoughts on the Future of Scholarly Communication." *Journal of Electronic Publishing* 13 (2). doi:10.3998/3336451.0013.208.

———. 2014. "Designing for Difference." *Differences* 25 (1): 177–88. doi:10.1215/10407391-2420039.

McWhirter, Andrew. 2015. "Film Criticism, Film Scholarship and the Video Essay." *Screen* 56 (3): 369–77. doi:10.1093/screen/hjv044.

Meade, Chris. 2013. "IF:BOOK – Future of the Book UK." http://www.ifbook.co.uk/.

Meadows, Jack. 2006. "The Users of E-Publishing and Their Communication Behaviour." In *Proceedings of the ELPUB2006 Conference on Electronic Publishing*. Sofia: IMI-BAS.

Meeks, Elijah. 2012. "Building a Scholarly Digital Object." *Digital Humanities Specialist*. March 19. https://dhs.stanford.edu/spatial-humanities/building-a-scholarly-digital-object/.

Meng, Haiyan, and Douglas Thain. 2017. "Facilitating the Reproducibility of Scientific Workflows with Execution Environment Specifications." *Procedia Computer Science*, International Conference on Computational Science, ICCS 2017, 12-14 June 2017, Zurich, Switzerland, 108 (January): 705–14. doi:10.1016/j.procs.2017.05.116.

Meng, Haiyan, Rupa Kommineni, Quan Pham, Robert Gardner, Tanu Malik, and Douglas Thain. 2015. "An Invariant Framework for Conducting Reproducible Computational Science." *Journal of Computational Science* 9 (July): 137–42. doi:10.1016/j.jocs.2015.04.012.

Mersch, Dieter. 2004. "Kunst und Sprache. Hermeneutik, Dekonstruktion und die Ästhetik des Ereignens." In *Ästhetik Erfahrung*, edited by Jörg Huber, 41–59. Wien: Ambra.

Meyer, Eric T., Monica E. Bulger, Avgousta Kyriakidou-Zacharoudiou, Lucy Power, Peter Williams, Will Venters, Melissa Terras, and Sally Wyatt. 2011. "Collaborative yet Independent: Information Practices in the Physical Sciences." 1991753. Rochester: Social Science Research Network. https://papers.ssrn.com/abstract=1991753.

Milloy, Caren, and Ellen Collins. 2016. "OAPEN-UK Final Report: A Five-Year Study into Open Access Monograph Publishing in the Humanities and Social Sciences." Final Report. JISC. https://scholarlycommunications.jiscinvolve.org/wp/2016/01/28/oapenukreport/.

MODE. 2012. "Glossary of Multimodal Terms." http://multimodalityglossary.wordpress.com/.

Mons, Barend. 2005. "Which Gene Did You Mean?" *BMC Bioinformatics* 6 (1): 142. doi:10.1186/1471-2105-6-142.

Mons, Barend, and Jan Velterop. 2009. "Nano-Publication in the E-Science Era." In *Workshop on Semantic Web Applications in Scientific Discourse (SWASD 2009)*. Vol. 523. Washington, DC: CEUR. http://ceur-ws.org/Vol-523/Mons.pdf.

Mons, Barend, Herman van Haagen, Christine Chichester, Johan T. den Dunnen, Gertjan van Ommen, Erik van Mulligen, Bharat Singh, et al. 2011. "The Value of Data." *Nature Genetics* 43 (4): 281–83. doi:10.1038/ng0411-281.

Moyle, Martin, and Panayiota Polydoratou. 2007. "Investigating Overlay Journals: Introducing the RIOJA Project." *D-Lib Magazine* 13 (9/13).

Mozilla Science Lab. 2013a. "Code as a Research Object." https://mozillascience.github.io/code-research-object/.

———. 2013b. "Code as a Research Object: A New Project." https://mozillascience.org/code-as-a-research-object-a-new-project.

Nentwich, Michael. 2003. "Cyberscience and Knowledge Representation." In *Cyberscience. Research in the Age of the Internet*, edited by Michael Nentwich, 253–315. Vienna: Austrian Academy of Sciences Press. http://www.austriaca.at/3188-7toc.
Newfield, Denise. 2013. "Transformation, Transduction and the Transmodal Moment." In *The Routledge Handbook of Multimodal Analysis*, edited by Carey Jewitt, 2nd ed., 100–114. London, New York: Routledge.
Newman, Paul, and Peter Corke. 2009. "Editorial Data Papers of High Quality Data Sets." *The International Journal of Robotics Research* 28 (5): 587–87. doi:10.1177/0278364909104283.
Neylon, Cameron. 2009. "Head in the Clouds: Re-Imagining the Experimental Laboratory Record for the Web-Based Networked World." *Automated Experimentation* 1 (January): 3. doi:10.1186/1759-4499-1-3.
———. 2012. "OA and the UK Humanities & Social Sciences: Wrong Risks and Missed Opportunities." *Science in the Open*. December 12. http://cameronneylon.net/blog/oa-and-the-uk-humanities-social-sciences-wrong-risks-and-missed-opportunities/.
van Noorden, Richard. 2014. "Publishers Withdraw More Than 120 Gibberish Papers." *Nature News*, February. doi:10.1038/nature.2014.14763.
Norris, Sigrid. 2009. "Modal Density and Modal Configurations." In *The Routledge Handbook of Multimodal Analysis*, edited by Carey Jewitt, 78–91. New York: Routledge.
———. 2011. *Identity in (Inter)Action, Introducing Multimodal (Inter)Action Analysis*. Berlin, Boston: De Gruyter Mouton.
Nowviskie, Bethany. 2015. "Digital Humanities in the Anthropocene." *Digital Scholarship in the Humanities* 30 (suppl_1): i4–i15. doi:10.1093/llc/fqv015.
Nüst, Daniel, Markus Konkol, Edzer Pebesma, Christian Kray, Stephanie Klötgen, Marc Schutzeichel, Jörg Lorenz, Holger Przibytzin, and Dirk Kussmann. 2016. "Opening Reproducible Research." In *EGU General Assembly Conference Abstracts*, 18:EPSC2016–7396. Vienna: SAO/NASA Astrophysics Data System. http://adsabs.harvard.edu/abs/2016EGUGA..18.7396N.
Nüst, Daniel, Markus Konkol, Edzer Pebesma, Christian Kray, Marc Schutzeichel, Holger Przibytzin, and Jörg Lorenz. 2017. "Opening the Publication Process with Executable Research Compendia." *D-Lib Magazine* 23 (1/2). doi:10.1045/january2017-nuest.
O'Halloran, Kay. 2004. *Multimodal Discourse Analysis: Systemic Functional Perspectives*. London; New York: Continuum.
———. 2008. *Mathematical Discourse: Language, Symbolism and Visual Images*. London, New York: Continuum.
———. 2011. "Multimodal Discourse Analysis." In *The Bloomsbury Companion to Discourse Analysis*, edited by Ken Hyland and Brian Paltridge, 120–37. Continuum Companions. London; New York: Bloomsbury Academic.
O'Halloran, Kay, and Victor Lim Fei. 2014. "Systemic Functional Multimodal Discourse Analysis." In *Interactions, Images and Texts: A Reader in Multimodality*, edited by Sigrid Norris and Carmen Daniela Maier, 11:135–50. Boston: de Gruyter Mouton.
O'Halloran, Kay, and Bradley A. Smith. 2011. "Multimodal Studies." In *Multimodal Studies: Exploring Issues and Domains*, edited by Kay O'Halloran and Bradley A. Smith, 1–15. Chichester: Routledge.
O'Hearn, JoLynn, May Chau, Laurie Bridges, Bonnie E. Avery, Jane Nichols, Ruth Vondracek, and Margaret Mellinger. 2017. "Future of the Journal."
O'Toole, Michael. 2006. "Opera Ludentes: The Sydney Opera House at Work and Play." In *Multimodal Discourse Analysis: Systemic-Functional Perspectives*, edited by Kay O'Halloran, 11–28. London: Continuum.
Odewahn, Andrew. 2015. "Embracing Jupyter Notebooks at O'Reilly." *O'Reilly Media*. May 7. https://beta.oreilly.com/ideas/jupyter-at-oreilly.

Odewahn, Andrew, Kyle Kelley, and Rune Madsen. 2014. "Publishing Workflows for Jupyter." http://odewahn.github.io/publishing-workflows-for-jupyter.

Open Humanities Press. 2015. "Open Humanities Press." http://openhumanitiespress.org/.

Open Knowledge Foundation. 2015. "The Open Definition – Open Definition – Defining Open in Open Data, Open Content and Open Knowledge." http://opendefinition.org/.

Open Phacts. 2012. "The Open PHACTS Nanopublication Guidelines." http://www.nanopub.org/guidelines/1.8/.

OpenAIRE plus, ed. 2013. "OpenAIRE Guidelines 3.0 Documentation." https://guidelines.openaire.eu/en/latest/.

Ossenbruggen, Jacco, Lynda Hardman, and Lloyd Rutledge. 2006. "Hypermedia and the Semantic Web: A Research Agenda." *Journal of Digital Information* 3 (1). http://journals.tdl.org/jodi/article/viewArticle/78/77.

Owen, John Mackenzie. 2002. "The New Dissemination of Knowledge: Digital Libraries and Institutional Roles in Scholarly Publishing." *Journal of Economic Methodology* 9 (3): 275–88. doi:10.1080/13501780220000015113.

———. 2006. *The Scientific Article in the Age of Digitization*. Dordrecht: Springer.

Palmer, Carole L., Lauren C. Teffeau, Carrie M. Pirmann, and OCLC Research. 2009. "Scholarly Information Practices in the Online Environment Themes from the Literature and Implications for Library Service Development." Dublin, Ohio: OCLC Research. http://www.oclc.org/research/publications/library/2009/2009-02.pdf.

Pampel, Heinz, and Sünje Dallmeier-Tiessen. 2014. "Open Research Data: From Vision to Practice." In *Opening Science*, edited by Sönke Bartling and Sascha Friesike, 213–24. Berlin: Springer. doi:10.1007/978-3-319-00026-8_14.

Pan, Ding. 2010. "An Integrative Framework for Continuous Knowledge Discovery." *Journal of Convergence Information Technology* 5 (3). doi:10.1.1.306.9546.

Parsons, Mark A., and Peter A. Fox. 2013. "Is Data Publication the Right Metaphor?" *Data Science Journal* 12: WDS32–WDS46.

Pavlopoulos, Georgios A., Evangelos Pafilis, Michael Kuhn, Sean D. Hooper, and Reinhard Schneider. 2009. "OnTheFly: A Tool for Automated Document-Based Text Annotation, Data Linking and Network Generation." *Bioinformatics* 25 (7): 977–78. doi:10.1093/bioinformatics/btp081.

Pebesma, Edzer, Daniel Nüst, and Roger Bivand. 2012. "The R Software Environment in Reproducible Geoscientific Research." *Eos, Transactions American Geophysical Union* 93 (16): 163–63. doi:10.1029/2012EO160003.

Peek, Robin P., and Jeffrey P. Pomerantz. 1998. "Electronic Scholarly Journal Publishing." *Annual Review of Information Science and Technology* 33.

Pellegrini, Tassilo. 2017. "Semantic Metadata in the Publishing Industry – Technological Achievements and Economic Implications." *Electronic Markets; Heidelberg* 27 (1): 9–20. doi:10.1007/s12525-016-0238-x.

Penev, Lyubomir, Donat Agosti, Teodor Georgiev, Terry Catapano, Jeremy Miller, Vladimir Blagoderov, David Roberts, Vincent Smith, Irina Brake, and Simon Ryrcroft. 2010. "Semantic Tagging of and Semantic Enhancements to Systematics Papers: ZooKeys Working Examples." *ZooKeys* 50 (1). doi:10.3897/zookeys.50.538.

Perez, Fernando, and Brian Granger. 2013. "An Open Source Framework for Interactive, Collaborative and Reproducible Scientific Computing and Education." https://ipython.org/_static/sloangrant/sloan-grant.html.

Perkel, Jeffrey M. 2018. "Data visualization tools drive interactivity and reproducibility in online publishing." *Nature* 554 (7690): 133–34. doi:10.1038/d41586-018-01322-9.

Peroni, Silvio. 2014a. "The Digital Publishing Revolution." In *Semantic Web Technologies and Legal Scholarly Publishing*, edited by Silvio Peroni, 7–43. Law, Governance and Technology Series 15. Berlin: Springer.

———. 2014b. "The Semantic Publishing and Referencing Ontologies." In *Semantic Web Technologies and Legal Scholarly Publishing*, 121–93. Law, Governance and Technology Series 15. Berlin: Springer.

Peters, Dale, and Norbert Lossau. 2009. "DRIVER: Building a Sustainable Infrastructure for Global Repositories." *The Electronic Library* 29 (2): 249–60.

Pettifer, Steve, Philip McDermott, James Marsh, David Thorne, A. Villeger, and Teresa K. Attwood. 2011. "Ceci n'est pas un hamburger: Modelling and Representing the Scholarly Article." *Learned Publishing* 24 (3): 207–20.

Pfaff, Claas-Thido, Birgitta König-Ries, Anne C. Lang, Sophia Ratcliffe, Christian Wirth, Xingxing Man, and Karin Nadrowski. 2015. "RBEFdata: Documenting Data Exchange and Analysis for a Collaborative Data Management Platform." *Ecology and Evolution* 5 (14): 2890–7. doi:10.1002/ece3.1547.

Pham, Quan, Severin Thaler, Tanu Malik, Ian Foster, and Boris Glavic. 2015. "Sharing and Reproducing Database Applications." *Proceedings of the VLDB Endowment* 8 (12): 1988–91. doi:10.14778/2824032.2824118.

Phelps, Thomas A., and Robert Wilensky. 1996. "Toward Active, Extensible, Networked Documents: Multivalent Architecture and Applications." In *Proceedings of the First ACM International Conference on Digital Libraries*, 9:100–108. New York: ACM. doi:10.1145/226931.226951.

van der Poel, K. G. 2007. "Verkenning van de interesse van wetenschappelijke onderzoekers." Utrecht: Surf Foundation.

Poo, Mu-ming, and Chung-I. Wu. 2017. "New Approaches to Publishing Scientific Reports at NSR." *National Science Review* 4 (4): 511–11. doi:10.1093/nsr/nwx073.

Poole, Alex H. 2015. "How Has Your Science Data Grown? Digital Curation and the Human Factor: A Critical Literature Review." *Archival Science* 15 (2): 101–39. doi:10.1007/s10502-014-9236-y.

Príncipe, Pedro, Najla Rettberg, Eloy Rodrigues, Mikael K. Elbæk, Jochen Schirrwagen, Nikos Houssos, Lars Holm Nielsen, and Brigitte Jörg. 2014. "OpenAIRE Guidelines: Supporting Interoperability for Literature Repositories, Data Archives and CRIS." *Procedia Computer Science*, 12th International Conference on Current Research Information Systems, 33: 92–94. doi:10.1016/j.procs.2014.06.015.

Puschmann, Cornelius, and Marco Bastos. 2015. "How Digital Are the Digital Humanities? An Analysis of Two Scholarly Blogging Platforms." *PLOS ONE* 10 (2): e0115035. doi:10.1371/journal.pone.0115035.

Puschmann, Cornelius, and Merja Mahrt. 2013. "Scholarly Blogging: A New Form of Publishing or Science Journalism 2.0." In *Science and the Internet*, edited by Alexander Tokar, Michael Beurskens, Susanne Keuneke, Merja Mahrt, Isabella Peters, Timo van Treeck, Katrin Weller, and Cornelius Puschmann, 1st ed., 171–182. Düsseldorf: Düsseldorf University Press.

Raatikainen, Panu. 2001. "Exploring Randomness and The Unknowable." *Notes of the AMS* 48 (9).

Ramsay, Stephen, and Geoffrey Rockwell. 2012. "Developing Things: Notes Toward an Epistemology of Building in the Digital Humanities." In *Debates in the Digital Humanities*, edited by Matthew K. Gold, 75–84. Minneapolis: University of Minnesota Press.

Rasch, Miriam. 2017. "State of the Art." Institute of Network Cultures. http://hdl.handle.net/20.500.11884/9c673d83-b009-4f5d-b43e-ea7b33c9ba8a.

Rees, Jonathan. 2010. "Recommendations for Independent Scholarly Publication of Data Sets." Creative Commons Workingpaper. San Francisco. http://neurocommons.org/report/data-publication.pdf.

Reilly, Susan, Wouter Schallier, Sabine Schrimpf, Eefke Smit, and Max Wilkinson. 2011. "Report on Integration of Data and Publications." http://epic.awi.de/31397/.

Renear, Allen, and Carole L. Palmer. 2009. "Strategic Reading, Ontologies, and the Future of Scientific Publishing." *Science* 325 (5942): 828–32. doi:10.1126/science.1157784.

Research Councils UK. 2015. "Big Data - Research Councils UK." http://www.rcuk.ac.uk/research/infrastructure/big-data/.

Rettberg, Najla, and Birgit Schmidt. 2012. "Repository Communities in OpenAIRE: Experiences in Building up an Open Access Infrastructure for European Research." In *Conference Papers of the 7th Open Repositories*. Edinburgh: University George Square.

de Ribaupierre, Hélène, and Gilles Falquet. 2014. "User-Centric Design and Evaluation of a Semantic Annotation Model for Scientific Documents." In *Proceedings of the 14th International Conference on Knowledge Technologies and Data-Driven Business*, 40:1–40:6. I-KNOW "14. New York: ACM. doi:10.1145/2637748.2638446.

Richards, Julian D. 2018. "Internet Archaeology and Digital Scholarly Communication." In *Cultural Heritage Infrastructures in Digital Humanities*, edited by Julian D. Richards, Agiatis Benardou, Erik Champion, Costis Dallas, and Lorna Hughes, 36–47. London: Routledge.

Robertson, Benjamin J. 2013. "The Grammatization of Scholarship." *Amodern*, no. 1 (February). http://amodern.net/article/the-grammatization-of-scholarship/.

Robertson, Tim, Markus Döring, Robert Guralnick, David Bloom, John Wieczorek, Kyle Braak, Javier Otegui, Laura Russell, and Peter Desmet. 2014. "The GBIF Integrated Publishing Toolkit: Facilitating the Efficient Publishing of Biodiversity Data on the Internet." *PLOS ONE* 9 (8). doi:10.1371/journal.pone.0102623.

Rodriguez-Gonzalez, Alejandro, Marcos Martinez-Romero, Mikel Egana Aranguren, and Mark D. Wilkinson. 2014. "Nanopublishing Clinical Diagnoses: Tracking Diagnostic Knowledge Base Content and Utilization." In *2014 IEEE 27th International Symposium on Computer-Based Medical Systems*, 335–40. Piscataway: IEEE. doi:10.1109/CBMS.2014.82.

Roos, Marco, Sean Bechhofer, Jun Zhao, Paolo Missier, David Newman, David De Roure, and M. Scott Marshall. 2010. "A Linked Data Approach to Sharing Workflows and Workflow Results." In *Leveraging Applications of Formal Methods, Verification, and Validation*, 340–54. Lecture Notes in Computer Science. Berlin, Heidelberg: Springer. doi:10.1007/978-3-642-16558-0_29.

Rowsell, Jennifer. 2013. *Working with Multimodality: Rethinking Literacy in a Digital Age*. London; New York: Routledge.

Ruiz-Iñiesta, Almudena, and Óscar Corcho. 2014. "A Review of Ontologies for Describing Scholarly and Scientific Documents." In *Proceedings of 4th Workshop on Semantic Publishing*. Vol. 1155. Anissaras: CEUR.

Sanchez, Alfredo, Yazmin Morales, and Arturo Flores. 2004. "Collaborative Environments for Digital Publishing." In *Proceedings of the Fifth Mexican International Conference in Computer Science*, 329–36. Piscataway: IEEE. doi:10.1109/ENC.2004.1342624.

Santana-Perez, Idafen, Rafael Ferreira da Silva, Mats Rynge, Ewa Deelman, María S. Pérez-Hernández, and Óscar Corcho. 2017. "Reproducibility of Execution Environments in Computational Science Using Semantics and Clouds." *Future Generation Computer Systems* 67: 354–67. doi:10.1016/j.future.2015.12.017.

Santana-Perez, Idafen, Rafael Ferreira da Silva, Mats Rynge, Ewa Deelman, María S. Pérez-Hernández, and Óscar Corcho. 2014. "A Semantic-Based Approach to Attain Reproducibility of Computational Environments in Scientific Workflows: A Case Study." In *Euro-Par 2014: Parallel Processing Workshops*, edited by Luís Lopes, Julius Žilinskas, Alexandru Costan, Roberto G. Cascella, Gabor Kecskemeti, Emmanuel Jeannot, Mario Cannataro, et al., 452–63. Lecture Notes in Computer Science. Berlin, Heidelberg: Springer. doi:10.1007/978-3-319-14325-5_39.

Saussure, Ferdinand de. 1959. *Course in General Linguistics*. New York: Philosophical Library.

Sayers, Jentery, and Craig Dietrich. 2013. "After the Document Model for Scholarly Communication: Some Considerations for Authoring with Rich Media." *Digital Studies/Le Champ Numérique* 3 (2). doi:10.16995/dscn.237.

Sayers, Jentery, Devon Elliott, Kari Kraus, Bethany Nowviskie, and William J. Turkel. 2015. "Between Bits and Atoms." In *A New Companion to Digital Humanities*, edited by Susan Schreibman, Ray Siemens, and John Unsworth, 1–21. Chichester: Wiley-Blackwell. doi:10.1002/9781118680605.ch1.

Schmidt, Nora. 2014. "Semantisches Publizieren im interdisziplinären Wissenschaftsnetzwerk. Theoretische Grundlagen und Anforderungen." Berlin: Humboldt University. https://edoc.hu-berlin.de/handle/18452/2773.

Schneider, Jodi, Paolo Ciccarese, Tim Clark, and Richard D. Boyce. 2014. "Using the Micropublications Ontology and the Open Annotation Data Model to Represent Evidence Within a Drug-Drug Interaction Knowledge Base." In *Proceedings of the 4th International Conference on Linked Science-Volume 1282*, 60–70. Aachen, Germany, Germany: CEUR.

Schneider, Jodi, Carol Collins, Lisa E. Hines, John R. Horn, and Richard D. Boyce. 2014. "Modeling Arguments in Scientific Papers to Support Pharmacists." In *ArgDiaP 2014: From Real Data to Argument Mining*. Warsaw: HAL. https://hal.archives-ouvertes.fr/hal-01076327/.

Schreibman, Susan, Ray Siemens, and John Unsworth, eds. 2016. *A New Companion to Digital Humanities*. Chichester: Wiley-Blackwell.

Sefton, Peter. 2009. "Towards Scholarly HTML." *Serials Review* 35 (3): 154–58. doi:10.1016/j.serrev.2009.05.001.

Seringhaus, Michael R., and Mark B. Gerstein. 2007. "Publishing Perishing? Towards Tomorrow's Information Architecture." *BMC Bioinformatics* 8 (January): 17. doi:10.1186/1471-2105-8-17.

Sernadela, Pedro, Eelke van der Horst, Mark Thompson, Pedro Lopes, Marco Roos, and José Luís Oliveira. 2014. "A Nanopublishing Architecture for Biomedical Data." In *8th International Conference on Practical Applications of Computational Biology & Bioinformatics (PACBB 2014)*, 277–84. Berlin, Heidelberg: Springer. doi:10.1007/978-3-319-07581-5_33.

Sernadela, Pedro, Phil Lopes, and José Luís Oliveira. 2013. "Exploring Nanopublications Integration in Pharmacovigilance Scenarios." In *2013 IEEE 15th International Conference on E-Health Networking, Applications and Services (Healthcom 2013)*, 728–30. Piscataway: IEEE. doi:10.1109/HealthCom.2013.6720773.

Shaw, Ryan, Michael Buckland, and Patrick Golden. 2013. "Open Notebook Humanities: Promise and Problems." In *Digital Humanities 2013 Book of Abstracts*. Lincoln: University of Nebraska. http://dh2013.unl.edu/abstracts/ab-297.html.

Shotton, David. 2009. "Semantic Publishing: The Coming Revolution in Scientific Journal Publishing." *Learned Publishing* 22 (2): 85–94. doi:10.1087/2009202.

———. 2012. "The Five Stars of Online Journal Articles - a Framework for Article Evaluation." *D-Lib Magazine* 18 (1/2). doi:10.1045/january2012-shotton.

Shotton, David, and Silvio Peroni. 2012. "FaBiO and CiTO: Ontologies for Describing Bibliographic Resources and Citations." *Web Semantics: Science, Services and Agents on the World Wide Web* 17 (December): 33–43. doi:10.1016/j.websem.2012.08.001.

Shotton, David, Alexandru Constantin, Silvio Peroni, Steve Pettifer, and Fabio Vitali. 2015. "The Document Components Ontology (DoCO)." *Semantic Web Journal*, no. Submitted Draft. http://www.semantic-web-journal.net/content/document-\%0020components-ontology-doco-0.

Shotton, David, Angelo Di Iorio, Silvio Peroni, Francesco Poggi, and Fabio Vitali. 2013. "Recognizing Document Components in XML-Based Academic Articles." In *Proceedings of the 2013 ACM Symposium on Document Engineering*, 181–84. ACM. doi:10.1145/2494266.2494319.

Shotton, David, Silvio Peroni, and Fabio Vitali. 2012. "Scholarly Publishing and Linked Data: Describing Roles, Statuses, Temporal and Contextual Extents." In *Proceedings of the 8th International Conference on Semantic Systems*, 9–16. New York: ACM. doi:10.1145/2362499.2362502.

Shotton, David, Katie Portwin, Graham Klyne, and Alisair Miles. 2009. "Adventures in Semantic Publishing: Exemplar Semantic Enhancements of a Research Article." *PLoS Comput Biology* 5 (4): 1–17. doi:10.1371/journal.pcbi.1000361.

Siebler, Kay. 2016. *Learning Queer Identity in the Digital Age, by Kay Siebler*. London: Palgrave Macmillan.

Sierman, Barbara, Birgit Schmidt, and Jens Ludwig. 2009. *Enhanced Publications. Linking Publications and Research Data in Digital Repositories*. Amsterdam: Amsterdam University Press. http://dare.uva.nl/document/150723.

Simukovic, Elena. 2012. "Enhanced Publications." Berlin: Humboldt Universität.

Singh, Ripudaman, Rostislav Chudoba, K. Gopal, and Carsten Koenke. 1998. "IMMJ: Interactive Multi-Media Journals in Science and Technology Prospects and Issues." *Ejournal* 8 (2).

Smith, Bradley A., Sabine Tan, Alexey Podlasov, and Kay O'Halloran. 2011. "Analyzing Multimodality in an Interactive Digital Environment: Software as a Meta-Semiotic Tool." *Social Semiotics* 21 (3): 359–80. doi:10.1080/10350330.2011.564386.

Smith, Vincent, Teodor Georgiev, Pavel Stoev, Jordan Biserkov, Jeremy Miller, Laurence Livermore, Edward Baker, et al. 2013. "Beyond Dead Trees: Integrating the Scientific Process in the Biodiversity Data Journal." *Biodiversity Data Journal* 1: e995. doi:10.3897/BDJ.1.e995.

Sofronijević, Adam. 2012. "Publishing Against the Machine: A New Format of Academic Expression for the New Scientist." In *Science and the Internet*, edited by Alexander Tokar, Michael Beurskens, Susanne Keuneke, Merja Mahrt, Isabella Peters, Cornelius Puschmann, Timo van Treeck, and Katrin Weller, 251–62. Düsseldorf: Düsseldorf University Press.

Sofronijević, Adam, and Aleksandra Pavlović. 2013. "Applicability of the Nano-Publication Concept for Fostering Open Access in Developing and Transition Countries." In *Proceedings of the 5th Belgrade International Open Access Conference*. Belgrade: National Library of Serbia.

Sollaci, Luciana B., and Mauricio G. Pereira. 2004. "The Introduction, Methods, Results, and Discussion (IMRAD) Structure: A Fifty-Year Survey." *Journal of the Medical Library Association* 92 (3): 364–71.

Van de Sompel, Herbert, and Carl Lagoze. 2007. "Interoperability for the Discovery, Use, and Re-Use of Units of Scholarly Communication." *CTWatch Quarterly* 3 (3): 32–41.

Van de Sompel, Herbert, Patrick Hochstenbach, and Tobias De Pessemier. 1997. "The Hybrid Information Environment and Our Intranet Solution to Access It." In *Proceedings of the Fourth SA Online 1997*. South Africe: SAOUG Archive. http://hdl.handle.net/1854/LU-1056689.

Van de Sompel, Herbert, Alberto Pepe, Matthew S. Mayernik, and Christine L. Borgman. 2010. "From Artifacts to Aggregations: Modeling Scientific Life Cycles on the Semantic Web." *Journal of the American Society for Information Science and Technology* 61 (3): 567–82. doi:10.1002/asi.21263.

Sørgaard, Pål, and Tone Irene Sandahl. 1997. "Problems with Styles in Word Processing: A Weak Foundation for Electronic Publishing with SGML." In *Proceedings of the Thirtieth Hawaii International Conference on System Sciences*, 6:137–46. Piscataway: IEEE. doi:10.1109/HICSS.1997.665495.

Stäcker, Thomas, Constanze Baum, Timo Steyer, Michael Kleineberg, Anne Baillot, Ben Kaden, Esther Chen, Niels-Oliver Walkowski, Christian Schwaderer, and Thomas Ernst. 2016. "Working Paper 'Digitales Publizieren'." *DHd Working Paper*. Wolfenbüttel: Herzog August Bibliothek. http://diglib.hab.de/ejournals/ed000008/startx.htm.

Star, Susan Leigh, and James R. Griesemer. 1989. "Institutional Ecology, "Translations" and Boundary Objects: Amateurs and Professionals in Berkeley's Museum of Vertebrate Zoology, 1907–39." *Social Studies of Science* 19 (3): 387–420. doi:10.1177/030631289019003001.

Steinkrüger, Philipp, ed. 2016. "RIDE | A Review Journal for Scholarly Digital Editions and Resources." Accessed October 25. http://ride.i-d-e.de/.

Stiegler, Bernard. 2006. "Anamnesis and Hypomnesis. Plato as the First Thinker of the Proletarianisation." *Ars Industrialis*. http://arsindustrialis.org/anamnesis-and-hypomnesis.

———. 2010. *Hypermaterialität und Psychomacht*. Zürich: Diaphanes.

———. 2011. "Digital as Bearer of Another Society." *Digital Transformation Review* 1 (July): 44–50.

———. 2012. "Die Aufklärung in the Age of Philosophical Engeneering." *Computational Culture*, no. 2 (September).

Stirling, Allan, and James Birt. 2014. "An Enriched Multimedia EBook Application to Facilitate Learning of Anatomy." *Anatomical Sciences Education* 7 (1): 19–27. doi:10.1002/ase.1373.

Stöckl, Hartmut. 2013. "Semiotic Paradigms and Multimodality." In *The Routledge Handbook of Multimodal Analysis*, edited by Carey Jewitt, 2nd ed., 275–86. London, New York: Routledge.

Stolley, Karl. 2016. "The Lo-Fi Manifesto, V. 2.0." *Kairos* 20 (2). http://kairos.technorhetoric.net/20.2/inventio/stolley/index.html.

Stribling, Jeremy, Max Krohn, and Dan Aguayo. 2005. "SCIgen - An Automatic CS Paper Generator." https://pdos.csail.mit.edu/archive/scigen/.

Suber, Peter. 2004. "Open Access Overview." June 21. http://legacy.earlham.edu/~peters/fos/overview.htm.

Svensson, Patrik. 2010. "The Landscape of Digital Humanities." *Digital Humanities Quarterly* 4 (1).

Takeda, Kenji, Graeme Earl, Jeremy Frey, Simon Keay, and Alex Wade. 2013. "Enhancing Research Publications Using Rich Interactive Narratives." *Philosophical Transactions of the Royal Society of London A: Mathematical, Physical and Engineering Sciences* 371 (1983): 20120090. doi:10.1098/rsta.2012.0090.

Thatcher, Sanford G. 1996. "Re-Engineering Scholarly Communication: A Role for University Presses?" *Journal of Scholarly Publishing* 27 (3): 197–207. doi:10.3138/JSP-027-04-197.

The White House. 2013. "Open Government Initiative." *The White House*. https://obamawhitehouse.archives.gov/open.

Thomas, Kluyver, Ragan-Kelley Benjamin, Pérez Fernando, Granger Brian, Bussonnier Matthias, Frederic Jonathan, Kelley Kyle, et al. 2016. "Jupyter Notebooks a Publishing Format for Reproducible Computational Workflows." In *Positioning and Power in Academic Publishing: Players, Agents and Agendas*, edited by F. Loizides and B. Schmidt, 87–90. Amsterdam: IOS Press. doi:10.3233/978-1-61499-649-1-87.

Thomas, William. 2007. "Writing A Digital History Journal Article from Scratch: An Account." *Digital History Project*. http://digitalhistory.unl.edu/essays/thomasessay.php.

Thompson, Emily. 2013. "Vectors Journal: The Roaring "Twenties - Editor's Introduction." *Vectors*, no. 7. http://vectorsjournal.org/projects/index.php?project=98.

Thompson, Mark, and Erik Schultes. 2012. "Using Nanopublications to Incentivize the Semantic Exposure of Life Science Information." In *Proceedings of the 5th International Workshop on Semantic Web Applications and Tools for Life Sciences*. Paris: CEUR.

Tinnell, John. 2015. "Grammatization: Bernard Stiegler's Theory of Writing and Technology." *Computers and Composition* 37 (Supplement C): 132–46. doi:10.1016/j.compcom.2015.06.011.

van der Tol, Maarten. 2001. "The Abstract as an Orientation Tool in Modular Electronic Articles." *Document Design* 2 (1): 76–88.

Treloar, Andrew E. 1999. "Rethinking the Library's Role in Publishing." *Learned Publishing* 12 (1): 25–31. doi:10.1087/09531519950146066.

Treusch-Dieter, Gerburg. 2001. "Das Ende einer Himmelfahrt. Vom Feuer der Vergöttlichung zur Vereisung des DNS. Eine Kult- und Kulturgeschichte des Autos." In *Technologien als Diskurse. Konstruktionen von Wissen, Medien und Körpern*, edited by Andreas Lösch, Dominik Schrage, Dierk Spreen, and Markus Stauff, 239–54. Diskursivitäten 5. Heidelberg: Synchron.

Vectors Journal, dir. 2008. *Vectors Journal Dynamic Backend Generator.* YouTube. https://www.youtube.com/watch?v=kkxSSBMPFtA.

"Vectors Journal." 2013. http://vectorsjournal.org/issues/index.php?issue=7.

Velterop, Jan. 2010. "Nanopublications The Future of Coping with Information Overload." *Logos* 21 (3): 119–22. doi:10.1163/095796511X560006.

Verhaar, Peter. 2009. "Report on Object Models and Functionalities." In *Enhanced Publications. Linking Publications and Research Data in Digital Repositories*, 40. Amsterdam: Amsterdam University Press.

Vernadskij, Vladimir Ivanovich. 1997. *Scientific Thought as a Planetary Phenomenon*. Moscow: Nongovernmental Ecological V. I. Vernadsky Foundation.

Visosevica, Tanja, and Amanda Myersb. 2017. "Video Essay: The Multimodal Assignment of Now." In *Proceedings of the 2nd Association for Visual Pedagogy Conference*, 167–171. Denmark: Aalborg University.

Voutsinos, Lavrentios. 2010. "A Web 2.0 Oriented Reference Design Pattern for Structuring and Standardizing Rich Internet Publications."

W3C Library Linked Data Incubator Group. 2011. "Use Case Enhanced Publications - Library Linked Data." February. http://www.w3.org/2005/Incubator/lld/wiki/Use_Case_Enhanced_Publications.

W3C Research Object for Scholarly Communication Community Group. 2013. "Research Object for Scholarly Communication Community Group." https://www.w3.org/community/rosc/.

de Waard, Anita, and Joost G. Kircz. 2008. "Modeling Scientific Research Articles – Shifting Perspectives and Persistent Issues." In *Open Scholarship: Authority, Community, and Sustainability in the Age of Web 2.0 - Proceedings of the 12th International Conference on Electronic Publishing*, 234–45. Toronto. doi:10.1.1.578.6751.

de Waard, Anita, and Gerard Tel. 2006. "The ABCDE Format. Enabling Semantic Conference Proceeding." In *SemWiki2006, First Workshop on Semantic Wikis - From Wiki to Semantics, Proceedings*, edited by Max Völkel and Sebastian Schaffert. Budva: CEUR.

Wark, Mckenzie. 2013. "Totality for Kids." *Vectors*, no. 7. http://vectorsjournal.org/issues/7/totality.

Waters, Colin N., Jan Zalasiewicz, Colin Summerhayes, Anthony D. Barnosky, Clément Poirier, Agnieszka Gałuszka, Alejandro Cearreta, et al. 2016. "The Anthropocene Is Functionally and Stratigraphically Distinct from the Holocene." *Science* 351 (6269). doi:10.1126/science.aad2622.

Weilenmann, Anne-Katharina. 2014. "A New Paradigm for the Scientific Article." *Information Services & Use* 34 (3–4): 315–19. doi:10.3233/ISU-140753.

Weiss, Rick, and Joy Zgorski. 2012. "Obama Administration Unveils "Big Data" Initiative." *The White House President Obama*. March 29. https://obamawhitehouse.archives.gov/the-press-office/2015/11/19/release-obama-administration-unveils-big-data-initiative-announces-200.

Weiten, Moritz, Günter Wozny, and Bernd Goers. 2002. "Wege zum Informationsmanagement für interdisziplinäre Forschungsprojekte und die Entwicklung eines prototypischen Systems." *Chemie Ingenieur Technik* 74 (11): 1545–53. doi:10.1002/1522-2640(20021115)74:11<1545::AID-CITE1545>3.0.CO;2-X.

Welch, Ian, Niklas Rehfeld, Euan Cochrane, and Dirk von Suchodoletz. 2012. "A Practical Approach to System Preservation Workflows." *Praxis der Informationsverarbeitung und Kommunikation* 35 (4): 269–80. doi:10.1515/pik-2012-0049.

Welt, Haus der Kulturen der. 2015. "Future Storytelling." *HKW*. September 16. http://hkw.de/en/programm/projekte/2014/future_storytelling/future_storytelling.php.

Wheary, Jennifer, Lee Wild, Christina Weyher, and Bernard Schutz. 1998. "Thinking in Electronic Terms." In *Proceedings. Socioeconomic Dimensions of Electronic Publishing Workshop*, 1998:83–87. Piscataway: IEEE. doi:10.1109/SEDEP.1998.730714.

Whyte, Angus, and Pryor. 2011. "Open Science in Practice: Researcher Perspectives and Participation." *International Journal of Digital Curation* 6 (1): 199–213. doi:10.2218/ijdc.v6i1.182.

Whyte, Angus, Sarah Callaghan, Jonathan Tedds, and Matthew S. Mayernik. 2013. "Perspectives on the Role of Trustworthy Repository Standards in Data Journal Publication." In *Abstracts of the International Association for Social Science Information Services and Technology Conference*. Cologne: IASSIST. http://www.iassistdata.org/conferences/2013/presentation/3657.

Willinsky, John, Alex Garnett, and Angela Pan Wong. 2012. "Refurbishing the Camelot of Scholarship: How to Improve the Digital Contribution of the PDF Research Article." *The Journal of Electronic Publishing* 15 (1). doi:10.3998/3336451.0015.102.

Wittek, Peter. 2014. "Reproducible Research, Literate Programming, IPython, and GitHub." May 16. http://peterwittek.com/reproducible-research-literate-programming-ipython-and-github.html.

Wittgenstein, Ludwig. 2006. *Philosophische Untersuchungen*. Frankfurt am Main: Suhrkamp.

Worthington, Simon. 2015. *Hybrid Lecture Player* (version 1.1). Hybrid Publishing Lab. https://github.com/consortium/hybrid-lecture-player.

———. 2016. "Hybrid Publishing Portfolio." Lüneburg: Leuphana Universität Lüneburg. https://hpg.io/portfolio.pdf.

Worthington, Simon, and Loraine Furter. 2014. *A Publication Taxonomy*. Lüneburg: Hybrid Publishing Consortium. https://research.consortium.io/docs/a_publication_taxonomy/a-publication-taxonomy.html.

Woutersen-Windhouwer, Saskia, and Renze Brandsma. 2009. "Report on Enhanced Publications State-of-the-Art." Amsterdam: Amsterdam University Press. http://dare.uva.nl/record/340461.

Xu, Hao. 2010. "Managing Ubiquitous Scientific Knowledge on Semantic Web." In *Advances in Computer Science and Information Technology*, edited by Tai-hoon Kim and Hojjat Adeli, 421–30. Lecture Notes in Computer Science 6059. Berlin, Heidelberg: Springer. doi:10.1007/978-3-642-13577-4_37.

———. 2011. "Managing Ubiquitous Scientific Knowledge Objects." Dissertation, Trento: University of Trento.

Xu, Hao, Jing Yu, Wei Liu, and Lan Huang. 2014. "A Review of Scientific Discourse Representation Models." *Koganai* 17 (5): 1691.

Yuan, Zhihao, Dai Hai Ton That, Siddhant Kothari, Gabriel Fils, and Tanu Malik. 2018. "Utilizing Provenance in Reusable Research Objects." *Informatics* 5 (1). doi:10.3390/informatics5010014

Zhao, Jun, José-Manuel Gómez-Pérez, Khalid Belhajjame, Graham Klyne, Esteban Garcia-Cuesta, Aleix Garrido, Kristina Hettne, Marco Roos, David De Roure, and Carole A. Goble. 2012. "Why Workflows Break and Combating Decay in Taverna Workflows." In *2012 IEEE 8th International Conference on E-Science*, 1–9. Los Alamitos: IEEE Computer Society. doi:10.1109/eScience.2012.6404482.

Zheng, Charles, and Douglas Thain. 2015. "Integrating Containers into Workflows: A Case Study Using Makeflow, Work Queue, and Docker." In *Proceedings of the 8th International*

Workshop on Virtualization Technologies in Distributed Computing, 31–38. VTDC "15. New York: ACM. doi:10.1145/2755979.2755984.

Zylinska, Joanna. 2011. "Project Objectives." *Living Books About Life*. May 11. http://www.livingbooksaboutlife.org/blog/2011/05/project-objectives/.

———. 2015. "Photomediations Machine." http://photomediationsmachine.net/.

Zylinska, Joanna, Kamila Kuc, Jonathan Shaw, Jonathan Varney, Michael Wamposzyc, and Gary Hall. 2015. "Photomediations: An Open Book." http://www.photomediationsopenbook.net/.